VICTORIAN
FICTION

VICTORIAN FICTION

A Guide to Research

> *By Robert Ashley, James D. Barry,*
> *Bradford A. Booth, Wayne Burns,*
> *Mildred G. Christian, C. L. Cline,*
> *Curtis Dahl, George S. Fayen, Jr.,*
> *W. J. Harvey, Jacob Korg,*
> *Ada Nisbet, Donald Smalley,*
> *and Lionel Stevenson*
>
> *Edited by Lionel Stevenson*

HARVARD UNIVERSITY PRESS
Cambridge, Massachusetts 1966

Preface

SPONSORED by the Victorian Literature Group of the Modern Language Association of America, this guide to research is designed as a companion volume to *The Victorian Poets*, produced under the same auspices in 1956.

Critical and scholarly attention to the Victorian novelists has developed so widely during the present generation that the need for some selection and evaluation of the mass of material is already apparent. The authors of the chapters in the present volume mention books and articles of earlier date whenever they retain value for modern students; but the larger part of the material discussed has been published during the past quarter of a century.

The choice of subjects was dictated by the quantity of material that offered itself for consideration and by the extent to which various figures could be regarded primarily as novelists. The task of selection was difficult in the later part of the Victorian period, when the number of competent novelists increased and there were no longer a few universally recognized as great masters. Robert Louis Stevenson has been omitted, in spite of his influence on romantic fiction, because his adult novels are few and of debatable rank. The absence of Samuel Butler is to be attributed not only to the limited extent of his work in fiction but also to the fact that his only novel was not published until after the close of the Victorian period, and exerted its effects in the twentieth century. The most conspicuous omission is Henry James; although he wrote his novels in England and occupied a commanding literary position there, he is still formally classified as an American writer.

The material is complete to the end of 1962. References to

a few important publications of 1963 are included in several chapters.

Thanks are due to Professors Gordon S. Haight and Richard L. Purdy for advice on the chapters on George Eliot and Thomas Hardy respectively, and to Professor James D. Barry for editorial suggestions.

LIONEL STEVENSON

Contents

BNYPL	*Bulletin of the New York Public Library*
BUSE	*Boston University Studies in English*
CBEL	*Cambridge Bibliography of English Literature*
CHEL	*Cambridge History of English Literature*
EC	*Essays in Criticism*
ELH	*Journal of English Literary History*
HLQ	*Huntington Library Quarterly*
JEGP	*Journal of English and Germanic Philology*
LQHR	*London Quarterly and Holborn Review*
MLN	*Modern Language Notes*
MLQ	*Modern Language Quarterly*
MLR	*Modern Language Review*
MP	*Modern Philology*
NCF	*Nineteenth-Century Fiction*
N&Q	*Notes and Queries*
PBSA	*Papers of the Bibliographical Society of America*
PMLA	*Publications of the Modern Language Association of America*
PQ	*Philological Quarterly*
PULC	*Princeton University Library Chronicle*
RES	*Review of English Studies*
SAQ	*South Atlantic Quarterly*
SP	*Studies in Philology*
TLS	*Times Literary Supplement*
UTQ	*University of Toronto Quarterly*
VNL	*Victorian Newsletter*
VQR	*Virginia Quarterly Review*
VS	*Victorian Studies*
YULG	*Yale University Library Gazette*

1

General Materials

Bradford A. Booth

In "THE ART OF FICTION" (1884) Henry James remarked, "Only a short time ago it might have been supposed that the English novel was not what the French call *discutable*." James's observation, taking its origin in a recognition of Walter Besant's pioneer, if elementary, treatise on the aesthetics of the novel, was intended to emphasize the fact that though some literary journals were devoted in very large part to reviews of novels, there was precious little serious criticism. He knew there had been writers of demonstrable ability — men such as G. H. Lewes, John Morley, and R. H. Hutton — critics of wide reading, keen intelligence, and sensitive responses to literary values. But unlike poetry and the drama, the novel had not enjoyed a tradition of close analysis; indeed, the criteria of good fiction were ambiguous and the vocabulary of its criticism was inadequate for anything but relatively superficial comment. The critics were often shrewd and observant, but their charming essays, frequently illumined by intuitive flashes, were darkened by plot summaries and the enumeration of "beauties." True, George Ford has found a passage in the *Prospective Review* (1851) in which the "appreciation of the handling of point of view in *David Copperfield* . . . reads like a paragraph from Lubbock's *The Craft of Fiction*," [1] and Richard Stang has recently argued that the work of some mid-Victorian critics has

[1] George H. Ford, *Dickens and His Readers* (Princeton, 1950), p. 128.

been undervalued.[2] Nevertheless, with all due regard for the insights of earlier critics and despite George Saintsbury's warning against the bias of contemporary partisanship, most readers of this symposium will probably conclude that the great bulk of significant work in Victorian fiction has been produced in the last thirty years through the development of new critical approaches and the energies of modern scholarship.

It is generally acknowledged that the change from the Victorian "appreciation" to the modern disciplined critical evaluation can largely be credited to the driving critical intelligence of James, who penetrated beyond plot and characters into meaning and the artful techniques by which meaning can be conveyed through the subtleties of suggestion and indirection. This development, however, did not come quickly. In 1913 Saintsbury, calling his history of the novel the first to deal with the Victorians, opened no new approaches and advanced few ideas that would have surprised David Masson or Frederic Harrison. Today the historian-critic, armed with new methods of analysis and a firm grasp of fictional techniques, attempts to apply fresh criteria to nineteenth-century fiction.

It is part of the new dignity of fiction that masterpieces which a half century ago were deemed beyond further analysis are now being re-examined and that fresh values are being discovered in them. The formulation of new critical concepts and the language by means of which they can be described is the achievement of our time. As a result we are well into a period of revolutionary change, in which for the first time novels are being read with meticulous care as works of art. It is significant that we have apparently arrived at the point where there is some demand for accurate texts. What the thoughtful poet or dramatist actually wrote has always been the subject of precise editorial inquiry, but the novelist could be represented in edition after edition as having written nonsense, and nobody protested. Corrupt texts have been

[2] Richard Stang, *The Theory of the Novel in England, 1850-1870* (New York, 1959).

the rule, even those under presumed editorial surveillance. Paragraphs and even chapters have been printed out of order, original errors have accreted new ones, and still these miserable texts appeared. Variorum editions of even the greatest novels are perhaps not to be expected, but scholarly, annotated texts such as James A. Work's edition of *Tristram Shandy* are long overdue. It is heartening, therefore, to know that a critical edition of Dickens has been launched. No doubt others will follow.

The last quarter century has been a period of tremendous scholarly accomplishment in Victorian studies. In addition to work on individual novelists, noted in the following chapters, research has been actively pursued in the general categories of bibliographies, histories, and special studies.

I. *Bibliographies*

Most scholars are convinced that adequate bibliographical aids are basic to any comprehensive studies in Victorian fiction. These, unfortunately, are not yet available, though some preliminary work has been done and more is in progress. *The Cambridge Bibliography of English Literature*, volume III (1941), offers titles, number of volumes, and dates (for the first edition only) of works by the better novelists. But these lists are often incomplete, are inconsistent in the record of serial publication, are not without error, and are of no help if one's inquiry takes him into minor or anonymous fiction. What is badly needed is an extension of Andrew Block's *The English Novel, 1740–1850: A Catalogue* (1939; rev. ed., 1961), which is itself, as Robert Colby has shown (*NCF*, 1962), both woefully incomplete for the period presumably covered and full of egregious errors. The only truly descriptive bibliography in the field is Michael Sadleir's two-volume *XIX Century Fiction* (1951). This work, one of the landmarks of bibliography, is based on the Sadleir library, now at the University of California, Los Angeles; but, contrary to frequent statements, it extends beyond the limits of the collection, particularly in the listing of series reprints. Nevertheless, Sadleir was necessarily selective, and his bibliography is no substitute for what is desperately needed: a checklist of every novel published. Some preliminary work has been done toward this end. Robert A. Colby of Queens College has compiled a list of novels, admittedly incomplete, up to 1862, the cut-off date of the second volume of the *English Catalogue*, with locations in British libraries. Such work is invaluable and should have organized support. Sara Keith has arranged by author and indexed by title the catalogues of Mudie's Circulating Library for 1848, 1858, 1869, 1876, and 1884, supplying publishers, publication dates, and catalogue notes. The 3000 titles in the list for 1848, 1858, and 1869, which are obtainable on microfilm, constitute the best available material on the popular novels of the mid-Victorian period. Similar work on the catalogues of the firm of Bentley, comprising the years 1829–90, 1892, 1894, and 1898, has been pursued by Royal A. Gettmann of the University of Illinois. An author and title index of the publications of this company, long active in the field of fiction, is available at the University of Illinois library.

Lucien Leclaire has attempted to group local-color novels on a county basis in a *General Analytical Bibliography of the Regional Novelists of the British Isles, 1800–1950* (1953), but the *CBEL* is actually much more complete. For example, Leclaire lists only 13 of Mrs. Oliphant's 97 novels. The value of the work rests in the index, which enables one to learn who wrote about a given county or area. Another bibliographical aid is Leo J. Henkin's "Problems and Digressions in the Victorian Novel, 1860–1900" (*Bulletin of Bibliography*, 1943–1950), which attempts a breakdown of fiction into various subject categories. This is a most useful compilation.[3]

[3] There are two Victorian periodicals which throw light into this dark area: Sampson Low's *Publisher's Circular* (1837), a fortnightly on which the *English Catalogue* was based and which purported to list every book published in Great Britain; and Whitaker's *The Bookseller* (1858), a monthly which is interesting for brief reviews, plot synopses, and so forth, aimed at the retailer and the circulating libraries. Neither of these was by any means impeccable, but the harried research in this field must do with what is available.

II. *Histories*

Since 1900 twenty-odd histories of the English novel have been published, eleven of these appearing in the last twenty-five years. The Victorian period bulking so large in the development of the novel, it is to be expected that many of these histories are concerned chiefly with that era. To discuss them all individually and at length is impossible. Nor would it be wise, for by their nature histories are addressed to unpracticed students and to general readers, not to specialists. Nevertheless, because they are written by professed experts they inevitably reflect changing critical approaches and emphases. To this extent they warrant attention.

The standard text is E. A. Baker's ten-volume *The History of the English Novel* (1924–1939), of which more than three volumes are devoted to the Victorian period. This comprehensive work, largely restricted to major writers, is descriptive rather than critical, and its few tentative judgments derive more from an impressionistic than a rigorously analytical approach. R. M. Lovett and Helen S. Hughes's *The History of the Novel in England* (1932), long the most popular college text, has been superseded by livelier and more accurate accounts. Pelham Edgar's *The Art of the Novel* (1933) is probably the first history to approach the Victorians from the point of view of technique, Edgar having been a close student of Henry James. Gordon Hall Gerould's *Patterns of English and American Fiction* (1942), more than half of which is devoted to the Victorians, takes the unique and eminently defensible position that it is useful to follow parallel developments in two literatures. Unfortunately, however, it has the crippling disadvantage of trying to do too much and is consequently thin. Edward Wagenknecht's *Cavalcade of the English Novel* (1943; rev. ed., 1954) is a serviceable work, particularly in the revised edition, by virtue of its excellent bibliographies. But some of the value of the work is lost as a result of Wagenknecht's devotion to very conservative literary views.

Five more histories appeared during the 1950's. Richard Church's *The Growth of the English Novel* (1951), written as one of the Home Study Books, is too brief, too elementary, and too crotchety to be of much scholarly interest. Arnold Kettle's two-volume *An Introduction to the English Novel* (1952–1953) is not a history but a series of always shrewd and often brilliant analyses of individual novels. Neither is it strictly an introduction, for few who come to Kettle's pages without a wide background of experience with fiction will carry away many of the fine things to be found there. The thesis which Kettle pushes (rather too hard, I believe) is that "the great novels of the nineteenth century are all, in their differing ways, novels of revolt." S. Diana Neill's *A Short History of the English Novel* (1952) attempts to answer the need for a comprehensive one-volume survey that will not neglect the twentieth century. The result is that the Victorians are given inadequate treatment. Aldous Huxley receives almost double the space allotted to Thackeray; D. H. Lawrence, almost six times the space allotted to Trollope. The magnitude of her task forces Miss Neill to scatter her shot very widely, and she is driven perforce to generalizations. Walter Allen's *The English Novel* (1955) is one of the best balanced of the one-volume surveys. Allen qualifies for his task by the experience of the novelist as well as that of the critic, and he approaches the Victorians without obvious biases or eccentric judgments. If there are no surprises in his treatment, it has the virtues of soundness and solidity. The most recent history is Lionel Stevenson's *The English Novel: A Panorama* (1960). Traditional in its approach and not so full in bibliographical material as is Wagenknecht's survey, this study, like Allen's, is notable for an even-tempered view of fiction that plays no obvious favorites and takes no extreme critical position. It is a careful, rational, highly competent history.

Examining these studies, one is tempted to suggest that the possibilities of the survey history have been about exhausted, and that future appraisals of Victorian fiction are likely to take the form of close analyses of individual texts.

III. *Essays and Interpretations*

A number of interesting studies of Victorian fiction have concentrated on one part of the period; others have based a series of brief interpretations upon a new concept of the novel, or have offered critical analyses with emphasis on methods and technique.

In the first category one finds Lord David Cecil's *Early Victorian Novelists* (1934), perhaps the most popular book of its kind, many times reprinted and currently available in paperback. Cecil is a traditional critic, urging no new theories or interpretations calculated to wash out all previous criticism, and rejecting the esoteric jargon which sometimes makes banal ideas seem original. He finds two kinds of novels — those before and after George Eliot — and he finds in all these works "an extraordinary mixture of strength and weakness." Their range of subject and variety of mood are wide, and they have creative imagination in "a supreme degree." Yet they "hardly ever stir those profounder feelings to which the very greatest art appeals." All this is so conventional as to suggest the complete absence of fresh insight. Nevertheless, the very qualities that make Cecil traditional have kept him from eccentric judgments. His large endowment of common sense, plus his alert perceptiveness to what the Victorians intended, gives his work unusual value. His reading of *Wuthering Heights*, for example, is for many readers the most lucid and most convincing study of that novel ever written.

Cecil is not highly regarded, however, by the *Scrutiny* critics, led by F. R. Leavis, whose *The Great Tradition* (1948) has been at once the most influential and the most controversial study in this field. Leavis contends that the great English novelists are Jane Austen, George Eliot, James, Conrad, and Lawrence. Dickens, Thackeray, Trollope, Meredith, and Hardy he finds unrewarding. The principal charges against them are that they do not trouble themselves about form and method, and that they do not create profoundly serious works of art. These indictments can perhaps in some measure be sustained, but Leavis seems to press the case beyond all reason. Thackeray, for example, "has (apart from social history) nothing to offer the reader whose demand goes beyond the 'creation of characters.' His attitudes and essential substance of interest are so limited that (though of course he provides incident and plot) for the reader it is merely a matter of going on and on; nothing has been done by the close to justify the space taken — except, of course, that time has been killed." Leavis' criteria permit him to include a chapter on *Hard Times,* apparently the best of Dickens' novels, and the expression of great admiration for Disraeli, who is "so alive and intelligent as to deserve permanent currency." It is impossible not to salute Leavis and his followers for the service which they have performed in demanding close attention to texts and in calling attention to the subtleties of conscious artistry, for the standards Leavis seeks to establish serve to frustrate loose relativism and fuzzy impressionism. But most Victorian scholars feel that he has defined the function of the novel very narrowly, and he has certainly alienated many fair-minded readers by asserting his own prejudices with the dogmatism of Sir Oracle.

An excellent study of early Victorian fiction is Kathleen Tillotson's *Novels of the Eighteen-Forties* (1954). The first part of Mrs. Tillotson's book is a compendium of information on the novel of the period: publication problems, subject matter, techniques, influences, and criticism. The second part is devoted to critical analyses of *Dombey and Son, Mary Barton, Vanity Fair,* and *Jane Eyre.* These essays at their best, as in the last named, are not only graceful and charming, but are full of penetrating aperçus, particularly in matters of the relation between structural patterns and artistic intent. There have been few general studies of *fin de siècle* novels, though W. C. Frierson's *The English Novel in Transition, 1885–1940* (1942) is useful.

Two collections of essays on the lady novelists of the period appeared in 1946: Laura L. Hinkley's *Ladies of Literature* and Lucy Poate Stebbins' *A Victorian Album.* Both of these are chatty and gossipy, rather than scholarly, but are not without interest, particularly Mrs. Stebbins' chapters on the minor novelists.

Significant studies which are only in part concerned with the Victorian field are too numerous to be separately cited. Some of the most valuable critiques will be discussed in the chapters on individual authors, but several of these volumes must be mentioned here. Dorothy Van Ghent's *The English Novel: Form and Function* (1953) contains analyses of seven Victorian novels. These are brilliant pieces, and though designed primarily for the student they handle so deftly and so knowingly the problems and procedures of paradox and irony, of symbolism and allegory, of the behavior of myth, the function of plot, and the activities of style that they constitute an advanced grammar of the novel and place Mrs. Van Ghent among our very best critics. Bruce McCullough's *Representative English Novelists: Defoe to Conrad* (1946) contains nine similar analyses. These are not so technical as Mrs. Van Ghent's, but by virtue of McCullough's alert common sense they are helpful in the exploration of meaning. Frank O'Connor's *The Mirror in the Roadway* (1956), with its five essays on Victorian fiction, is one of the most exciting of these books. The approach is refreshingly undogmatic, and the critical perceptions are remarkable for their originality and steady good taste. O'Connor not only knows the clichés of formal criticism — and how to avoid them — but he has that rare quality of lean and compact statement. No other critic of our time has thrown out so many useful suggestions for the interpretation of Victorian fiction.

One might also mention Malcolm Elwin's *Old Gods Falling* (1939), which includes two chapters on George Moore and two on Stevenson, plus discussions of Rider Haggard and other minor figures. Elwin pursues the biographical approach, often sacrificing scholarship to the drama and color of his novelists and their work. The approach is much the same as that of his *Victorian Wallflowers* (1934), in which Ainsworth, Wilkie Collins, Mrs. Henry Wood, Blackmore, and Ouida are made to yield perhaps more than their quota of oddity. V. S. Pritchett's two collections, *The Living Novel* (1947) and *Books in General* (1953), offer brief and penetrating studies of many Victorian novelists. John Holloway's *The Victorian Sage* (1953) describes Disraeli, George Eliot, and Hardy as artists seriously interested in man's fate, and suggests that in their attempt to define essence they contributed notably to "prophetic" literature. An early symposium volume, *The English Novelists* (1936), edited by Derek Verschoyle, with seven essays on Victorians, is of dubious value because the articles are written by people who, however well known, often have few qualifications for their assignments. This is not true of *From Jane Austen to Joseph Conrad* (1958), edited by Robert C. Rathburn and Martin Steinmann, Jr. The twenty-two essays in this volume cover with scholarly authority various aspects of major novelists and novels.

IV. *Studies in Forms and Types*

Though the social or humanitarian novel remains one of the most characteristic types of the Victorian age, it has not per se received much attention, and Louis Cazamian's *Le Roman social en Angleterre, 1830–1850* (1903), remains after a half century the chief text for a subject that calls for more study. Nevertheless, the novel continues to be recognized as a mirror of society, and various aspects and attitudes of Victorian life have been traced through their representation in fiction.

E. M. Delafield in *Ladies and Gentlemen of Victorian Fiction* (1939) comments amusingly on the Victorian domestic scene, though her heavy reliance on examples from Charlotte Yonge suggests that she is more concerned with entertainment than with an accurate social record. A good deal of information not readily accessible elsewhere is to be found in Amy Cruse's *The Victorians and Their Books* (1935), which takes a different road to the same destination. Much of interest is to be found in Margaret Dalziel's *Popular Fiction a Hundred Years Ago* (1957), which describes the substratum of lowbrow works on which the masterpieces were erected. But the best guide to public taste in Victorian fiction is Richard D. Altick's *The English Common Reader* (1957), a superb account of what was read and why. This is social history of a vital kind.

The status of women is also social history. It becomes literary history as well when scholars examine the role played by the heroine in popular novels. Robert P. Utter and Gwendolyn B. Needham in *Pamela's Daughters* (1936), devoting most of their study to Victorian fiction, assume a playful attitude toward their material and like Miss Delafield emphasize the more absurd examples of prissiness, silliness, and general helplessness of swooning femininity. A more recent, and on the whole more serious, work is Patricia Thomson's *The Victorian Heroine: A Changing Ideal* (1956). Although this study sets out to examine only the period 1837–1873, there are of necessity so many glimpses beyond these arbitrary limits that we have, in effect, a social history of the century. The chief subjects discussed are social workers, governesses, the education of women, the rights of women, and what was delicately called the Social Evil. Though the study is basically serious, it is written in a vein of dry understatement that would have amused some of the better novelists who are pilloried.

The Victorian hero has come under even closer surveillance than the heroine. Mario Praz's *The Hero in Eclipse in Victorian Fiction* (1956), a challenging but vulnerable study that has received much attention, examines the conservative, bourgeois, and "Biedermeier" aspects of the age, particularly as reflected in Dickens, Thackeray, Trollope, and George Eliot. Dickens is seen as the shallow and somewhat devious apostle of jollity and goodness, whose fictional reticences contrast sharply with the latitude of his private morality. His heroes are only sepulchral monuments with mild, stupid faces. Thackeray is "the apostle of mediocrity," whose rejection of the heroic is the negation of the epic spirit. Trollope, "the most typical representative . . . of the Biedermeier spirit," rejecting heroes, deceptions, and surprises as well as the picturesque and sensational, is a realist who gratified the

sense of recognition. His antiheroic point of view, his sharp
eye for sham and deceit, and his "ironical bourgeois common
sense" make him a quietly effective satirist. George Eliot's
work best supports Praz's thesis, for her adoption of the commonplace, her antiheroic philosophy, and her intimism *do*
represent a changing concept of character in Victorian fiction.
The interest in the so-called sensation novel, widespread a
generation ago — witness W. C. Phillips' *Dickens, Reade and
Collins — Sensation Novelists* (1919) and S. M. Ellis' *Wilkie
Collins, Le Fanu and Others* (1931) — has yielded to scholarship in the earlier Gothic form, though there is, of course,
some overlapping. This is particularly true in the area of
supernatural fiction, of which there has been one recent and
noteworthy study: Peter Penzoldt's *The Supernatural in Fiction* (1952). This work is limited to British short stories and
is bibliographically inadequate, treating only a few selected
writers where fuller coverage might be expected, but Penzoldt illuminates his subject with more than ordinary skill.
Bringing to his task a good deal of psychiatric training, he
analyzes both ghostly tales and their authors with often
startling results, yet he wisely refrains from pushing this type
of inquiry beyond the limits of its usefulness. Interest in
supernatural fiction is further shown by the publication of
a number of collections of the work of minor writers: for
example, Mrs. Riddell's *Weird Stories*, Rhoda Broughton's
Twilight Stories, a great deal of Le Fanu, and occasional
stories by Mary Elizabeth Braddon, Mrs. Molesworth, and
Catherine Crowe.

V. *Studies in Technique*

The most significant aspect of the twentieth-century novel,
that which most sharply differentiates it from the Victorian,
is its concern with problems long considered the province of
the philosopher and the psychologist. The Victorian novel
expressed itself, for the most part, in terms of the bourgeois
attitude toward life, which conceives meanings and values as
imposed by authority — family, church, or state. The modern

novel, by contrast, viewing man as the creator of his own existence, propounds a new concept of human reality: the consciousness of experience. With the novelist's assumption of what Leon Edel calls the mind's eye view there has been an inward turning of the attention to examine not society and its varied external relationships to the individual but the human consciousness itself. How to transform this often inchoate material of the mind into a valid and ordered interpretation of life has been the novelist's problem. In our day it is clear that the most significant writers have sought to do so by conceiving the novel in terms of symbol, image, and myth, and critics have trained themselves to read novels in these terms.

With this background scholar-critics, re-examining the masterpieces of Victorian fiction, have discovered values which had not previously been suspected and subtleties which had commonly been denied the early practitioners. There is as yet no extended study of symbolism in fiction, but in his chapter "Supreme Fictions" in *The Literary Symbol* (1935) William York Tindall points out that all great novels are to some extent symbolic, and that Dickens, Meredith, and Hardy, among others, developed symbols thematically in a way that anticipates the richness and precision of the technique of the twentieth century. J. Hillis Miller's recent critical study of Dickens emphasizes that writer's pervasive use of symbols, and Tindall reminds us of Conrad's constant awareness of the rapprochement between symbolism and art.

The ancillary study of myth, another preoccupation of modern criticism, also touches the Victorians. Richard Chase, whose *Quest for Myth* (1948) is the chief study of the concept of myth in literature, contends that in fiction the prestige of symbolism has declined.[4] Though his interest lies principally in modern poetry, he has driven scholars by the challenge of his work to re-examine basic texts. He has done so himself, notably in "The Brontës, or Myth Domesticated," in *Forms of Modern Fiction* (1948), where he argues that the Brontës'

[4] See also Harry Levin's essay *Symbolism and Fiction* (Charlottesville, 1956).

tremendous displacement of the domestic values toward the tragic and mythical, though it falls short of ultimate achievement, gives their work a margin of superiority over that of other Victorian novelists.

The principal change to be observed over the last generation in studies of the technique of fiction has been a progression from general to specific, from sweeping comments on the handling of plot and characters to detailed analyses of technique, such as the management of point of view, interior monologue, and time. In these modern studies the Victorian novelist has been useful primarily in providing *l'exemple horrible*. The change can perhaps be dated from 1918 when Joseph Warren Beach published his epoch-making *The Method of Henry James*, the pioneer attempt to organize the theory of a consistent point of view. Percy Lubbock in *The Craft of Fiction* (1921) emphasizes to what extent the Victorian novelist sacrificed reality by authorial intrusion. Yet he is broad enough to grant the virtue of consistency whatever the patterns. E. M. Forster in *Aspects of the Novel* (1927) is less disturbed by a wavering point of view in the nineteenth-century novel. To Lubbock's attack on this aspect of *War and Peace*, he replies that such infringement of the "rules" is of no importance if the novel comes off: "All that matters to the reader is whether the shifting of attitude and the secret life are convincing." This is perhaps the last apologia for the unfocused Victorian novel. Norman Friedman, whose "Point of View in Fiction: The Development of a Critical Concept" (*PMLA*, 1955) is the most comprehensive treatment of the subject, lists some twenty-odd references in the last fifteen years (among them Beach, Tate, and Schorer), all very hard upon the Victorian novelists' shortcomings in this matter of technique. Two other familiar texts, old but still useful, Edwin Muir's *The Structure of the Novel* (1928) and Van Meter Ames's *The Aesthetics of the Novel* (1928), are concerned with larger issues. Irène Simon's *Formes du roman anglais de Dickens à Joyce* (1951) approaches the chief Victorian novelists from the perspective of a disciple of Louis

Cazamian, balancing the subjective data gathered by one's immediate reaction to a work of art against the objective facts discovered by historical research.

The Victorians made little contribution toward the solution of another technical problem: the handling of time, which Henry James declared to be the stiffest responsibility facing the novelist. In *Time and the Novel* (1952) A. A. Mendilow points out that the eighteenth-century novelists — particularly Sterne, who in *Tristram Shandy* so remarkably anticipated the fascination which this concept has had for the twentieth century — recognized the possibilities of the time shift and made interesting experiments. The Victorians, on the other hand, because of the static symmetry of the old self-contained plot, were not stimulated to new approaches. Today, Mendilow maintains, the Victorian sense of the dominant patterns of life has been succeeded by a conviction of the dynamic formlessness of life, which has a variable flow. For the novelists, therefore, the rigid Victorian stylizations will no longer suffice. It should be added, however, that this does not hold true for Conrad, who, as Edward Crankshaw has shown, is one of the most notable experimenters in time relationships.

Yet another technical matter which has attracted attention is rhythm. Here the Victorian novelists did pioneering work, though their successors went on to much more complicated forms. E. K. Brown in *Rhythm in the Novel* (1950) shows how the elementary use of repetition of phrase in *Middlemarch* is developed into the artful repetition of incident, character, and situation, dependent on a sequence of time, in *The Well-Beloved* and other novels. These kinds of more or less obvious rhythm become complex when the novelist begins to employ symbols, both fixed and, to use Brown's term, expanding (that is, when the symbol continues to develop new layers of meaning). The expanding symbol, useful when the novelist is attempting to render a subtle or elusive feeling, was beyond Thackeray or Trollope, who communicated meaning within the conventional elements in the structure of the novel — story, people, place, and comment. It remained for Proust and E. M. Forster to develop the expanding symbol.

The elusive quality of style — so vague, so nebulous, so indefinable — has been increasingly subject to close examination in recent years (most studies in stylistics before 1920 have succumbed to methodological obsolescence). Many of the current problems are posed and methods explored in *Style in Prose Fiction,* edited by Harold C. Martin (1959), a collection of essays from the program of the English Institute, 1958. All but one of the papers deal with English and American fiction of the nineteenth century, and the selective bibliography which is included offers the best available guide to the growing literature of this important subject.

Many recent critics of fiction have discarded the terms by which Victorian novelists discussed their work. Trollope, who wrote more formal criticism than any other of the mid-Victorian novelists, evaluated novels in terms of plot, characters, style, dialogue, and so forth. Until James's prefaces became well-known, critics generally followed suit. But I. A. Richards in *Practical Criticism* (1930), Queenie D. Leavis in *Fiction and the Reading Public* (1932), and Denys Thompson in *Reading and Discrimination* (1934) hold that discussion of these abstractions is pointless, that such terms are without merit in criticism, the business of which is to test the quality of an author's mind by subjecting selected passages to analysis for "sense, feeling, tone, and intention." The older concepts, it is argued, do not convey the resonance of a novel; they are merely the instruments by which a novelist expresses his sensibility. Lately, similar remarks have been made by John Holloway and by Arnold Kettle, who maintains that "you cannot really separate say 'character' from 'plot,' 'narrative' from 'background.' " One cautionary voice, that of Douglas Grant in "The Novel and Its Critical Terms" (*EC,* 1951), suggests that to discuss the novel in terms of the author's sensibility only, without regard to its historical context, is dangerous. Some critics continue to believe that to assess fairly the purposes and techniques of the Victorian novelists it is imperative that the critic understand what *they* meant by the terms they used. The new vocabulary of fiction is the basis of two other books in which the Victorian novel is frequently discussed: Robert Liddell's *A Treatise on the Novel* (1947) and *Some Principles of Fiction* (1953). As points of reference with regard to contemporary practices, the work of Dickens, George Eliot, and Hardy is brought under particular study.

One voice has recently been raised to assert the value of the older criticism. In *The Theory of the Novel in England, 1850–1870* (1959) Richard Stang studies the criticism that appeared in some of the major Victorian periodicals. Though many readers will feel that Stang is inclined to overestimate the significance of his findings and to inflate intelligent journalism into major criticism, his work emphasizes the fact that much useful digging in this relatively neglected area remains to be done. Perhaps the same conclusion is to be drawn from Miriam Allott's *Novelists on the Novel* (1959), in which important statements by the practitioners themselves on such matters as the nature of prose fiction, the genesis of a novel, the craft of fiction, and so forth, are arranged in a chronological scheme, together with perceptive material by the editor.

VI. *Special Studies*

The proliferation of scholarship in Victorian fiction in our time has been such that it is scarcely possible to cover all the relevant books and quite impossible even to touch upon the articles which are concerned with general considerations rather than individual authors. It is necessary, however, to note the significant special studies, if only to indicate some of the lines which research has taken.

Science and the clash of ideas have contributed notably to fiction and to the study of fiction. Three excellent studies in this area, not nearly so well known as they should be, are the work of a distinguished French scholar, Madeleine L. Cazamian. In a three-part study, *Le Roman et les idées en Angleterre*, Mme. Cazamian has written importantly of the influence of social and intellectual history upon the novel. The first of these, *L'Influence de la science, 1860–1890* (1923), traces the effect of the new science upon, chiefly, George Eliot, Butler, Gissing, and Hardy. The second, *L'Anti-intellectualisme et l'esthétisme, 1880–1900* (1935), treats not only Morris, Pater, Wilde, and Moore as would be expected, but at some length Arthur Machen. The last study, *Les Doctrines d'action et l'aventure, 1880–1914* (1955), discusses, among the Victorian novelists, Stevenson, Meredith, Conrad, and Kipling. These are first-rate studies, written from the vantage point of an informed and sensitive foreign critic. Unfortunately for students whose French is rusty, they have not been translated. Another competent investigator of the scientific influence is Leo J. Henkin, whose *Darwinism in the English Novel, 1860–1910* (1940) describes the impact of the theories of evolution and natural selection upon some one hundred novels. On a somewhat different but nevertheless scholarly level is J. O. Bailey's *Pilgrims through Space and Time* (1947), a study of science fiction and utopian fiction.

Anglo-French literary relations have been signalized by two valuable investigations. W. C. Frierson's *L'Influence du naturalisme français sur les romanciers anglais de 1885 à 1900* (1925) charts the force of Zola and others in determining an important shift in English perspectives. Marian Gladys Devonshire, looking at the obverse of the medal in *The English Novel in France, 1830–70* (1929), records various editions, translations, reviews, and critiques. It would be useful to have such information for other periods and other literatures. The vital Russian influence is briefly but usefully charted in Gilbert Phelps's *The Russian Novel in English Fiction* (1956).

There have been two attempts to survey the political novel. M. E. Speare's *The Political Novel* (1924) is devoted in large measure to a study of Disraeli, though there are briefer sections on Trollope, George Eliot, Meredith, and Mrs. Humphry Ward. Less satisfactory is Joseph L. Blotner's monograph *The Political Novel* (1955), which not only attempts too much but does so under the misapprehension that it is the first work in this field.

Several quite different works may be cited in conclusion. Frances Theresa Russell's *Satire in the Victorian Novel* (1920) is a pioneer study that remains useful, for no one else has adressed himself to this formidable subject. Walter L. Myers' *The Later Realism* (1927) is an interesting and valuable examination of the effect of late Victorian thought on the theory of characterization; that is, on the ways in which science, philosophy, and psychology changed Victorian concepts of the nature of man and thus the fictional portraits of man in action. Joseph E. Baker's *The Novel and the Oxford Movement* (1932) is based on a study of some 125 novels which reflect in varying degrees the religious controversies of the early part of the period. A more recent treatment of the religious novel, Margaret Maison's *The Victorian Vision* (1962), covers the later period more fully, but it retraces much of the same ground without adequate recognition of Baker's work. Susanne Howe's *Novels of Empire* (1949), studying the literature of colonization through works by Haggard, Henty, Olive Schreiner, Trollope, Henry Kingsley, and others, offers too broad a panorama and fritters out into a catalogue, but it is useful in suggesting a line of inquiry which, more rigorously pursued, might provide a touchstone of one aspect of the age.

Finally, the attention of students is drawn to three journals in the field. The files of *Nineteenth-Century Fiction*, founded in 1945, contain a considerable portion of the recent critical literature on the novelists of the period. *English Fiction in Transition*, which covers 1880–1920, is particularly valuable for the bibliographical aids to which it is largely, but by no means exclusively, devoted. *Modern Fiction Studies*, despite its title, frequently treats novelists who produced their major work during the Victorian period. The success of these periodicals, with their overlapping interests, attests the current lively demand for scholarly studies in Victorian fiction.

Brander Matthews, writing in 1908, acknowledged that "in the age of Victoria the novel established itself as the literary form most alluring to all men of letters." Nevertheless, "the prosperous parvenu of literature" was not everywhere taken seriously, though the time had clearly arrived when it would profit by an informed criticism. Matthews particularly recommended, it may be of interest to note, the economic interpretation of literary history as a rich field for research. This call to scholarly arms was not immediately answered, but by the early twenties the critical ranks were reasonably full and marching forward on many fronts. Their members have rapidly grown in recent decades, until today the study of Victorian fiction is one of the most active of scholarly fields. Much has been done, and well done; but Brander Matthews would no doubt be astonished to learn that it is the consensus of leading scholars, more than half a century after his remarks, that we have not yet dug very widely, and that Victorian fiction remains one of the most challenging and rewarding areas for research.[5]

[5] I am indebted to Appleton-Century-Crofts for permission to reprint a few sentences from my article "The Novel" in *Contemporary Literary Scholarship*, edited by Lewis Leary (© Copyright 1958 Appleton-Century-Crofts) and to The Regents of the University of California for permission to reprint some material from my "Current Books" columns in *Nineteenth-Century Fiction*.

2 🦢

Benjamin Disraeli
Edward Bulwer-Lytton

Curtis Dahl

Victorian fiction minces in with dandiacal
steps. Two dandies, Benjamin Disraeli, later prime minister
and first Earl of Beaconsfield, and Edward George Earle
Lytton Bulwer Lytton, later (to complicate the name even
further) first Baron Lytton of Knebworth, were the popular
novelists of their day. Though it has now been a long time
since critics have considered them major writers, they continue to stimulate critical interest as representatives of literary
currents of the early Victorian period and especially as forerunners of trends in fiction important in the work of greater
Victorian novelists. Thus nineteenth-century criticism of
these two brilliantly cravatted novelists was in large part
evaluative, whereas twentieth-century criticism has for the
most part been historical.

Both writers were active in many fields other than fiction.
Bulwer was dramatist, poet, critic, essayist, historian, translator, pamphleteer, and politician. Similarly, Disraeli was
statesman, politician, orator, political theorist, poet, wit, and
dandy. In all these aspects they have received critical attention, Bulwer, of course, primarily as dramatist and Disraeli
primarily as statesman. The research here reviewed is only
that which is in some way connected with fiction. This distinction is fairly easy to make with Bulwer, though such a book

as Charles H. Shattuck's *Bulwer and Macready, A Chronicle of the Early Victorian Theatre* (1958) on Bulwer's fruitful dramatic association with the great Victorian actor throws light on the genesis of several of his novels from abortive plays. With Disraeli, however, the distinction is far more difficult. Since his novels are to a large extent political utterances, almost every study of Disraeli as political theorist or statesman is partially based on them and in turn helps to explain them.

DISRAELI

I. *Bibliography*

The most nearly complete bibliography of Disraeli as a novelist is that in Michael Sadleir, *XIX Century Fiction, A Bibliographical Record* (2 vols., 1951). Other useful bibliographies are George Angus' "Contributions to a Bibliography of Benjamin Disraeli" (*N&Q*, 1893), and the chapter on Disraeli in Sadleir's *Excursions in Victorian Bibliography* (1922).

II. *Editions and Letters*

The best edition of the works of Disraeli is that variously called the Empire and Earl's Edition published with a critical introduction by Edmund Gosse and a biographical preface by Robert Arnot (20 vols., 1904–1905). This edition includes a number of the speeches and pamphlets. Of the novels alone the standard editions are the Hughenden (11 vols., 1881) and the Bradenham (12 vols., 1926). The latter has incisive, helpful, though brief introductions by Philip Guedalla. The introductions by Lucien Wolf to the Century Edition (1904) contain much valuable information.

From various periodicals J. Logie Robertson gathered in 1891 a volume of *Tales and Sketches by the Right Honourable Benjamin Disraeli. The Dunciad of Today*, edited by Michael Sadleir (1928), is a reprint of two anonymous contributions to *The Star Chamber* of 1826; Sadleir's introduction (reprinted in *Things Past*, 1944) persuasively follows most of the early biographers but not Monypenny and Buckle in arguing that these two pieces can justifiably be included in the Disraeli canon. In *Texas Studies in English* (1943) C. L. Cline, who has perhaps published more research than anyone else on Disraeli the novelist, has reprinted "The Unfinished Diary of Disraeli's Journey to Flanders and the Rhineland" — a useful appendix to the second part of *Vivian Grey* and an interesting revelation of pre-Victorian taste in the fine arts.

Like many of the Victorians Disraeli was a lively correspondent. His letters, especially the early ones to his sister, amusingly reveal the social milieu out of which several of the novels came. In 1885 Ralph Disraeli edited *Lord Beaconsfield's Home Letters, Written in 1830–31* and in 1886 *Lord Beaconsfield's Correspondence with His Sister, 1832–52* (republished in one volume in 1887 as *Lord Beaconsfield's Letters* and again in 1928 as *Home Letters, Written by Lord Beaconsfield, 1830–52*, with an introduction by Augustine Birrell). *Letters from Benjamin Disraeli to Frances Anne, Marchioness of Londonderry, 1837–61* (ed. Marchioness of Londonderry, 1938) and *The Letters of Disraeli to Lady Bradford and Lady Chesterfield* (ed. Marquis of Zetland, 2 vols., 1929) have little to do with the novels, but "A New Sheaf of Disraeli Letters: Hitherto Unpublished Correspondence with His Sister Sarah," edited by Clarence I. Freed in *American Hebrew* (1927), gives a number of personal and literary insights into them. Lady Blessington's letters to Disraeli printed in *N&Q* (1947) by C. L. Cline illuminate the important friendship between her and Disraeli, and "Benjamin Disraeli's Letters to Robert Carter" (*PQ*, 1952), ed. Hubert H. Hoeltje, present sidelights on the Goldwin Smith controversy and on Disraeli's enormous popularity in America. Carter was editor of *Appleton's Journal*. In "Disraeli's Fan Mail" (*NCF*, 1954), Bernard R. Jerman documents from letters at Hughenden the popular reception of Disraeli's novels.

III. *Biography*

Biographical studies of Disraeli are like the sands of the sea in number and range from virulent political diatribe through measured analysis to sickeningly feminine fictionalizing. The great mine of information is, of course, the thorough, ponderous, yet fascinating official biography by William Flavelle Monypenny and George Earle Buckle. With its detailed narrative, its reprinting of countless documents, and its sensible criticism *The Life of Benjamin Disraeli* (6 vols., 1910–1920, I–II by Monypenny, III by Monypenny and Buckle, IV–VI by Buckle; reissue in 2 vols. with minor corrections, 1929) is still the most useful source for information about Disraeli the man or Disraeli the novelist.

Despite the pre-eminence of Monypenny and Buckle, several of the earlier biographies still have value for the student of the novels. *The Right Honourable Benjamin Disraeli* (1852), by George H. Francis, and *The Right Honourable Benjamin Disraeli, M.P., A Literary and Political Biography* (1854), by Thomas Macknight, reveal attitudes toward Disraeli in the earlier portion of his career. Francis directs his fire at the amusing extravagance of Disraeli's style, while Macknight roundly damns the novels as the moral and political wickedness of an atheistical hypocrite. Athanase Cucheval-Clarigny's *Lord Beaconsfield et son temps* (1880) is a sprightly, understanding summary of his life; in contrast, Francis Hitchman, *The Public Life of the Right Honourable Earl of Beaconsfield* (2 vols., 1879), which supplies a large mass of detailed information, is ponderous and slow. Two much more important biographies are those by Georg Brandes (*Benjamin Disraeli, Jarl af Beaconsfield. En litteraer Carakteristik*, 1878; trans. Sturge, 1880) and James Anthony Froude (*Lord Beaconsfield*, 1890). Brandes, whose book is more of a psychological study than a biography, tries to show that Disraeli's political career was almost wholly an outgrowth of the Tory radicalism expressed in his novels. Though stimulating, Brandes is apt to be more impressionistic than accurate.

Froude's book is also politically motivated. It is a study of Disraeli from a largely Carlylean point of view, with primary emphasis among the novels laid on the Young England group. Walter Sichel's *Disraeli, A Study in Personality and Ideas* (1904), though an analysis of Disraeli's intellectual development, surprisingly is weak on the novels; Oscar A. H. Schmitz in *Die Kunst der Politik: Lord Beaconsfield* (1914) convincingly argues a close relationship between Disraeli the statesman and Disraeli the artist; and F. Carroll Brewster's *Disraeli in Outline* (1890) is useful for its summaries of the plots of the novels.

The biographies succeeding Monypenny and Buckle have for the most part been either popularizations or special studies based on new interpretations. Recently, however, Bernard R. Jerman, making use for the first time of abundant material from the Austen-Layard family and from the Disraeli archives at Hughenden, has added to our understanding of the novelist by retelling in *The Young Disraeli* (1960) the story of Disraeli's life through 1837. With sound critical judgment he shows how Disraeli's hitherto unexplained financial and amorous entanglements relate to his early novels. He also explains fully for the first time the role played by Disraeli's early Egeria, Sara Austen.

The next best recent biographical study is the brief *Disraeli* (1936) by Harold Beeley — a concise, intelligent, and well-ordered summary of the pertinent facts about the novels together with good criticism of them. "E. T. Raymond" (Edward Raymond Thompson) in *Disraeli: Alien Patriot* (1925) uses the novels to try to prove his thesis that the "real" Disraeli was a shrewdly calculating, untrustworthy Oriental alien whose greatness lay in the objectivity toward English life and affairs that his differentness gave him. The biographies by Sir E. G. Clarke (1926) and D. L. Murray (1927) are readable but relate only slightly to the novels. Of even more popular biographies Elswyth Thane's *Young Mr. Disraeli* (1936) must really be judged as fiction, André Maurois' *La Vie de Disraëli* (1927; trans. Miles as *Disraeli, A Picture of the Victorian Age*, 1927) is dramatic rather than critical, and

Hesketh Pearson's *Dizzy, The Life and Personality of Benjamin Disraeli, Earl of Beaconsfield* (1951) refuses to treat Disraeli seriously as a novelist. Pearson's satire, however, is refreshing.

A number of articles treat specific aspects of Disraeli's life. Lucien Wolf in *Transactions of the Jewish Historical Society of England* (1902–1905) explodes the romantic account of the origin of the Disraeli family which the novelist propagated and used in his novels, but see Cecil Roth's *Benjamin Disraeli* (1952) for corrections to Wolf. In *The Pageantry of Life* (1900) Charles Whibley passes from the subject of Disraeli as a dandy to a valuable criticism of the deftness, "style," and dramatic quality of Disraeli's fiction. On a deeper level Stanley B. James, writing in the *Catholic World* (1941), sees Disraeli's career as a tragedy in that for the sake of worldly fame and power he compromised his profound, almost Catholic, prophetic vision of an organic society based on an established religion. Both Montagu Frank Modder's "Young Disraeli in Scotland" (*LQHR*, 1932) and Emily Morse Symonds' ("George Paston") "The Young Disraeli and His Adventures in Journalism" (*Cornhill Magazine*, 1932) recount the frequently amusing negotiations with Murray and Lockhart that lie behind *Vivian Grey*. "With Disraeli in Italy," by J. A. Lovat-Fraser (*Contemporary Review*, 1930), shows how Disraeli's Italian tour of 1826 provided background for a number of the novels. Finally, in *RES* (1943) C. L. Cline dates and clarifies from documents at Hughenden the relationship between Disraeli and Thackeray that led to the satirical portrait of the latter in *Endymion*.

IV. *General Criticism*

Four book-length general surveys of the novels have been written, each one taking a different tack. The first of these, Philipp Aronstein's "Benjamin Disraeli's Leben und dicterische Werke" (*Anglia*, 1895), is an orderly, complete treatment that emphasizes the novels' satiric power. Aronstein's chapters on such subjects as Disraeli and the Jews and Disraeli and Carlyle are informative, and his bibliography is highly useful. Of Hildegard Seikat's *Die Romankunst Disraelis* (1933) only a small fraction is in print, and that fraction seems mechanical. In view of her title her conclusion that Disraeli has little novelistic art is disappointing. Not even professing originality or depth, Muriel Masefield's *Peacocks and Primroses: A Survey of Disraeli's Novels* (1953) is an entertaining popular recapitulation of Disraeli's biography and the "pageant of English life" from 1826 to 1880 as seen through his novels. Though useful as an introduction, it is largely mere rehearsal of plot. The most recent general survey to appear, *The Monstrous Clever Young Man: The Novelist Disraeli and His Heroes* (1959), by Arthur H. Frietzsche, argues convincingly that Disraeli has created a single, largely autobiographical hero whom he develops through a series of novels in which the basic pattern is similar.

Disraeli's stature as not a major but a second-string novelist has encouraged many critics to try to polish him off neatly in a brief essay. Most of these essays are thin and repetitive, but a few offer important new angles of critical vision. Of the essays published before 1925 two of the best are Leslie Stephen's "Mr. Disraeli's Novels" in *Hours in a Library, Second Series* (1876), and Stuart P. Sherman's "The Disraelian Irony" in *Points of View* (1924), both urging a lighthearted appreciation of the novels. Stephen argues that Disraeli's skill lies in the tantalizing ambiguity with which he carefully hides where he is serious and where he is ironic. Particularly in a book like *Tancred* Disraeli purposely and amusingly bewilders his reader. Sherman, too, emphasizes the comic, satiric, and ironic aspects of the novels and sees Disraeli as a showman who is covertly making fun of the aristocracy at the same time that he is praising it — a debatable but provocative thesis. In a characteristically graceful essay (printed as a general introduction to the Empire or Earl's Edition of the novels, 1904–1905, and reprinted in *Transactions of the Royal Society of Literature*, 1918) Edmund Gosse contends that even in the novels Disraeli the man is more important than any of his literary creations. Other valuable essays are those by R. E.

Gordon George on the unity of the novels, *Nineteenth Century* (1924); by Walter Sichel on "Disraeli as a Landscape Painter" in the novels, *Time* (1888); by Eugène-Melchior de Vogüé on the imperialism of Disraeli in contrast to the imperialism of Kipling, *Revue des deux mondes* (1901); and by Frederic Harrison on the way in which Disraeli's fame as a statesman has obscured his merit as a satirist, *Studies in Early Victorian Literature* (1895).

Of the more recent general studies John Holloway's chapter in *The Victorian Sage* (1953) is by far the most stimulating. Though with the warnings of Stephen and Sherman sounding in one's ears one cannot perhaps wholly accept Holloway's thesis that in the novels there is a close and meaningful unity of purpose buttressed both by the light satire and by the serious discussions of ideas, Holloway's arguments from style and plot are cogent. With a great deal of success he relates the often seemingly absurd artificiality of Disraeli's diction to an inner core of meaning. Three years before the appearance of Holloway's book, Eric Forbes-Boyd in "Disraeli the Novelist" (*Essays and Studies of the English Association*, 1950) had also urged that Disraeli's affectation, his flamboyance of style, his operatic exaggeration, was a deliberate artistic technique, but Forbes-Boyd had not followed this insight into any such rounded conclusion as Holloway's. Another excellent general essay is Frank Swinnerton's "Disraeli as a Novelist" (*London Mercury* and *Yale Review*, 1928), which contends that Disraeli in his first few novels discovered that he could not write a great romantic novel, recognized the fact, and deliberately dropped to the political novel, in which he became supreme. The break, according to Swinnerton, came after *Henrietta Temple*.

No review of the general criticism of Disraeli's novels should neglect to mention Anthony Trollope's thorough condemnation of them as "tinsel" and "pasteboard" with the "flavour of hair-oil" (in his *Autobiography*) or Thackeray's delightful parody " 'Codlingsby,' by B. Shrewsberry, Esq." A recent article, by Sir H. J. d'Avigdor-Goldsmid, *London*

Magazine (1960), is interesting as an opinion by a present-day Member of Parliament. Paul Bloomfield's pamphlet in the "Writers and Their Work" series (1961), a readable general panorama with helpful scattered comments but no real thesis, is unusually favorable toward the earlier novels and accords scant justice to the wit and sophisticated satire of the later ones. The most recent of all general studies is the chapter "Benjamin Disraeli, The Romantic Egotist" in Stephen R. Graubard, *Burke, Disraeli, Churchill: The Politics of Perseverance* (1961). Though oriented largely toward politics and biography and though plodding in style, Graubard's chapter is of value in emphasizing in the novels the repeated theme of individual heroism, of "the dimensions and possibilities of success" and the value of youth and heroic achievement, as expressed through Disraeli's often unbelievable heroes.

Specific aspects of the novels have also received attention. Since Disraeli's are the prime exemplars of the type, much has been made of his development of the political novel. H. D. Traill, for instance, in an essay "The Political Novel" in *The New Fiction* (1897) traces the genre from Disraeli, and M. E. Speare in *The Political Novel: Its Development in England and America* (1924) places primary emphasis on him. Another kind of political analysis, implicit in many of the articles and biographies already mentioned, is that which turns to the novels for light on Disraeli's political and social views. Three German critics have analyzed the relationship between the novels and Disraeli's international policies: Bruno Bauer, *Disraeli's romantischer und Bismarck's socialistischer Imperialismus* (1882); Boris Segalowitsch, *Benjamin Disraelis Orientalismus* (1930); and Hans Rühl, *Disraelis Imperialismus und die Kolonialpolitik seiner Zeit* (1935). The social ideas of the novels, best treated by Louis Cazamian in the sixth chapter of *Le Roman social en Angleterre, 1830–1850* (1903), have also been considered in Otto Thoma, *Das englische Verfassungs- und Gesellschaftsideal in den politischen Romanen Benjamin Disraelis* (1913) and more recently, as a result of the modern revival of interest in conservatism, in Albert Tucker, "Disraeli and the National Aristocracy" (*Canadian Journal of Economics*, 1962). The question of religion obviously looms large in the novels. Disraeli's religious views are treated briefly in Joseph Ellis Baker's *The Novel and the Oxford Movement* (1932) and at greater length with special reference to *Lothair* in Irmgard Herrmann's *Benjamin Disraelis Stellung zur katholischen Kirche* (1932). The fullest, though perhaps not the most perceptive, treatment of the subject is in Arthur H. Frietzsche, *Disraeli's Religion: The Treatment of Religion in Disraeli's Novels* (1961), which traces in the novels the "stumbling" path of Disraeli's successive enthusiasms for Judaism, Catholicism, and Anglicanism and argues that *Lothair* can be read as in large part Disraeli's own spiritual autobiography. In contrast to Frietzsche's conception that Disraeli's religious beliefs have only a rough pattern is Clyde J. Lewis's argument in "Disraeli's Conception of Divine Order" (*Jewish Social Studies*, 1962), that Disraeli's social and political ideas are coherently based on one basic religious idea.

Over the years one of the subjects that have most consistently aroused the interest of commentators has been Disraeli's relationship to Judaism and the Jews. The best of the many treatments of this theme are Joseph Caro, "Benjamin Disraeli, Juden und Judentum" (*Monatsschrift für Geschichte und Wissenschaft des Judentums*, 1932); Cecil Roth's excellent passages in his brief biography, *Benjamin Disraeli, Earl of Beaconsfield* (1952); and Montagu Modder, "The Alien Patriot in Disraeli's Novels" (*LQHR*, 1934), the basic theme of which is that the novels reflect the struggle of the Jews in Victorian times to gain recognition of their rights and talents. Lesser studies on the same subject are chapter VII of David Philipson, *The Jew in English Fiction* (1889); chapter VI of Maurice Muret, *L'Esprit Juif* (1901); and chapter V of Otto Friedrich, *Weise von Zion* (1936).

The artistic background out of which Disraeli's novels arose has also received critical attention. German influences on his work have been rewardingly discussed by Jean-Marie

Carré in *Goethe en Angleterre* (1920), Susanne Howe in *Wilhelm Meister and His English Kinsmen* (1930), and Felix Gilbert in "The Germany of *Contarini Fleming*" (*Contemporary Review*, 1936). Gilbert's article is particularly useful in combatting the tendency to read many of the novels too autobiographically. Carré argues that it is the Goethean thought that gives the real interest to Disraeli's stylistically mediocre and slow-moving novels.

Another literary trend that has received merited attention is that of the society novel. The antecedents of both Bulwer and Disraeli in this genre are well described in Matthew Whiting Rosa's *The Silver-Fork School: Novels of Fashion Preceding "Vanity Fair"* (1936). On the same general subject H. B. Samuel in "Two Dandy Novels" (*Academy and Literature*, 1904) has made a revealing distinction between the dominant literary emphasis in *Pelham* and the dominant political emphasis in *Vivian Grey*. The whole question of dandyism in both novelists has, however, been best treated in a lively and readable book by Ellen Moers, *The Dandy: Brummell to Beerbohm* (1960), which despite its title is really a literary study. Chapter IV, "Disraeli," points out that in *Vivian Grey* and to a lesser extent in the other novels Disraeli has created an unusual type of dandy, one who longs for political power.

Other literary relationships have also been noted. Lionel Stevenson's "Stepfathers of Victorianism" (*VQR*, 1930), for instance, is an exceedingly clear-sighted and succinct comparison between Disraeli and Bulwer in the light of their Romantic antecedents and their influence on the succeeding Victorian period. Of Disraeli's debt to the Romantics, however, the most thorough treatment is Johanna Kohlund, *Benjamin Disraelis Stellung zur englischen Romantik* (1913). Disraeli's own influence on an American author is treated by Ruth L. Hudson in "Poe and Disraeli" (*American Literature*, 1937), who convincingly argues that several of Poe's stories were intended as burlesques of novels by Disraeli. To counterbalance these studies of literary origins the student should keep in mind Frietzsche's previously mentioned *The Mon-*

strous Clever Young Man and also Friedrich Karl Otto's *Autobiographisches aus Disraeli's Jugendromanen* (1913).

Finally, one should not forget the numerous "keys" to the real prototypes of the fictional characters in the novels. Identifying Disraeli's characters has been an international pastime from before the first appearance of *Vivian Grey* up to the present. Perhaps the most elaborate keys are those published by H. Pereira Mendes and R. W. Howes in 1904 and 1907 respectively. The best approach to the whole problem, however, is through the indexes to *N&Q*.

V. *Studies of Individual Novels*

Detailed studies of individual novels by Disraeli have been rare, and those that have appeared have tended to be of only peripheral interest. Little, for instance, has been written about the early novels. In "The Publication and Reception of Disraeli's *Vivian Grey (Quarterly Review*, 1960), it is true, R. W. Stewart provides details as to the composition, the secrecy surrounding the authorship, the portrayal of Murray and Lockhart as Carabas and Cleveland, and the unfavorable reviews of that first novel. Also C. L. Cline in "Benjamin Disraeli on the Grotesque in Literature" (*RES*, 1940) reprints from the original manuscript Disraeli's own defense of the drinking scene in the book, and Maria Caspar by a careful study of the contemporary German background corrects in *Disraelis Vivian Grey II als politischer Schlüsselroman* (1928) the English "keys" to the German parts of the story. In "The Failure of Disraeli's *Contarini Fleming*" (*N&Q*, 1942) C. L. Cline examines the financial history of that book from accounts preserved at Hughenden and suggests that its relative failure helped turn Disraeli from a literary to a political career. A. Brandl in a brief note "Zur Quelle von Disraelis *Alroy*" (*Archiv*, 1925) points out as a source of that novel Rabbi Benjamin of Tudela's itinerary, an English translation of which was published in 1840. *Henrietta Temple* has received notice of another kind in Anthony Powell's introduction to his reprinting of it in *Novels of High Society from the*

Victorian Age (1947): Powell emphasizes the shrewd psychology and eighteenth-century spirit of the novel. And three critics have studied the delineations of Shelley and Byron in *Venetia*. Herbert Bruce Hamilton's *Byron in Disraeli's Novel Venetia* (1884) is pedestrian; Richard Garnett's "Shelley and Lord Beaconsfield" (*Essays of an Ex-Librarian,* 1901), identifies the possible sources of Disraeli's new information about Shelley and emphasizes the fact that Disraeli was one of Shelley's very early admirers; and Gustav Hahn's *Lord Beaconsfields Roman Venetia ein Denkmal Byrons und Shelleys* (1898) lauds the novel for its poetic picture of the two great poets.

As might be expected, Disraeli's dazzling political trilogy has aroused considerably more critical interest. A striking article on *Coningsby* is "A Political Novel: Disraeli Sets a Lively Pace" (*TLS,* 1959), in which Maurice Edelman forcefully contends that the novel's power lies in its relationship with real politics: its drama springs from the confrontation of social classes or estates rather than from the clash of individuals. Two other valuable studies of the same novel are Eugène Forçade's excellent review of it as primarily a political manifesto in "De la Jeune Angleterre" (*Revue des deux mondes,* 1844) and Walter Allen's laudatory introduction to the Chiltern Library edition (1948). André Maurois in the introduction to the World's Classics edition (1931) sums up well the difficulty faced by Disraeli in his attempt to mingle fiction and history, and Arthur H. Frietzsche in "Action Is Not for Me: Disraeli's Sidonia and the Dream of Power" (*Proceedings of the Utah Academy of Sciences, Arts, and Letters,* 1959–1960) points out in Sidonia Disraeli's odd conception of a hero who supposedly has huge influence and deep wisdom but who takes no part in action and whose arguments for Jewish racism could equally well support anti-Jewish racism. In two minor notes C. L. Cline has identified references to *Coningsby* by Thackeray, Trollope, and Samuel Butler ("*Coningsby* and Three Victorian Novelists," *N&Q,* 1944), and D. J. Greene, citing amazingly close parallels, has argued that Thackeray's Becky Sharp was suggested by Mrs.

Guy Flouncey ("Becky Sharp and Lord Steyne — Thackeray or Disraeli?" *NCF*, 1961).

Though *Sybil* has received less attention, it has been treated excellently by H. D. Traill in the introduction to an edition published by Macmillan in 1895 and competently by Walter Sichel in his introduction to the World's Classics edition (1925). Robert Hamilton's comment on the novel, "Disraeli and the Two Nations" (*Quarterly Review*, 1950), supports Disraeli's conservatism as an ideal applicable to our time too. Of *Tancred* the best discussion is still James Russell Lowell's review in the *North American Review* (1847), later reprinted in *The Round Table* (1913) — a witty and high-spirited picture of Disraeli and Bulwer as seen by an American in the 1840's. It makes great fun of the fashionable novel and is also an attack on Young England's glorification of the past and on the use of fiction for political propaganda. *Tancred* is seen as far too grandiose. The best answer, of course, to such criticism is to view the novel as intentionally flamboyant, as Gosse does, or as unified by an overriding purpose, as Holloway does.

Something of the same kind of approach is taken to *Lothair*, the first of the two late novels, in an amusing review "Le Roman politique en Angleterre" (*Revue des deux mondes*, 1870), by P. Challemel-Lacour, who concentrates on the difficulty of drawing the line between fantasy and seriousness in the book. But the primary discussion of *Lothair* has centered on its religious ideas. Frietzsche's *Disraeli's Religion* has been mentioned above. A fresh approach has been provided by H. Somerville, who argues not wholly convincingly in "Disraeli and Catholicism" (*The Month*, 1932) that the novel is not an attack on the Catholic Church but that, on the contrary, Disraeli shows in it great respect for Catholics and Catholicism. Somerville sees Disraeli like Newman in reaction against the secular materialism of the age. If Somerville is surprising in viewing *Lothair* as sympathetic to Catholicism, G. W. E. Russell astonishes even more in *Portraits of the Seventies* (1916) by proving that some of the more absurdly melodramatic Italian incidents in the book are based on real events. Research, one must conclude, can do anything! Rowland Grey in "Disraeli in Fancy Street" (*Cornhill Magazine,* 1929) has discussed the author's self-portraiture in *Endymion.*

BULWER-LYTTON

I. *Bibliography*

Since even the canon of his writings, particularly of his contributions to periodicals, is not yet established, much bibliographical research remains to be done on Bulwer. There is great need for a complete and accurate bibliography. The best now available is that in Michael Sadleir's *XIX Century Fiction, A Bibliographical Record* (2 vols., 1951). Archie R. Bangs convincingly makes one addition to the Bulwer canon in attributing to Bulwer a brief novel entitled *Mephistophiles in England; or, The Confessions of a Prime Minister (PMLA,* 1932). A study of American and British magazines would probably reap a large though perhaps not valuable harvest.

II. *Editions and Letters*

There is no wholly complete edition of Bulwer's works. Though there are dozens of editions of the novels alone — three of the important ones being the Library Edition (40 vols., Edinburgh and London, 1859–1874), the New Library Edition (40 vols., Boston, 1892–1893), and the New Knebworth Edition (29 vols., London, 1895–1898) — only one edition has been published that satisfactorily includes the poetry and nonfiction too: the Knebworth Edition (37 vols., 1873–1877).

A complete collection of Bulwer's correspondence is also lacking and is much to be desired not alone because of its importance to the study of Bulwer but also because of Bulwer's contacts with nearly every major author from the reign of George IV until Bulwer's death in 1873. Aside from the letters published in *The Life, Letters, and Literary Remains*

(2 vols., 1883) by his son, the first Earl of Lytton ("Owen Meredith"), the largest published collection is *The Letters of the Late Edward Bulwer, Lord Lytton, to His Wife*, published in 1884 by Louisa Devey, Rosina Bulwer's literary executrix. These are useful in correcting the official family version of the early years and break-up of the marriage. Frederick Gillen has edited the letters to Charles Kent ("Mark Rochester") in the Boston Public Library, *More Books* (1947), letters which, though brief, give an interesting insight into Bulwer's literary and political affairs. Sarah Dickson's "The Bulwer-Lytton Collection" in *PULC* (1946) on the Morris Parrish Collection, and the note entitled "Letters of Edward Bulwer-Lytton, Baron Lytton, to Richard Bentley, 1829–73," *Bodleian Library Record* (1948), are useful descriptions of collections. No description or catalogue has as yet been published of the mass of letters and manuscripts at Knebworth.

III. *Biography*

The basic sources for biography of Bulwer are *The Life, Letters, and Literary Remains* by his son, the first Earl of Lytton, and *The Life of Edward Bulwer, First Lord Lytton* (2 vols., 1913) by his grandson, the second Earl. The first of these, though it reaches only to 1831, is a mine of letters and thitherto unpublished fragments and includes a fairly extensive fragment of autobiography. The second is the standard life, a thoroughly workmanlike job which includes much of the material of the first life but carries the story through to the end. It contains little criticism. A good comparison of and comment on these two lives is provided by Edmund Gosse's review of the latter in the *Fortnightly Review* (1913). Though the grandson's life is not so pious as the son's, it nevertheless should still be balanced in regard to the marriage and ensuing scandal by the altogether too partisan and too defamatory book stating Rosina's grievances, *A Blighted Life* (1880), probably not written by Rosina but based on information supplied by her, and Louisa Devey's similar volume, *The Life of Rosina, Lady Lytton* (1887, suppressed). *The Unpublished Letters of Lady Bulwer Lytton to A. E. Chalon, R.A.*, edited by S. M. Ellis (1914), add little to the controversy. Other of the earlier lives also still have considerable value. Two written in 1873, the year of Bulwer's death, are Thomson Cooper's *Lord Lytton, A Biography*, which includes valuable references to critical opinions of Bulwer's work expressed at the time of his death, and Jan ten Brink's "Lord Edward Bulwer Lytton" (*Litterarische Schetsen en Kritieken*, V, 1882), an informed and thorough Dutch analysis. In *Edward Bulwer, First Baron Lytton of Knebworth, A Social, Personal, and Political Monograph* (1910) T. H. S. Escott follows the dangerous procedure of drawing biography out of the novels, but he was one of the first to note how Bulwer was a pioneer in several important literary trends, and his discussion of Bulwer's essays enters into a field too much ignored by both earlier and later critics. In 1913 William Alfred Frost in *Bulwer Lytton: An Exposure of the Errors of His Biographers* prepared the way for the Earl of Lytton's standard biography by correcting misstatements in the preceding biographies.

Though stimulating, later biography has by no means been definitive. Michael Sadleir's *Bulwer: A Panorama. I. Edward and Rosina, 1803–1836* (1931; also published as *Bulwer and His Wife: A Panorama*), a fragment of what would if completed have been the most detailed and solidly based biography, is the best study of the background of much of the early fiction. It is very full on Bulwer's relationship with Lady Caroline Lamb. Yet it perhaps has too much detail, too much imaginative reinterpretation, and too much amateur psychologizing. One regrets that Sadleir's biography was never completed, but one can understand why. Evidently an offshoot of his research on Bulwer is his *Blessington-D'Orsay, A Masquerade* (1933; rev. ed., 1947), which has much to say about the relationship between Bulwer and Lady Blessington. Entirely different from Sadleir's often diffuse volumes is the Earl of Lytton's second biography of his grandfather. This brief volume in the English Novelists series (1948) is an admirable summary of Bulwer's life together with a swift, accurate survey of the novels. The critical remarks are eminently sane, though they perhaps overpraise the Caxton series. Sidelights on Bulwer can, of course, be found in the lives and letters of Disraeli, Carlyle, Thackeray, Dickens, Macready, and most of the other literary figures of the era.

IV. *General Criticism*

During his lifetime Bulwer came in for an inordinate amount of both praise and vilification. Carlyle's stinging satire in *Sartor Resartus*, Thackeray's in the *Punch* parody "George de Barnwell" and in *The Yellowplush Correspondence*, Tennyson's in "The New Timon and the Poets," and John Wilson's in *Noctes Ambrosianae* was more than balanced by the adulation of such friendly critics as L.E.L., Henry F. Chorley, R. H. Horne, Margaret Oliphant, and Benjamin Jowett, and by the tremendous reputation he won for himself, particularly in America and Germany (see, for instance, the German articles on Bulwer by Heinrich Laube in *Moderne Charakteristiken*, 1835, and Julian Schmidt in *Bilder aus dem geistigen Leben unserer Zeit*, 1870). Since his death critics have been less rabid for or against him. The one book-length study of his work, E. G. Bell's *Introductions to the Prose Romances, Plays, and Comedies of Edward Bulwer, Lord Lytton* (1914), is laudatory. Unfortunately it is little more than a series of brief summaries of the novels with an explanation of the moral lesson in each, and its principal value lies in its careful noting of textual changes from edition to edition.

Of the general critical essays on Bulwer's fiction, most emphasize his constant effort to achieve popularity. For example, in a vigorous attack, "Lord Lytton's Novels" (*Nineteenth Century*, 1901), Walter F. Lord attributes Bulwer's success with the public — but not with the critics — to his carrying on in prose the Byronic tradition and to his remarkable command of supernatural machinery. On the other hand, in "The Novels of Lord Lytton" (*Critic*, 1903), Francis Gribble says that his secret was a combination of sentiment, melodramatic effect, and knowledge of the world that made him the grandfather of the penny adventure novel. In the same vein Lewis S. Benjamin ("Lewis Melville") in *Victorian Novelists* (1906; see also "The Centenary of Bulwer-Lytton," *Bookman*, 1903) argues that florid style, false sentiment, and poor psychology weaken his early novels but that in his later books he began to lose his artificiality and to think more deeply and see more clearly. A much more kindly article by Lionel Stevenson, "Stepfathers of Victorianism" (*VQR*, 1930), demonstrates that Bulwer and Disraeli both added a strain of realism to the Byronic elements which they inherited and thus made a new amalgam that pointed forward to Reade and Dickens. To the tantalizing critical question of how so apparently bad a novelist as Bulwer can still retain his readers as he has done, at least with respect to *The Last Days of Pompeii,* Desmond MacCarthy in "The Padded Man" (*Experience*, 1935) unfortunately has been able to give no more satisfactory answer than his predecessors; he can only say that Bulwer has a vitality and gift of interesting the ordinary reader that has been underrated.

Since Bulwer's main historical importance is as a literary pioneer in fiction, specialized studies have dealt with the several kinds of novels into which Bulwer blazed the way which greater novelists were later to follow. In *Le Roman social en Angleterre, 1830–1850* (1903) Louis Cazamian studies Bulwer as one of the first social novelists of the Victorian period and points out how *Paul Clifford*, which Cazamian calls a Utilitarian novel, looks forward to Dickens. Alec Lucas in "*Oliver Twist* and the Newgate Novel" (*Dalhousie Review*, 1954), Régis Messac in "Bulwer Lytton et Dostoïevski: de Paul Clifford à Rashkolnikof" (*Revue de littérature comparée*, 1926), and Keith Hollingsworth in *The Newgate Novel, 1830–1847* (1963) have seen Bulwer as a pioneer in the novel with the criminal hero. Messac's thoughtful analysis is particularly perceptive in attributing the weakness of

Eugene Aram and *Paul Clifford* to Bulwer's recoiling from his own conception of a good man drawn to crime for a "good" reason. Messac argues convincingly that Dostoyevsky was influenced by Bulwer. Hollingsworth points out the relationship of Bulwer's crime novels to the contemporary movement for legal reform.

As Carlyle recognized, another kind of novel in which Bulwer was a pioneer was the novel of fashion. Matthew Whiting Rosa has given this aspect of his fiction considerable attention in *The Silver-Fork School* (1936). Less important comments on the same subject are those by Leon H. Vincent in *Dandies and Men of Letters* (1913) and H. B. Samuel in "Two Dandy Novels" (*Academy and Literature*, 1904) — both primarily concerned with *Pelham*. The most illuminating study of that novel and of Bulwer himself in that respect, however, is certainly that in Ellen Moers, *The Dandy: Brummell to Beerbohm* (1960). Moers argues that *Pelham*, which she views as a manual of Regency dandyism, is Bulwer's best novel and also makes the excellent suggestion that the ostensibly historical *The Last Days of Pompeii* really reflects the "last days" of Regency society.

Bulwer has also attracted attention as historical novelist and novelist of the occult. Indeed, one of the most thorough recent studies of him is Hellmuth Seifert's excellent *Bulwers Verhältnis zur Geschichte* (1935). In "History on the Hustings: Bulwer-Lytton's Historical Novels of Politics" (*From Jane Austen to Joseph Conrad*, edited by Robert C. Rathburn and Martin Steinmann, Jr., 1958) Curtis Dahl shows that in typical Victorian fashion Bulwer uses history to comment on the political questions of his own time. Bulwer, who was always interested in the occult, would probably be pleased and perhaps amused to learn that his novels of the occult may have been central in the founding of the Theosophical Society by Mme. Blavatsky. This, at least, is the thesis of S. B. Liljegren in "Quelques romans anglais, source partielle d'une religion moderne" (*Mélanges d'histoire littéraire, générale et comparée, offerts à Fernand Baldensperger*, 1930), and the same author's *Bulwer-Lytton's Novels and Isis Unveiled*

(1957). By citing epigraphs and quotations Liljegren convincingly shows that much of Mme. Blavatsky's Egyptian and Rosicrucian lore was based on Bulwer's novels such as *The Last Days of Pompeii, Zicci, Zanoni, A Strange Story,* and *The Coming Race.* C. Nelson Stewart's brief monograph *Bulwer-Lytton as Occultist* (1927) supports the same thesis. The relationship of Bulwer's interest in the occult to the controversy over scientific materialism and Darwinian evolution and the foreshadowing of modern psychology in his interest in the occult are studied by Joseph L. Fradin in " 'The Absorbing Tyranny of Every-day Life': Bulwer's *A Strange Story*" (*NCF*, 1961).

Bulwer was a theoretical critic of fiction as well as a novelist. As early as 1864 Nassau W. Senior in his *Essays on Fiction* pointed out the importance of Bulwer's theory to an understanding of his novels. Harold H. Watts clarified just what that theory was by analysis of Bulwer's essay "On Art in Fiction" in "Lytton's Theories of Prose Fiction" (*PMLA*, 1935). This trend of study has recently been brought to a head by Michael Lloyd in his excellent "Bulwer-Lytton and the Idealising Principle" (*English Miscellany*, 1956). Lloyd's article is extremely important to an understanding of Bulwer's successes and failures as a novelist, and his conclusion that *Zanoni* represents, paradoxically, the antithesis in life of what Bulwer preached in art is striking. On a much lower plane, unfortunately, is the thematic study by Gustav Busch, *Bulwers Jugendliebe und ihr Einfluss auf sein Leben und seine Werke* (1899–1900).

Source and influence hunting in Bulwer has been in large measure a German preserve. Unfortunately much of it, like Karl Beger's *Die historischen Quellen zu Bulwers Roman "Devereux"* (1912) and Karl Jakob's *Die historischen Quellen von Bulwers Roman "The Last of the Barons"* (1908), is pedestrian and lacks criticism. Johannes Müller, in *Bulwers Roman "The Last of the Barons"* (1907), does point out interesting analogues to the story of the alchemist Adam Warner. A good summary of the literary, particularly the Gothic, background of *The Last Days of Pompeii* is given by Erich Zim-

merman in his *Entstehungsgeschichte und Komposition von
Bulwers "The Last Days of Pompeii"* (1914). Curtis Dahl in
"Bulwer-Lytton and the School of Catastrophe" (*PQ*, 1953)
and "Recreators of Pompeii" (*Archaeology*, 1956) has shown
the background of the same novel in the numerous literary
and pictorial works on Pompeii preceding it and in the cult
of catastrophe that was a major aspect of both art and literature from the 1780's to the 1840's. Source studies of three
other novels are: Albert Warncke, *Miss Mitfords und Bulwers
englische Rienzibearbeitungen im Verhältnis zu ihren Quellen und zu einander* (1904); Franz Heinrich's *Laurence
Sterne und Edward Bulwer* (1904); and Cornel Dumbacher's
careful *Bulwers Roman "Harold, the Last of the Saxon
Kings," eine Quellenuntersuchung* (1911).

More general influences on Bulwer have been studied in
three works on his relationship with German literature. Jean-
Marie Carré, *Goethe en Angleterre* (1920), and Susanne
Howe, *Wilhelm Meister and His English Kinsmen* (1930),
have much of value to say about Bulwer. One of the most intelligent and well-organized source studies specifically on Bulwer is August Hermann Goldhan's long article "Über die Ein-
wirkung des Goethischen Werthers und Wilhelm Meisters
auf die Entwicklung Edward Bulwers" (*Anglia*, 1894). Goldhan emphasizes Goethe's influence on both Bulwer's thought
and his emotional attitudes. Finally, the previously mentioned
article by Archie R. Bangs on *Mephistophiles in England*
(*PMLA*, 1932) serves as a good study of Bulwer's debt to
Goethe.

V. *Studies of Individual Novels*

In addition to the source studies, there are a few, but only
a few, research articles on specific novels by Bulwer. Most of
these are of peripheral importance. Charles Duffy, *N&Q*
(1943), suggests that Thomas Campbell may well have written
a parody or continuation of *Pelham* under the title *Pelham's
Widow*. Keith Hollingsworth, *MLN* (1951), advances evidence to show that William Jerdan suggested to Bulwer the

idea of satirizing public figures of the day in the guise of highwaymen in *Paul Clifford*. V.R. in *N&Q* (1935) tries to explain why in the same novel Bulwer so bitterly attacked the *Athenaeum*. Herman S. Ficke, *Texas Studies in English* (1926), advances the interesting theory that *A Strange Story* is a major source of H. Rider Haggard's *She*. The reception, particularly in America, of *The Last Days of Pompeii* is well summed up by Arthur Bartlett Maurice in the *Bookman* (1903), with quotations from Poe, Sumner Lincoln Fairfield, and others. The best introduction to the same novel is the sound, balanced, yet appreciative one by Edgar Johnson in the Limited Editions Club edition (1956). More such critical and scholarly essays on novels by Bulwer are much to be desired.

3 ₷

Charles Dickens

Ada Nisbet

THE STORY GOES that a woman packing books for the boys at the front during World War I complained to Shaw, "Surely Dickens is a washout!" Whether or not the Shavian reply, "Mont Blanc is a washout to people who have not sufficient breath to climb Primrose Hill," was prophetic of a hardier stock to come, no one can deny that the years since 1918 have seen a phenomenal rise in the number of ardent scramblers over Dickensian terrain. An extravagant irony, in itself Dickensian, lies in the fact that the stick buried at the turn of the century by a procession of solemn Mr. Moulds is once again as lively a rocket as that set off by Samuel Pickwick in 1836.

The multiplicity of writings on Dickens in the past thirty years discourages any hope of making this survey more than a relief map indicating major promontories.[1] A check of Victorian bibliographies (in themselves highly selective) reveals the Gradgrindian facts that exclusive of the *Dickensian* 50 more articles on Dickens were published in the 1940's than in the 1930's and 130 more in the 1950's than in the 1940's. And the *Guide to Doctoral Dissertations in Victorian Literature*,

---

[1] This survey covers through 1962 and includes a few of the numerous more recent publications.

1886–1958 (comp. Richard D. Altick and William R. Matthews, 1960) indicates a parallel growth, showing a rise from 7 dissertations in the 1930's to 11 in the 1940's to 32 in the 1950's.

Fortunately, others have already tackled the job of bringing some kind of order and perspective out of this chaos. Foremost among these is George H. Ford, whose *Dickens and His Readers: Aspects of Novel-Criticism since 1836* (1955) is indispensable to the Dickensian novice and expert alike, for it not only charts the complex currents of Dickens' reputation in England, but illuminates the history of critical taste from his own day to the present. Ford has not limited his study to reviews, but has drawn from diaries, autobiographies, biographies, letters, memoirs, and critical essays, and on every page exercises a discerning judgment that keeps the narrative in firm control. Along the same lines but much less comprehensive and judicious is Irma Rantavaara's earlier study, *Dickens in the Light of English Criticism* (1944). Another useful survey, limited to a selective review of major biographies and critical works, is the British Council pamphlet *Charles Dickens* (1953; rev. 1960, 1963) by K. J. Fielding. Fielding packs an immense amount of information and acute evaluation into thirty-eight pages, and his bibliography will be found a reliable guide for the Dickensian initiate. Other reviews of briefer scope are Morton D. Zabel, "Dickens: The Reputation Revised" (*Nation*, Sept. 17, 1949), reprinted in *Craft and Character in Modern Fiction* (1957); Fred W. Boege, "Recent Criticism of Dickens" (*NCF*, 1953); and Edgar Johnson, "The Present State of Dickensian Studies" (*VNL*, 1955). The three major surveys of Dickens' foreign reputation are *Dickens et la France: Etude d'une interaction littéraire anglo-française* by Floris Delattre (1927), *Dickens' Works in Germany, 1837–1937* by Ellis N. Gummer (1940), and the bibliography of Russian translation and criticism compiled by IU. Fridlender and I. Katarsky, *Charl'z Dikkens, bibliografiia russkikh perevodov i kriticheskoi literatury na russkom iazyke, 1838–1960* (1962).

I. *Manuscripts* [2]

The holograph manuscripts of most of the major novels, together with many of the working notes and proofs, were willed by Dickens to John Forster and are now in the Forster Collection at the Victoria and Albert Museum. The collection contains only the 1847 preface to *Pickwick*, the 1848 preface to *Nicholas Nickleby*, and 31 chapters of *Oliver Twist*, but it has the full manuscripts and most of the corrected proofs of all the other novels except *Great Expectations* and *Our Mutual Friend* as well as those of *American Notes, Pictures from Italy* (incomplete), *The Chimes, Sketches of Young Couples,* Chapters II and VI of *A Child's History of England,* the diaries for 1838–1841, journalistic miscellanea, and publishers' records. The manuscript of *Great Expectations* is in the Wisbech Literary Institute, Cambridgeshire; that of *Our Mutual Friend* in the Pierpont Morgan Library, New York. Also at the Morgan Library are the manuscripts of all the Christmas Books except *The Chimes* and *The Haunted Man,* as well as *Sketches of Young Gentlemen,* "Hunted Down," "Holiday Romance," one page of *Nickleby,* a scrapbook of the periodical issues of *Great Expectations* with holograph alterations, and a few articles and business agreements. *The Haunted Man* is at the Pforzheimer Foundation, New York. Miscellaneous articles and speeches, Chapter XII of *A Child's History,* and a letterpress book of business correspondence for *All the Year Round* are in the Huntington Library, California. Six leaves of *Pickwick* are at the British Museum. Princeton University Library has recently acquired the "Office Book" for *Household Words,* an invaluable aid to identification of contributors.[3] The Berg Collection at the New York Public Library owns a number of important manuscripts including the unique pocket diary for 1867 which has figured so prominently in the search for informa-

---

[2] Useful notes on the manuscripts will be found in William Miller and T. W. Hill, *Dickensian,* 1917; K. J. Fielding, *VNL,* 1958; and John Butt, *YULG,* 1962.

[3] Unfortunately the whereabouts of the companion book for *All the Year Round,* consulted by F. G. Kitton (see *Minor Writings,* p. vii), is unknown.

tion on the Dickens-Ternan story, a book of memoranda (1855–1870),[4] a page of *Pickwick*, 4 pages of *Oliver Twist*, 18 minor but complete manuscripts, 22 publishers' agreements, and the corrected proof sheets for *Our Mutual Friend*. A number of early publishers' agreements, a petty cash book kept by Dickens in 1828, the corrected proofs for thirty chapters of *Copperfield*, and several smaller pieces are at the Harvard library. The Free Library of Philadelphia has 30 pages of corrected proof for *Chuzzlewit*, a half page of *Nickleby*, five shorthand notebooks made up by Dickens in teaching shorthand to Arthur Stone, and various minor items. Besides a number of miscellaneous papers and documents, the Dickens House in London owns one page of *Pickwick* and 39 pages of *Nickleby*. The Rosenbach Foundation Museum, Philadelphia, has 24 pages of *Pickwick* and 103½ pages of *Nickleby* (the major portions of the extant manuscripts of those two novels) as well as an account book kept by the business manager of the reading tours of 1861–1863 and 36 original documents connected with *Household Words* and *All the Year Round* including half-yearly statements of profits and partnership agreements. The only significant manuscripts other than letters known still to be in private hands are the 22 pages of *Nickleby* and 12 pages of *Pickwick* in the collection of the Comtesse de Suzannet, a number of publishers' agreements held by Henry Charles Dickens, and the items in the extensive personal collection of Colonel Richard Gimbel, part of which is housed at Yale University, including "The Mudfog Papers," "The Perils of Certain English Prisoners," single pages of *Oliver Twist* and *Pickwick*, a portion of the corrected proofs of *Drood*, and a number of minor articles, pro-

---

[4] Forster in the *Life* describes the notebook's contents in some detail in the chapter "Hints for Books Written and Unwritten," excerpts from which are reprinted in the *Nonesuch Letters* as an appendix. See also the account by the notebook's onetime owner in *Mrs. J. Comyns Carr's Reminiscences*, ed. Eve Adam (1926), and the discussions by Harry B. Smith, *Harper's*, 1924; George Ford, *NCF*, 1952; Felix Aylmer, *Dickensian*, 1954; Pansy Pakenham, *Dickensian*, 1955; and William J. Carlton, *Dickensian*, 1959. The memoranda record ideas for stories and articles and are especially important for the study of *Little Dorrit* and *Our Mutual Friend*. K. J. Fielding is preparing the notebook for publication in *BNYPL*. The pocket diary for 1867 still awaits an editor.

logues, and contracts. Major Dickens collections also possess notable examples of original drawings, inscribed and annotated volumes, and copies of Dickens' personal reading editions with holograph alterations and notations.

The five great depositories of letters are the Pierpont Morgan Library (1360 letters), the Huntington Library (970), the Free Library of Philadelphia (900), the New York Public Library (500), and the Dickens House (434). Most notable among the smaller collections are those at the Victoria and Albert Museum, the British Museum, the John Rylands Library, the Brotherton Library at Leeds, the Rosenbach Foundation Museum, the Boston Public Library, the libraries of Harvard, Texas, and Princeton universities, and the private collections of the Comte de Suzannet and Colonel Richard Gimbel. Dickens' practice of burning letters written to him leaves few extant letters of the other half of his vast correspondence. The most extensive collection of such letters is a group of 143 at the Huntington Library, all but a few of which were written in 1841; the Huntington also has extensive material associated with Dickens such as 96 letters of Georgina Hogarth and 162 letters concerning the farewell banquet given to Dickens before his departure for America in 1867.[5] The New York Public Library has 30 letters written to Dickens and the Morgan Library has 60 as well as a group of letters from Mrs. Dickens to assorted correspondents and a number from other members of the Dickens family.

II. *Bibliography*

In 1947 Philo Calhoun and Howell J. Heaney, in their *Dickensiana in the Rough*, stated categorically, "There is no accurate and complete Dickens bibliography." The statement still stands. Should a bibliographer appear, he would find *Dickensiana in the Rough* an invaluable Baedeker. Originally published in *PBSA* (1947) as a review of William Miller's *The Dickens Student and Collector: a List of Writings Relat-*

---

[5] See Franklin P. Rolfe's useful listing of the Huntington Library collection of letters from and to Dickens in *HLQ*, 1938.

ing to Charles Dickens and His Works, 1836–1945 (1946; supps., 1947, 1953), this pamphlet is a devastating exposé of Miller's ineptness as a bibliographer; and yet *The Dickens Student and Collector,* for all its omissions, confusions, and inaccuracies, remains the most comprehensive list of books, pamphlets, reviews, and articles about Dickens likely to appear in print. Miller was a dedicated Dickensian, one of the founders of the Dickens Fellowship as well as of the *Dickensian* itself, but obviously no scholar. His work nevertheless rescues from oblivion a mass of ephemera (3189 entries) collected over half a century, including what is probably a unique listing of musical items.

Miller acknowledges his indebtedness to an earlier indefatigable Dickensian, Frederic G. Kitton, and adopts the subject arrangement and chronological pattern of Kitton's *Dickensiana: A Bibliography of the Literature Relating to Charles Dickens and His Writings* (1886), a more limited work but superior to Miller's in its annotation and illustrative quotations. Kitton in his turn was indebted to two earlier bibliographies: James Cook's (1879) and Richard Herne Shepherd's (1880). Kitton was also the author and compiler of two other pioneer volumes: *The Novels of Charles Dickens: A Bibliography and Sketch* (1897) and *The Minor Writings of Charles Dickens: A Bibliography and Sketch* (1900). Other earlier bibliographies, not all of whose entries were incorporated by Miller, are John P. Anderson's list published in Frank T. Marzials, *Life of Charles Dickens* (1887), Sir John Alexander Hammerton's *The Dickens Companion: A Book of Anecdote and Reference* (1910), and the British Museum's *Dickens: An Excerpt from "The General Catalogue of Printed Books"* (1926; reissued, 1960, to cover all entries on Dickens to 1955).

The standard bibliographies of works by Dickens are John C. Eckel, *The First Editions of the Writings of Charles Dickens* (1913; rev. and enl. ed., 1932) and Thomas Hatton and Arthur H. Cleaver, *A Bibliography of the Periodical Works of Charles Dickens: Bibliographical, Analytical and Statistical* (1933), both brought out in limited editions. As

Calhoun and Heaney point out (*Dickensiana in the Rough,* p. 5), neither is complete or wholly reliable, an opinion corroborated in *TLS* (Jan. 26, 1933), *Dickensian* (Spring, 1933), and *Publisher's Weekly* (March 31, 1934). Some valuable corrections will be found in Michael Sadleir's notes on the Dickens entries in his *XIX Century Fiction* (1951), but as he admits, the details of parts publication, variations in illustrations as plates were replaced, and other bibliographical problems are vastly complicated and perhaps irresolvable. No less suspect are the bibliographies of American editions, chief of which are William Glyde Wilkins, *First and Early American Editions of the Works of Charles Dickens* (1910); Herman Le Roy Edgar and R. W. G. Vail, "Early American Editions of the Works of Charles Dickens" (*BNYPL,* 1929); and the entries on Dickens in Isidore R. Brussel, *Anglo-American First Editions, 1826–1900* (1935). Several valuable footnotes by Frank Weitenkampf on the bibliographical confusions of American illustrated editions will be found in *BNYPL* (1945), *American Collector* (1948), and *Boston Public Library Quarterly* (1953).

As the work most bibliographically controversial as well as most beloved by collectors, *Pickwick* has received the greatest attention from bibliographers. Among these are Percy H. Fitzgerald, *The History of Pickwick. With a Bibliography* (1891); George W. Davis, *The Posthumous Papers of the Pickwick Club: Some New Bibliographical Discoveries* (1928); and John C. Eckel, *Prime Pickwicks in Parts; Census with Complete Collation, Comparison and Comment* (1928). However, Hatton and Cleaver's description remains generally accepted as the most nearly definitive. Later corrections and commentary will be found in Logan Clendening, *A Handbook to Pickwick Papers* (1936), in J. Christian Bay's *The Pickwick Papers; Some Bibliographical Remarks* (1936; rev., 1938; reprinted in *The Fortune of Books,* 1941), in the articles devoted to the subject that have appeared in the *Dickensian* over the years, and in *A Centenary Bibliography of the Pickwick Papers,* by William Miller and E. H. Strange (1936), the last particularly useful for its quotations from reviews.

A selection of the most significant from a host of articles dealing with the bibliographical problems of other individual works would include F. J. H. Darton's discussion of *Sketches by Boz* in *Dickens: Positively the First Appearance. A Centenary Review* (1933); Eric Allen Osborne's *The Facts about "A Christmas Carol"* (1937); Calhoun and Heaney's "Dickens' 'Christmas Carol' after a Hundred Years: A Study in Bibliographical Evidence" (*PBSA*, 1945); Richard Gimbel's "The Earliest State of the First Edition of Charles Dickens' *A Christmas Carol*" (*PULC*, 1958); William B. Todd's comments on the *Carol* in *Book Collector* (1961); and the discussion of the rarity of the first book edition of *Great Expectations* in "Court of Appeals" (*New Colophon*, 1948–1949). Also useful, especially to Droodians, are the bibliographies of Droodiana such as that of J. Cuming Walters in *The Complete Edwin Drood: The History, Continuations, and Solutions, 1870–1912* (1912); B. W. Matz's in *The Problem of "Edwin Drood"* by Sir W. Robertson Nicoll (1912), continued by Winifred Matz (*Dickensian*, 1928–1929); and Albert A. Hopkins' description of Dr. Howard Duffield's famous Grolier Club exhibit (*Dickensian*, 1932).

The appeal of Dickens to the collector has led to the publication of descriptive catalogues of such famed collections as those of the Comte de Suzannet, Morris L. Parrish, Edwin W. Coggeshall, Thomas Hatton, William M. Elkins, Charles J. Sawyer, William Andrews Clark, and others; the most recent publication of this kind is the handsome catalogue of the Dickens collection at the University of Texas (1961). These, as well as the many other auction and booksellers' catalogues of Dickensiana, are often of value to scholars, especially when they list and quote from unpublished letters which have disappeared. Library exhibit catalogues or brochures are sometimes of interest. A notable example is the Yale exhibition of selected items from the collection of Colonel Richard Gimbel, described by him in *YULG*, 1962; another is the pamphlet *Reading for Profit: The Other Career of Charles Dickens; An Exhibition from the Berg Collection* (preprinted from *BNYPL*, 1958), in which John D. Gordan, curator of the Berg Collection, describes a brilliantly conceived exhibition of letters, annotated prompt books, photographs, and contemporary announcements in a running commentary which tells the story of Dickens as public performer with more dramatic effectiveness than any biography.

Only the most useful of special catalogues and bibliographies can be noted here. John Harrison Stonehouse's listing of the books in Dickens' own library, reprinted from Sotheran's *Price Current of Literature* in his *Catalogue of the Library of Charles Dickens from Gadshill* (1935), although far from a comprehensive index of Dickens' reading, is one of the few available keys. Of comparable interest because of Dickens' close friendship with Forster are the catalogues of the Forster Collection brought out by the Victoria and Albert Museum which cover the printed books (1888), the paintings and manuscripts (1893), and the Dickens exhibition of 1912 (1912). Others in special areas are the bibliography of the reading editions published in J. H. Stonehouse, *Sikes and Nancy* (1921); Dorothy Pierce's "Special Bibliography: The Stage Versions of Dickens' Novels" (*Bulletin of Bibliography and Dramatic Index*, 1936); the bibliographies of illustrations in J. A. Hammerton, *The Dickens Picture-Book: A Record of Dickens Illustrators* (1910) and in Thomas Hatton's more definitive census of the illustrations supervised by Dickens, published in *Retrospectus and Prospectus: The Nonesuch Dickens* (1937), to which G. S. Layard supplies some useful footnotes in his two chapters on Dickens in *Suppressed Plates, Wood Engravings, &c.* (1907).

None of the Dickens dictionaries and works of reference is complete or without inaccuracies, but in the absence of a modern scholarly work the most useful are Gilbert A. Pierce, *The Dickens Dictionary* (1872; 2d ed., with additions by W. A. Wheeler, 1894; latest ed., 1926); F. G. De Fontaine, *A Cyclopedia of the Best Thoughts of Charles Dickens* (1873; enl. ed., *The Fireside Dickens*, 1883); Alexander J. Philip, *A Dickens Dictionary* (1909; 2d. ed., with W. L. Gadd, 1928); Arthur L. Hayward, *The Dickens Encyclopaedia* (1924); and Percy Fitzgerald, *The Pickwickian Dictionary and Cyclopaedia* (1902).

III. *Editions*

During Dickens' lifetime and as long as the copyright held, Chapman and Hall was the only authorized publisher of complete editions, the first of which was that known as the Cheap Edition (17 vols., 1847–1868), with an intervening Library Edition (22 vols., 1857–1859). The Charles Dickens Edition (21 vols., 1867–1875) has been generally accepted as the most authentic in text, since it contains the last revisions of Dickens himself; but, as John Butt has pointed out ("Editing a Nineteenth-Century Novelist," *English Studies Today*, 1961), this is the text which set in motion a plethora of minor inaccuracies. The most complete standard edition is the Gadshill (38 vols., 1897–1908), announced as edited by Andrew Lang, who furnished the introductions, but actually edited by B. W. Matz. Besides being the first complete edition, the Gadshill was the first truly edited one and the first to include all the original and many additional illustrations. In it Matz collected and identified a number of the minor periodical works (also published separately as *Miscellaneous Papers*) and included the speeches and poems; in a deluxe issue of 1903 Forster's *Life* was added. The more elaborate National Edition (40 vols., 1906–1908), with the Matz text, which the Nonesuch *Retrospectus and Prospectus* (1937) in its description and evaluation of the four major preceding editions called "until now the best of all editions" and "the one into which Chapman and Hall poured all their resources," was a limited edition of 750 sets and so is not readily available except in cheap and inferior reprints. It is especially valuable for its facsimile reproductions of the wrappers for monthly installments and the inclusion of all Dickens' variant prefaces. A brief description of all Chapman and Hall complete editions will be found in Matz's *Two Great Victorian Writers* (1905).

The Macmillan Edition (21 vols., 1892–1925), with introductions by Charles Dickens the younger, is the most widely used of the editions that appeared after the copyright elapsed. Other editions are valuable not so much for their texts as for introductions by such people as Gissing, Chesterton, and

Shaw. Probably the most extravagant and ambitious ever to be launched is the tri-level Complete Works brought out by the New York publisher George D. Sproul (G. G. Harrap was the London publisher) under the editorship of Frederic G. Kitton. Plans called for a St. Dunstan Edition of 15 sets of 130 folio volumes each, to be printed on Italian parchment and sold for $1000 a volume, a Bibliophiles' Edition of 50 sets of 112 volumes on "special hand-made paper," and an Autograph Edition of 250 sets of 56 volumes on "white hand-made paper." The project was apparently abandoned in 1908 after Kitton's death. Though auction records exist for the St. Dunstan edition of *Pickwick* (5 vols.) [6] I have been able to locate only the 15 published volumes of the Autograph Edition (1902–1908) which include five novels, *Reprinted Pieces*, and *Master Humphrey's Clock*. This edition is of interest not only for Kitton's annotations and bibliographical and topographical notes, but also for the introductions by such people as Gissing, Saintsbury, Henley, Dobson, and Dowden, and especially for the assemblage of fine reproductions of original and extra illustrations. The 364 illustrations in the three volumes of *Pickwick*, for example, vie with Joseph Grego's *Pictorial Pickwickiana* (1899) and with Chapman and Hall's famed "topical edition" of *Pickwick* (eds., C. Van Noorden and Charles Plumptre Johnson, 1909) in offering a history of Pickwickian illustrations as well as of graphic taste in the nineteenth century.

The Nonesuch Edition, designed and planned by Francis Meynell and edited by Arthur Waugh, Walter Dexter, Thomas Hatton, and Hugh Walpole (23 vols., 1937–1938), is the handsomest of the complete editions but, like the other limited editions, is not generally obtainable. The coup of the Nonesuch publishers was the purchase from Chapman

---

[6] The University of Texas owns a proof copy of Vol. I, printed on vellum. For accounts of Sproul's plans for his "Millionaire's" edition, see *Publisher's Weekly*, Feb. 8, 1902, and *Book-Lover*, 1903. The Autograph Edition (not to be confused with the "Autograph Edition" edited by Richard Garnett and published by Chapman and Hall in 1900) is described by Kitton in the *Prospectus of the Autograph Edition of the Writings of Charles Dickens in Fifty-six Volumes* (1903).

and Hall of the steel plates and wood engravings from which
the original illustrations were printed and the distribution
of one of these to each of the 877 purchasers of the sets limited
to this number, with even an original drawing in some instances thrown in. To the scholar, the unique value of the
Nonesuch Edition is the inclusion of the three volumes of
Dickens' letters, collected and edited by Walter Dexter. The
most convenient and inexpensive modern edition, and the
only complete one of the major works now in print, is the
New Oxford Illustrated Dickens (21 vols., 1947–1958), with
critical introductions of uneven merit; recommended are
those of Humphry House (*Oliver Twist*), Kathleen Tillotson
(*Barnaby Rudge*), and Lionel Trilling (*Little Dorrit*).

The *New Oxford Illustrated Dickens* does not meet the
need for a genuinely critical edition. Happily, the Clarendon
Press has announced the launching of such an edition under
the joint editorship of John Butt and Kathleen Tillotson,
both known for their pioneering textual studies of a number
of Dickens' novels. According to Butt (*English Studies Today*,
1961), the editors plan to compare the manuscripts, proof
sheets, and various book and parts editions in order to arrive
at a definitive text for each novel and to call attention to significant revisions.

Separately published individual volumes and collected editions of the poems, plays, readings, short stories, and periodical contributions, as well as the volumes edited or prefaced
by Dickens, such as *The Memoirs of Joseph Grimaldi*, are
too numerous to list here and should be checked in the *CBEL*.
Unfortunately there is no accepted canon of the minor works
and bibliographical chaos reigns in respect to them. Certainly an important editorial job that needs to be done is the
identification and editing of the contributions to *Bentley's
Miscellany, Examiner, Daily News, Morning Chronicle,
Household Words, Household Narrative,* and *All the Year
Round.* Matz's *Miscellaneous Papers* is selective, as are Dickens' own volumes of reprinted materials, *The Uncommercial
Traveller* and *Reprinted Pieces.* The importance of these
largely unexplored writings to an understanding of Dickens'

social and political views has been pointed out by Monroe Engel in "The Politics of Dickens' Novels" (*PMLA*, 1956) and by P. A. W. Collins in a series of articles (*NCF*, 1960; *Dickensian*, 1960; and *Review of English Literature*, 1961). The model for the gathering and editing of such materials could be K. J. Fielding's *The Speeches of Charles Dickens* (1960), the most scholarly current edition of any special field of Dickens' minor works. Not only does Fielding include fifty-one more speeches than found in any earlier edition, but his exhaustive comparison of variant versions invalidates most of the earlier texts, and his introduction and notes make important contributions to both biographical and critical study of Dickens.

No scholar is likely to be unaware of the numerous modern reprints of individual novels, of interest either for their special format and illustrations (by such artists as Arthur Rackham, C. E. Brock, Mary Petty, Frederick Banbery, Ronald Searle, and Edward Gorey) or for introductions by such critics as C. Day Lewis, George H. Ford, E. K. Brown, J. B. Priestley, Clifton Fadiman, Edward Wagenknecht, Alec Waugh, Morton D. Zabel, J. I. M. Stewart, Monroe Engel, J. Hillis Miller, Edgar Johnson, and Graham Greene. G. Robert Stange offers a useful evaluation of a group of Dickens reprints in paperback or inexpensive hardback in *College English* (1959). Strangely, though individual novels have been brought out by any number of publishers, *Nicholas Nickleby, Barnaby Rudge, Martin Chuzzlewit, Little Dorrit,* and *Our Mutual Friend* remain "unpaperbacked" though all are available in Nelson's Classics.

IV. *Letters*

The collection of Dickens' letters which was the accepted standard for half a century is that which Humphry House nicknamed the "Mamie-Georgie" edition, compiled and edited by Dickens' daughter Mamie and his sister-in-law Georgina Hogarth. Two volumes appeared in 1880, a supplementary volume in 1882; these three volumes were condensed and rearranged in two volumes in 1882, and a one-volume edition appeared in 1893. Since changes, additions, deletions, and rearrangement occurred with each new edition, the reader must be on his guard. As a bereaved-family project, intended to correct and supplement Forster, it suffers from innumerable editorial suppressions, telescopings, and distortions, generally designed to avoid or soft-pedal unpleasant events in the life of Dickens or what the editors considered his less admirable traits. It may well have been at this time that many letters were destroyed and others subjected to the defacement by shears or to the heavy inking-out of words and passages which mars many extant manuscripts.[7]

The edition of the letters brought out by the Nonesuch Press in 1938 was an event of major importance, even though its publication as part of the limited and expensive 23-volume *Nonesuch Dickens* has curtailed its widespread use. Even more distressing, although the number of letters was increased to 5163 from the Mamie-Georgie's 900, and although many suppressed passages were restored, the Nonesuch not only is far from complete but contains many inaccuracies, telescopings, and bowdlerizations of its own and is even, in some instances, less accurate than earlier texts. The scholar who wants to be sure of his text must still consult the original manuscripts.

With all its faults, however, it is impossible to overestimate the importance of the *Nonesuch Letters*. Wedded as it was to the biographical revelations of Gladys Storey and Thomas Wright which appeared at about the same time, it led to the quickening of interest in Dickens as man and artist that has burgeoned at a Malthusian rate down to the present. And it remains, next to the novels themselves, the primary source for study of Dickens until the new and definitive Pilgrim Edition now in progress can supersede it. The Pilgrim Edition, made possible by a grant from the Pilgrim Trust Fund, received a serious setback in 1955 with the death of the initiator and editor, Humphry House, but is now going forward

[7] For a good account of this edition of the letters, see Arthur A. Adrian, *Georgina Hogarth and the Dickens Circle*, pp. 206–227.

under the coeditorship of Madeline House and Graham Storey. This is to be an unbowdlerized, fully annotated and indexed edition of upwards of 10,000 letters, all the diaries and publishers' agreements presently available, and many letters written to Dickens. Until this massive edition of ten to eleven volumes, the first of which (through 1839) has been announced for 1964, is completed, studies of many aspects of Dickens must be held tentative and inconclusive.

The Nonesuch Edition includes, generally in fuller and more accurate texts, Dickens' letters which had appeared in individual volumes to such correspondents as Mark Lemon, Thomas Beard, Wilkie Collins, Henry Kolle, John Macrone, John A. Overs, W. H. Wills, Charles Lever, and Maria Beadnell, but some of these collections have notes and critical introductions that are worth consulting; and F. W. Dupee's volume of *Selected Letters of Charles Dickens* (1960) has a lively introduction (reprinted in *Partisan Review*, 1960). Among the volumes which contain letters not in the Nonesuch, the most important is *Mr. and Mrs. Charles Dickens: His Letters to Her* (1935), edited by Walter Dexter. These were the letters Mrs. Dickens left with her daughter, Kate Perugini, with the hope that they would eventually be published "to show the world that Dickens once loved her." After consultation with G. B. Shaw, who claimed credit for opening Kate's eyes "to the fact that there was a case for her mother as well as her father" (see *Time and Tide*, July 27, 1935), Mrs. Perugini decided against destroying the letters. Another major supplement to the Nonesuch is the volume of 280 letters from Dickens to Angela Burdett Coutts (later Baroness Burdett-Coutts) edited by Edgar Johnson and published in America under the rather misleading title *The Heart of Charles Dickens* (1952), in England as *Letters from Charles Dickens to Angela Burdett-Coutts* (1953). As the most extensive extant correspondence Dickens carried on with anyone outside his family, these letters illuminate areas of his activities and attitudes previously all but unknown, particularly those touching on social welfare and reform since in them Dickens was acting as adviser to England's wealthiest philanthropist. Users must be reminded, however, that although more complete than the earlier edition of Charles C. Osborne (1931), Johnson's volume offers less than half the total number of letters in the collection (now at the Pierpont Morgan Library), and that some of the most interesting await publication in the Pilgrim Edition.

Also of interest is the group of 44 early letters from Dickens to Forster published by K. J. Fielding and Gerald G. Grubb (*BUSE*, 1956). Although these letters, which had escaped discovery until 1937, are disappointing in their sketchiness and, as Grubb remarks, "tell us more about Forster than . . . Dickens," they are an important find because so few of Dickens' letters to Forster have survived from a correspondence that Grubb estimates as at least 2000 letters. Of these Forster turned over only 145 to the Victoria and Albert Museum and only a handful are extant elsewhere. According to Percy Fitzgerald (*John Forster, by One of His Friends*, 1903, p. 16), the many passages from the letters quoted by Forster in his biography of Dickens were cut out of the originals and pasted on the manuscript later destroyed by the printer.

Many small caches as well as single letters have appeared in print since the *Nonesuch Letters*. The most important include Franklin P. Rolfe's "Additions to the Nonesuch Edition of Dickens' Letters" (*HLQ*, 1941) and "More Letters to the Watsons" (*Dickensian*, 1942); "Unpublished Letters to Lady Holland," anonymously edited by Walter Dexter (*Dickensian*, 1940); "Dickens and America: Some Unpublished Letters," by Richard D. Altick (*Pennsylvania Magazine of History*, 1949); "Hood and Dickens: Some New Letters," by Alvin Whitley (*HLQ*, 1950); "Some Unpublished Correspondence of Dickens and Chapman and Hall," by Gerald G. Grubb (*BUSE*, 1955); and the series of letters to Philoclès Régnier published in two installments by Sylvère Monod (*Etudes anglaises*, 1958).

V. *Biography*

The two indispensable full-scale biographies of Dickens are the earliest, *The Life of Charles Dickens* by his close friend and business adviser John Forster, published at intervals in three volumes (1872–1874), and the latest, *Charles Dickens: His Tragedy and His Triumph* by Edgar Johnson, published in two volumes in 1952.

In its own day Forster's *Life* was attacked as distorted, some referring to it as Forster's "Life with Dickens" because it emphasized his own friendship with the novelist, played down Dickens' relations with friends like Wilkie Collins, and all but ignored Mrs. Dickens. Others protested that it described too many of Dickens' "warts": his attitude toward his parents, his interest in sales and profits, the "hysterical restlessness" (as Harriet Martineau described it) of his later years. William J. Carlton's recent discovery of a cache of letters written to Forster upon the appearance of the biography makes possible a number of what Carlton calls "Postscripts to Forster" (*Dickensian,* 1962). As these and other new facts have come to light, criticism of Forster's work has changed. The objection now is that too much was omitted, that Forster not only suppressed all reference to the Ternan scandal and other events of his subject's personal life, but offered little revelation of the "inner" Dickens. And yet, with all its reticences and half-truths, Forster's biography holds the immense advantage of having been written by a fundamentally intelligent and honest man who probably knew Dickens more intimately than any other contemporary. It has been the spring from which all later biographers, including Edgar Johnson, have drawn many essential facts.

The most useful edition of Forster's *Life* is that published in one thick volume in 1928, edited and copiously annotated by J. W. T. Ley. Ley's introduction assesses Forster's strengths and weaknesses as a biographer and surveys major contributions to Dickensian biography between 1874 and 1928, singling out three to whom "the heaviest debts are owed": B. W. Matz, Frederic G. Kitton, and Robert Langton. Matz had preceded Ley as editor of Forster (included in the Memorial Edition of 1911), was the editor of the Gadshill and National Editions, the assiduous collector of Dickens' periodical contributions (published as *Miscellaneous Papers*), the first editor of the *Dickensian,* and the author of numerous minor books and articles on Dickens. Frederic G. Kitton, whose activities as bibliographer and editor have already been mentioned, was an equally industrious Dickensian. His biography *Charles Dickens: His Life, Writings, and Personality* (1902) added little to known facts; but two other works, *Charles Dickens by Pen and Pencil, Including Anecdotes and Reminiscences Collected from His Friends and Contemporaries,* followed by a *Supplement* and a portfolio of "Additional Illustrations" (1889–1891), and *Dickens and His Illustrators* (1899), in spite of minor inaccuracies, are important source books for graphic and anecdotal Dickensiana. Langton's *The Childhood and Youth of Charles Dickens* (1883; rev. and enl. ed., 1891) stemmed from the author's dissatisfaction with Forster's cursory handling of the early years, dissatisfaction which led to an intensive search for new facts. The volume is a valuable supplement to Forster.

Since Langton, several minor works have followed the same procedure of investigation into various aspects of Dickens' life and family connections before the publication of *Pickwick.* The most valuable of these include *Green Leaves: New Chapters in the Life of Charles Dickens* by John Harrison Stonehouse (1930–1931; rev. ed., 1931); *Charles Dickens, Shorthand Writer* by William J. Carlton (1926); and *The Dickens Ancestry: Some New Discoveries by Leslie C. Staples, with an Account of the Barrows of Bristol by William J. Carlton* (1951), a reprint of articles from the *Dickensian.*

The most important biographical developments between Forster and Johnson are those concerned with the violently debated role of Ellen Ternan in Dickens' life. Except for the appearance of her name in Dickens' will and a possible reference to her by the abbreviation "E" in a quoted letter, Forster's *Life* makes no mention of the young actress and says little about the circumstances of Dickens' separation from his wife. My own volume, *Dickens and Ellen Ternan* (1952), attempts to survey all the bits of "evidence," both factual and conjectural, and so may serve as an introduction to pertinent materials up to the publication of Johnson's biography. Its only contribution of consequence supplementary to Johnson is the publication of obliterated passages from letters in the Huntington Library which contain the only definitely personal references to Ellen in Dickens' hand that have yet come to light.

The first important disclosure of the Ternan episode appeared in the article "98 Years Ago To-day Charles Dickens Began His Honeymoon" (London *Daily Express*, April 3, 1934). The following year the author, Thomas Wright, brought out *The Life of Charles Dickens*, in which the story of Dickens' love for the obscure young actress was told in greater detail. The abuse heaped upon Wright for bringing the scandal into the open prompted him to further investigations which he was unable to complete before his death in 1936; some of these findings appeared in the posthumous *Thomas Wright of Olney: An Autobiography* (1936).

The first to use these disclosures in a full-length biography was Hugh Kingsmill [Lunn], who welcomed their timely appearance in support of his own iconoclastic views and incorporated them in *The Sentimental Journey: A Life of Charles Dickens* (1934). Three years later, though unaware of Wright's or Kingsmill's work, a seeming vindicator of both appeared in the person of Miss Gladys Storey, who wrote *Dickens and Daughter* (1939) in fulfillment of a promise made to Kate Perugini, Dickens' second daughter. *Dickens and Daughter* is not the work of a scholar or professional writer, but there is little justification for the vehement attacks which greeted its publication, since the source of the facts presented was Mrs. Perugini herself, the single intimate witness whose testimony has been recorded. Fair-minded critics admit that, for all the charges of sensationalism and distortion heaped upon both Wright and Storey by those who wanted to disbelieve their statements, neither has yet been proved wrong in any important point; and though neither has been proved right, subsequent discoveries have gone far in the direction of doing so.

Wright died before the *Nonesuch Letters* came out and Miss Storey was apparently unaware of its publication. Dame

Una Pope-Hennessy's *Charles Dickens* (1945) was the first biography to take advantage of the new materials of the Wright-Storey volumes and the *Nonesuch Letters*. Written by a more competent writer and scholar than either Wright or Storey, this was the best biography since Forster, and although not without conspicuous weaknesses, it remains the only biography that has tried to do justice to Mrs. Dickens, the forgotten figure in the Dickensian carpet.

Three other biographies followed Dame Una's in quick succession: Hesketh Pearson's *Dickens: His Character, Comedy, and Career* (1949), Jack Lindsay's *Charles Dickens: A Biographical and Critical Study* (1950), and Julian Symons' *Charles Dickens* (1951). Pearson's adds little to Pope-Hennessy since it tapped no new source materials, but it is a livelier and more smoothly flowing narrative, avoiding its predecessor's dull summaries of novel after novel, and it may well remain the one-volume favorite in the field. Pearson's experience in the theater gives a special vitality to his treatment of the histrionic side of Dickens. Lindsay's volume, attempting far more in the way of relating biography and criticism than any earlier work, is provoking in both meanings of the word. Certainly Lindsay as a critic is superior to both Pope-Hennessy and Pearson; he had read everything that Dickens wrote, often with refreshingly original insight. But the Lindsay vision of the outer and inner world of Dickens is too frequently distorted by the Marxian-Freudian blinders he insists upon wearing. Julian Symons' biography, one of the brief volumes of the English Novelists series, follows Lindsay's lead in emphasizing the psychological approach; substituting Emil Kraepelin for Freud, Symons writes up Dickens as the case history of a manic-depressive.

This brings us to the second "indispensable" biography, the one that will certainly stand as standard until such time as major discoveries may call for a new one. The reader will find in Johnson's *Charles Dickens: His Tragedy and Triumph* a combination of biography and criticism that has been highly commended for its richly documented account, the result of an examination of masses of published and unpublished materials on a scale hitherto unattempted. And Johnson writes with a rare accomplishment of style that has pleased Book-of-the-Month-Club readers and scholars alike. His criticism has been less well received, mainly because it fails to add as much to our understanding of Dickens the writer as the biography does to knowledge of his life, and because of a pervasive overpartiality that attributes greater wakefulness to Dickens than Horace allowed Homer. Johnson, like most biographers of Dickens, presents him much as Dickens saw himself because he depends largely upon Dickens' own writings and letters (and on Forster, which is much the same thing). The fact that Dickens destroyed most of the letters written to him, and that members of his family destroyed or defaced many of his letters they considered damaging to his "public image," raises the question of how possible it is for any biography of Dickens to be a complete portrait.[8] But Johnson's partisanship is an "am'able weakness" in a work which, by reason of exhaustive research, meticulous documentation, and readability stands as a major achievement.

Though Johnson's success may discourage any full-scale biography for some time, unexplored bypaths remain. Not surprisingly, the one to Ellen Ternan's door continues to attract explorers, among them Felix Aylmer, who stepped from the stage to play a real-life Inspector Bucket in pursuit of the elusive young lady. His *Dickens Incognito* (1959) received wide notice before its most sensational "discovery" — relating to the presumed birth of a child — was exposed by Graham Storey in a letter to the London *Sunday Times* (Dec. 13, 1959) as a misreading of records. But Aylmer's haste in jumping from conjecture to conclusion in this matter does not cancel the significance of some of his other findings. His canny reading of cryptographic entries in Dickens' pocket diary for 1867 led him to the discovery of Slough as the prob-

---

[8] For questions raised about Johnson's interpretation of a single episode, see Gordon N. Ray, "Dickens versus Thackeray: The Garrick Club Affair" (*PMLA*, 1954), Johnson's answer followed by Ray's reply (*PMLA*, 1956), and a third opinion by Harry Stone (*Dickensian*, 1957).

able residence of Dickens and Ellen prior to Peckham; and he presents a convincing reconstruction of Dickens' movements as recorded in the diary.

Tantalizingly few other pieces of the Ternan jigsaw have dropped into place since Johnson's biography. K. J. Fielding's re-examination of the much debated Helen Thomson letter in his "Charles Dickens and His Wife: Fact or Forgery?" (*Etudes anglaises*, 1955), supplemented by W. J. Carlton's discussion (*N&Q*, 1960), offers sound evidence that the controversial letter from Mrs. Dickens' aunt, important as giving more of her side of the separation scandal than is found elsewhere, is genuine. In two other articles (*NCF*, 1952, 1955), Fielding examines the scandal behind the "Violated Letter," concluding that the rumors which stirred Dickens to extreme action probably concerned Georgina rather than Ellen. Valuable information about Ellen and her little-known family appears in the series "The Theatrical Ternans" (*Dickensian*, 1958–1961) by another sedulous detective, Malcolm Morley. Morley's extensive research in theatrical records has enabled him to fill in details of the personal and professional life of the Ternans aside from their connection with Dickens, so that the wraiths that were Frances and Tom Ternan, Fanny, Maria, and Nelly begin to take on substance. The latest book to treat the Dickens-Ternan story, C. G. L. Du Cann's *The Love-Lives of Charles Dickens* (1961), presented as a barrister's expert examination of evidence, is an undocumented, irresponsible account so full of inaccuracies, contradictions, and cross-purposes that it cannot be taken seriously. With ironic legerdemain Du Cann attempts to establish as fact a mass of highly questionable gossip about other "affairs" at the same time that he discards as unacceptable the considerable evidence supporting the Dickens-Ternan relationship.

Two biographies have appeared since Johnson's, neither of which claims to supersede it. K. J. Fielding's *Charles Dickens: A Critical Introduction* (1958) is described by its author as "not an attempt to give the full story of Dickens's life, but to provide an account of his career as an author." It can be recommended as the best brief introduction to the work and life of Dickens, sound in its facts and astute in its criticism. The second is J. B. Priestley's *Charles Dickens: A Pictorial Biography* (1961), embellished with 132 excellent illustrations, a work that is gracefully written and contains some interesting personal comment but is not, except pictorially, a significant contribution.

W. H. Bowen's privately printed *Charles Dickens and His Family: A Sympathetic Study* (1956) began as a study of Dickens' medical history and grew into an account of Dickens, his parents, grandparents, wife, in-laws, brothers, sisters, and children. The title is provocative because so much remains to be learned about many members of the family, but this undocumented account, based on outdated printed sources, adds little (with the possible exception of the medical discussion) to our knowledge. A much sounder study of aspects of Dickens' relations with his family is Arthur A. Adrian's thoroughly documented *Georgina Hogarth and the Dickens Circle* (1957). Reviewers (particularly English reviewers) have found Adrian's peripheral discoveries minimal compared with his mountainous research, but the Dickens specialist cannot afford to ignore the smallest newborn mouse. The superior latter half of the book deals with the fresh materials of Georgina's letters written after Dickens' death, from which emerge portraits of the family as Georgina saw them, especially of the children about whom so little is known. The earlier half presents the familiar facts of Dickens' life in a semifictionalized rearrangement as if viewed by Georgina. Adrian does little to clarify Georgina's enigmatic part in the separation proceedings; what facts are known about her are given, but many readers would interpret them less sympathetically. In the course of three hundred pages devoted to a woman of little importance except for what her story can contribute to our understanding of Dickens, Adrian ignores the provocative undertones of Georgina's role as wife-and-mother substitute for a repudiated sister, so that the most important questions about Georgina–Agnes Wickfield–Esther Summerson remain unanswered.

Adrian's most valuable sources were the unpublished diary

of Annie Fields in the Massachusetts Historical Society Collection and the Hogarth-Fields correspondence in the Huntington Library. The publisher James T. Fields and his wife were Dickens' closest American friends in his later years. For the scholar without access to the unpublished materials, both Fields's *In and Out of Doors with Charles Dickens* (1876) [9] and his wife's *Memories of a Hostess: A Chronicle of Eminent Friendships Drawn Chiefly from the Diaries of Mrs. James T. Fields* (ed. M. A. De Wolfe Howe, 1922) will be found useful to the study of Dickens' relations with America and Americans, many aspects of which remain to be explored. Another reminiscencer describes Dickens' second visit in *Pen Photographs of Charles Dickens's Readings: Taken from Life by Kate Field* (1868; new and enl. ed., 1868; illus. ed., 1871), an account supplemented by extracts from the author's diary in *Kate Field: A Record* by Lilian Whiting (1899). H. W. L. Dana, Longfellow's grandson, describes Dickens' exchange of courtesies with England's favorite American poet in "Longfellow and Dickens: the Story of a Trans-Atlantic Friendship" (*Cambridge Historical Society Publications,* XXVIII, 1943), drawing upon the Craigie Collection of largely unpublished correspondence now in the Houghton Library, Harvard University; the relationship is explored in greater depth by Edward Wagenknecht in "Dickens in Longfellow's Letters and Journals" (*Dickensian,* 1955). Other accounts of the visits to America include that by George W. Putnam, American secretary for the tour of 1842 (*Atlantic Monthly,* 1887), and the two works dealing with the reading tours, *Charles Dickens as I Knew Him* (1885) by George Dolby, manager of the later tours, and *Charles Dickens as a Reader* (1872) by William Charles Kent. Three early compilations, haphazardly documented and far from definitive, attempt to deal more broadly with the American

[9] This is largely a reprint of the chapter on Dickens in Fields's *Yesterdays with Authors* (1872). See also his *Biographical Notes and Personal Sketches* (1881) and "Our Whispering Gallery" in *The Atlantic Monthly* (Jan.–Dec. 1871). Good accounts of the Fields's relations with Dickens will be found in *Fields of The Atlantic Monthly* by James C. Austin (1953) and *The Rise and Fall of James Ripley Osgood* by Carl J. Weber (1959).

experiences: William Glyde Wilkins' *Charles Dickens in America* (1911), Joseph Jackson's *Dickens in Philadelphia* (1912), and Edward F. Payne's *Dickens Days in Boston; A Record of Daily Events* (1927); another work by Wilkins, his collection of graphic ephemera, *Dickens in Cartoon and Caricature* (1924), draws largely, though not exclusively, upon American sources.

A few modern scholars have been exploring special aspects of Dickens' relations with America.[10] Robert B. Heilman's "The New World in Dickens's Writings," in two parts (*Trollopian*, 1946–1947), provides the most general introduction to the subject. Gerald G. Grubb attacks the question of whether or not Dickens lost money in the Cairo speculation (presumed to be the origin of Eden in *Chuzzlewit*) in "Dickens' Western Tour and the Cairo Legend" (*SP*, 1951), a subject followed up by Howard G. Baetzhold (*Dickensian*, 1959). In the three-part article "The Personal and Literary Relations of Dickens and Poe" (*NCF*, 1950) Grubb explodes some of the folklore on that subject. Leo Mason has written on various aspects of the Dickens-Poe relationship in five articles in the *Dickensian* (1940, reprinted in pamphlet form; 1943; 1946; 1951), I have contributed a footnote to Grubb (*NCF*, 1951), and H. W. Webb has added a further note to the subject (*NCF*, 1961). Washington Irving has attracted the interest of such Dickensian investigators as Ernest Boll (*MLQ*, 1944), W. C. Desmond Pacey (*American Literature*, 1945), and Christof Wegelin (*MLQ*, 1946).

The subject of Dickens and slavery has provoked the most significant work related to the American experiences. Louise H. Johnson's discovery of Dickens' heavy borrowing (if not plagiarizing) from Theodore Weld's *American Slavery as It Is* in "The Source of the Chapter on Slavery in Dickens's *American Notes*" (*American Literature*, 1943) is a major contribution. Arthur A. Adrian, in "Dickens on American Slavery: A Carlylean Slant" (*PMLA*, 1952), and John O.

---

[10] A check of the index volumes of the *Dickensian* will lead to innumerable items relating to Dickens and America, including those in the "American Number" (1942) commemorating Dickens' first visit.

Waller, in "Charles Dickens and the American Civil War" (*SP*, 1960), take up other aspects. Harry Stone probes deeper into the tricky subject of Dickens' ambiguous attitudes in "Charles Dickens and Harriet Beecher Stowe" (*NCF*, 1957), which brings to light an interesting letter of Dickens to Lord Denman's widow. In another article, "Dickens' Use of His American Experiences in *Martin Chuzzlewit*" (*PMLA*, 1957), Stone charts the metamorphosis of autobiographical fact into fiction. My own article "The Mystery of 'Martin Chuzzlewit' " (in *Essays Critical and Historical Dedicated to Lily B. Campbell*, 1950) relates the critical reception of *American Notes* to the popular reception of *Martin Chuzzlewit*.

Aspects of Dickens' publishing and business relations with Americans are discussed by William E. Buckler, *"Household Words* in America" (*PBSA*, 1951); Gerald G. Grubb, "Personal and Business Relations of Charles Dickens and Thomas Coke Evans" (*Dickensian*, 1952) and "The American Edition of *All the Year Round*" (*PBSA*, 1953); and Lawrence H. and Caroline W. Houtchens, "Contributions of Early American Journals to the Study of Charles Dickens" (*MLQ*, 1945). Articles on Dickens and the international copyright question have been written by K. J. Fielding (*Bulletin of the British Association for American Studies*, 1962) and Lawrence H. Houtchens *(American Literature*, 1941).

Dickens' activities as editor at home have been dealt with extensively by Gerald G. Grubb, who in 1940 wrote his doctoral dissertation on Dickens as a journalist. The most important of his contributions are the series of articles on Dickens as editor (*Booker Memorial Studies*, ed. Hill Shine, 1950; *NCF*, 1951–1952); the exchange of opinion with William E. Buckler on Dickens' financial dealings with contributors to his periodicals: Grubb (*PMLA*, 1943), Buckler (*PMLA*, 1951), Grubb (*Dickensian*, 1955); the annotated publication of Dickens' correspondence with Chapman and Hall (*BUSE*, 1955); and several other articles noted elsewhere. Percy Fitzgerald's *Memories of Charles Dickens. With an Account of "Household Words" and "All the Year Round" and of the Contributors Thereto* (1913) offers a firsthand ac-

count of Dickens' relations with his writers. His difficulties
with Richard Bentley are presented in *Dickens vs. Barabbas;
Forster Intervening* (ed. Charles J. Sawyer, 1930) and in David
A. Randall's valuable report on the Bentley correspondence
now deposited in the Berg Collection of the New York Public Library (*TLS*, Oct. 12, 1946). Biographies of Dickens'
several publishers as well as recent studies of publishing history in the nineteenth century should be checked for accounts of Dickens' relations with his own publishers as well
as those with that numerous tribe of Grub Street operators
Thomas Hood called the "Bookaneers." Royal A. Gettmann's
A Victorian Publisher: A Study of the Bentley Papers (1960)
and Arthur Waugh's *A Hundred Years of Publishing: Being
the Story of Chapman & Hall, Ltd.* (1930) are of special importance; as Waugh remarks, the first portion of his book "becomes something not easily distinguishable from yet one more
narrative of 'Boz's' titanic and 'inimitable' career" (p. xiv).

The related subject of Dickens' relations with his illustra-
tors (also frequently stormy) has not received any truly schol-
arly attention except possibly the brief discussion by Arthur
Waugh in *Retrospectus and Prospectus: The Nonesuch
Dickens* (1937). We have only the early anecdotal accounts of
Edgar A. Browne, *Phiz and Dickens as They Appeared to
Edgar Browne* (1913), Kitton's *"Phiz": A Memoir* (1882) and
Dickens and His Illustrators (1899), and the cursory treatments given the Cruikshank-Dickens story in various biographies of Cruikshank, none of which, excepting Ruari Mc-
Lean's slim contribution to the "English Masters of Black-
and-White" series (1948), is a modern work. It is amazing in
this age when biographers seem to be dredging for minnows
that Blanchard Jerrold's outdated two volumes on Cruikshank, published in 1882, still stand as the only full-scale
biography. Nor has any work of significance appeared on the
history of Dickensian illustration and its relation to public
response to the novels. Albert Johannsen's handsome volume
Phiz Illustrations from the Novels of Charles Dickens (1956)
points up how much could be learned from a scholarly study
along these lines.

Two early works dealing superficially with a series of contemporaries, W. T. Shore's *Charles Dickens and His Friends* (1909) and J. W. T. Ley's *The Dickens Circle: A Narrative of the Novelist's Friendships* (1918), are of slight scholarly importance, but give leads that could be profitably explored. The biographies of close friends like William Macready, Wilkie Collins, and John Forster are, of course, of prime importance. Unfortunately, the two books on Forster, Percy Fitzgerald's *John Forster, by One of His Friends* (1903) and Richard Renton's *John Forster and His Friendships* (1912) are undistinguished; Dickens scholars have reason to look forward to J. Lee Harlan's biography of Forster, now in progress. William Henry Wills, who spent many years in close association with Dickens as subeditor of *Household Words* and *All the Year Round,* would seem to be another figure who deserves more attention from those interested in Dickens than he has received.

The best listing of the pleasant but largely uninformative accounts of "life with father" by children and grandchildren will be found in Edward Wagenknecht's *The Man Charles Dickens* (1929). J. C. Maxwell has pointed up the value of reminiscences by even the relatively obscure in his discussion of Eleanor E. Christian's diary in *Englishwoman's Domestic Magazine* (1871; reprinted with extensive alterations, *Temple Bar,* 1888), a diary containing one of the most interesting of contemporary accounts of Dickens' volatile temperament.

Any explorer of the bypaths of Dickensian biography will have reason to be grateful for the second cumulative index to the *Dickensian,* through the volume for 1960. Many professional scholars have tended to dismiss the *Dickensian* as the organ of amateur enthusiasts, but they do so now at their peril, for many first-rate critics and scholars contribute regularly. Even in the early days, as Humphry House observed, "the serious work of collecting new evidence about Dickens's life *in general* (apart from special subjects like the matter of Ellen Ternan) was carried on by them and by nobody else" (*All in Due Time,* p. 231). Such contributions, together with those to *N&Q,* have filled in many bits and pieces of biographical information. The *Dickensian* has also done the scholar yeoman service by noting references to Dickens in newly published volumes of Victoriana as they appear. Earlier volumes including accounts of Dickens' relations with prominent contemporaries are listed in *CBEL* under "Personal Recollections and Memoirs," a list richly supplemented by Wilhelm Dibelius' "Erinnerungen" in the bibliography of his *Charles Dickens* (1916).

VI. *Criticism*

If the critic has been properly defined as one who "conducts his education in public," the public education of Dickens' critics has been remarkable for its stammering indecisions and inconsistencies. Much Dickens criticism is devoted to second thoughts and rediscovery, as evidenced in such recurrent titles as "Corrected Impressions" (Saintsbury, 1895), "Charles Dickens Revisited" (William A. Sibbald, 1907; Hilaire Belloc, 1927), "The Return to Dickens" (Wilbur Cross, 1912; Bernard Darwin, 1940), "Charles Dickens Comes Back" (George Dangerfield, 1934), "Dickens Once Again" (A. Compton-Rickett, 1937), "On Re-reading Dickens" (St. John Ervine, 1942), and "New Judgment" (J. B. Priestley, 1944). Perhaps reflective of an increase in more precise critical probing, titles since the 1940's indicate a shift from general reassessment to that of specific novels, as in "*Oliver Twist* Reexamined" (Colm Brogan, 1948), "On Rereading *Great Expectations*" (Howard Mumford Jones, 1954), "A Re-examination of *Edwin Drood*" (William W. Bleifuss, 1954), "*A Tale of Two Cities* Reconsidered" (G. Robert Stange, 1957), and "Little Nell Revisited" (Mark Spilka, 1960).

The fact is that polarity of response characterizes almost every assessment of Dickens from that of the first reviewer of *Pickwick* to such recent works as *The Imagination of Dickens* (1961) in which A. O. J. Cockshut states frankly that the questions he seeks to answer are "How did a man with such a coarse mind become a master of his art?" and "How was it possible . . . to be a best-seller and a true classic at the same time?" The observation echoes such earlier comments as "No novelist of any period is more sensationally unequal than Dickens" (David Cecil, *Early Victorian Novelists; Essays in Revaluation*, 1934, p. 27); "The question [is] whether Dickens is great enough to carry his colossal faults" (G. M. Young, *Daylight and Champaign*, 1937, p. 30); "I swallow Dickens whole and put up with the indigestion" (V. S. Pritchett, *New Statesman*, 1944, p. 143); "One is tempted to define the work of Dickens as a blazing volcano of genius almost entirely surrounded by a morass of imbecility" (Hesketh Pearson, *Dickens*, 1949, p. 185); "My own experience in reading Dickens . . . is to be bounced between violent admiration and violent distaste" (Kingsley Amis, *Spectator*, 1956, p. 23); "The genius and the rubbish exist side by side in the same novel" (R. C. Churchill, *From Dickens to Hardy*, 1958, p. 119). The difficulty would seem to be summed up in J. B. Priestley's blunt statement that "Dickens is not an easy subject . . . It is far easier to be adequate on a Henry James than it is on Dickens" (*Saturday Review*, 1925, p. 343).

The paradox of Dickens' power to attract and repel points up the problems that face any historian of Dickens criticism. The significant cleavages occur not so much between critics as in them. An approver of Dickens' social criticism disapproves his imaginative flights of fancy; an admirer of his poetic imagination dislikes his propagandizing; a reader who delights in the comic genius of his early novels deplores the brooding melancholy of his later ones; one who is moved by the power of his sense of the macabre and the demonic has no taste for his irrepressible extravagances of comic character and language. Most criticism ends by being a Rorschach key to the critic's own taste and predispositions.

Ample evidence of the rich variety of critical approach to Dickens is offered in anthologies like *The Dickens Critics* (ed. George H. Ford and Lauriat Lane, Jr., 1961), *Dickens and the Twentieth Century* (ed. John Gross and Gabriel Pearson, 1962), and the several student casebooks that have been devoted to Dickens. The difficulties of attempting to pin critics "wriggling on the wall" are pointed up in the comments of Ford, Johnson, Miller, Monod, and Peyrouton on the changing status of Dickens among critics in *Dickens Criticism, Past, Present, and Future Directions: A Symposium* (ed. Noel C. Peyrouton, 1962). Even so Odyssean a guide as Ford in *Dickens and His Readers* could be challenged in almost his every attempt to categorize the critics he discusses. As John Gross has observed, "the critic who hopes that he can encompass Dickens's achievement without sometimes contradicting himself would do better to look for another author" (*Dickens and the Twentieth Century*, p. xvi).

No modern scholar is unaware of the importance of Edmund Wilson's essay "Dickens: The Two Scrooges" (in *The Wound and the Bow,* 1941).[11] Wilson's brilliant use of the then new materials in Wright's and Storey's biographies and the *Nonesuch Letters,* which led him to a revaluation of Dickens' novels, is a salutary lesson for those who question the critical contribution of historical scholarship. Wilson's view of an author whom dons and Bloomsbury critics had abandoned to the Philistines has served as a catalyst to so much subsequent criticism of Dickens that it is now customary to refer to individual critics as pre- or post-Wilsonian. Admittedly, much recent discussion of Dickens is derivative of Wilson, but much has also pushed on into areas he left untouched, and there is now even a healthy reaction against him for not having discovered more than he did twenty years ago. That Wilson stands at the watershed between the new view of Dickens and the old, which may at its most superficial level be equated with the preference for the late "dark" novels over the early more comic ones, must not obscure the fact that, as Ford's *Dickens and His Readers* and Richard Stang's *The Theory of the Novel in England, 1850–1870* (1959) reveal, many writers before Wilson had illuminating things to say. The point is worth stressing because some of

---

[11] The essay is a merging of lectures delivered at the University of Chicago in 1939 and first published in the *Atlantic Monthly* and the *New Republic* in 1940. It has been conveniently brought out in paperback in *Eight Essays* (1954).

the discoveries and opinions of earlier critics turn up in modern learned journals as the latest thing in revolutionary insight into Dickens.

Wilson mentions three predecessors, Gissing, Chesterton, and Shaw, with special tribute to Gissing. All three shared a passion for Dickens, but each was drawn to him for different reasons. Gissing, one of the closest to a naturalist that England produced, defended Dickens' brand of realistic vision against critics of the realist school like G. H. Lewes and Henry James in two important works, *Charles Dickens: A Critical Study* (1898) and *Critical Studies of the Works of Charles Dickens* (New York, 1924; London title, *The Immortal Dickens*, 1925). The latter is a reprint of the nine essays Gissing wrote for the unfinished Rochester Edition, to which should be added his essay on *David Copperfield* written for the Autograph Edition (1903). Chesterton, a lover of Dickens' comic genius and "Great Gusto," defended him against Gissing, whom Chesterton accused of making the author of *Pickwick* over into his own gloomy image.[12] Out of the lifelong outpouring of books and essays on Dickens by Chesterton, whom Lionel Trilling has described as "a far greater critic than his present reputation might suggest" (*A Gathering of Fugitives*, 1956, p. 41), the most important are the biography, *Charles Dickens: A Critical Study* (1906; reprinted with an introduction by Alexander Woollcott as *Charles Dickens: The Last of the Great Men*, 1942) and his introductions to the Everyman Edition reprinted in *Appreciations and Criticisms of the Works of Charles Dickens* (1911; reissued as *Criticisms and Appreciations*, 1933). Shaw's broader but in general more superficial vision took in both Dickens' humor and his deep sense of social wrong — and, as everyone knows, Shaw placed Dickens in the triumvirate of English geniuses, outranked only by Shakespeare and Shaw. The fact that his commentary on Dickens is scattered in ob-

[12] And yet Gissing, who was one of the first to compare Dickens and Dostoyevsky, saying of *Crime and Punishment* that "Dickens might well have written the whole book," ironically stresses similarities in their comic powers (*Charles Dickens*, pp. 292-293).

scure publications may explain the relative neglect of critics; the section on Dickens in *CBEL* makes no mention of Shaw, nor does Rantavaara's *Dickens in the Light of English Criticism* (1944). His most important criticism will be found in the introductions to *Hard Times* (Waverley Edition, 1911) and to *Great Expectations* (Limited Editions Club, 1937; repr., London, 1947).[13]

The G. H. Lewes autopsy on Dickens as a writer (*Fortnightly Review*, 1872; discussed by Gordon Haight, *PMLA*, 1956), together with Henry James's review of *Our Mutual Friend* in the *Nation* (1865; reprinted in *Views and Reviews*, 1908), James Fitzjames Stephen's series of reviews, the most famous that of *A Tale of Two Cities* (*Saturday Review*, Dec. 17, 1859), and possibly Walter Bagehot's early review of the Cheap Edition (*National Review*, 1858), all unsympathetic in spite of the ubiquitous tributes to Dickens' "genius," are the most important early evaluations if only because their views dominated sophisticated opinion for a half century or longer. Their picture of Dickens as an erratic genius warbling his subliterate woodnotes wild became the norm against which any more original approach, such as that of Gissing, Chesterton, Shaw, or Wilson, had to take the offensive. Certainly the stereotype was handed down, by way of such standard reference works as Leslie Stephen's catabolically influential contribution to the *Dictionary of National Biography* (1888), Saintsbury's discussion in *CHEL* (1917), and, with some qualifications, Ernest Baker's in *The History of the English Novel* (1936), to too many of the superficial histories of English literature and accounts in anthologies that still dominate undergraduate opinion. The *Encyclopaedia Britan-*

[13] See *The Mystery of the Unhappy Ending: A Correspondence* (1937) for a highly amusing *New Yorkerish* exchange between Shaw and the publishers of this volume in which Shaw among other things mentions that he cannot write the preface until he has read a new book about an actress (probably Wright's biography of Dickens) whom he "suspects of having suggested the character of Estella." For comment on Shaw as critic of Dickens, see Humphry House's excellent "G.B.S. on *Great Expectations*" (*Dickensian*, 1948; reprinted in *All in Due Time*, 1955); and the discussions of Edgar Johnson (*Shaw Bulletin*, 1953; reprinted in *VQR*, 1957) and Hugh Kingsmill (in *Progress of a Biographer*, 1949).

nica has been a notable exception to this list. William Minto's article in the ninth edition (1877), which, as observed by Ford, "anticipates part of Edmund Wilson's interpretation," and Chesterton's in the fourteenth (1941; recently brought up to date by K. J. Fielding) have been a valuable antidote to the patronizing realists.

There are a number of pre-Wilsonian critics with whom the serious student should be acquainted. Edwin P. Whipple, a neglected American interpreter of the major novels, contributed a series of perceptive introductions to the New Illustrated Library Edition of Dickens (New York, 1876–1877; published concurrently in the *Atlantic Monthly* and later collected in the two-volume *Charles Dickens: The Man and His Work*, 1912). Alice Meynell's essays in the *Atlantic Monthly* (1903) and *Dublin Review* (1912; many times reprinted in her collected essays) are important landmarks in the appreciation of Dickens as a serious artist. Andrew Lang's review of Gissing (*Longman's Magazine*, 1898) makes an interesting comparison with his own introductions to the Gadshill Edition launched a year earlier, introductions which sparked Swinburne's contemptuous onslaught in the *Quarterly Review* (1902; reprinted, 1913, with an essay on *Oliver Twist* that was written for the abortive Autograph Edition), and the less famous objections of W. E. Henley (*Pall Mall Magazine*, 1899), with Francis Thompson serving as an anonymous referee (in "Mrs. Boythorn and Her Canary," *Academy*, 1902). Lang, who was really Swinburne's whipping boy for "G. H. Lewes & Co.," replied in the *Morning Post* (July 12, 1902).[14] This battle over the specifics of Dickens' reputation at the turn of the century played a counterpoint in brass to the still echoing stringed-instrument discussion of the "art of fiction" carried on in the 1880's by James, Besant, and Stevenson, and cannot be properly interpreted apart from it.

[14] Numerous essays on Dickens will be found in Lang's volumes of collected essays and in his contributions to contemporary periodicals, conveniently listed by Roger L. Green in the *Dickensian* (1944); see also Green's defense of Lang as "Real Reader of Dickens" (*Dickensian*, 1961).

One of the ablest defenders of Dickens against what W. E. Henley called "the scorn of the Superior Person" (*Outlook*, March 5, 1898) was R. Brimley Johnson in his discussion of aesthetic criticism of Dickens in *Book Monthly* (1906), but the virus was long a-dying, if, indeed, it has ever died. Two years after Johnson, Paul Elmer More in his Shelburne essay on "The Praise of Dickens" (5th series, 1908) objected to the lack of the "aristocratic element" in Dickens, an attitude which dominated the 1920's when the reputation of Dickens along with everything else Victorian was at its nadir. Virginia Woolf, priestess of the Bloomsbury group attacked by Wilson for its myopic snobbery, carried the family tradition of prejudice against Dickens into the twentieth century in the influential essays on *David Copperfield* (in *Nation & Athenaeum*, Aug. 22, 1925, followed by a letter to the editor, Sept. 12; both reprinted in *The Moment and Other Essays*, 1947) and on *Bleak House* (in "Phases of Fiction,"*Bookman*, 1929; reprinted in *Granite and Rainbow*, 1958). Interestingly, in an earlier review article (*TLS*, March 27, 1919), when writing anonymously, Mrs. Woolf had been much less astringent, even observing that "It can only be a question whether any other English novelist, save Scott, has a right to be called Shakespearian."

In spite of Bloomsbury, however, a group of champions came forward in the 1920's. Oliver Elton's discussion in his classic *Survey of English Literature* (1920), expanded into *Dickens and Thackeray* (1924), is a remarkably modern evaluation. George Santayana's essay on Dickens in the *Dial* (1921; reprinted in *Soliloquies in England*, 1922) — in spite of such severities as that Dickens "had no *ideas* on any subject" and was insensitive to "religion, science, politics, art" — pays tribute to the special qualities of Dickens' artistic genius; his views are best summarized in his well-known contribution to the ubiquitous "Dickery-Thackens" controversy — that comparing them "is like comparing the grape with the gooseberry; there are obvious points of resemblance, and the gooseberry has some superior qualities of its own; but you can't make red wine of it." Another defender, Sir Arthur Quiller-

Couch, dared defy the prevailing Oxbridge contempt for
Dickens by delivering a series of five lectures at Cambridge
later published in *Charles Dickens and Other Victorians*
(1925) which did not apologize for ranging over Shakespeare,
Dante, Molière, Tolstoy, and Dickens with no discriminatory
change of tone. The lectures begin with the warning that
"You must get it out of your minds that Dickens was, in any
sense at all, a cheap artist playing to the gallery" and go on
to touch matters of such modern critical concern as the deep
humiliation of the blacking factory, the artistry of Dickens'
language, the world created by his own imagination, the way
Dickens "strove to make himself a better artist." A brief
essay by Hugh Walpole might also be mentioned for its surprising emphasis upon the brooding power of the later novels
which, in Walpole's words, "have not been sufficiently studied
in their strange and almost uncanny relationship to certain
aspects of the modern novel" (*The Eighteen-Seventies*, ed.
Harley Granville-Barker, 1929). In spite of such defenders,
however, it must be admitted that by far the most influential
downgrading of Dickens in the 1920's was the brief discussion by E. M. Forster in *Aspects of the Novel* (1927) with its
now familiar critical segregation of "flat" and "round" characters and its verdict that "Dickens' people are nearly all
flat." Edwin Muir immediately challenged the oversimplifi-
cation in *The Structure of the Novel* (1928) and Lionel Trilling damned it as "an obfuscation of the actual facts of char-
acter-contrivance" (*E. M. Forster*, 1943, p. 167), but recurring
challenges down to the present are testimony to its influence.

Criticism in the 1930's runs very thin, with only two general
books, Sir Osbert Sitwell's *Dickens* (1932), supplemented by
an essay in *Trio* (1938), and Stephen Leacock's critical biography (1933),[15] neither of which makes any significant contribution to criticism or biography. Lord David Cecil's chapter on Dickens in *Early Victorian Novelists* (1934; republished with a new foreword as *Victorian Novelists*, 1958) is

---

[15] Leacock's criticism in the earlier "Fiction and Reality: A Study of the
Art of Charles Dickens" (*Essays and Literary Studies*, 1916) is superior to
that in the biography, called a "potboiler" by Ford.

more important than either Sitwell or Leacock, but shows the weakness of insufficient knowledge about Dickens inevitable in Dickensian criticism prior to 1940.

SOCIAL REALISM. Actually, the best book of the 1930's is Thomas A. Jackson's *Charles Dickens: The Progress of a Radical* (1937). This work makes the first serious effort to trace the social commentary through all the novels, though Jackson's procrustean Marxism weakens the interpretations of what he finds. Like Jackson, a number of other enthusiasts had tried to make something of a socialist of Dickens, including E. W. Pugh, *Charles Dickens: The Apostle of the People* (1908), W. W. Crotch, *Charles Dickens: Social Reformer* (1913), and Cumberland Clark, *Dickens and Democracy, and Other Studies* (1930). More recent doctrinaires have left their readers, as R. J. Cruikshank has observed, with the "bemused feeling that *Das Kapital* was written by an economist called Karl Dickens and *Great Expectations* by a German emigré named Charles Marx who is buried at Highgate" (foreword to *The Humour of Dickens*, 1952). Cruikshank probably had Jack Lindsay's biography of Dickens (1950) especially in mind, but more recent critics such as Ian Milner in "The Nature of the Hero in Dickens and the Eighteenth Century Tradition" (*Philologica*, 1957) and Arnold Kettle in "Dickens and the Popular Tradition" (*Zeitschrift für Anglistik und Amerikanistik*, 1961) [16] are more insistently Marxist than Lindsay as, of course, are the many Soviet commentators discussed below. That Dickens does not fit neatly into the fellow-traveler pattern cut out for him by the Marxists is due mainly to their simplification of his plague-on-all-your-houses position. Fabian Shaw did not make this mistake. Although he found in *Hard Times* "Karl Marx, Carlyle, Ruskin, Morris, Carpenter rising up against civilization

[16] Kettle's paper, first read at an East German seminar, stirred lively controversy when it appeared in *Carleton Miscellany* (1961); see the correspondence (Spring 1962) and Kettle's reply (Fall 1962). Kettle's essays on *Oliver Twist* in *An Introduction to the English Novel* (1951) and on *Our Mutual Friend* in *Dickens and the Twentieth Century* (1962) are less stridently Marxist, as is Jack Lindsay's discussion of *Barnaby Rudge* in the latter anthology.

as a disease" (introduction to *Hard Times*, 1911), and called *Little Dorrit* a "more seditious book than *Das Kapital*," Shaw at the same time labeled Dickens an "unphilosophic radical" and warned readers that they might as well "look for a nautilus in a nursery" as look for Karl Marx in his novels (introduction to *Great Expectations*, 1937).

Nor did the two writers who share honors with Edmund Wilson in initiating the mature stage of Dickensian criticism in the 1940's make Jackson's mistake. These are the novelist and bitter social critic George Orwell, and the Oxford scholar Humphry House. In his essay on Dickens in *Inside the Whale* (1940; reprinted in *Dickens, Dali, and Others* — English title, *Critical Essays* — 1946), Orwell concludes that Dickens was a moral reformer but not in any sense a political revolutionist, a judgment reminiscent of what Louis Cazamian called Dickens' "Philosophie de Noël." Unlike Wilson, Orwell sees little growth or change in Dickens, but in certain respects the English critic shows greater awareness of deep-seated British attitudes and mores than does the American Wilson. Humphry House brings to his thorough acquaintance with Dickens and his novels a scholar's knowledge of Victorian social and political history — something no one had done before him and few since. The result is that *The Dickens World* (1941), in spite of the modifications and extensions that new information inevitably calls for, stands as a classic not only of Dickensian study but, as David Daiches has pointed out, of sociological criticism in general (*Critical Approaches to Literature*, 1956, pp. 366–370). Though House follows Shaw and Orwell in recognizing that Dickens was no revolutionary but a man very much of his time and class, he is closer to Wilson than Orwell in noting Dickens' growing obsession with the theme of money's corrosive power, and in seeing other changes that took place in Dickens and in the novels; as he puts it, "In *Pickwick* a bad smell was a bad smell; in *Our Mutual Friend* it is a problem" (p. 135).

The first fruits of the studies of Wilson, Orwell, and House are seen in Lionel Stevenson's "Dickens's Dark Novels, 1851–1857" (*Sewanee Review*, 1943). Stevenson's probing extension of Wilson's thesis of the self-vision embedded in Dickens' social vision points up how difficult it is to isolate particular aspects of Dickens for praise or condemnation without doing violence to the complex whole. Much modern criticism does just that, by narrowing its sights to one novel or one Dickens, or even to one Dickens in one novel. The example of two critics arriving at diametric views of Dickens through failure to recognize what V. S. Pritchett has described as "the multitude of his disparate selves" (*New Statesman*, 1944) is instructive. Anthony West, in his severe review of Edgar Johnson's biography (*New Yorker*, 1953; reprinted in *Principles and Persuasions*, 1957) and in his pulverizing answer to Mary McCarthy's rather unsophisticated objection to that review (see *Reporter*, March 3 and 31, 1953), builds a case against Dickens on isolated evidence of his unreliability and ambiguity as a social commentator. In contrast, F. R. Leavis finds in *Hard Times*, a novel which Stephen Leacock called "an amalgam of Jack the Giant-Killer, Ricardo's Political Economy and the Sermon on the Mount" (*Charles Dickens*, 1933, p. 144), sufficient evidence of mature social vision to allow Dickens entrance into *The Great Tradition* (1948), albeit through the servant's entrance of an appendix. Ironically, Leavis admires a novel which preaches "Fancy" and "Imagination" for its Gradgrindian reflection of its time, while West prepares a documented brief to attack Dickens for not being Gradgrindian enough. It is true that Leavis' famous essay calls attention to generally unappreciated merits in *Hard Times*, especially those of language and imagery, but it fails to appreciate the presence of those same merits in greater fullness in other Dickens novels. Now, fifteen years later, Leavis has taken up a second novel, *Dombey*, after a "very long abstention" and is again surprised to discover what critics had been trying to tell him all along, that "there is a greater Dickens than the traditional cult has tended to recognize" (*Sewanee Review*, 1962). Even more recently Leavis has extended his admiration to *Little Dorrit*, remarking with some vehemence in a letter of objection to Peter Fison's statement that "Dr. Leavis, of course, doesn't like

Dickens" (*Spectator*, Dec. 28, 1962) that he "would without hesitation surrender the whole *oeuvre* of Flaubert for *Dombey and Son* or *Little Dorrit*" (*Spectator*, Jan. 4, 1963). The confession drew from the editor of the *Dickensian* the exclamation, "Well might it be said that there is more joy in heaven . . ." (May 1963, p. 92).

It is still possible to examine profitably special aspects of Dickens' social commentary, if the part makes no pretense to be the whole. A challenge to West's view, for example, is found in Monroe Engel's documented examination of *Household Words, Household Narrative*, and *All the Year Round* in "The Politics of Dickens' Novels" (*PMLA*, 1956; incorporated into *The Maturity of Dickens*, 1959), though Engel's apparent ignorance of the Office-Book for *Household Words*, which would have eliminated guesswork as to authorship of contributions to that journal, admittedly weakens some of his evidence. John Holloway offers a similar challenge as well as a sound corrective to Leavis' closet-reading of *Hard Times* [17] in his essay on the novel in *Dickens and the Twentieth Century*, an example of the kind of clearvisioned judgment that can result from a careful job of research into what Dickens had been reading, writing, and saying at the time he was "creating" a piece of fiction.

Dickens' activities in connection with Baroness Burdett-Coutts's establishment of Urania Cottage, a home for fallen women, and other philanthropies have attracted discussion; first, in the early work by Edward F. Payne and Henry H. Harper, *The Charity of Charles Dickens* (1929), and more recently, following the publication of the Dickens-Coutts correspondence by Edgar Johnson, in Clara B. Patterson, *Angela Burdett-Coutts and the Victorians* (1953), and in articles by P. A. W. Collins (*Social Casework*, 1959), Rachel Marks (*Social Service Review*, 1953), and K. J. Fielding (*Dickensian*, 1961). Margaret Kiddle takes up the related sub-

[17] Remonstrances have become commonplace; see C. B. Cox, who calls Leavis a "Positivist critic" (*Critical Quarterly*, 1959, p. 330); A. J. A. Waldock (*Southerly*, 1948); K. J. Fielding (*MLR*, 1953); Dingle Foot (introduction to the New Oxford Illustrated edition of *Hard Times*, 1955); Raymond Williams (*Culture and Society*, 1958); and Angus Wilson (*Critical Quarterly*, 1960).

ject of Dickens and Caroline Chisholm in *Historical Studies, Australia and New Zealand* (1945). Collins has also been exploring Dickens' ideas on education. In his valuable annotated bibliography, *Dickens's Periodicals: Articles on Education* (1957), he laid the foundation of his comprehensive study of the subject, *Dickens and Education* (1963), in which a number of his earlier articles on various aspects of the subject are incorporated. Other treatments are those of A. A. Adrian (*NCF*, 1950) and John Manning in his *Dickens on Education* (1959) with its valuable bibliography of earlier contributions to the subject.

Another work by Collins, *Dickens and Crime* (1962), with the professional distinction of having been published as one of the Cambridge Studies in Criminology, examines all aspects of Dickens' ideas and attitudes (which prove to be more complex and inconsistent than generally conceded) on crime, criminals, and legal procedure. Earlier works on the subject of Dickens and the law had for the most part been written by dilettantes. Of these Alfred Trumble, *In Jail with Dickens* (1896), Ada B. Teetgen (*Contemporary Review*, 1923), Paul C. Squires (*Journal of Criminal Law and Criminology*, 1938), and William S. Holdsworth, *Charles Dickens as a Legal Historian* (1928) stand as the best of a poor lot. The most provocative of more recent discussions emphasize Dickens' interest in law, crime, and criminals from a psychological rather than a sociological point of view. Similarly, earlier trivialities on Dickens' doctors have given way to serious examinations of the amazingly accurate descriptions of disease to be found in his novels. Among the most useful of these are Sir Russell Brain, "Charles Dickens: Neuro-psychiatrist" (*London Hospital Gazette*, 1942) and "Dickensian Diagnoses" (*British Medical Journal*, 1955; reprinted in *Some Reflections on Genius*, 1960); C. G. Strachan, "The Medical Knowledge of Charles Dickens" (*British Medical Journal*, 1924); A. and P. Plichet, "Charles Dickens et ses observations neuropsychiatriques" (*La Presse medicale*, 1956); James A. Brussel, "Charles Dickens: Child Psychologist and Sociologist" (*Psychiatric Quarterly Supplement*, 1938); Richard A. Hunter and Ida Macalpine, "A Note on Dickens's Psychiatric Reading" (*Dickensian*, 1957); and Isaak Oehlbaum, *Das pathologische Element bei Charles Dickens* (1944). Those interested in the subject will find notations of earlier articles in the catalogues of the U.S. Surgeon-General's Library which began publication in 1880.

A favorite topic of Dickensites, revealing their uneasiness about it, has been Dickens and religion, a subject which deserves more searching examination than it has received. Both Tolstoy and Dostoyevsky admired Dickens as the most Christian of English novelists, and a modern Italian writer, Mario Buzzichini, has written on "Dickens, Buon Cristiano" (*Pan*, 1934), but few English readers have had the same reaction. John Laird calls Dickens' ambiguous creed "philanthropical moralism . . . without much benefit of clergy" (*Philosophical Incursions into English Literature*, 1945, pp. 153–154), and Leavis raises the question of whether Dickens really understood "the part played by religion in the life of nineteenth-century industrial England" (*The Great Tradition*, 1948, p. 245). No one has yet answered the question satisfactorily. Most of the early works on the subject are inconsequential with the possible exception of William Kent's *Dickens and Religion* (1930). The best of more recent discussion will be found in the chapter on religion in Humphry House's *The Dickens World*; in the incidental commentary of such critics as Lionel Trilling and J. Hillis Miller; in G. Ingli James, "Dickens: An Essay in Christian Evaluation" (*Blackfriars*, 1957); and, surprisingly, in Sherman Eoff, *The Modern Spanish Novel* (1961, pp. 21–37). Other useful discussions include those of J. M. Connell (*Hibbert Journal*, 1938), Arthur A. Adrian (*NCF*, 1955), Steven Marcus (*New Statesman*, 1961), N. C. Peyrouton (*Dickensian*, 1963), and A. O. J. Cockshut's analysis of the cathedral imagery in *Drood* in *Dickens and the Twentieth Century*. More sociological than religious in focus are the explorations of Dickens' attitudes toward Jews by Lauriat Lane, Jr. (*TLS*, July 20, 1951; and *PMLA*, 1958), Harry Stone (*VS*, 1959; reprinted with some changes, *Midstream*, 1960), and Edgar Rosenberg in

From Shylock to Svengali: Jewish Stereotypes in English Fiction (1960).

Evaluation of Dickens as social observer is naturally concomitant to evaluation of him as social critic. Innumerable books and articles have tracked the Pickwickians in and out of real stagecoaches, inns, and beds, and have found originals for everyone from Jingle to Grewgious. Such antiquarian titbits are of minimal value to the scholar, though recent studies such as David M. Bevington's "Seasonal Relevance in *The Pickwick Papers* (*NCF*, 1961), the textual analyses of John Butt and Kathleen Tillotson in *Dickens at Work* (1957), and discussions like Robert Browning's of *Sketches by Boz* in *Dickens and the Twentieth Century* increase respect for Dickens' sensitive response to the world he knew and throw significant light on his craftsmanship. The best of the many antiquarian books listed in *CBEL* and in Miller's *Student and Collector* include A. L. Hayward, *The Days of Dickens* (1926); E. Beresford Chancellor, *The London of Charles Dickens* (1924) and *Dickens and His Times* (1932); the several works of Walter Dexter and William Kent; and *In the Steps of Charles Dickens* by William Addison (1955). For identification of characters the standard work is still Edwin W. Pugh, *The Charles Dickens Originals* (1912), though subsequent to Pugh contributors to the *Dickensian* and to *N&Q* have suggested numerous supplementary identifications; one of the most prolific of these sleuths, J. H. McNulty, brought his contributions together in *Concerning Dickens and Other Literary Characters* (1942). Of more general interest and value are studies like O. F. Christie, *Dickens and His Age* (1939); Ivor Brown, *Dickens in His Time* (1963); R. J. Cruikshank, *Charles Dickens and Early Victorian England* (1949), which sketches the background of social, political, and cultural events, allowing the reader to relate Dickens to that background in his own way; and Richard Aldington's "The Underworld of Young Dickens" in *Four English Portraits* (1948), which raises antiquarianism to the level of sensitive study of Dickens. The general run of such works, however, is at a sad level of what someone has called "scrupulous inaccuracy" and as a consequence has brought the whole approach into disrepute.

IMAGINATION AND SYMBOLISM. In 1920 Chesterton protested against both "the man who could prove that Micawber never lived, and the man who could prove in what particular street he lodged" (*Charles Dickens Fifty Years After*, p. 1). As an antirealist, Chesterton recognized that both ultra- and anti-Dickensians subscribed to the realist dogmas that had dominated criticism of the novel for half a century, dogmas that he considered inapplicable to Dickens' "best of all impossible worlds" (*The Last of the Great Men*, p. 205). About the same time J. B. Priestley, protesting against the realist Gissing's view of Dickens, cited Henry Cockton's exposé of private asylums in *Valentine Vox* as equal to anything similar in Dickens, but pointed out that the superiority of Dickens to the unread Cockton lay in his creation of "a world of his own . . . governed by an imagination that transfers it into an entirely new sphere" (*Saturday Review*, Sept. 26, 1925). Mark Schorer's division of novels into antipodal types, the "documentary" and the "evocative," the latter "reaching towards the condition of poetry" (*Society and Self in the Novel*, 1956) is but one of numerous manifestations that could be cited of the critical revolution of the past two decades. And, as Ford has pointed out in *Dickens and His Readers*, this revolution, or counterrevolution as he calls it, could be precisely documented by charting the course of the parallel counterrevolution in criticism of Dickens.

It is now commonplace to recognize that for all his talent as "a special correspondent for posterity," as Bagehot called him, Dickens' genius lies in his extraordinary imaginative powers. The words most frequently met with in recent discussions are "imagination," "fantasy," "poetry," "symbol," "myth," "archetype," and "genius." Rise in critical esteem for Dickens is clearly related to the general shift from admiration for verisimilitude (external or psychological) to admiration for imagination and symbol, a shift that has been variously referred to as "the flight from reality," or "the discovery of the soul," or the movement from "mimesis" to "mythopoeism." [18] Ironically, Dickens himself insisted in many of his prefaces that his creations were true to life, but the discussions of Ford and Stang offer ample evidence of Dickens' advice to others respecting the importance of imagination in novel writing, as do studies like Monroe Engel's "Dickens on Art" (*MP*, 1955; incorporated into *The Maturity of Dickens*) and the discussions of P. A. W. Collins in *English Studies* (1961) and the *Dickensian* (1956), as well as the selections from Dickens in Miriam Allott, *Novelists on the Novel* (1959).

Lewes, Taine, Saintsbury, Swinburne (the first to call the Thames the real protagonist of *Our Mutual Friend*), George Barlow, Robert Buchanan, Hermann Heuer, and a host of others had noted Dickens' use of the oblique and richly suggestive methods of the poet, but with few earlier exceptions modern readers are giving first place to this aspect of Dickens for the first time, and his current stature as a novelist depends upon his qualities as a poet and artist rather than upon what William R. Thayer, as early as 1894 (in the *Forum*), condemned as "epidermism." Like the sociological critics, the psychological critics and the symbolists take their cue from Edmund Wilson as they explore the imaginary gardens into which Dickens put his real toads. "The task of criticism," writes Morton D. Zabel, "lies exactly in the discernment of this vision and poetry . . . Where biographical research aids the restitution of this larger and greater Dickens it makes a radical contribution to criticism" (*Craft and Character in Modern Fiction*, 1957, p. 13).

Prompted, like Wilson before him, by new developments in Dickensian biography, Lionel Trilling in a brilliant study of *Little Dorrit* probed the subtleties of Dickens' symbolic handling of the theme of society versus the individual, observing that the novel "at its best is only incidentally realistic; its finest power of imagination appears in the great general

---

[18] For a good introduction to the "Battle of the Books" over realism in the key period, 1880–1915, with valuable bibliographies, see *Realism and Romanticism in Fiction* (ed. Eugene Current-Garcia and Walton R. Patrick, 1962).

images whose abstractness is their actuality" (*The Opposing Self*, 1955, p. 65).[19] And three of the book-length critical studies of Dickens which have appeared since Wilson [20] follow the same lead, albeit with individual permutations. J. Hillis Miller, an acknowledged disciple of Trilling and Georges Poulet, in *Charles Dickens: The World of His Novels* (1958) moves the examination of Dickens' idiosyncratic vision from the psychological to the Jungian or "visionary" level, and follows his metaphysical "search for identity" through six novels. In the course of his study it becomes clear that Miller's interest in Kafka and in Kierkegaardian existentialism (see his "Franz Kafka and the Metaphysics of Alienation" in *The Tragic Vision of the Christian Faith*, ed. Nathan A. Scott, 1957) both enriches and distorts his understanding of Dickens. Monroe Engel, who is more at ease as a sociological than as psychological or literary critic, in *The Maturity of Dickens* (1959) attempts without much success to unravel the complex relationship of Dickens' public and private vision. And A. O. J. Cockshut in *The Imagination of Charles Dickens* (1961) grapples with this "non-U" genius in blunt, undisguisedly "U" fashion, with the air of a George Henry Lewes who has read Edmund Wilson. Cockshut rises superior to the Freudian, Jungian, Kierkegaardian, mythopoetic and other Didi-Gogoian "nonsense" of his fellow critics, and yet concludes that it was the intensity of Dickens' poetic imagination, not his social conscience, that made him a writer of the first order. But even though each of these recent books has intelligent, stimulating, and frequently perceptive things to say — and Miller's in particular is a book that should not be ignored by the serious student in spite of its difficult and jargon-addicted style [21] — none is

[19] The essay on *Little Dorrit* appeared earlier as an introduction to the New Oxford Illustrated Edition of the novel (1953) and also in the *Kenyon Review* (1953). Trilling's review of Edgar Johnson's biography of Dickens (*The Griffin*, 1953; reprinted in *A Gathering of Fugitives*, 1956) makes it clear that the biography triggered his reconsideration of Dickens.

[20] *The Flint and the Flame: The Artistry of Charles Dickens* by Earle Davis (1963) appeared too late for discussion here.

[21] Miller's introduction to the Rinehart *Oliver Twist* (1962) shows a definite advance in lucidity. For a clarification of some of his major ideas,

quite the comprehensive evaluation of Dickens as literary artist we have been waiting for. Perhaps such an evaluation will be forthcoming as soon as twentieth-century critics overcome their reluctance to acknowledge Dickens' full stature and, as noted recently by Peter Fison in a review article headed "Killed and Dissected" (*Spectator*, 1962), "stop apologising for him."

Shorter studies that stand in what could loosely be called the Trilling tradition include C. A. Bodelsen's "Some Notes on Dickens' Symbolism" (*English Studies*, 1959); Robert Morse's discussion of *Our Mutual Friend* and other novels in the *Partisan Review* (1949); Dorothy Van Ghent's study of *Great Expectations* in *The English Novel: Form and Function* (1953); Norman Friedman's (*BUSE*, 1957) and Louis Crompton's (*NCF*, 1958) analyses of *Bleak House*; and Julian Moynahan's "The Hero's Guilt: The Case of *Great Expectations*" (*EC*, 1960), supplemented by his defense against critics of his psychological approach such as Louis Crompton and Barbara Hardy (*EC*, 1960–1961). Critical interest in *Great Expectations* has been especially lively and controversial. G. Robert Stange (*College English*, 1954) and John H. Hagan, Jr. (*NCF*, 1954) offer contrasting interpretations of the novel, while the multiplicity of possible interpretations is brought into sensible focus by K. J. Fielding in "The Critical Autonomy of *Great Expectations*" (*Review of English Literature*, 1961). Two other essays on single novels, less metaphysical than Morse, Van Ghent, or Moynahan but dealing with some of the same problems, are Arnold Kettle's on *Oliver Twist* in *An Introduction to the English Novel* (1951) and Kathleen Tillotson's on *Dombey* in *Novels of the Eighteen-Forties* (1954), the latter emphasizing the technical artistry of Dickens' use of symbols, and recently followed up by Harry Stone in his discussion of the music-staircase imagery in *Dombey* (*College English*, 1963).

Of others that take up various aspects of Dickens' "im-

---

consult R. D. McMaster's review, "Dickens, Jung, and Coleridge" (*Dalhousie Review*, 1959). Miller's own review of Cockshut (*VS*, 1961) is interesting for its illumination of the differences in their approaches.

aginative world," often repetitive, a highly selective list would include such introductions as Morton D. Zabel's to *Bleak House* (1956) and *A Tale of Two Cities* (1958), both reprinted in *Craft and Character in Modern Fiction* (1957), and that of George H. Ford to *David Copperfield* (1958); Sister M. Corona Sharp's (*University of Kansas City Review*, 1961) and R. D. McMaster's (*Dalhousie Review*, 1960) studies of *Our Mutual Friend*; McMaster's "Man into Beast in Dickensian Caricature" (*UTQ*, 1962) and his analysis of *Little Dorrit* (*Queen's Quarterly*, 1961); G. Armour Craig's discussion of *Bleak House* in *Society and Self in the Novel* (1956) and the sensitive two-page analysis of a single scene from that novel by C. B. Cox (*Critical Quarterly*, 1960); James K. Gottshall's "Devils Abroad: The Unity and Significance of *Barnaby Rudge*" (*NCF*, 1961); Charles R. Forker's "The Language of Hands in *Great Expectations*" (*Texas Studies in Literature*, 1961); Angus Wilson's "Dickens and the Divided Conscience" (*Month*, 1950); Harry Stone's studies of the fairy-story elements in *Great Expectations* (*Kenyon Review*, 1962) and in *The Haunted Man* (*SAQ*, 1962), a subject also explored by J. C. Reid with special emphasis upon *The Old Curiosity Shop* in his *The Hidden World of Charles Dickens* (1961); and John Bayley's provocative challenge to the admirers of the late novels in his essay on *Oliver Twist* in *Dickens and the Twentieth Century*. John Killham's discussion of *Pickwick* in *Dickens and the Twentieth Century* provides a footnote to all these admirers of Dickens as poet and myth-maker by condemning the whole approach and urging a return to considerations of plot and character, an opinion echoed by fellow contributor William Empson in his objection that "the devices which are called symbolic are precisely the same as those which were called theatrical; . . . calling them by the new name does not give any help in deciding which of them is good" (p. 15).

SELF-REVELATION. David Daiches in his discussion of Edmund Wilson as "psychological critic" (*Critical Approaches to Literature*, 1956) distinguishes between Wilson's approach to a work from the writer's life [22] and the more "dangerous" approach from the work to the author. Jack Lindsay and more recently Julian Symons use both approaches, but they are perhaps more representative of the latter, and a number following their lead have pushed on to psychiatric speculations which, provocative as they may be to readers of a post-Freudian generation, are often even more dangerous since they tend to depend more upon knowledge of psychological theories than knowledge of either the novels or the facts of Dickens' life. Chief among these are Leonard F. Manheim, editor of *Literature and Psychology* and author of two articles, "The Personal History of David Copperfield" and "The Law as Father" (*American Imago*, 1953, 1955), drawn from his unpublished thesis, "The Dickens Pattern: A Study in Psychoanalytic Criticism"; and Mark Spilka in "*David Copperfield* as Psychological Fiction" (*Critical Quarterly*, 1959), in "Little Nell Revisited" (*Papers of the Michigan Academy*, 1960), and in his book and his several articles on Dickens and Kafka discussed below. Less extreme in their view of Dickens Agonistes but along the same line are Ernest Boll, "Charles Dickens in *Oliver Twist*" (*Psychoanalytic Review*, 1940); Warrington Winter, "Dickens and the Psychology of Dreams" (*PMLA*, 1948); Edmund Bergler, "*Little Dorrit* and Dickens' Intuitive Knowledge of Psychic Masochism" (*American Imago*, 1957); Jonathan Bishop, "The Hero-Villain of *Oliver Twist*" (*VNL*, 1959); and Steven Marcus, "Who is Fagin?" (*Commentary*, 1962). Perhaps the most sensationally psychoanalytic is Leslie A. Fiedler's discussion of Dickens and Dostoyevsky as nymphet-obsessed "child-rapists" in his series of articles in *The New Leader* (1958; reprinted in *No! in Thunder*, 1960).

Many, of course, have raised objections to irresponsible psychologizing, including Louis Cazamian, "Psycho-Analysis and Literary Criticism" in *Three Studies in Criticism* (1924);

[22] Not to be confused with such a "psychological" approach as H. B. Fantham's of Dickens' (and Mrs. Dickens') endocrine, thyroid, parathyroid, adrenal, and pituitary glands (*Character and Personality*, 1934); see also P. C. Squires, "The Case of Dickens as Viewed by Biology and Psychology" (*Journal of Abnormal Psychology*, 1936).

Lionel Trilling, "Art and Neurosis" in *The Liberal Imagination* (1941); and Humphry House, who in 1948 condemned the effect of "an imperfect apprehension of the findings and gropings of psychology" on modern biography, in which "the search for the ego has led to the neglect of the superego" (*All in Due Time*, 1955, p. 261). In spite of such extremes as Fiedler, however, the most illuminating psychological studies of Dickens have been those directed to his childhood (about which he himself said so little) and to his attitude toward children. Few critics of whatever school have failed to note how continuously and obsessively Dickens drew from the deep well of his childhood experience, and yet this important subject has not yet received the full or close attention it deserves. Interestingly, creative writers seem to have been specially drawn to it: J. B. Priestley writes on it in *Literature and Western Man* (1960), as does John Cowper Powys in *Visions and Revisions* (1915; reprinted, 1955); Edward Sackville-West in *Inclinations* (1949) has a chapter on "Dickens and the World of Childhood" and Graham Greene's essay on "The Young Dickens" in *The Lost Childhood and Other Essays* (1951) has become a classic.[23] Greene emphasizes Dickens' deep and gripping awareness of the child's world of horror and nightmare, an awareness which R. D. McMaster in "Dickens and the Horrific" (*Dalhousie Review*, 1958) relates to his reading as a child. Harry Stone in a number of articles noted elsewhere — and especially in his recently published "Dark Corners of the Mind: Dickens' Childhood Reading" (*Horn Book*, 1963), with its charming illustrations from early chapbooks — has also made provocative use of Dickens' childhood reading, drawing from his comprehensive but as yet unpublished dissertation on Dickens' reading in general (UCLA, 1955); except for this study, the highly significant subject of Dickens' reading, about which circulate so many critical clichés, has been dealt with only in such superficial guides as James S. Stevens, *Quotations and Refer-*

[23] Originally an introduction to the Hamish Hamilton edition of *Oliver Twist* (1950); see V. S. Pritchett's excellent review of it in the *New Statesman* (1950; reprinted in *Books in General*, 1953).

ences in Charles Dickens (1929) and T. W. Hill, "Books that Dickens Read" (*Dickensian*, 1949).

CRAFTSMANSHIP. The findings of the symbolists and psychoanalysts have not supported the Chestertonian notion that Dickens was a genius and therefore did not need to be a "novelist." Discovery of his controlled use of symbol and autobiography reveals that he was much more of a conscious artist than was sensed by even the most enthusiastic of his earlier votaries. Steven Marcus believes that true respect for Dickens as an artist had to wait until the work of Joyce, Proust, Faulkner, and Kafka made his techniques more familiar (*New Statesman*, 1961). Although Ford's and Stang's surveys show instances of early flickers of awareness, the first extended investigations of Dickens as literary craftsman are the textual studies of John Butt and Kathleen Tillotson. In a series of separate articles which were brought together and supplemented in their collaborative volume *Dickens at Work* (1957), these two scholars set themselves the task of examining Dickens' "methods and conditions of work" in seven major novels and *Sketches by Boz* through close examination of manuscripts, number plans, proof sheets, serial and book texts, letters, and instructions to illustrators. Butt had also examined the origin and design of *A Christmas Carol* in the *Dickensian* (1954) and written two studies of *Great Expectations* (*Durham University Journal*, 1948, and *Dickensian*, 1949), only portions of which appear in *Dickens at Work*.

Butt and Tillotson's revolutionary approach to Dickens as an artist worthy of the most precise textual study had been preceded by only a handful of minor studies such as "The Strange Story of a Dickens Misprint" by Wilfred Hargrave (*Connoisseur*, 1902; reprinted in *Book-Lover*, 1903); Fritz Fiedler's study of *A Christmas Carol* (*Archiv für das Studium der neueren Sprachen*, 1922); two articles by Gerald G. Grubb, "On the Serial Publication of *Oliver Twist*" (*MLN*, 1941) and "Dickens' Pattern of Weekly Serialization" (*ELH*, 1942); the study of the manuscript of *Our Mutual Friend* by Ernest Boll (*MP*, 1944); and by some parallels in the important work of the French scholar Sylvère Monod (*Dickens romancier,* 1953). Of special interest are those portions of the major novels deleted from the manuscripts by Dickens which appear in print for the first time in the *Dickensian* (1952–1954) under the title "Shavings from Dickens's Workshop." Of the textual studies Boll's is useful since *Dickens at Work* includes no discussion of *Our Mutual Friend,* though Boll falls far below the Butt-Tillotson standard. A few "shavings" from the latter were published as early as 1874 in Kate Field's account in *Scribner's Monthly* of the only novel manuscript in America, as well as in an article in *Massey's Magazine* (1896). More recently Robert Morse has discussed the structural problems of *Our Mutual Friend* in *Partisan Review* (1949) and Francis X. Shea has examined the variations between the original manuscript and the first printed edition in his unpublished dissertation (see *Dissertation Abstracts,* 1961).

C. P. Snow (*New Statesman,* 1957) and Bruce Harkness (*Studies in Bibliography,* 1959) have deplored the general neglect of textual study on the part of Dickens critics, but the trail-blazing work of Butt, Tillotson, and Monod, epitomized in plans for the forthcoming critical edition of Dickens by the Clarendon Press, has gone far to cancel charges of neglect. The authors of *Dickens at Work* have continued to illuminate Dickens' craftsmanship in a series of short studies: Butt on *Bleak House* (*Critical Quarterly,* 1959), *Little Dorrit* (*UTQ,* 1959), *Martin Chuzzlewit's* illustrations (*Review of English Literature,* 1961), and Dickens' manuscripts (*YULG,* 1962); and Tillotson on *Oliver Twist* (*Essays and Studies,* 1959) and *Dombey* (in *Novels of the Eighteen-Forties,* 1954). It is true, however, that though it may be hoped that all Dickensian criticism has profited from such textual study, not many others have so far turned in the same direction. Exceptions would include the articles on monthly and weekly serialization by K. J. Fielding (*Dickensian,* 1958); a series of rather fumbling studies by Archibald C. Coolidge, Jr., drawn from his unpublished dissertation on "Serialization in the Novels of Charles Dickens" (see *Dissertation Abstracts,*

1956), appearing in *Mississippi Quarterly* (1961), *Dickensian* (1961), *SAQ* (1962), and *North Dakota Quarterly* (1962); and the extension of Butt's discussion of *Bleak House* by P. A. W. Collins (*NCF*, 1960), George J. Worth (*JEGP*, 1961), and Trevor Blount (*RES*, 1963).

Although not precisely textual, a great number of Dickensian studies have been devoted to problems of structure. Ford's discovery of an anonymous contributor to the *Prospective Review* of 1851 who discussed "point of view" in Dickens long before James or Lubbock, as well as Stang's examples of such discussions in the 1850's and 1860's, underscores the fact that it is the rare reader who finds what he does not expect to find, and few have expected to find a conscious use and control of "point of view" in Dickens. More recent discussions of the subject include M. E. Grenander's comments on point of view in *Bleak House* (*NCF*, 1956), those of Robert B. Partlow, Jr., on *Great Expectations* (*College English*, 1961), and Frederick W. Boege's general discussion (*PMLA*, 1950).

Perhaps inevitably, structural studies of *Edwin Drood* have been most numerous. Edmund Wilson, whose discussion of *Drood* is the culmination of his "Dickens: The Two Scrooges," points to the work of W. Robertson Nicoll (*The Problem of Edwin Drood*, 1912), Aubrey Boyd (*Washington University Studies*, 1921), and Howard Duffield (New York *Bookman*, 1930) as the most important of his predecessors. Nicoll's study was based on Dickens' revisions of the original draft; the Collins edition of the novel (1956), with an introduction by C. Day Lewis, reprints the revisions along with excerpts from John Forster's and Wilson's commentary on *Drood*. Since Wilson the most comprehensive study is Richard M. Baker's *The Drood Murder Case: Five Studies in Dickens's "Edwin Drood"* (1951; reprinted from *NCF*, 1948–1949). Other interesting discussions are those of V. S. Pritchett in the *New Statesman* (1944; reprinted in *The Living Novel*, 1946); Michael Innes [J. I. M. Stewart] in his introduction to the Chiltern edition of the novel (1952); George H. Ford's "Dickens's Notebook and *Edwin Drood*" (*NCF*, 1952); and

Malcolm Morley in a series of articles in the *Dickensian* (1957) on the stage solutions to the mystery. There has also been a lively battle running in the pages of the *Dickensian* for the past several years between the "undertakers" (Pansy Pakenham, T. S. Blakeney, and others), who believe Drood is dead, and the "resurrectionists" (William Bleifuss, Gavin Brend, and Felix Aylmer), who believe he is still alive.

Various aspects of Dickens' craftsmanship have also been the focus in studies of other individual novels, such as that of *Barnaby Rudge* by Harold F. Folland (*PMLA*, 1959) and those of *Martin Chuzzlewit* by Joseph Brogunier (*Dickensian*, 1962), Edward B. Benjamin (*PQ*, 1955), and Barbara Hardy (*Dickens and the Twentieth Century*, 1962), Miss Hardy playing something of a devil's advocate in the matter of praise of Dickens' sense of structure, a subject also treated in her "Change of Heart in Dickens's Novels" (*VS*, 1961). Dorothy Van Ghent in "The Dickens World: The View from Todgers's" (*Sewanee Review*, 1950) also analyzes aspects of technique in *Chuzzlewit*, especially Dickens' use of animism, a subject discussed with more general reference by Priscilla Gibson (*NCF*, 1953) and R. D. McMaster (*UTQ*, 1962). *Bleak House* has been the subject of several studies, most notably those of Robert A. Donovan (*ELH*, 1962) and W. J. Harvey (*Dickens and the Twentieth Century*). The most valuable contributions to structural study of *Great Expectations* are those of John H. Hagan, Jr. (*ELH*, 1954), Thomas E. Connolly (*PQ*, 1955), Andrew P. Drew (*Dickensian*, 1956), James H. Broderick and John E. Grant (*MP*, 1958), Sylvère Monod (*Dickensian*, 1960), and Mary Edminson (*NCF*, 1958), the last especially useful for its establishment of the date of action of the novel.

A variety of artistic problems in *David Copperfield* are taken up by Earle R. Davis (*University of Wichita Studies*, 1941), E. K. Brown (*Yale Review*, 1948), and Gwendolyn B. Needham (*NCF*, 1954); Needham is challenged in some of her conclusions by William H. Marshall in "The Image of Steerforth and the Structure of *David Copperfield*" (*Tennessee Studies in Literature*, 1960). Several modern editions

of *Copperfield* make valuable contributions to the study of
its form and technique, such as George H. Ford's (1958),
called by G. Robert Stange "the best available edition" and
the most truly "edited" one of any Dickens novel (*College
English*, 1959, p. 180). Acknowledging indebtedness to John
Butt's textual studies, Ford gives the serial division into installments and includes an appendix of omitted passages.
More recently Edgar Johnson has brought out an edition
(1962) which incorporates *in situ* the passages removed in
proof and the serial parts divisions. Sylvère Monod, whose
translated edition of *Copperfield* (Paris, 1956) offers valuable
textual commentary, calls attention to the useful notes of
an obscure early editor, E. Kibblewhite (Oxford edition,
1916).

Certainly, as pointed out in Ernest Alan Horsman's provocative general analysis *Dickens and the Structure of the
Novel* (1959), an important aspect of Dickens' craftsmanship
is his handling of language. Oliver Elton in a discussion of
his "wordcraft" remarks that the best of Dickens' characters
are "triumphs of style" (*A Survey of English Literature*, II,
217), a tribute which few, disparagers or defenders, have
failed to echo. And yet, although every critic of Dickens
has had something to say about "Dickensian style" and a
few, like J. Hillis Miller, have given it rewarding attention,
no completely satisfactory or comprehensive study of Dickens'
use of language has yet appeared. Ford points out that the
best of the early treatments, most of which were sophomoric,
was David Masson's essay comparing Dickens and Thackeray
(*North British Review*, 1851; later expanded and published
in his *British Novelists and Their Styles*, 1859). Foreign
scholars have been the more active in this area, perhaps not
surprisingly in view of the translator's need for special sensitivity in matters of diction, though it is something of a
surprise that a Japanese Dickensian, Tadao Yamamoto, has
given the subject the most assiduous attention in *Growth and
System of the Language of Dickens: An Introduction to a
Dickens Lexicon* (1950; rev. ed., 1952). Of similar interest
is Evgeny Lann's discussion of Dickens' early style and the

problems of translating *Pickwick* into Russian in *Literaturnyi kritik* (1939). In view of the long tradition of German interest in linguistics as well as in Dickens, German studies of his language and literary style are to be expected. Early works will be found listed in Ellis N. Gummer, *Dickens' Works in Germany, 1837–1937* (1940); the two most important since 1937 are *Die erlebte Rede im englischen Roman des 19. Jahrhunderts* (1948) by the Swiss scholar Lisa Glauser, notable for its discussion of interior monologue, and Ludwig Borinski's excellent study of the "dark novels" in *Neueren Sprachen* (1957). The best short study in French is Sylvère Monod's "L'Expression dans *Our Mutual Friend*: manière ou maniérisme?" (*Études anglaises*, 1957). The few stylistic studies written in English by foreign scholars include Knud Sørensen, "Subjective Narration in *Bleak House*" (*English Studies*, 1959), and C. A. Bodelsen, "The Physiognomy of the Name" (*Review of English Literature*, 1961). There is some brief commentary in Mario Praz, *The Hero in Eclipse in Victorian Fiction* (trans., 1956).

Recent developments in semantic studies may bring about more serious study of Dickens' language by English and American scholars. The British grammarian Randolph Quirk has taken an initial step in his brief but illuminating *Charles Dickens and Appropriate Language* (1959) and in his contribution to the Dickens number of *Review of English Literature* (1961), "Some Observations on the Language of Dickens." The latter, which takes up Dickens' handling of interior monologue and stream of consciousness appears to owe an unacknowledged debt for some of its illustrative materials to Harry Stone's "Dickens and Interior Monologue" (*PQ*, 1959), in which Stone draws particularly from the minor stories and sketches for unstereotyped illustrations, and makes some interesting Joycean analogies. Stone in his turn may have taken a cue from Jacob Isaacs who was the first, so far as I have been able to discover, to note the strong Joycean flavor in the speech of such feminine characters as Mrs. Nickleby and Mrs. Lirriper [24] (see *An Assessment of Twentieth-Cen-*

---

[24] Stone pays special attention to "Mrs. Lirriper's Lodgings," which Isaacs

tury Literature, 1951, pp. 97–101); or Quirk and Stone may both be indebted to T. W. Hill's supplementary note to Donal O'Sullivan's discussion of Dickens and Thomas Moore (*Studies*, 1948, p. 342). More recently, Jean McClure Kelty, in apparent ignorance of all her predecessors, comments on the more obvious examples of interior monologue and stream of consciousness in "The Modern Tone of Charles Dickens" (*Dickensian*, 1961). Other treatments will be found in Richard Stang, *The Theory of the Novel in England* (pp. 99–103), Fred W. Boege (*PMLA*, 1950), and Marvin Rosenberg (*JEGP*, 1960). All these discussions recall Graham Greene's description of the language of *Great Expectations* as "A secret prose giving that sense of a mind speaking to itself with no one there to listen . . . delicate and exact poetic cadences, the music of memory, that so influenced Proust" (*Lost Childhood*, p. 52).

A peripheral subject, the naming of characters, has received both literary and linguistic attention in such discussions as those of W. F. Peacock (*Belgravia*, 1873), E. De Laski (*American Journal of Psychology*, 1918), Elizabeth Hope Gordon (*University of Nebraska Studies in Language, Literature, and Criticism*, 1917), Lionel Stevenson (*Dickensian*, 1936), Kelsie B. Harder (*Names*, 1959), and C. A. Bodelsen (*Review of English Literature*, 1961), but the most exhaustive treatment of the subject is that of Charlotte Sennewald in *Die Namengebung bei Dickens, eine Studie über Lautsymbolik* (1936).

Dialect in Dickens has also been more thoroughly investigated by the German philologists Franz, Westendorpf, and Grünewald (see Gummer) than by English or American scholars. In spite of the testimony of such authorities as Gissing who praised Dickens' keen ear for the speech of his day, especially that of his "idiotic women" whose "phrases

---

calls "one of Dickens' most neglected masterpieces" (p. 98). The short stories in general have been neglected by critics; Stone's discussion here and those of "George Silverman's Explanation" in *SP* (1958) and *The Haunted Man* in *SAQ* (1962), together with Morton D. Zabel's general commentary in the introduction to his anthology *Charles Dickens' Best Stories* (1959), are the only noteworthy exceptions.

might have been taken down by a phonograph" (*Charles Dickens*, 1898, p. 178), the question of the accuracy of Dickens' use of dialect has long been debated. Numerous notes on the subject have appeared in *N&Q* and the *Dickensian* as well as discussions in such works as Ernest Weekley's *Adjectives and Other Words* (1930); William Matthews' *Cockney Past and Present* (1938); and Julian Franklyn's *The Cockney: A Survey of London Life and Language* (1953). And of course the Shavian comments in the notes to *Captain Brassbound's Conversion* are well known; these notes prompted the Danish study by Joseph Saxe, *Bernard Shaw's Phonetics: A Comparative Study of Cockney Sound-Changes* (1936), which set itself to explore "to what extent Shavian phonetics differ from the Dickensian species, as perpetuated by 'Punch'." The only more recent treatments of any importance are K. J. Fielding's note on the East Anglican dialect of *David Copperfield* (*TLS*, April 30, 1949), Louise Pound's "The American Dialect of Charles Dickens" (*American Speech*, 1947), and Anne Lohrli's "Dickens's *Household Words* on American English" (*American Speech*, 1962).

Certainly the serious work of John Butt, Kathleen Tillotson, Sylvère Monod, and all the others who have been looking afresh at the whole matter of methods of publication in the nineteenth century, Dickens' practices in particular, calls for a reassessment of the long-entrenched opinions about Dickens' carelessness as a writer. A great deal of water has gone under many bridges in the quarter century since Mrs. Q. D. Leavis could praise Mrs. Radcliffe over Dickens because she "makes an appeal less to the nerves than to the imagination" and "does achieve a total effect" impossible for "the novelist who made his living by cheap serial publication" (*Fiction and the Reading Public*, 1939, pp. 154, 157).

LURE OF THE THEATER. Angus Wilson has observed that "Dickens' greatest natural gift was his ear" ("Charles Dickens: A Haunting," *Critical Quarterly*, 1960). Students of his language agree that the life of his characters lies in their speech, and that the key to the power Dickens holds over his readers may be the oral quality of the whole body of his writing. Butt and Tillotson point out that the relationship with his readers was "not unlike that of an oral story-teller," and their studies of the weekly or monthly exchange between Dickens and his public document what biographers and critics had long noted: his very special sensitivity to audience response — "his lifelong love-affair with his reading public," as Mrs. Tillotson puts it, "which, when all is said, is by far the most interesting love-affair of his life" (*Dickens at Work*, p. 75). Chesterton blamed this many-headed mistress for making "rather a mess of his private life" (*Come to Think of It*, 1930, p. 254), and Frank O'Connor has called the affair "a highly unseemly relationship" in a discussion in which he objects on aesthetic grounds to this "intrusion of the audience" (*The Mirror in the Roadway*, 1956). Critics more frequently object to "author intrusion," though recently this Jamesian bogy has been receiving able defense from scholars like Mrs. Tillotson (*The Tale and the Teller*, 1959) and Wayne C. Booth (*The Rhetoric of Fiction*, 1961), and Arnold Kettle looks upon the twentieth-century isolation of the novelist from his public as an alarming development (*An Introduction to the English Novel*, 1953, II, 64). Another commentator, Gabriel Pearson, who considers Dickens a case history of social revolution, sees the drama of Dickens' relation with his public resolving itself in the melodramatic climax of the public readings in which Dickens acted out with his audience "the hidden conflicts and compulsions of the age" so that "his audience, or rather his lover's passion for it, destroyed him." Pearson does touch on the literary side of the love affair when he adds, "but not before his artist's passion had, beneath the guise of the performer, moulded it and recreated it, and, in the process, the imaginative landscape of Nineteenth-Century England" ("Dickens and His Readers," *Universities and Left Review*, 1957).

Many commentators, like Pearson, have seen in the public readings something of Dickens' near pathological need for contact with his audience. Such studies of the readings as John D. Gordan's *Reading for Profit* (1958) and J. H. Stonehouse's *Sikes and Nancy* (1921), Walter Dexter's series of accounts of the readings in the *Dickensian* (1941–1943), and the discussions of Theresa and Richard Murphy (*Quarterly Journal of Speech,* 1947, 1955) and Robert Woodall (*Contemporary Review,* 1958) focus more on the biographical or psychological origins of the phenomenon than on its artistic consequences. Some hint of the ore to be mined by a comparison of the various reading texts with the original passages in the novels is found in John D. Gordan's edition of the unique Berg copy of the Gamp reading (*Mrs. Gamp: A Facsimile of the Author's Prompt Copy,* 1956), in which he examines Dickens' corrections, deletions, and additions made from 1858 to 1868 and compares these with six other printed editions. An extension of this kind of collation to other reading editions could isolate some of the specifics that account for audience response to Dickens (see L. A. Kennethe's useful account of Dickens' personal copies in the *Dickensian,* 1943). Aspects of such response might also be illuminated by a comparison of Dickens' versions with the arrangements of Emlyn Williams (*Readings from Dickens,* 1953), the public performance of which was praised by Eric Bentley for bringing home to modern audiences Dickens' mastery of language as no silent reading could (*The Dramatic Event,* 1954, p. 125).

Ford notes that the "warm bond between author and public was reinforced by the personal tone of *Household Words* and *All the Year Round*" (*Dickens and His Readers,* p. 160), to which might be added that of his speeches and letters. A reviewer of Fielding's edition of the *Speeches* observed that Dickens addressed his hearers in installments much as his novels were composed (*New Statesman,* 1960), and F. W. Dupee in the introduction to his *Selected Letters of Charles Dickens* (1960) says that readers breathe "an exhilarating air of vast public acclaim" that "follows him around all his days like a brass band." The possibly deep and permanent influences upon his art of the public response first to his writings and then to his public readings still challenge investigation.

Still another aspect of Dickens' contact with his public, that of his lifelong interest in the theater as amateur actor, play-wright, and playgoer, has also been much commented upon. But since no comprehensive study of the relationship of drama and novel from 1740 has yet been written, and since, as Bernard Bergonzi has reminded us, "We are in need of a critical theory of melodrama" (*Dickens and the Twentieth Century*, p. 69), the ground remains untilled for a proper study of the complex fusions in Dickens of the dramatic and the melodramatic, the genuinely tragic or comic and the merely theatrical. There is the important critical problem of how far the techniques and conventions of the stage, as well as the acting of such favorites as Charles Mathews and Mac-ready, affected his art. Dickens' phenomenal rise to popularity is inextricably related to the decline of the drama in the nineteenth century as well as to the qualities of audience communication in his own work which undoubtedly sprang from his conviction that "Every writer of fiction . . . writes, in effect, for the stage" (*Speeches*, ed. K. J. Fielding, p. 262). Some of the right questions have been posed in scattered short studies, the most valuable of which are R. C. Churchill, "Dickens, Drama and Tradition" (*Scrutiny*, 1942; incor-porated in part in *English Literature in the Nineteenth Century*, 1951); Marvin Rosenberg, "The Dramatist in Dick-ens" (*JEGP*, 1960); Archibald C. Coolidge, Jr.'s two essays on melodrama and sensationalism in Dickens (*VNL*, 1961); and John Oliver Perry, "The Popular Tradition of Melo-drama in Dickens" (*Carleton Miscellany*, 1962). Of the many earlier book-length studies on Dickens and the theater, in-cluding those by T. E. Pemberton, S. J. Adair Fitzgerald, Alexander Woollcott, F. J. H. Darton, and Karla König, only J. B. van Amerongen's *The Actor in Dickens* (1926) is of much critical importance.

Among the questions not yet satisfactorily resolved is how a novelist often compared with Shakespeare could have taken seriously the bad plays he wrote, acted in, and attended, almost all of the type of melodrama defined by Chesterton as creating "people so morally simple as to kill their enemies in Oxford Street, and repent on seeing their mother's photograph" (*Charles Dickens*, p. 117). The ultimate question is, of course, as it is with Shakespeare, how much weight should be given to the pyrotechnics of disguises, lost heirs, mistaken identities, unmasked villains, and all the rest of it, in any final appraisal. Spadework on Dickens' dramatic taste has been done by Dutton Cook (*Longman's*, 1883), G. H. Clarke (*Queen's Quarterly*, 1945), and Gilbert Highet (in *People, Places, and Books*, 1949). Walter Dexter's accounts of Dickens' writings for the stage and appearances as an actor (*Dickensian*, 1937, 1939–1940) and especially William J. Carlton's identification and discussion of Dickens' contributions to the *Morning Chronicle* in "Charles Dickens, Dramatic Critic" (*Dickensian*, 1960) are useful introductions to the subject. Dickens' many speeches for the General Theatrical Fund should also be consulted for their frequent references to actors and plays.

A promising area of investigation as yet unexplored is the multitude of contemporary dramatizations of the novels, all of them appallingly bad. A comparison of these with the novels themselves should lead to some interesting conclusions about Dickens' alleged lack of discrimination and catering to the degraded theatrical taste of his day. Besides the listings in Allardyce Nicoll's *History of English Drama* and the 190 published adaptations Miller's *Student and Collector* offers, other useful lists have been compiled by Dorothy Pierce (*Bulletin of Bibliography*, 1936), Frank Hugh Rand, *Les Adaptations théatrales des romans de Dickens en Angleterre, 1837–1870* (1939), and Malcolm Morley in a series of accounts in the *Dickensian*. The best listing of American stage versions to 1900 will be found in the unpublished dissertation of Walter S. Lazenby, Jr. (see *Dissertation Abstracts*, 1962). F. Dubrez Fawcett's *Dickens the Dramatist: On Stage, Screen and Radio* (1952) is a general survey which should be supplemented by the contributions of Ian F. Finlay and Edward Wagenknecht to the *Dickensian* (1958). Fawcett's extension of listings to include modern adaptations offers materials for arriving at some kind of evaluation of the elements of theatricalism in Dickens (as well as for contributing a chapter to theatrical history) through a comparison of what a Victorian adaptor like Edward Stirling, say, did with Dickens and what David Lean has done. Margaret G. Ortman in her discussion of Dickens in *Fiction and the Screen* (1935, pp. 115–136) takes only a hesitant and inconclusive step in this direction. Much more important is Sergei Eisenstein's classic discussion of what motion pictures have learned from Dickens in "Dickens, Griffith, and the Film Today" (*Film Form*, 1949; newly trans. and ed. by Jay Leyda, 1957); aside from his central topic, Eisenstein makes a major contribution to the study of Dickens as artist and literary craftsman.

PRECURSORS AND IMITATORS. Even though none but an extreme idolater is likely to take seriously Macready's verdict that the murder of Nancy as read by Dickens was "worth ten Macbeths" or Tolstoy's and Francis Jeffrey's that Little Nell is equal to Cordelia, it is undeniable that no name has been more frequently bracketed with that of Dickens than Shakespeare's, by such critics as Shaw, Santayana, T. S. Eliot, and a host of others; even Henry James in the midst of his objections to Dickens and Balzac admitted, "They have no rivals but each other and Shakespeare" (*French Poets and Novelists*, 1884, p. 147). On the popular level, too, the linking was commonplace, as evidenced in the long series of cartoons, "The Shakespeare-Dickens Combination Company," which ran from November 16, 1894, to February 23, 1895, in *Lika Joko*. And yet, although there have been a few short studies such as Cumberland Clark, *Shakespeare and Dickens: A Lecture* (1918; reprinted in *Dickens and Other Studies*, 1930), Howard Duffield, "The Macbeth Motif in *Edwin Drood*" (*Dickensian*, 1934), Elmer Edgar Stoll, "Heroes and Villains: Shakespeare, Middleton, Byron, Dickens" (*RES*, 1942), Edward P. Vandiver, Jr., "Dickens' Knowledge of Shakespeare" (*Shakespeare Association Bulletin*, 1946), and Wilhelm Dibelius' early study in *Shakespeare-Jahrbuch* (1916) supplemented by his discussion in *Charles Dickens* (1916), there has been no comprehensive study of the influence of Shakespeare upon Dickens or of the many fascinating parallels in their respective careers.[25] And although many have noted Dickens' affinity to the Jacobean dramatists, the only article I know of treating a particular dramatic predecessor other than Shakespeare is "Jonson and Dickens: A Study in the Comic Genius of London," by Evelyn Simpson (*Essays and Studies*, 1944), which does little exploring of direct influence.

It is true that source-stalking deserves the suspicion with which many look upon all parallelizing, if firm and positive results are looked for. But the chase itself can still contribute much of critical importance to the study of an author. Virginia Woolf once complained against W. Walter Crotch's scramble after sources in *The Secret of Dickens* (1919) that "If everybody is somebody else, would it not be simpler to call them all Charles Dickens and have done with it?" but she had to admit that "in his hunt up and down the centuries . . . Mr. Crotch starts a great many hares which are well worth pursuing, whether we catch them or not" (*TLS*, March 27, 1919). The right kind of study of Dickens' precursors on the one hand and imitators on the other could bring into significant focus the unique qualities that set a Dickens apart from a Pierce Egan or a William De Morgan. Or a close examination of the imitable tricks of style and tone caught by a deliberate plagiarizer like Reynolds in *Pickwick Abroad*, or by parodists like Albert Smith in his "Dombey and Son Finished" or Robert Benchley in "Christmas Afternoon," could serve as a touchstone for the discovery of what is inimitable in Dickens.

Among the most widely suggested literary influences aside from Shakespeare, the Bible, and the *Arabian Nights* are

[25] Besides the technical and artistic similarities, there is the parallel of their obscure middle-class background and lack of formal education. Two Victorian parodies of the Shakespeare-Bacon controversy used Dickens as a foil; one by Andrew Lang claimed that "Boz" was an anagram for Herbert Spencer (*Macmillan's*, 1886) and the other proved by cryptograms that Gladstone was the real author of the novels (*Cornhill*, 1888); both satirized the Baconians by arguing that Dickens was no gentleman and therefore "couldn't-uv" written such masterpieces.

Cervantes, Lesage, Defoe, Fielding, Smollett, Sterne, the
Gothic novelists, Godwin, the essayists Goldsmith, Lamb,
Addison, and Steele, and the poets Burns and Thomas Moore.
But again no extended study has been given these affinities
or those with more immediate predecessors, even though the
names of Scott, Hood, Hook, Egan, Charles Mathews, Reynolds, Surtees, Marryat, Hunt, Ainsworth, Bulwer-Lytton,
and Irving have been regularly tossed about by biographers,
critics, and literary historians. Were *Pickwick*'s ingredients,
as the *Athenaeum* reviewer in 1836 contended, "two pounds
of Smollett, three ounces of Sterne, a handful of Hook, a dash
of a grammatical Pierce Egan"? And are there not some few
spoonfuls of *Jorrocks' Jaunts* and Bell's *Life in London*?
Just how much did *Sketches by Boz* owe besides the title to
Irving's *The Sketch Book*? Or *Oliver Twist* to *Snarleyyow*
and *Paul Clifford*? And so on and on, down to the works
which have faced definite charges of plagiarism, such as *A
Tale of Two Cities*, so charged by supporters of the claims
of Watts Phillips' *The Dead Heart*, and *Edwin Drood*, by
supporters of Robert Lytton's *The Disappearance of John
Ackland*.[26] As Chesterton observed, "We talk of great models,
but good literature is sometimes based on bad literature and
great men sometimes model themselves on small ones" (*The
Outline of Literature*, ed. John Drinkwater, 1924, III, 804);
Chesterton's proposal that some brave soul "wander in that
wilderness of waste-paper" has so far had no takers equal to
the challenge.

The most comprehensive treatment of sources in general
will be found in Fritz Fiedler, "Dickens' Belesenheit" (*Archiv*

[26] The controversy over Phillips, begun by Emma Watts Phillips in *Watts Phillips: Artist and Playwright* (1891), has been discussed by John Coleman (*New Review*, 1889), J. A. Falconer (*MLN*, 1921), Sir John Shuckburgh in an introduction to *A Tale of Two Cities* (1949), and Carl R. Dolmetsch (*Dickensian*, 1959). The claims of "Owen Meredith" were first noted by Andrew Lang in *The Puzzle of Dickens's Last Plot* (1905) and J. Cuming Walters (*Athenaeum*, April 14, 1906, followed up in *The Complete Edwin Drood*, 1912); and have been attacked or defended by M. A. Ellis (*N&Q*, April 30, 1921), Frederick Page (*N&Q*, March 11, April 8, 1944; *Dickensian*, 1946), and Aurelia Harlan in *Owen Meredith: A Critical Biography of Robert, First Earl of Lytton* (1946).

für das Studium der neueren Sprachen und Literaturen, 1920)
and in Dibelius' two works: *Englische Romankunst* (1910)
and *Charles Dickens* (1916), though as Baker warns Dibelius
is often overimaginative in his source-hunting. Other German studies explore the sources for individual novels: Curt
Böttger, *Charles Dickens' historischer Roman 'A Tale of Two
Cities' und seine Quellen* (1913) and Alfred Ulrich, *Studien
zu Dickens' Roman 'Barnaby Rudge'* (1931). Good explora-
tory studies are Lionel Stevenson's "The Second Birth of
the English Novel" (*UTQ*, 1945) and Earle Davis' "Dickens
and the Evolution of Caricature" (*PMLA*, 1940); Baker,
Elton, and Saintsbury (*CHEL*) also discuss sources in some
detail. Individual studies of varying degrees of importance
include Albert Winter on Addison (*Joseph Addison als
Humorist in seinen Einfluss auf Dickens' Jungendwerke,*
1899); Marie Hamilton Law on Defoe's *History of the Devil*
(*PMLA*, 1925); Donal O'Sullivan on Thomas Moore (*Stud-
ies,* 1948); Paul C. Kitchen on Thomas Holcroft (*Schelling
Anniversary Papers,* 1923); Archibald C. Coolidge, Jr., on
Mrs. Radcliffe (*Dickensian,* 1962), on Hazlitt (*Mississippi
Quarterly,* 1962), and on Dickens and the comic tradition,
especially Hazlitt and Fielding (*VN*, 1960); Frank Wilson on
Fielding and Smollett (*Dickens in seinen Beziehungen zu
den Humoristen Fielding und Smollett,* 1899); Frans D.
Wierstra on Smollett (*Smollett and Dickens,* 1928); William
Woodman Huse, Jr., "Pickle and Pickwick" (*Washington
University Studies, Humanistic Series,* 1922); and the discus-
sion of Dickens in F. W. Boege, *Smollett's Reputation as a
Novelist* (1947). Both Alex Lucas' "*Oliver Twist* and the
Newgate Novel" (*Dalhousie Review,* 1954) and Sherman
Eoff's "*Oliver Twist* and the Picaresque Novel" (*SP*, 1957)
are disappointing treatments of provocative subjects.

Among studies of Dickens' more immediate predecessors
are P. Morand on Surtees (*Nouvelles littéraires,* 1935); the
running debate in letters to the *TLS* (April 19–June 14,
1934) proposing sources for Jingle's speech; Alvin Whitley's
note (*Dickensian,* 1956), R. Baird Shuman's three articles
(*N&Q*, 1959), and J. C. Reid's recent book (1963) on Thomas

Hood; Myron F. Brightfield's discussion of Dickens in *Theodore Hook and His Novels* (1928); Robert Browning's comparison of *Sketches by Boz* with the work of Hook, Hunt, Egan, and Poole (*Dickens and the Twentieth Century*, 1962); and treatments of Carlyle by Philipp Arontsein (*Anglia*, 1896), Mildred G. Christian (*Trollopian*, 1947), Arthur A. Adrian (*PMLA*, 1952), George H. Ford (*UTQ*, 1948; *Dickens and His Readers* also has a good corrective discussion of the relations between Dickens and Carlyle), and Lawrence H. Houtchens in his unpublished thesis on "Carlyle's Influence on Dickens" (Cornell, 1931). Jack Lindsay discusses Carlyle's and also Bulwer-Lytton's influence in his essay on *Barnaby Rudge* in *Dickens and the Twentieth Century*; more extended treatment of Bulwer-Lytton will be found in his biography of Dickens, the only Dickensian biography which treats sources with any imaginative sensitivity. In a lively controversy over Irving's influence on Dickens, Christof Wegelin (*MLQ*, 1946) has challenged the findings of Ernest Boll (*MLQ*, 1944) as "amiable hyperbole" (see also W. C. D. Pacey, *American Literature*, 1945), and yet a check of the first reviews of *Pickwick* will show that almost all of them noted echoes of Irving.[27]

Of Dickens' contemporaries, Wilkie Collins has been by far the most widely discussed. A partial explanation for this interest may lie in an early work, Walter C. Phillips' *Dickens, Reade, and Collins, Sensation Novelists* (1919; reprinted, 1962), which started most of the hares that have been attracting scholar-huntsmen ever since. Phillips, among the first to treat Dickens seriously as a conscious artist, explores not only the mutual indebtedness of Collins and Dickens, but also their shared indebtedness to the Gothic tradition. Besides the attention given the subject by Collins' two biographers, Kenneth Robinson (1952) and Nuel Pharr Davis

[27] Background studies worth consulting for Dickensian relationships with the minor literature and journalism of the early Victorian period include Richard D. Altick, *The English Common Reader: The Mass Reading Public, 1800–1900* (1957), Keith Hollingsworth, *The Newgate Novel, 1830–1847* (1963), and Louis James, *Fiction for the Working Man, 1830–1850* (1963).

(1956), others who have joined in the chase include Earle Davis, *Charles Dickens and Wilkie Collins* (*University of Wichita Studies*, 1945); Henry J. W. Milley, "Wilkie Collins and 'A Tale of Two Cities' " (*MLR*, 1939); T. S. Eliot (*TLS*, Aug. 4, 1927; reprinted in *Selected Essays*, 1932); Malcolm Elwin (*London Mercury*, 1931); Arthur A. Adrian (*HLQ*, 1953); Harry Stone (*Dickensian*, 1957); and Harland S. Nelson (*VNL*, 1961). See also Robert P. Ashley, "Wilkie Collins Reconsidered" (*NCF*, 1950) and "Wilkie Collins and the Dickensians" (*Dickensian*, 1953), the latter answered by K. J. Fielding in the following issue. The degree of indebtedness on both sides could be clarified by a closer study of their collaborations than any yet made. Of particular interest, for example, is the Morgan Library manuscript of *The Frozen Deep* with Dickens' numerous autograph emendations; Collins' marginalia on his copy of Forster's *Life of Dickens*, reproduced in *Pall Mall Gazette* (Jan. 20, 1890), are also of peripheral interest.

Discussions of Dickens' relations with other contemporary novelists such as Charles Lever, Elizabeth Gaskell, George Eliot, Poe, Thackeray, and Trollope have in general been of more biographical than critical interest. Exceptions include the brief note on the similarities between *Bleak House* and *Felix Holt* by M. H. Dodds (*N&Q*, 1946); an unpublished dissertation on Dickens and Thackeray by Edward Eugene Irwin (See *Dissertation Abstracts*, 1961); and three articles in the *Trollopian*: Ernest Boll's "The Infusion of Dickens in Trollope" (1946), Lionel Stevenson's "Dickens and the Origin of *The Warden*" (1947), and Bradford Booth's "Trollope and 'Little Dorrit' " (1948). Most attempts along this line, however, such as Leo Mason's "*Jane Eyre* and *David Copperfield*" (*Dickensian*, 1947), encourage wariness of the whole approach.

Those placed by their contemporaries in the immediate line of succession from Dickens include Gilbert, Butler, Wilde, Besant, Stevenson, Mark Twain, George Moore, Hall Caine, Frank Norris, Bret Harte, Dreiser, and Kipling. Yet few of these relationships have attracted critical interest.

Except for the tenuous suggestions thrown out by Thomas Stephenson (*Gilbert and Sullivan Journal*, 1930) and Jane W. Stedman (*Dickensian*, 1962), the subject of Gilbert's possible indebtedness to Dickens remains unexplored in spite of Hesketh Pearson's attestation that "no other author aroused his unqualified enthusiasm" (*Gilbert: His Life and Strife*, 1957, p. 38), and although there exist a number of other concrete evidences of Gilbert's interest in Dickens, such as his dramatization of *Great Expectations* in 1871. As for Mark Twain, Walter Blair's comparison of *A Tale of Two Cities* and *Huckleberry Finn* (*MP*, 1957) and a brief discussion in Albert E. Stone, Jr., *The Innocent Eye: Childhood in Mark Twain's Imagination* (1961), appear to be the only attempts to explore a promising subject. Stephen Leacock's essay in the *Yale Review* (1934) and W. H. Auden's in the *Listener* (Oct. 1, 1953) compare Mark Twain and Dickens, and Karl Brunner's "Dickens und Mark Twain in Italien" (*Festschrift für Walther Fischer*, 1959) points out contrasts in the use each made of his experience in Italy, but none makes much reference to possible literary indebtedness. In the case of Dickens' profound influence upon Kipling, Ann Matlack Weygandt's detailed discussion in *Kipling's Reading and Its Influence on His Poetry* (1939) will be found useful. Ironically, the twentieth century has discovered that Henry James, the last one his contemporaries would have called Dickensian, did not entirely escape the shadow of Dickens. Ford's survey (*Dickens and His Readers*, pp. 203–212) shows that in spite of the Master's harsh judgment of Dickens (first published in the *Nation*, Dec. 21, 1865), there is evidence in his letters and memoirs of indebtedness to Dickens and of a change in James's attitude toward realism, a point also noted by Donald Emerson, "Henry James and the Limitations of Realism" (*College English*, 1960). Those who have discussed the Dickens-James relationship include T. M. Phillips (*Manchester Quarterly*, 1919), H. Blair Rouse (*NCF*, 1950), Q. D. Leavis (*Hudson Review*, 1955), and Oscar Cargill (*PMLA*, 1956). Even F. R. Leavis acknowledges the debt, however reluctantly, in the brutal observation that *The Bos-*

tonians is "*Martin Chuzzlewit* redone by an enormously more intelligent and better educated mind" (*The Great Tradition*, 1948, p. 134).

Ford Madox Ford, in commenting upon the "enormously evident" influence of Dickens upon *The Princess Casamassima* and *Evan Harrington*, said that it was "as difficult for any one born shortly before 1850 to escape the influence of the author of *Little Dorrit* as it is for all of us, born since 1603, to avoid that of the authors of *Lear* — and the Authorised Version" (*Thus to Revisit*, 1921, p. 42). And Fred Lewis Pattee devoted an entire chapter of *The Feminine Fifties* (1940) to describing Dickens as the leading influence upon American fiction, noting that "*Harper's Magazine* was founded in 1850 with Dickens its major reason for being" (p. 68). Yet when we come to the particulars of such influence upon modern authors we again find there has been more casual throwing about of names than close study — perhaps because, as G. H. Ford observes, the problem is "infinitely complex" and can become "an elaborate exercise in walking upon eggs" (*Dickens and His Readers*, p. 210). The shift in critical opinion of Dickens has been paralleled by a shift in the recognition of descendants. Shaw, Gissing, and Conrad clearly established their indebtedness by their own statements. Shaw, whose criticism of Dickens has already been noted, admitted that a "concordance of his own writings would reveal the Dickens allusions as running from four to one against any other writer" (*Dickens and His Readers*, p. 233). John Mason Brown in a review of Hesketh Pearson's *G. B. S.* (*Saturday Review*, 1942) observed of Shaw that "You must try to conceive, if you can, Charles Dickens and John Bunyan being one man." Others have commented upon the resemblances between the two writers, notably J. B. Priestley (*Dickensian*, 1932), Arnold P. Drew (*N&Q*, 1955), and Harold F. and Jean R. Brooks (*Dickensian*, 1963). Like Shaw, Gissing in "Dickens in Memory" (*Critic*, 1902; reprinted in *Critical Studies*, 1924) and Conrad in *A Personal Record* (1925) speak with warmth of their imaginative response to Dickens, a response noted in the case of Conrad by Frederick R. Karl (*N&Q*, 1957) and by F. R. Leavis in *The Great Tradition*.

In the 1920's J. D. Beresford felt called upon to defend Wells, Bennett, and Galsworthy against Virginia Woolf's charge that they were all inferior imitators of Dickens and Thackeray ("The Successors of Charles Dickens," *Nation and Athenaeum*, 1923). Before the 1940's these three, to whom could be added J. B. Priestley and William De Morgan, were the novelists most often referred to as "Dickensian." Later the names of Conrad, Henry James, Lawrence, and Joyce appear with increasing frequency. V. S. Pritchett remarked in 1944, "There is more of Dickens, to my mind, in James Joyce's *Ulysses* than in books like *Kipps* or *Tono Bungay*" (*New Statesman*), an opinion echoed by Morton D. Zabel in 1949: "Shaw . . . like Dostoevsky, Henry James, Proust, and Joyce, shows the real impact of Dickens on the modern imagination rather than the DeMorgans, Wellses, and Priestleys usually taken to be his descendants" (*Craft and Character in Modern Fiction*, p. 11). Zabel's statement recalls Baker's admission at the close of his discussion of Dickens' faults that the absence of similar faults "in the very fine writer who was hailed as the second Dickens left only a William de Morgan" (*The History of the English Novel*, VII, 326). The title of the article in *TLS* (Nov. 18, 1939), "Last of the Dickensians: William De Morgan" should have read "Last of the Old Dickensians."

Few special studies of the new Dickensians have appeared, though all are discussed at some length by Ford and references dot the paragraphs of current Dickensian criticism. The name of Dickens also occurs with increasing frequency in the biographies and critical studies of various modern authors, many of which references are conveniently noted in the *Dickensian* under the heading, "The Influence of Dickens: Collected from Recent Books," a feature initiated in 1932. The parallels between Joyce and Dickens, especially in such analogies as the speech of Jingle and Bloom, have become commonplace since first noted by Wyndham Lewis (*The Art of Being Ruled*, 1926); Harry Levin discusses them in some detail in *James Joyce* (1941) and critics like Jacob Isaacs, Harry Stone, and Randolph Quirk, as already pointed out, move the discussion into more subtle areas than Bloom's indebtedness to Jingle. Critics are especially fond of linking their subjects in a triangular relationship with Dickens and European writers like Dostoyevsky, Proust, and Kafka. Several have been discovering Dickensian traits in the American novelists Fitzgerald, Faulkner, and Steinbeck, as evidenced in Norman Friedman, "Versions of Form in Fiction — *Great Expectations* and *The Great Gatsby*" (*Accent*, 1954); A. E. Le Vot, "*Our Mutual Friend* and *The Great Gatsby*" (*Fitzgerald Newsletter*, 1962); Leslie Fiedler, "William Faulkner: An American Dickens" (*Commentary*, 1950); James T. Stewart, "Miss Havisham and Miss Grierson" (*Furman Studies*, 1958); and Hugh Holman's discussion of Steinbeck as "A Narrow-Gauge Dickens" (*New Republic*, 1954).

In 1904 W. E. Henley observed, "Dickens had many 'sedulous apes'; but there never was an ape of them all who did more than suggest the trick of his foot as he walked, or the shadow of his hat on the wall" (Introduction to Dickens' *Reprinted Pieces*, Autograph Edition), and it may be that loyal Dickensians would agree that all descendants of the Inimitable are "narrow-gauge." The disengaged scholar or general reader may, in his turn, justifiably rebel against much of the metaphysical speculation that yokes two favorites with violence together. But for all this, the impact of Dickens upon other artists — not all, by any means, minor — is as undeniable as it has been phenomenal. In the last analysis the testimony of the writers themselves is the most significant. Not only have Gissing, Shaw, Conrad, and many others so testified, but the attraction Dickens has had for writers of this generation like Orwell, Greene, and Joyce Cary is evident in much that they have written about him as well as in what they have written. In the one instance of Angus Wilson, reviewers and critics have frequently noted Dickensian qualities in his work, and Augustin Martin, in commenting upon Dickens' "immensity of genius to comprehend . . . society in all its forms," goes on to say that "the only modern

English novelist who seems to have this comprehensiveness of grasp is Angus Wilson" (*Studies*, 1960, p. 206). But certainly Wilson's personal statement in "Charles Dickens: A Haunting" (*Critical Quarterly*, 1960) is the most moving of tributes to the power that one creative artist can exercise upon the imagination of another.

FOREIGN INFLUENCE. English and American critics have been slow to recognize Dickens' impact upon European authors. In 1939 Edmund Wilson protested, "The Bloomsbury that talked about Dostoevsky ignored Dostoevsky's master, Dickens" (*The Wound and the Bow*, p. 1), and more recently George H. Ford has reaffirmed the irony of Dickens' influence upon the very Continental authors who displaced him in England as the most admired of novelists (*Dickens and His Readers*, p. 217). That Europeans are aware of what Renan called the "vaste échange où chacun donne et reçoit à son tour, où l'écolier d' hier devient le maître d'aujourd'hui" (*Questions contemporaines*, 1868, p. 113) is evidenced by such documented surveys of the reputation and literary influence of Dickens as Floris Delattre, *Dickens et la France: Etude d'une interaction littéraire anglo-française* (1927); Ellis N. Gummer, *Dickens' Works in Germany, 1837–1937* (1940); and the 327-page bibliography of Russian translation and criticism compiled by IU. Fridlender and I. Katarsky, *Charl'z Dikkens, bibliografiia russkikh perevodov i kriticheskoi literatury na russkom iazyke, 1838–1960* (1962).

Delattre's *Dickens et la France* exemplifies Renan's statement; it lists and evaluates the French translators and critics of Dickens and, in a particularly interesting chapter on Dickens and French naturalism, reveals the French running far ahead of the English in critical appreciation of Dickens. Though less interested than Gummer in literary sources and more skeptical of specific influences, Delattre nevertheless quotes Remy de Gourmont's statement "Quant à Dickens, c'est de son oeuvre qu'est sorti notre réalisme" (from *Promenades littéraires*, 1904, p. 328), and takes brief note of similarities if not indebtedness in the works of Hugo, Balzac,

Sand, Sue, Champfleury, Zola, France, Bernard, Hémon, and
Proust. The only writer Delattre treats at length here and
also in his discussion of Dickens in *De Byron à Francis
Thompson* (1913), is Alphonse Daudet, the "Dickens français," commenting that the "interpénétration" of the two
writers was so profound as to be without parallel (p. 163).
Henry James similarly noted strong resemblances, which he
termed "nothing so gross as imitation" but "conscious sympathy" (*Partial Portraits*, 1888, p. 222). Certainly Daudet
has been the French writer most widely recognized as in the
Dickensian tradition. Besides William Angus Munro's
*Charles Dickens et Alphonse Daudet, romanciers de l'enfant
et des humbles* (1908), Louis Weizmann's *Dickens und Daudet in deutscher Übersetzung* (1880), and John Garrett's edition of parallel selections, *Dickens and Daudet* (1930), a
number of briefer discussions have appeared: Louis Delzons
(*L'Artiste*, 1888), F. Baldensperger (*Revue germanique*,
1908), the anonymous "Dickens and Daudet" (*Cornhill Magazine*, 1891), and K. Boehm in *Zeitschrift für englischen und
französischen Unterricht* (1925).

Aside from Delattre there has been little scholarly interest
in Dickens' influence in France in spite of the novelist's personal attachment to everything French and his acquaintance
with most of the "greats" of nineteenth-century literary
France, including Dumas, Lamartine, Gautier, Scribe, Sue,
and Hugo (whom he particularly admired). Although the
noting of similarities between Dickens and the author of
Comédie humaine has become commonplace, André Joubert
denied any real affinity (*Correspondant*, 1872), and little substantial evidence that either Dickens or Balzac was directly
influenced by the other exists, though Jack Lindsay's "Note
on Balzac" (*Charles Dickens*, p. 453) poses some interesting
questions. Discussions like James's in *French Poets and
Novelists* (1884) and more recent treatments by Emile Cam-
maerts (*Contemporary Review*, 1929) and Jared Wenger
(*PMLA*, 1947), as well as Henriette Roland Holst's comparative study of Tolstoy, Balzac, and Dickens in *Romankunst als Levensschool* (1950), draw comparisons rather than

describe specific influences. Of these Wenger's is the most stimulating, with an excellent discussion of Dickens' masochistic and sadistic women. Stuart Atkins had preceded Wenger in taking up the question of possible Dickensian influence upon Zola (*MLQ*, 1947), a subject with challenging possibilities, though the predictable lines of influence would seem to be made less predictable by Zola's description of Dickens as "si vibrant et si intense comme évocateur de la vie extérieure, mais si pauvre comme analyste de l'homme et comme compilateur de documents humains!" (*Le Naturalisme au théâtre*, 1923, p. 69). Short essays have been written about two minor French novelists: Albert Mousset and Georges Meyer examine Tristan Bernard's debt to Dickens in an early article in *La Grande revue* (1913), and Raymond Jean points out the influence of *Sketches by Boz* upon Nerval's *Nuits d'octobre* (*Revue de littérature comparée*, 1955).

Modern Dickens scholars have occasionally mentioned Paul de Kock (whom Tolstoy called "the French Dickens"), Huysmans, and a few others, but have been most interested in Proust, especially in the marked similarities of style and language. Edmund Wilson in *Axel's Castle* (1931) and Osbert Sitwell in *Trio* (1938) were among the first to note resemblances in the two novelists. More recently Edgar Johnson has compared Swann's craving for Odette with Pip's for Estella (*Charles Dickens*, p. 992). And Mario Praz regards Proust's anthropomorphism as directly derived from Dickens (*La Casa della Fama*, 1952, p. 272). Sylvère Monod calls Proust one of Dickens' "plus grands successeurs" and points out the English novelist's handling of time and memory and his complex psychological associations of persons, places, and odors as examples of impressive "notations proustiennes" (*Dickens romancier*, pp. 74, 341, 455). Raphaël Cor's *Un Romancier de la vertu et un peintre du vice: Charles Dickens–Marcel Proust* (1928) is a reprint of articles published separately (that on Dickens in *Mercure de France*, 1920). Except for a few comments in the preface Cor fails to discuss the two authors in relation to each other; he does, however, cite some interesting parallels between Dickens and Anatole France (p. 51).

The Gummer survey of Dickens in Germany, less critically penetrating but more scholarly than Delattre, is indispensable as a bibliographical guide to contemporary and modern criticism and translation as well as to Dickens' influence upon German novelists. Gummer opens with the statement that "the immediate and lasting success of Dickens' works in Germany is without parallel," and the thoroughness of his record of that success down to 1937, especially of Dickens' influence, renders detailed repetition unnecessary. Gummer devotes a full chapter each to Gustav Freytag, Otto Ludwig, Wilhelm Raabe, Fritz Reuter, Friedrich Spielhagen, and Gustav Frenssen, and takes briefer notice of Alexander von Ungern-Sternberg and Marie von Ebner-Eschenbach. In a supplementary discussion of the other side of the exchange ("Dickens and Germany," *MLR*, 1938) Gummer notes Dickens' minimal knowledge of German writers. Since 1937 German interest in the subject has suffered almost total eclipse, Helmut Viebrock's discussion of the use of animism in Dickens and Hoffmann (*English Studies*, 1962) being the only exception worthy of notice.

An interesting early French review of Frenssen's *Jörn Uhl* by Téodor de Wyzewa (*Revue des deux mondes*, 1901) calls attention to many echoes of *David Copperfield* in the novel and goes on to pay tribute to Dickens as the most powerful influence of his day upon German, French, and Russian novelists. An anonymous author discusses Dickens and Raabe in *TLS* (July 20, 1922), and William Brighty Rands ("Matthew Browne") in "From Faust to Mr. Pickwick" (*Contemporary Review*, 1880) rambles through fourteen pages of sentimental tribute to Mr. Pickwick as a moral Gretchen. More recently, except for Howard W. Church's detailed tracing of the influence of *David Copperfield* upon Frenssen's *Otto Babendiek* (*Germanic Review*, 1936), Frank A. Gibson's "Dickens and Germany" (*Dickensian*, 1947) which calls attention to the influence on Theodor Fontane among

others, an inconclusive discussion of Dickens and Georg
Büchner by Rudolf Majut (*MLR*, 1955), and a few scattered
references to Thomas Mann, English and American critics
have devoted themselves almost exclusively to Kafka among
the descendants of Dickens writing in German.

Next to Dostoyevsky, Kafka has been the favorite of modern critics seeking to establish lines of Dickensian inheritance, especially those of the "search for identity" school.
The most prolific of these, Mark Spilka, followed up his
dissertation on Dickens and Kafka (Indiana, 1956) with three
studies of the influence of *David Copperfield* on *Amerika*
(in *Franz Kafka Today*, ed. Angel Flores and Homer Swan-
der, 1958; in *Critical Quarterly*, 1959; and in *American
Imago*, 1959), and with articles on *David Copperfield* and
The Metamorphosis (*Comparative Literature*, 1959), "*Great
Expectations*: a Kafkan Reading" (*Twelve Original Essays
on Great English Novels*, ed. Charles Shapiro, 1960), and
"Dickens and Kafka: 'The Technique of the Grotesque' "
(*Minnesota Review*, 1961). Spilka's full-length study, *Dickens
and Kafka: A Mutual Interpretation* (1963), is an adroit synthesis and expansion of these earlier studies. Since Spilka
had been preceded by Rudolph Vasata (in *Central European
Observer*, Feb. 9, 1945, and in *The Kafka Problem*, ed. Angel
Flores, 1946), by E. W. Tedlock, Jr. (*Comparative Literature*,
1955), and by Roy Pascal (*Listener*, 1956), who deal with
many of the same analogies, as well as by Kafka himself who
points out in his diaries a number of specific parallels between *David Copperfield* and *Amerika*, the subject of Dickens and Kafka would seem to have been exhausted were it
not for "the kind of modern taste," as John Gross puts it,
"which only becomes interested in the Circumlocution Office
if Kafka is invoked" (*Dickens and the Twentieth Century*,
p. x). Actually some of the most acute commentary on Dickens as a forerunner of Kafka has come not from Kafka specialists but from Dickens specialists in incidental discussions,
such as Ford's on *The Just and the Unjust* and *The Trial*
(*Dickens and His Readers*, pp. 254–256); J. Hillis Miller's
on the Kafkaesque theme and atmosphere of *Little Dorrit*

(*Charles Dickens: The World of His Novels*, pp. 233–234); and Julian Symons' general comments in *Charles Dickens* (pp. 90–91). A recent discussion of *The Trial* and *Bleak House* by Murray Krieger, in "The World of Law as Pasteboard Mask" (*The Tragic Vision*, 1960, pp. 138–140), even reaches the conclusion that Dickens is better than Kafka.

The Fridlender and Katarsky bibliography is an impressive record of Russian interest in Dickens since the translation of *Pickwick* in 1838. The chronological entries, which cover translations, criticism, and references to Dickens in the works of Marx, Engels, Lenin, and others, are in Russian, but a table of contents, an index, and a summary of Katarsky's introduction on Dickens' impact upon Russian literary life are in English. A fifty-page appendix contains short articles on such subjects as Dickens and tsarist censorship, manuscripts of Russian theatrical versions, translators of Dickens, and influences on Russian poetry. The bibliography unquestionably opens up areas of Russian interest in Dickens all but unknown to the non-Slavic world, particularly that of Communist reaction to Dickens. Westerners are more aware of the impact upon the literary giants of the nineteenth century, particularly of that upon Dostoyevsky.

The critical revolution accompanying "the discovery of the soul" opened the eyes of modern critics to similarities between Dickens and writers like Kafka and Dostoyevsky, especially in symbolic revelations of nightmare fears and animal brutalities lying just beneath man's surface consciousness. Few critics have failed to follow Edmund Wilson's lead in linking Dickens and Dostoyevsky. Both Tolstoy and Gissing had preceded Wilson in such linking, as had Osbert Sitwell, though with different emphases, and B. G. Reizov had discussed *Pickwick*'s influence on *The Village of Stepanchikovo* in *Iazyk i literatura* (1930). A later essay, George Katkov's "Steerforth and Stavrogin: On the Sources of *The Possessed*" (*Slavonic and East European Review*, 1949), continues the search for specific parallels, though Michael A. Futrell in the most detailed examination of the subject (*English Miscellany*, 1956) believes that both Reizov and Katkov

overstate their cases and ignore the complexities posed by
the number and variety of influences operating in Dostoyevsky's work. Ironically, Futrell shows that the early novels,
especially *The Old Curiosity Shop,* had far greater influence
than the later ones which modern readers find so strikingly
Dostoyevskian, as reflected in such comments as André Gide's
in 1943, "Dans l'atroce il rejoint presque Dostoievsky; et
c'est alors que je le préfère. Il ne m'amuse pas du tout dans
Pickwick" (quoted in Sylvère Monod, *Charles Dickens,* 1958,
p. 91). And Futrell's emphasis upon Dostoyevsky's great admiration for Little Nell should be noted by those who, like
Aldous Huxley in *Vulgarity in Literature* (1930), praise
Dostoyevsky and deplore Dickens' sentimentality. Critics
who have contributed significantly to the general subject
of Dostoyevsky and Dickens include Alexandra Wexler
(*Deutsche Rundschau,* 1962), Rex Warner, in *The Cult
of Power* (1947), and Lindsay, Trilling, Fiedler, Symons,
Ford, and Joyce Cary in works already mentioned. And, as
Peter Fison has observed recently in a review of *Dickens and
the Twentieth Century,* "Dostoievsky skulks in the wings"
of most modern criticism of Dickens (*Spectator,* 1962).

Other Russian novelists frequently linked with Dickens
are his early contemporary Gogol (whom Dickens read and
admired in Turgenev's French translation), Tolstoy, and
Turgenev, though nothing of first importance has been
written on any one of these relationships. Besides two early
comparisons of Gogol and Dickens — Vladimir Nabokoff's
"Charles Dickens: A Russian Appreciation" (*Dickensian,*
1912; translated by the author from *Retch,* 1912) and C. M.
Bowen's "*Dead Souls* and *Pickwick Papers*" (*Athenaeum,*
1916) — there is only the single study by Michael A. Futrell,
"Gogol and Dickens" (*Slavonic and East European Review,*
1956). The best account of Tolstoy's enthusiastic reaction
to Dickens, supplementary to his own numerous comments
on the creator of Little Nell in *What Is Art?* (1898) and in
his letters and journals, is that of Nikolay Apostolov in
Family Views of Tolstoy (ed. Aylmer Maude, 1926).[28] Biogra-

[28] Among the Tolstoyan comments on Dickens that Apostolov quotes, the

phers such as Ernest J. Simmons and Nikolai N. Gusev are
in general agreement that the Russian novelist's earliest
writings, *Childhood, Boyhood,* and *Youth,* offer clear evidence of Dickens' influence, but the only critical treatment
of the subject is Henriette Roland Holst's comparative study
of Tolstoy, Balzac, and Dickens in *Romankunst als Levensschool* (1950).[29] Turgenev was well known to Dickens, who
published in *Household Words* (1855) four of the *Sportsman's Sketches* translated by William Hepworth Dixon from
Charrière's *Memoires d'un seigneur russe.* Royal A. Gettmann points out that Dickens used the *Sketches* as war propaganda to confirm accounts of barbarism and tyranny under
Nicholas I (*Turgenev in England and America,* 1941). There
is debate about whether Dickens (who owned a set of his
works) ever met Turgenev, though Turgenev recorded that
he was "reduced to the ecstasies of a calf" when he attended
three of the readings in 1863 (quoted in Gilbert Phelps, *The
Russian Novel in English Fiction,* 1956, p. 45). Arnold Bennett disapprovingly admitted that Turgenev "put Dickens
above Balzac, and was never tired in his praise" (*Fame and
Fiction,* 1901, p. 223) and Henry James, bewildered by the
Russian master's admiration for Dickens, stated that he
"often meant, but accidentally neglected to . . . ask him
to explain his opinion" (*The Art of Fiction,* 1948, p. 113);
both Bennett and James failed to see what Vogüé noted as
early as 1886 in his *Le Roman russe,* that Russian realism
owed much to Dickens and little to Balzac. Among less widely
known Russian novelists who have been compared with Dickens are Vladimir Korolenko who testifies to the impact of
the English author in the essay "My First Acquaintance with
Dickens" (see Boris Gilenson, *Dickensian,* 1937), Nikolai
Chernyshevsky whose comments on Dickens and Thackeray
have been reviewed by M. L. Seliverstov in *Dikkens i Tek-*

one that Dickens' novels "are a bond of union between man in America and
man in Petersburg" may interest modern political coexistentialists (I, 177).

[29] The most comprehensive survey of the subject was presented by Victor
O. Burniak in a paper delivered at the American Association for the Advancement of Slavic Studies at Stanford University, April 27, 1963; a condensed version of this paper will be published in *NCF.*

kerei v otsenke Chernyshevskogo (1954), Alexander Herzen, Maxim Gorky, and the Hebrew and Yiddish writers Perez Smolenskin and Shalom Jacob Abramowitz ("Mendele mocher seforim").

Ever since Sam Weller's appearance in the fourth number of *Pickwick* readers have hailed him as a Dickensian Sancho Panza. Early reviewers and almost all biographers and critics since Taine, as well as Dostoyevsky, who admired both for the triumph of being comic without losing the reader's sympathy (*Letters*, trans. Ethel Colburn Mayne, 1951, pp. 142–143), have linked *Don Quixote* and *Pickwick*, and yet no clear lines of inheritance have been established. The few treatments of the subject, such as the dilettantish discussions of "Matthew Browne" (*Contemporary Review*, 1880), T. A. Lyon (*New Statesman*, 1935), and an early article by H. S. Ashbee (*Revue hispanique*, 1899), as well as incidental commentary in such studies as Frank Wadleigh Chandler, *The Literature of Roguery* (1907) and Walter Starkie, "Cervantes y la novela inglesa" (in *Homenaje a Cervantes*, ed. Francisco Sánchez-Castañer, 1950), add little to what the general reader can discover for himself. The best discussion will be found in the chapter on "Cervantes en Dickens" in Ramón Pérez de Ayala, *Principios y fináles de la novela* (1958), with an especially valuable comparison of *Rinconete y Cortadillo* and *Oliver Twist*. Sherman Eoff draws some interesting general analogies in "*Oliver Twist* and the Spanish Picaresque Novel" (*SP*, 1957), but avoids the crucial question of Dickens' own awareness of the tradition.

As for Dickens' impact upon Spanish writers, one of the most frequently recognized as Dickensian is Benito Pérez Galdós, whose own tribute to Dickens as his master will be found in the preface to his translation of *Pickwick* (see *La Nación*, March 9, 1868), a translation which introduced Dickens to the Spanish public. Marcelino Menéndez y Pelayo, writing in 1897, noted striking similarities in the work of the two novelists, especially in the "dreamlike qualities, in the wealth of detail seen as through a microscope . . . in the depiction of exceptional states of consciousness, madness, sleepwalkers, seers, and strange types of all sorts" (*Estudios y discursos de crítica histórica y literaria*, 1952, V, 103). The only extended discussion of Dickens' influence on Galdós is Effie Erickson's in *Hispania* (1936), but significant commentary will also be found in Leslie B. Walton, *Pérez Galdós and the Spanish Novel of the Nineteenth Century* (1927) and in Ricardo Gullon's 300-page introduction to Galdós' *Miau* (1957) as well as in his *Galdós novelista moderno* (1960). Vernon A. Chamberlain's discussion of Galdós in *Hispanic Review* (1961) is also of interest for its comments on the Spanish novelist's indebtedness to Dickens for his use of "muletilla" or speech crutches. Dickensian traits have also been noted in Pío Baroja and in José María de Pereda, the "modern Cervantes," whose *Sotileza* is compared with *David Copperfield* in a provocative and detailed discussion by Sherman H. Eoff (*The Modern Spanish Novel*, 1961, pp. 21–50). Portuguese novelist Júlio Dinis is also sometimes compared with Dickens, as are a number of Latin American writers including Lucio Vicente López of Argentina and Brazilian authors Raul Pompéia, Inglês do Souza, and Machado de Assis. Of these Machado de Assis, Brazil's most noted nineteenth-century novelist, is the most important. As one of the first to introduce Dickens to Brazil, translating *Oliver Twist* in 1870 and writing a number of critical articles on him, Machado de Assis has long been recognized as a descendant of the English writer; comments on aspects of his indebtedness will be found in Eugênio Gomes, *Espêlho contra Espêlho* (1949, pp. 66–77), and Agrippino Grieco, *Machado de Assis* (1959).

A major Dutch link with Dickens has been that connecting him with the genre painters, first pointed up, as noted by Kenneth Allott (*Victorian Prose*, 1956, p. xlii), in Kingsley's phrase "Dutch painting and Boz" in *Alton Locke*; it has been discussed briefly by Bagehot, Mario Praz, R. J. Cruikshank, and others, more fully by Ian F. Finlay in "Dickens's Influence on Dutch Literature" (*Dickensian*, 1957). Finlay also calls attention to the direct influence of *Sketches by Boz* upon Nicolaas Beets' *Camera obscura* (1839), "the most popu-

lar work in the whole of Dutch literature," and he goes on
to treat such minor writers as Johannes Kneppelhout, J. P.
Hasebroek, C. E. Van Koesveld, and Bernard Gewin as in
the Dickensian tradition. To this list L. Verkoren in "Dickens in Holland" (*Dickensian*, 1959) adds the names of Justus
van Maurik, J. J. Cremer, and Godfried Bomans, and em-
phasises the "unmistakable" influence of Dickens upon "the
greatest Dutch prose-writer of the nineteenth century, Eduard Douwes Dekker."

The only Scandinavian writer whose relations with Dickens have received extended attention is Hans Christian Andersen in Elias Bredsdorff, *Hans Andersen and Charles Dickens: A Friendship and its Dissolution* (1956), a work ineptly
translated from the author's *Andersen og Charles Dickens*
(1951) and more valuable for its biographical than for its
critical contribution.[30] Likenesses in stylistic characteristics
such as animism are so marked as to have drawn the attention of reviewers of Andersen's first book of fairy tales, translated into English in 1846. Andersen had been an emotional
admirer of Dickens since 1839, the year of *Nickleby*'s translation into Danish, and he admitted that *The Wood Nymphs*
and "The Beetle" were directly inspired by "Boz." Critics
have noted strong Dickensian elements in *The Two Baron-
esses* and others of Andersen's novels and short stories, but
on Dickens' side there was little more than an admiration
for the fairy stories (especially "The Little Mermaid") of
the man he described, after the inopportune visit of five
weeks during the trying domestic crisis of 1857, as "a cross
between Pecksniff and the Ugly Duckling" (quoted in Edward Wagenknecht, *The Man Charles Dickens*, p. 151). Two
writers, Martin Lamm in his biography of Strindberg (1940)
and Jack Lindsay in his *Charles Dickens* (1950), have given

[30] Even as biography the account needs to be supplemented by Wilkie
Collins' account of Andersen's visit to Gadshill in *My Miscellanies* and his
thinly disguised satire of Andersen as Herr von Müffe in "The Bachelor
Bedroom" (*All the Year Round*, Aug. 6, 1859); recent biographies of Collins,
especially that of Nuell Pharr Davis (1956), contain many details of this
pathetic-comic relationship omitted by Bredsdorff. Bredsdorff makes no mention of the earlier publication of many of the letters by Ejnar Munksgaard
(1937), nor of Wilhelm Bernhardt's notes to a German edition of Andersen's own account, *Ein Besuch bei Charles Dickens im Sommer 1857* (1895).

accounts of Strindberg's lifelong interest in Dickens beginning with the writing of his first novel, *The Red Room*, inspired by reading Dickens in Swedish. Lindsay remarks that it was "through Dostoevsky and Strindberg, on whom he had a profound effect at key moments of their development," that Dickens' "influence broadly enters the whole European stream" (p. 419).

China's introduction to the novels of Dickens through the translations of Lin Shu, who admired the Englishman as equal to the Chinese literary idol Ssa-ma Ch'ien, established Dickens firmly in prerevolutionary China as the most popular of western authors. Lin Shu, who knew no English, nevertheless translated 171 works from English into classical Chinese by having them explained to him by friends who had read them in English or some other language. In answer to those who might call this kind of translation grotesque, Arthur Waley has recently stated his opinion that Lin Shu made Dickens "a better writer" in the process ("Notes on Translation," *Atlantic Monthly*, 1958). Waley notes that through Lin Shu's translations of Western fiction in the early nineteenth century, "Chinese fiction was revitalized when it was at its last gasp" (p. 110). The Revolution of 1917 turned writers from the use of classical Chinese to the living language of the people, and Mao Tse-tung's enunciation of the principles of socialist realism in 1942 turned them to the pledge, in Mao Tun's words, to "remould our thoughts to serve the masses" (*Chinese Literature*, 1953, p. 13). Mao Tun is only one of the several major novelists of Communist China who have come under the influence of Dickens. Chih Tsing Hsia in his *A History of Modern Chinese Fiction, 1917–1957* (1961) calls attention to Dickensian influences in such other authors as Shen Ts'ung-wen, Chang T'ien-i (especially in his farcical satire "The Strange Knight of Shanghai") and, above all, Lao Shê who discovered Dickens when he studied in England in the 1920's and, before returning to his own country, launched his literary career with two highly Dickensian comic novels, *The Philosophy of Lao Chang* and *Chao Tzu-yueh*.

The fact is that even though little of scholarly or critical importance has been written on Dickens' foreign influence outside of France, Germany, and Russia, whenever the literary histories of whatever country are looked into, Dickens is there. As only two examples, look into Julius von Farkas' *Der ungarische Vormärz: Petöfis Zeitalter* (1943) and you will find a description of literary Hungary in the 1840's when the works of Dickens "lieszen vor den Augen der jungen Schriftsteller eine neue Welt erstehen"; besides Petöfi, who was such an admirer of Dickens that he read *Martin Chuzzlewit* on his honeymoon, Farkas mentions such Hungarian writers as Tompa, Jósika, Kúthy, Kemény, and Arany as having come under the powerful influence of Boz (pp. 171–172). And then look into the volume of critical essays comparing the literatures of East and West (in Arabic) by Muhammad Jamal al-Din al-Ramadi (Cairo, [1962?]), and you will find an account of Dickensian influence upon such modern Arabic novelists as Ṭāhā Ḥuysayn, Maḥmūd Taymūr, and Tawfīq al-Ḥakīm. We all know that Conrad discovered Dickens by reading *Nickleby* in Polish and had a particular love for *Bleak House* which he read "innumerable times, both in Polish and English" (*A Personal Record*, 1912). But we have to be told that another Polish novelist, Bolesław Prus (Aleksander Głowacki) used *Bleak House* as the model for his own *Emancypantki* (see J. Kulczycka-Saloni's discussion in *Prace Polonistyczne,* 1947), and the possible Conrads of other nationalities who never went on to master English remain for the most part undiscovered. Whether one looks upon parallel-hunting as valueless or as a lens through which to explore the mysteries of literary cross-fertilization, an undeniable excitement springs from the record of the far-flung impact of one man's written word in such casual epithets as "the Italian Dickens" given to Salvator Farina by Remy de Gourmont,[31] or "the German Dickens" to Jean Paul (by a recent TLS reviewer), or "the Brazilian Dickens" to a Machado de Assis, or "the French Dickens" to a Daudet, or "the Dickens of the People's Republic" to a Lao Shê.

---

[31] In *Les Matinées espagnoles,* 1885; see also *Scottish Review,* 1887.

FOREIGN CRITICISM. Critical and scholarly interest in Dickens outside of England and America has naturally been most active in those countries where his influence has been greatest. Floris Delattre's *Dickens et la France* (1927) is an indispensable guide to the great body of French criticism of Dickens from Philarète Chasles in 1839 to his own *Dickens* (1924), a volume of translated selections with introduction and notes. Here one need speak of only the two most important critics, Hippolyte Taine and Louis Cazamian, both of whom made contributions significant beyond considerations of nationality. Taine's essay on Dickens in the *Revue des deux mondes* (1856) could be called "The Two Scrooges" of the nineteenth century in that it was the first extended criticism in any language to treat Dickens as a major writer; its later inclusion as one of the two chapters on the novel (the other on Thackeray) in Taine's *Histoire de la littérature anglaise* (1863–1864; trans. 1871–1874) gave Dickens a prestige that was to influence all later criticism. Ironically, the positivist father of the sociological approach to literature dismisses Dickens' humanitarianism as sentimental morality but praises him for his poetic imagination.[32] Written just after the publication of *Hard Times* and thus antedating the so-called "dark" novels, the essay strikes another remarkably modern tone in its neglect of Dickens' humor (not even mentioning *Pickwick*) and its fascinated interest in the novelist's love of the macabre and horrific; indeed such comments as those on the hallucinations of Jonas Chuzzlewit after the murder might have been written for *American Imago*: "The play of these shattered reasons is like the creaking of a door on its rusty hinges; it makes one sick to hear it. We find in it, if we like, a discordant burst of laughter, but we discover still more easily a groan and a lamentation, and we are terrified to gauge the lucidity, strangeness, exaltation, violence of imagination which has produced such creations" (1871, II, 346).

[32] Taine admitted that at the time he wrote the essay on Dickens, the earliest piece of writing to be incorporated in the *Histoire*, he knew little about Dickens' life and so may have held fewer of the doctrinaire presuppositions which, as Harry Levin points out in his excellent discussion of Taine (*Accent*, 1956), influenced much of his criticism.

If Taine did not apply to Dickens his theories on the intimate relationship between literature and its milieu, his disciple Louis Cazamian did, in a work that has become a landmark in criticism of the English novel. *Le Roman social en Angleterre (1830–1850): Dickens–Disraeli–Mrs. Gaskell–Kingsley* (1904; rev. ed., 1935) [33] uses Dickens as the point of departure for a searching comparison of the social philosophies expressed in fiction with those of the reigning socioeconomic theorists. That such reputable critics as House, Orwell, Fielding, Monod, and Tillotson work in the same tradition testifies to Cazamian's stature and authority. The nature of that tradition is epitomized in the now familiar phrase "la philosophie de Noël" with which Cazamian characterizes Dickens' individualistic, nondoctrinal attitude toward social reform, an attitude which he traces from Carlyle through Dickens to Ruskin, and sees as ultimately having an impact less practical than "psychologique." Cazamian's discussions of *Bleak House* and *Hard Times* are of special interest; points made in the latter are often echoed in modern objections to Leavis' view of the novel. Cazamian's more recent opinions, as expressed in his review of Sylvère Monod's *Dickens romancier* (in *Etudes anglaises*, 1954), hint that biographical revelations have undermined his respect for the man Dickens and that the novelist's mixture of strengths and weaknesses as a writer makes him, in Cazamian's words, "un des exemples les plus embarrassants de dualité littéraire" (p. 126).

Simultaneously with the publication of Delattre's review of criticism appeared the essay on Dickens by André Maurois, France's most popular commentator on English literature. This essay, the first of a series of lectures published in Mau-

---

[33] The revised edition made few changes despite Cazamian's admission that much more was known about England's social history than when he wrote his doctoral thesis in 1903. In spite of its importance to the study of the English social novel, Cazamian's work has never been translated except for an abridgement of the section on Dickens in *Studies in Dickens* (ed. Mabell S. C. Smith, 1910, pp. 74–97); eight pages of comment on Dickens appear in the translated edition (1927) of Legouis and Cazamian's *Histoire de la littérature anglaise* (1924).

rois' *Etudes anglaises* (1927), is urbane and intelligent, but makes no contribution comparable to that of Taine or Cazamian. An English translation of the lecture appeared first in three installments in the *Forum* (1928–1929) and then in the single volume *Dickens* (1934) with a slightly revised and expanded text to accommodate such new developments in Dickensian biography as the Ternan disclosures. Maurois, who has published other essays on Dickens in the *Revue de Paris* (1934), *Nouvelles littéraires* (1937), and *L'Angleterre romantique* (1953), is evaluated as a critic of Dickens by A. W. Fox in *Papers of the Manchester Club* (1932). Emile Chartier ("Alain") in "Dickens étudié par un Français" (*Proceedings and Transactions of the Royal Society of Canada*, 1925) and in essays in *Nouvelle revue française* (1939) and *Revue de Paris* (1940), the latter two reprinted in *En lisant Dickens* (1945), echoes Taine in emphasizing the power of the imaginative elements in Dickens; a translation of the essay in the *Revue de Paris* on "Imagination in the Novel" is included by Ford and Lane as the sole example of Continental criticism in *The Dickens Critics*. But Chartier knew no English, and in the opinion of Monod ("Alain, lecteur de Dickens," *Mercure de France*, 1957) his dependence upon bad translations influences his Dickens, who becomes "à la fois francisé et philosophifié" (p. 120). Another modern critic, Léon Lemmonier, followed articles on "Actualité de Dickens" (*Mercure de France*, 1936) and "Génie de Dickens" (*French Review*, 1938) with a biography, *Dickens* (1946; trans., 1947), introducing the findings of Wright, Storey, and Wilson to French readers.

By far the most important present-day French writer on Dickens is Sylvère Monod, Professor of English literature at the University of Caen. Monod's *Dickens romancier; étude sur la création littéraire dans les romans de Charles Dickens* (1953) at once established him as a scholar more familiar with primary source materials than many of his English and American confreres. His announced thesis, "une protestation contre l'opinion très répandue que Dickens n'a pas de technique" (p. xix), reveals the affinity of his approach with that of Butt and Tillotson, some of whose articles preceded his book though their *Dickens at Work* came later. Monod, too, draws his conclusions from a close analysis of manuscripts, proof, printed texts, memoranda, and letters to Forster, presenting them chronologically with a minimum of biographical narrative. Also of critical importance are Monod's translations of three major novels for the *Classiques Garnier: Oliver Twist* (1957), *David Copperfield* (1957), and *Great Expectations* (1959), with introductions, notes, and bibliographies of an excellence that makes them superior to most present editions of the novels in English. He has also translated *Nouveaux contes de Noël* (1957), *Pickwick* (1958), and *Barnaby Rudge* (1962), the last two with introductions and notes by Pierre Leyres (Leyres edited these and also *Hard Times* for Gallimard's "Bibliothèque de la Pléiade"). Monod's small volume *Charles Dickens* (1958) is a popular illustrated introduction to Dickens. He has also contributed regularly to both French and English critical journals, the most important of which contributions are noted elsewhere in this survey.

Gummer's *Dickens' Works in Germany* is an exhaustive and on the whole reliable guide to criticism written in German before 1937. I have run across only three items not listed: Gerbert Eulenberg's essay on Dickens in his *Neue Bilder* (1912); the more important discussion by Bernhard Fehr in *Die englische Literatur des 19. und 20. Jahrhunderts* (1923); and a brief note in the *Archiv für das Studium der neueren Sprachen* (1919) by Alois Brandl, called the "Taine of Germany," founder in 1892 of the school of Dickensian scholarship which was to culminate in the work of his most brilliant student, Wilhelm Dibelius. Gummer singles out Dibelius as the leading contender for first place among German critics of Dickens, saying of his *Charles Dickens* (1916), "There is nothing to equal it in any language" (p. 158), a verdict underscored by H. V. Routh when he hailed the second edition in 1926 as "the event of the year" (*Year's Work in English Studies*, 1926). Dibelius' comprehensive volume, still unfortunately untranslated, was the first truly scholarly work on Dickens; its bibliography alone is a landmark in Dickensian studies. As Gummer points out, his preliminary introduction grew to such proportions after twelve years of research that he published it as an independent 900-page study, *Englische Romankunst* (1910; 2nd ed., 1922). Shorter studies by Dibelius appeared in *Englische Studien* (1910), *Anglia* (1911), and *Shakespeare-Jahrbuch* (1916). An important contemporary criticism of Dibelius and others of the "Schules Brandls" will be found in Eduard Eckhardt, "Zur Charakteristik von Charles Dickens," *Germanisch-romanische Monatsschrift* (1914).

Gummer says little of a second German critic, Wilhelm Dilthey, recently discovered in the wake of modern interest in psychological criticism. Adolph Zech, in a detailed evaluation of Dilthey (*Stanford Studies in English Language and Literature*, 1941, pp. 321–325), calls him "the leading literary critic of the nineteenth century" whose new approach emphasized that the critic must understand not only the work and its *Zeitgeist* but the author as well, and not only the author's life but also his personality and inner self. Dilthey's planned book on Dickens was never completed, but even though he does not get to the later novels in his fragmentary essay "Charles Dickens und das Genie des erzahlenden Dichters," first published in *Westermanns Monatschefte* (1877) and reprinted in *Die grosse Phantasiedichtung und andere Studien zur vergleichenden Literaturgeschichte* (1954), the application of his revolutionary "Erlebnis" theory to Dickens' childhood experiences and to the early novels marks him as significantly ahead of his time. Scattered comment on Dickens will also be found in Dilthey's *Einleitung in die Geistewissenschaften* (1883), *Dichterische Einbildungskraft und Wahnsinn* (1886), and *Das Erlebnis und die Dichtung* (1906).

In contrast to the long neglected Dilthey, the Austrian critic Stefan Zweig's comments on Dickens are well known through the wide translation and reprinting of his *Drei Meister: Balzac, Dickens, Dostojewski* (1920), reissued as the first volume of *Die Baumeister der Welt* (1920). An English translation of the essay on Dickens appeared as early as 1923 in the *Dial*, followed by the translations *Three Masters* (1930) and *Master Builders* (1939). The work was translated into all the major Continental languages and stirred comment as far away as Peru (see Gonzalo Otero Lora, "Stefan Zweig, critico," *Mercurio Peruano*, 1929). Zweig also uses a psychological rather than a scholarly or literary approach, stating in his preface that the subtitle of his essays could have been "The Psychology of the Novelist." But he is more of a Strachean "tourist critic" (as Strachey was described in a recent *TLS*) than Dilthey, and although he emphasizes the English novelist's triumph as humorist and visual genius, his oversimplified analysis of Dickens the man as a typical "Biedermeier" in smug tune with his age has had an undue and on the whole unfortunate influence upon much later criticism.

Gummer notes a sharp drop in German discussion of Dickens after World War I, a lack of interest which has continued to the present. There have been a handful of dissertations, a scattering of articles and chapters in longer works (some of which are noted elsewhere), and the monograph *Charles Dickens und das Theater* by Karla König (1932), but no book-length study has appeared. The most important contributions are the two chapters on Dickens in Horst Oppel's *Die Kunst des Erzählens im englischen Roman des 19. Jahrhunderts* (1950) and his discussion of *Our Mutual Friend* in *Neueren Sprachen* (1962); Rainulf Stelzmann's "*The Mystery of Edwin Drood*: Ein neuer Lösungsversuch," *Archiv für das Studium der neueren Sprachen* (1957);Ludwig Borinski's "Dickens' Spätstil," *Neueren Sprachen* (1957); and Heinz Reinhold's two articles: "Charles Dickens' Roman 'A Tale of Two Cities' und das Publikum," *Germanisch-romanische Monatsschrift* (1955), and "Kritik an den religiösen und moralischen Anschauungen in Dickens' Werken im 19. Jahrhundert," *Anglia* (1958). Two studies of Dickens' travels abroad are also of interest: Liselotte Thalmann, *Charles Dickens in seinen Beziehungen zum Ausland* (1956), and Karl Brunner's discussion of Dickens and Mark Twain in Italy, noted above. Of less importance are articles by T. Klein (*Zeitwende*, 1940), K. Hillebrand (*Altes Europa*, 1941), Wolfgang Colden (*Geist und Tat*, 1956), and chapters on Dickens in Willi Bredel, *Sieben Dichter* (1950), and in Wolfgang Schmidt-Hidding, *Sieben Meister des literarischen Humors in England und Amerika* (1959).

There are a number of excellent bibliographical guides in German, among which Anself Schlosser's *Die englische Literatur in Deutschland, 1895–1934* (1950) is particularly useful for its comprehensive listing of English and translated editions published in Germany. For the famous Tauchnitz editions, many of which predated English book editions, see *Fünfzig Jahre der Verlagshandlung Bernhard Tauchnitz, 1837–1887* (1887). Gummer calls attention to the mass of correspondence between Dickens and Tauchnitz, almost certainly destroyed by the bombing of Leipzig and unfortunately never published except for the few letters included in K. Otto, *Der Verlag Bernhard Tauchnitz, 1837–1912* (1912). A sound study of the Dickens-Tauchnitz relationship (and, in fact, of the whole subject of translation and foreign publication) is long overdue; J. Y. Southon's brief discussion of the Tauchnitz *A Christmas Carol* (*Dickensian*, 1912) and P. H. Muir's notes (nos. 53 and 55) on *David Copperfield* and a number of other novels (*Book Collector*, 1955) indicate the contribution such a study could make to the understanding of Dickens' publishing procedures as well as of his impact abroad.

Since the translation of *Pickwick* into Russian in 1838, Dickens has been the most popular of English authors in both tsarist Russia and the Soviet Union. In 1844 *Literaturnaia Gazeta* reported that he was known to every educated reader in Russia, and R. J. Cruikshank tells of the astonishment of the British during the Crimean War at finding "among the abandoned treasures of an army in headlong flight copies of *The Pickwick Papers*" (*Charles Dickens and Early Victorian England*, p. 69). In the *Dickensian* for 1937, quoting from *Izvestiia* that "Dickens has become one of the most beloved authors with Soviet readers, and the number of his volumes available in Soviet libraries hardly meets the demand," Walter Dexter noted that, in contrast to the seventy thousand copies of his works published in the ten years before the Revolution, one million appeared in the nineteen years after. In the *Dickensian* for 1961 Boris Gilenson writes that seven and one-half million copies of the novels have been sold since the Revolution and that the sixth edition of the collected works (of which nineteen of the planned thirty volumes have appeared) is selling at the rate of six hundred thousand per volume, "one of the highest figures for fiction in the Soviet Union." Perhaps the ultimate tribute was the appearance of a portrait of Dickens on a recently issued Soviet postage stamp.

Soviet critical interest from the beginning has centered on Dickens as social critic and "revolutionist," in spite of Nadezhda Krupskaya's report that Lenin walked out of a performance of *The Cricket on the Hearth* because he could not stomach its bourgeois sentimentality (*Memories of Lenin*, 1942, p. 299). According to the novelist Michael Sholokhov, Dickens is popular with the Soviet reader "because of his anxiety over social problems" (*Dickensian*, 1935), a view underscored by the anonymous Russian author of "Dickens in Russia: A Moral Educator" (*TLS*, Sept. 7, 1940), Sir Arthur Bryant (*Illustrated London News*, Aug. 22, 1959), and Nina Diakonova (*Soviet Literature*, 1962). It is therefore not surprising that in line with Khrushchev's pronouncement that "art belongs to the sphere of ideology" (*The Great Strength of Soviet Literature and Art*, 1962), current governmental encouragement of Dickensian studies in the universities and teacher-training institutes points up the propagandistic value of linking Dickens with Marx and Engels as a contemporary observer of the miseries of the proletariat under bourgeois capitalism. Gilenson notes that some of the Revolution's most important forerunners, such as the critics and critic-novelists Belinsky, Herzen, Chernyshevsky, Korolenko, and Gorky, admired Dickens for being one of the first to dedicate his fiction to social and humanitarian ends. The highly influential views of Belinsky, who expressed enthusiastic appreciation of the social significance of Dickens' novels as early as 1847 (in an article on Russian literature) are discussed by F. G. Ovchinnikova in *Uchenye zapiski Leningradskogo Pedagogicheskogo Instituta imeni Gertsena* (1955).

Only the most important of recent Russian studies can be listed here. Such reference works as the *Literaturnaia Entsiklopediia* (1930) and the *Dictionary Catalog of the Slavonic Collection of the New York Public Library* (1958) contain bibliographies of translations, biographies, and critical works; the monumental Fridlender-Katarsky bibliography of Dickens has already been described; Ernest L. Radlov's "Dikkens v Russkoi Kritike" (*Nachala*, 1922) is a helpful review; and there is an excellent survey of Russian revolutionary-democratic criticism of Dickens by Z. T. Grazhdanskaia in *Uchenye zapiski Moskovskogo Oblastnogo Pedagogicheskogo Instituta* (1953).

Of the early works on Dickens the most available in England or America are those by Aleksandr Kirpichnikov on Dickens as a pedagogue (1881), Aleksei Pleshcheev (1891), A. Annenskaia (1892), S. Orlovskii (1904), Ernst L. Radlov (1922), Anatolii Vasil'evich Lunacharskii and Rozaliia Shor (1931), Lunacharskii's critical preface (in English) to his translation of *Pickwick* (1935), and M. E. Elizarova's discussion of "Realism of Dickens and the Problem of the Comic" in *Iz istorii realizma XIX veka na Zapade*, ed., F. P. Shiller (1934). Modern studies include Evgeny L'vovich Lann's biographical novel *Dikkens* (1946; previewed by Lydia Evseyeva in the *Dickensian*, 1945), which should be supplemented by Lann's interesting account of the difficulties he faced as translator of *Pickwick* in *Literaturnyi kritik* (1939); Tamara Isaakovna Sil'man, *Dikkens. Ocherki tvorchestva* (1948; 2nd ed., 1958) and her chapter on Dickens in *Iz istorii angliiskogo realizma*, ed., Ivan Ivanovich Anisimov (1941); Valentina Vasil'evna Ivasheva, *Tvorchestvo Dikkensa* (1954); N. P. Mikhal'skaia, *Charl'z Dikkens* (1959); and I. M. Katarsky, *Dikkens* (1960). The last, a biography of 265 pages, is of first importance. Ivasheva (of Moscow University) is the most dominantly propagandistic, addressing herself to the rescue of Dickens from the neglect and misinterpretation of Western (especially American) critics, which she ascribes to their culpable disapproval of his attacks upon capitalism. Sil'man's studies, though not ignoring the social message in Dickens, concentrate on his creative method and are more sensitive to his political ambivalence. Briefer studies of some importance include T. Shaskolskaia's discussion of Dickens and Carlyle in *Uchenye zapiski Leningradskogo Pedagogicheskogo Instituta imeni Gertsena* (1940); Magdalina Aleksandrovna Neresova, *Tvorchestvo Charl'za Dikkensa* (in *Vsesoiuznoe Obshchestvo*, 1957); and A. A. Bel'skii's study of political satire in *Little Dorrit* in *Uchenye zapiski Cheliabinskogo Pedagogicheskogo Instituta* (1956). Most of these studies welcome Dickens with a bear hug of party-line affection, though the degrees of that affection vary and sometimes he is attacked for being not a true revolutionary but, in Lenin's phrase, a "vulgar sociologizer." Many discuss other aspects of the novels as well, sometimes with fresh perception, but when even *Pickwick* is seen as an example of how Dickens used laughter "as a means of relieving the horrors of life and mitigating the acuteness of class contradictions" (Lunacharskii in the foreword to *Pickwick*, 1935, p. x), the hug is as unstabilizing to *Pickwick's* dignity as salmon to that of Mr. Snodgrass.[34]

The critical approach to Dickens in other Communist countries is much the same as that in Soviet Russia. The Chinese, who read their Dickens as children in Lin Shu's classical translations, have begun to translate him into modern Chinese and into a good Communist. This will be seen in introductions to the new translations such as that of Hsu Tien-hung to *David Copperfield*, published in 1942, the year of Mao's pronouncement of the idealogical role of literature and art, and also in two articles in recent issues

[34] It is gratifying that Kenneth Tynan has found the Russian theater less politically slanted. "Shaw, Wilde, and Dickens, "he observes, "are played with absolute fidelity to the letter and spirit of the text" (*Tynan on Theatre*, 1964, p. 266).

of *Wen hsüeh p'ing lun* (1962), one by Yang Yao-min on special characteristics of Dickens' writing and thinking, and one by Fan Ts'un-chung on Dickens' criticism of the United States. And though less conspicuously propagandistic, most postwar criticism in European Communist countries looks at Dickens from the perspective of socialist realism. The shift of perspective is interestingly revealed in the writings of the most brilliant of Marxist critics, the Hungarian aesthetician György Lukács, whose rise and fall in official Communist favor has captured worldwide attention. Although Lukács has not written a book on Dickens, his critical works are worth looking into for the many references to Dickens, since an aside by the writer Thomas Mann called "the most important literary critic of today" is worth more than a chapter by a lesser man. Lukács' only works available in English are *Studies in European Realism: A Sociological Survey of the Writings of Balzac, Stendhal, Zola, Tolstoy, Gorki, and Others* (1950; trans. Edith Bone, with a foreword by Roy Pascal) and *The Historical Novel* (1962; trans. Hannah and Stanley Mitchell; American edition with a preface by Irving Howe). The only early Hungarian discussion of Dickens I have run across is *Charles Dickens: élete és muvei* (1913) written by an English Hungarian scholar, Arthur B. Yolland.

The most important prewar study by a Polish scholar is Roman Dyboski's *Charles Dickens: życie i twórczość* (1936), with a valuable bibliography of Polish translations. Besides the Kulczycka-Saloni discussion of Prus and Dickens already mentioned, a short article in Polish on Dickens and Trollope by I. Dobrzyczak (in *Tygodnik Powszechny*, 1946) is worth noting. Two Bulgarian pamphlets, *Dickens and America* (1939) and *From Lamb to Dickens* (1948), both written in English by Rusi Roussev, should also be mentioned; the first of these points up how little the America described by Dickens has changed in its "abuse of freedom," "preoccupation with material things," and "racial prejudices"; the second discusses Lamb's influence upon Dickens. UNESCO has recently celebrated Dickens' sesquicentennial by the issue of a pamphlet bibliography, *Dickens in Rumania* (1962); compiled by Alexandru Dutu and Sorin Alexandrescu, this bibliography includes a chronological listing of translations (1884–1961) and a brief list of periodical articles, short discussions in books, and one critical study of Dickens as a friend of the oppressed: *Un prieten al celor asupriti: Charles Dickens* by Vera Calin (1951). The weekly or monthly national bibliographies of Poland, Czechoslovakia, Bulgaria, and Yugoslavia are useful for their listings of translations as well as critical articles and notes as they appear; most of these began publication in the 1950's, though Bulgaria's (for books only) began in 1897. Czechoslovakian interest has naturally centered on Kafka and Dickens. Vasata and others whose work is discussed in the German section above resent treatment of Kafka as German; "Kafka's language was German," complains Vasata, but he "never became a German, not even a Deutschbohme or an Austrian" ("Kafka — A Bohemian Writer," *Central European Observer*, 1946). Finally, if any more evidence is needed on how Dickens has traveled around the world in 150 years, it has been supplied by Nícifor Naumov, Yugoslavian author of articles on "Dickens and His Time" (*Polet*, 1950) and "Dickens' Pecksniff" (*Politika*, 1955), who kindly sent me the bibliography of his unpublished dissertation on "Dickens in Yugoslavia" listing 150 articles, reviews, and critical introductions by Yugoslavian authors.

The dean of English literary study in Italy is Mario Praz, founder and editor of *English Miscellany*. Certainly the sixty-page section on Dickens in his *La crisi dell'eroe nel romanzo vittoriano* (1952), translated by Angus Davidson as *The Hero in Eclipse in Victorian Fiction* (1956), is the most important Italian contribution to Dickensian studies. Praz's major thesis of the decline of the "Romantic" hero into the virtuously mediocre "Biedermeier" hero of the Victorian novel, as applied to Dickens, strikes few notes that had not been sounded by Cazamian, House, Orwell, and especially Zweig,[35] but the contrapuntal theme of the rela-

[35] See Angus Wilson's "The Heroes and Heroines of Dickens" (*Review of*

tionships between art and literature is provocative and illuminating. And though the analogy of the Dutch genre painters seems to support his Biedermeier thesis, Praz's extension of the discussion to the fanciful grotesques of Gothic art and Hogarthian-Rowlandsonian caricature,[36] to Caravaggio, and even to the Surrealist collages of Max Ernst leads him to the detection of chiaroscuric elements in Dickens seemingly inconsistent with his first appraisal of the novelist as a Philistine dedicating his "wholly external" art (p. 187) to keeping a bourgeois audience happy and undisturbed. For the overinsularized English or American reader, the value of *The Hero in Eclipse* is that Praz places Dickens in a European context with a rich play of comparative reference to such writers as Soulié, Sue, Hugo, Proust, De Jouy, Janin, Borel, Tolstoy, Dostoyevsky, Garzhin, Stendhal, d'Aurevilly, Baroja, Huysmans, and many others.

Other Italian studies, none of which have been translated, are Carlo Izzo's *Autobiografismo di Charles Dickens* (1954), with a seventeen-page bibliography, and his essay on Dickens' present status in Italy in *Cultura e scuola* (1961). Two critical prefaces are of interest: Gabriele Baldini's to a volume of selections from Dickens published in the series "Il fiore delle varie letterature" (Milan, 1946) and Cesare Pavese's to his translation of *David Copperfield* (1939), reprinted in *La letteratura americana e altri saggi* (1951). The most important earlier studies are Emilia Errera's *Carlo Dickens* (1895; reprinted with other essays and a preface by

---

English Literature, 1961) for a view of Dickens' bourgeois heroes which recognizes that "Dickens aspired to a respectable middle-class radicalism attacking particular social evils, and ended as a middle-aged revolutionary with a peculiar hostility to the middle classes" (p. 12). Much earlier, Chesterton anticipated Praz in noting the disappearance of the hero after Carlyle, but in contrast saw the eclipse as a sign of increased understanding of society and self and of greater dissatisfaction with both (see *Charles Dickens: The Last of the Great Men*, esp. p. 9).

[36] Frederick Antal makes some good points about Dickens and Hogarth in *Hogarth and His Place in European Art* (1962), and F. R. Leavis (especially in his essay on *Dombey* in *Sewanee Review*, 1962) and others glance at it, but for the most part the fascinating subject of Dickens and the whole tradition of graphic caricature remains unexplored.

A. Orvieto, 1903); Silvio Spaventa Filippi's *Carlo Dickens* (1911; 2nd ed., 1924; reprinted in *L'umorismo e gli umoristi ed altri saggi*, 1932); shorter studies by Eugenio Camerini in *Nuova antologia* (1870) and *Nuovi profili letterari* (1875) and by Gino Bassi in *Rassegna nazionale* (1916); and commentary on Dickens as humorist and satirist by Tullo Massarini in *Storia e fisiologia dell'arte di ridere* (1902; III, 322–332) and by Federico Olivero in *Studi su poeti e prosatori inglesi* (1925). The subject of Dickens and Italy has been taken up by G. Rabizzani (*Il Marzocco*, 1911; reprinted in *Bozzetti di letterature italiana e straniera*, 1914), Federico Cannavò (*Nuova antologia*, 1918), and Lorenzo Vigo Fazio (*Le Lettere*, March 1, 1920; reprinted in *Saggi, discorsi*, 1926). Of these Cannavò's discussion with its detailed commentary on *Pictures from Italy* is the most valuable.[37]

The Dickensian enthusiasm of Spain and Latin America, evidenced in the writings of Galdós, Machado de Assis, and others already discussed, and in the listing of translations in "Los Libros de Dickens en España" by Juana de José Prades (*El Libro Español*, 1958), has apparently failed to stir comparable critical interest. Prades lists only a few short accounts in various literary histories. Several more important items deserve notation here. Spanish studies include José Méndez Herrera's critical introduction and notes to his translation of Dickens' *Obras Completas* (6 vols., 1948–1952); Unamuno's analysis of the autobiographical "actualities" in *David Copperfield* published in *Repertorio Americano* and reprinted as "Leyendo a Dickens" in his collected essays *De esto y de equello* (1953); and the seven chapters on Dickens in Ramòn Pérez de Ayala, *Principios y finales de la novela* (1958). An article in Portuguese, "Dickens e a Religião" by Manuel d'Almeida (*Brotéria*, 1956), has little critical value. Of Latin American studies, the most important is the Peruvian work *La Critica social in las novelas de Dickens*, by Giulianna Mariani (1960). Another book-length study, *Dickens y Sar-*

---

[37] These might be compared with the interesting discussion of Henry Massoul in "Trois voyages à l'Italie: Charles de Brosses, Charles Dickens, Maurice Maeterlinck" (*Mercure de France*, 1924, pp. 110–124).

miento: ostros estudios (1928) by Argentinian Rafael Alberto Arrieta, is a fascinating comparison of Dickens' reaction to the United States in 1842 with Sarmiento's in 1847–1848. A briefer Argentinian study by Pablo Rojas Paz, "Dickens, Londres y los niños," appeared in *Nosotros* (1941). An essay on Dickens written in 1920 by Brazilian critic Gilberto Amado first appeared in his *A Dansa sobre o abysmo* (1932) and later in *Tres estudios: Dickens y el humorisme, Goethe, Anatole France* (1936), a volume of his essays translated into Spanish by J. Rosendo Pinilla G. Another brief article, "Carlos Dickens. Su carácter. Sus obras," is worth noting for its early date and because it was written by Mexico's celebrated novelist Ignacio M. Altamirano for the initial volume (1869) of his periodical *El Renacimiento*.

Of the Dutch, who have recently launched their own *Dickensian,* Leslie Staples, secretary of the Dickens Fellowship, has remarked that they "have given the best informed members to the fellowship. They know much more about Dickens than we English, and no one can become a member of our Netherlands branches unless he has passed an examination on *The Works*" (Chicago *Tribune,* Feb. 18, 1962). Lists of translations will be found in Brinkman's *Catalogus der Boeken* and in L. Verkoren, "Dickens in Holland" (*Dickensian,* 1959), which also includes a few critical works such as J. B. van Amerongen's *The Actor in Dickens* (1926) and Frans Dirk Wierstra's *Smollett and Dickens* (1928). Verkoren's observation that another Dutch critic, Frans Coenen, in his *Charles Dickens en de Romantiek* (1911) praises Dickens as a Romantic and a "poet," a prose Wordsworth who lifts the ordinary events of human experience to poetic heights, indicates that Coenen would suffer no ostracism by critics of a half century later. Surprisingly, Verkoren does not mention one of the most provocative of the early studies, Jan ten Brink's detailed discussion of Dickens' early novels through *Nickleby,* published as Volume IV of his *Litterarische schetsen en kritieken* (1883); ten Brink compares Dickens favorably with Flaubert and other novelists and praises his gift for psychological analysis, especially of the criminal mind. Other studies not mentioned by Verkoren are Herman Jansonius' discussions of Dickensian characters in *Some Aspects of Business Life in Early Victorian Fiction* (1926); Syna De Vooy's rather superficial commentary on *Hard Times* as a "sociological novel influenced by the Industrial Revolution" in *The Psychological Element in the English Social Novel of the Nineteenth Century* (1927); D. De Lange's analysis of "The Dickens Phenomenon" in *Het Verschijnsel Charles Dickens. Een poging Tot Begrijpen* (1951); and a number of the Dutch dissertations listed by Altick and Matthews in their *Guide to Doctoral Dissertations.*

The most important recent discussion of Dickens in Dutch is H. L. Prenen's "Charles Dickens en de Caricatuur" in *De Lach in de Literatuur* (by J. H. Plokker, et al., 1955). This work begins with a devastating attack upon Henriette Roland Holst's view of Dickens in her comparative study of Tolstoy, Balzac, and Dickens, *Romankunst als Levensschool* (1950), and goes on to pay tribute to the supremacy of the English as humorists and to analyze the accomplishment of Dickens as caricaturist. Along with her attack on her countrywoman's study for its ultrasocialistic and completely humorless approach (epitomized in Mrs. Holst's comment that *Pickwick* falls flat after the first chapter!) Dr. Prenen criticizes the realists and naturalists of the late nineteenth century for their narrow definition of realism and for relegating Dickens to the literary slums between Buffalo Bill and Nick Carter because his realism is not cut to their pattern. The article also comments on Dickens' relation to the graphic caricaturists of the eighteenth and early nineteenth centuries, and draws an interesting parallel between Goya and Dickens. An important critical study in Flemish by M. E. Melpaire ran in seven installments in *Dietsche warande en Belfort* (1928–1929).

Of the Scandinavian countries, Denmark has shown the liveliest critical activity, with the studies of Carl A. Bodelsen of first importance. Besides his major work, *Dickens og hans bøger* (1957), and a pamphlet publication of two radio addresses, *To Radioforedrag om Dickens* (1941), Bodelsen has contributed significant articles to English scholarly journals, including "Some Notes on Dickens' Symbolism" (*English Studies,* 1959) and "The Physiognomy of the Name" (*Review of English Literature,* 1961). Most noteworthy among other Danish studies are Peder Hesselaa, "Dickens' Skaebne, den kritiske Litteratur fra 1870 til vore Dage" in *Festskrift til Valdemar Vedel* (1935); an early biography by Alfred Ipsen (1912); a provocative work centering on a discussion of Dickens' houses and localities, *Man laeser Dickens* (1949) by art historian Christian Elling; a brief but penetrating critical preface to *Great Expectations* by Ove Jørgensen for the Gyldendals Bibliotek (1929); Knud Sørensen's "Subjective Narrative in *Bleak House*" (*English Studies,* 1959); and the studies of Hans Christian Andersen already noted. Sweden has contributed a significant work by Martin Lamm: *Dickens och hans romaner* (1947), a series of critical essays on individual novels originally intended as prefaces to Swedish translations; "Pickwick Notes" (written in English) by Wilhelm Peter Uhrström in *Studier i Modern Språkvetenskap: Nyfilologiska sällskapet* (1931); and two earlier studies of less consequence: Ida Buergel Goodwin's *Charles Dickens: småfolkets skildrare* (1912) and Erik Lindstrom's *Charles Dickens* (1930). Of the three Norwegian biographies of Dickens — by Leonard Sandberg (1912), Gerhard Gran (1925), and Andreas Paulson (1930) — none makes a contribution comparable to that of Bodelsen or Lamm. The most recent critical study by a Norwegian is Gösta Langenfeldt's "Charles Dickens' sociala kritik" (*Edda,* 1952). Finland's outstanding Dickensian scholar is Irma Rantavaara, author of *Dickens in the Light of English Criticism* (1944) and *Charles Dickens, elämäkerta* (1946). A brief survey of Finnish interest in Dickens will be found in Marta Eneberg, "Charles Dickens i sin samtids Finland" in *Historiska och litteraturhistoriska studier* (1960).

Lafcadio Hearn, almost sole interpreter of English literature to the Japanese from 1890 to 1903, advised his students against reading Dickens (except for *A Tale of Two Cities* and the short stories which he preferred to the novels) because Dickens was so English they could not hope to understand him (see *Interpretations of Literature,* 1915, and *A His-*

tory of English Literature, 1927). Hearn's discouragement may account for the absence of critical Dickensian interest in Japan until the postwar period. The most important works are the linguistic studies of Tadao Yamamoto: *Growth and System of the Language of Dickens: An Introduction to a Dickens Lexicon* (1950; rev. ed., 1952), with the separately published index compiled by Chiaki Higashida and Michio Masui (1952); two studies of Dickens' language written in Japanese, *Dikkenzu no Eigo* (1951) and *Dikkenzu no Buntai* (1960); and an article on a Dickens lexicon in *Anglica* (Tokyo, 1962). Yamamoto acknowledges indebtedness to his teacher Sanki Ichikawa, especially to Ichikawa's "A Study of Dickens' Slang and Colloquialism" in *Studies in English Grammar* (trans. Eibumpō Kenkyū, 1912). Another study in English is *Harold Skimpole by Charles Dickens. Huntiana,* edited with notes by Yasuo Yamato (1931). Untranslated studies include a volume of essays, *Dikkenzu Shōsetsu-ron,* by Kōichi Miyazaki (1959); critical articles by Yūzō Aoki in *Eī-Bei Bungakushi Kōza* (1962) and Takashi Katō (on historical study in Dickens and on Dickens and his social background) in *Eibungaku Kenkyū* (1953); and monographs by Takeo Teranishi (1934), Shunji Ebiike (1955), and Akira Honda (1934). Honda has also written an article on Dickens and America for *Arubion* (1949) and a critical introduction to his translation of *A Tale of Two Cities* (1961). A checklist of the numerous Japanese translations from 1868–1955 will be found in *Meiji Taishō Shōwa hon'yaku* (1959), a bibliography of foreign literature translated into Japanese compiled by the National Diet Library, Tokyo.

The difficulties of pursuing Dickens into the labyrinths of Oriental languages have proved insurmountable, although the casual discovery of lively discussions of the Dickens-Ternan affair, first in Arabic in Mahmūd al-Samrah's volume of critical essays (Beirut, 196–?, pp. 133–141) and then in Bengali in *Lekhakedera prema* by Bholanath Mukhopadhyay (1962), is perhaps enough to spur a more qualified pursuer. Another Indian, P. G. Sathyagirinathan, has obligingly written in English on "Dickens and the Poor Law" (*Mysore*

University Half-Yearly Journal, 1943), as has Egyptian scholar
Nur Sherīf on "The Victorian Sunday in *Little Dorrit* and
Thyrza" (*Cairo Studies in English,* 1960), but it is the sight
of *Pickwick, David Copperfield,* and many others of the
novels translated into Bengali, Assamese, Gujarti, Hindi,
Kannada, Malayalam, Marathi, Tamil, Telugu, and Urdu
that should assure the partisan Dickensian that his belief in
the immortality of Dickens is even truer than turnips or
taxes is.

It may be that too intensive a search for records of what
readers of every nationality have had to say about Dickens
will place one among those whom Helen Gardner in her incisive diagnosis of modern pathocriticism accuses of being
unable "to plead justifiable ignorance of the researches or
opinions of a Chinese or Peruvian professor" (*The Business
of Criticism,* p. 5), but the podsnappery that would dismiss
with a wave of the hand such other countries as there may
happen to be is equally distasteful. Such a relief map of
criticism outside the Anglo-American Club as attempted
here is intended as a compromise between the two extremes.

EPILOGUE ON HUMOR. This survey of the multitudinous seas
of Dickens criticism, much of it incarnadined by the dark
moods and personal rebellions of those writing it, cannot be
concluded without calling attention to what long threatened
to become an ironic conspiracy of silence. Voices are now rising in increasing numbers to protest that the oversolemn preoccupation with the Existentialist, Kierkegaardian, Jungian,
Freudian, Marxian, Etceteran undertones in Dickens, and
the relentless tracing of the paragenesis of such elements in
favorites like Dostoyevsky, Proust, and Kafka, have led to the
neglect of the one element in Dickens which as his unique
achievement has most resisted imitation, his humor. The la-
ment of a *Blackwood's* reviewer of 1857, "In that wilderness
[of *Little Dorrit*], we sit down and weep when we remember
thee, O Pickwick," is echoed by readers who try to enjoy their
Buzfuz in the midst of the psychoanalyzers of William Dorrit.
Modern critics appear to be dividing into advocates of *Pick-*

wick and the early novels, and those of *Little Dorrit* and the later ones, a division reflected in the titles of the two most widely read modern biographies, Hesketh Pearson's *Charles Dickens: His Character, Comedy, and Career,* and Edgar Johnson's *Charles Dickens: His Tragedy and Triumph.*

Just as Edmund Wilson was given credit for awakening interest in Dickens as a serious artist, he is now being blamed for the neglect of Dickens as a comic genius. William Ross Clark accuses him of turning Dickens into "a melancholy misfit drifting helplessly unanalyzed in a pre-Freudian world" [38] and protests, against Wilson's "distorted concept," that Dickens' incorrigible and irrepressible humor invades even the most morbid of his scenes. Others note apprehensively the spread of the virus. Fred W. Boege in his review of criticism from 1940 to 1953 comments that "Wilson ignored the humor in Dickens, but Lindsay smothers it in four hundred pages of . . . joyless writing" (*NCF,* 1953). R. C. Churchill, observing that there is no reason why "post-Jamesians" cannot enjoy Dickens, objects vehemently to Monroe Engel's unsmiling description of Mrs. Gamp as "an example of the callous brutality bred by poverty" (*Spectator,* Nov. 13, 1959), and states his own position with emphasis in *From Dickens to Hardy* (1958): "In the field of comedy I put Dickens above Shakespeare, Ben Jonson, Fielding, and Smollett, though recognizing, as he did himself, that he owed much to them" (p. 120). Reviewers accused J. Hillis Miller of being gloomy even about *Pickwick* though they were rebuked by Augustine Martin who noted that Miller analyzes *Pickwick* "with a splendid dead-pan humour that conveys the critic's own enjoyment of this incomparable comedy" *(Studies,* 1960); Miller's own praise of K. J. Fielding (*NCF,* 1959) and A. O. J. Cockshut (*VS,* 1961) for their appreciation of Dickens as a supreme comic artist would seem to bear Martin out. Other reviewers have tended to regret Fielding's clear preference for

[38] "The Rationale of Dickens' Death Rate" (*BUSE,* Autumn, 1956), p. 95; Clark betrays a partiality for his own phrase, repeating it with slightly altered punctuation in "The Hungry Mr. Dickens" (*Dalhousie Review,* Autumn, 1956), p. 250.

the early novels, but a number agree with Miller about Cockshut, Steven Marcus remarking that his was the "best discussion of Dickens' humour I have seen" (*New Statesman*, 1961).

In his own defense against charges that he started the fad
for looking at Dickens through a glass darkly,[39] Wilson noted
in the foreword to the revised edition of *The Triple Thinkers*
(1948) that when he wrote "Dickens: The Two Scrooges" the
neglect was all on the other side, a statement corroborated by
Walter Allen in a review of Pearson's biography the same
year, in which he protested that Pearson's view of Dickens
failed to recognize that "Just as much a part of him as his
humour and his fine indignation are his abiding obsession
with violence and his marvellous sense of symbolism. His
was a nightmare universe, and if we are to look for affinities
with him among other writers, we shall find them in Dostoevsky rather than in Fielding or Smollett" (*New Statesman*,
1949). But by 1954 George Ford's exhaustive review of
Dickens criticism prompted him to reverse Allen's emphasis
in the observation, "If Dickens' work has more in common
with the kind of writing represented by Kafka, Dostoevsky, or
Faulkner than his Victorian critics recognized (had the comparison been possible), he has also more in common with
Smollett and Surtees than some of his more humorless
twentieth-century critics have recognized" (*Dickens and His
Readers*, p. 4).

No general biography or book of criticism fails to mention
Dickens' humor, of course, and some early writers like Chesterton and Priestley have given it full recognition and praise.
But, although a number of early treatises, especially German
dissertations, are devoted to aspects of the subject, Dickens'
humor has so far attracted no full-scale critical study and
only a scattering of essays and articles. It is of interest that
John Gross, coeditor of *Dickens and the Twentieth Century*,

[39] Ironically, on the eve of writing the essays that were to start critics
looking for social and psychological symbols in Dickens, Wilson in an amusing
contribution to the *Nation* which he signed "Edmund Wilson (not
Christopher Morley)," January 29, 1938 (reprinted in *The Shores of Light*,
1952) complained against the "philosophico-social" and "politico-social"
criticism of the 1930's and pleaded for a return to reading "for pleasure."

gives Wilson credit for knowing Dickens was a humorist, commenting, "Only someone who misses the point about Dickens would want to start explaining his jokes; a tactful man like Mr. Wilson simply offers his salute and lets the subject drop" (p. xii); and yet it is a disappointment that all eighteen of the essays in the anthology prove to be equally tactful, even John Killham's discussion of *Pickwick*. The tact, of course, may be prompted by the awareness that it takes a Chesterton to overcome the difficulty of talking about Dickens' humor. Lord David Cecil once remarked, "A man might as well praise a bird for having wings" (*Early Victorian Novelists,* p. 46); certainly the business of analyzing humor is a thankless task, since it cannot avoid giving the impression of having clipped the bird's wings as Keats said philosophy would an angel's. It may well be that this has more to do with the scholarly neglect of the subject than Edmund Wilson's launching of the graveyard school. As Angus Wilson has observed, the difficulties of analyzing the "deeper, free level of memory" probably account for the fact that "Dickens's most characteristic genius, his humour, has so daunted all his many analysers" (*The Wild Garden,* 1963, p. 140). A case in point is Archibald C. Coolidge, Jr.'s "Dickens's Humor" (*VNL,* 1960), which takes up some important aspects of the subject, but is such heavy going as to belie the platitude that it is impossible to write a dull book about Dickens.

Others have taken up the subject with varying degrees of success. C. B. Cox's "In Defense of Dickens" (*Essays and Studies,* 1958) pleads forcefully for a return to appreciation of Dickens' comic art, pointing out that it is in his comedy that Dickens shows his "profound sense of the human predicament" and that his recognition of "a fundamental absurdity and a fundamental glory in human experience is . . . the essence of that vision which makes him a great novelist." In another article, "Comic Viewpoints in *Sketches by Boz*" (*English,* 1959), Cox shows how Dickens' humor is saved from cynicism by the warmth of his sympathy with his characters. Douglas Bush in "A Note on Dickens' Humor," after remarking that modern critics "do not seem to be very much aware that Dickens is one of the world's greatest humorists," goes on to discuss one minor facet of his humor — the "theatrical quality of his comic characters' self-dramatization" (*From Jane Austen to Joseph Conrad*, ed. Robert C. Rathburn and Martin Steinmann, Jr., 1958). Two early comparative studies illuminate special aspects of Dickens' humor: Gordon McKenzie's "Dickens and Daumier" (*Studies in the Comic*, by B. H. Bronson, et al., 1941) and Evelyn Simpson's "Jonson and Dickens: A Study in the Comic Genius of London" (*Essays and Studies*, 1944). A more recent study by Sheila M. Smith, "Anti-Mechanism and the Comic in the Writings of Charles Dickens" (*Nottingham Renaissance and Modern Studies*, 1959), is one of the few attempts at analysis of the strengths and weaknesses of Dickens' humor in general. One of the most discerning discussions is V. S. Pritchett's "The Humour of Dickens" (*Listener*, June 3, 1954),[40] which begins with a calm statement of disagreement with those who consider the serious and later Dickens more important than the comic Dickens, and then goes on to discuss possible sources and to explore the specifics of the humor that is known to all the world as "Dickensian." Finally, a strong reminder has come from Lauriat Lane, Jr., in his preface to *The Dickens Critics* (1961) that "criticism loses sight of Dickens' sense of humor only at the risk of losing sight of its own — the worst fate for a critic of Dickens. Dickens' humor is part of his artistic method, of course, but humor is so strong and universal in Dickens' novels that it becomes part of his meaning as well" (p. 11).

Ironically it is a Frenchman, Sylvère Monod, who has devoted more attention to Dickens as comic genius than most recent critics writing in English. In *Dickens romancier* (1953) he comments upon the mass of "Droodiana" pouring from the press, "Le ton général de cette littérature est alarmant. Il est effroyablement sérieux. Les auteurs semblent oublier

---

[40] Reprinted with some alterations as "The Comic World of Dickens" in *Avon Book of Modern Writing, No. 2* (ed. William Phillips and Philip Rahv, 1954) and in *The Dickens Critics* (ed. George H. Ford and Lauriat Lane, Jr., 1961).

qu'il s'agit d'un roman, de personnages imaginaires, et du plus grand humoriste, peut-être, de tous les temps" (p. 467). He sounds a similar warning in his review of Edgar Johnson in which he accuses Johnson of failing to appreciate the humor of Dickens (*Etudes anglaises*, 1954) and again in the words with which he concludes "A French View of Dickens's Humour" (*Review of English Literature*, 1961): "There is no proper way of enjoying Dickens's humour. But someone who does not enjoy it one way or another should not make English literature his subject any more than one who does not enjoy Shakespeare's poetry." Monod's gentlemanly hint that there are people who should not write about Dickens recalls that voluble group with a Q. D. Leavis contempt for laughter who maintain they "cannot read Dickens" — a group of whom St. John Ervine remarked, "There is something seriously wrong with people who cannot read Dickens. Either their minds are out of order or they are suffering from moral obliquity. In either case, I don't wish to meet them, and I hope they fall over something and break both their legs" (*Listener*, Sept. 22, 1955).

R. C. Churchill has observed that "James might have written a Gampless *Chuzzlewit*, as Dickens might have poured the full flood of his sentimentality into *What Maisie Knew*, but this, after all, is merely to say that the two novelists are great for entirely different reasons" (*Spectator*, Nov. 13, 1959). The statement is a warning against dogmatisms of whatever school, which are the death of responsible criticism. Dickens has had his share of big-endian, little-endian debate, and of what Helen Gardner condemns as "Mr. X's modifications of Mr. Y's criticism of Mr. Z's article" (*The Business of Criticism*, p. 3), all of which threatens to turn Dickens into the "intolerable institution" Virginia Woolf predicted his admirers would make him (*TLS*, March 27, 1919). But Dickens will outlive all this as he outlived the years of critical neglect, and he will continue to take up more columns of the *Oxford Dictionary of Quotations* than any other writer except Shakespeare and to outsell all other Victorian novelists in paperback. Few would deny, however, that modern criticism, whether or not it stirs our enthusiastic acceptance, has brought more mature appreciation of Dickens' multiple and diverse achievements. Certainly the critical climate is healthier today than at the turn of the century when Arnold Bennett's attack on Dickens in "My Literary Heresies" (*T. P.'s Weekly,* 1904) found no challenger but a Will Evans writing for *The Amalgamated Engineer's Journal* (Oct. 1904). It may be, as has been charged, that all critics of Dickens are really talking about themselves, but the increase in the number of talkers at least indicates an increase in the number who have discovered him worth reading. As Bernard Darwin said when critical interest in Dickens was just beginning to gain momentum, "Mr. Pickwick once took another glass of punch just to see whether there was any orange-peel in it, because orange-peel always disagreed with him; and we can now read all Dickens yet again just to see if we were wrong about him" (*TLS,* Sept. 8, 1945).

4

William Makepeace Thackeray

Lionel Stevenson

THE STATUS of Thackeray is perhaps more equivocal than that of any other major Victorian novelist. Most historians of literature still echo his contemporaries in assigning him an importance second only to Dickens; and thanks to the diligence of Gordon N. Ray the student is now provided with an unsurpassed apparatus of documentation and ancillary knowledge. On the other hand, a few influential modern critics deny Thackeray almost all merit as a novelist, and several of them attack him with a peculiar sort of personal animus which at least testifies to his continuing power to evoke a lively response.

Among his five major novels, only two have been made available in the paperback editions which are the current gauge of academic respectability in the United States. A review of the existing scholarly publication on Thackeray and his works will indicate that the divergence of opinion is by no means of recent origin, and that some of the present points of controversy were first raised several generations ago.

I. *Bibliography*

The earliest attempt toward a detailed listing of Thackeray's writings was made in 1881 by R. H. Shepherd, *The Bibliography of Thackeray: The Published Writings in Prose and Verse and the Sketches and Drawings from 1829 to 1880.* This served to call attention to the complexity of the problem, arising from Thackeray's prolonged period of anonymous or pseudonymous journalism. A revised and enlarged edition was appended to Shepherd's reprint of some of Thackeray's miscellaneous writings, *Sultan Stork and Other Stories and Sketches* (1887). A useful but not elaborate bibliography was included in the final volume of the Biographical Edition of Thackeray's works in 1899.

The only ambitious and exhaustive bibliography is *A Thackeray Library: First Editions and First Publications, Portraits, Water Colors, Etchings, Drawings, and Manuscripts, Collected by Henry Sayre Van Duzer* (1919). This work has the usual merits and defects of a compilation made by a wealthy hobbyist. It is sumptuous in format and thorough in its information about the material in Van Duzer's collection or anything closely related to it. He states that of the four novels that appeared in monthly parts he "examined a score of copies" as a basis for his collation. His claim on the title page, however, that "a few additional items are included, forming a complete Thackeray bibliography," is modified in the introduction by the admission that he has omitted "the many publications of Thackeray and Thackerayana in the United States," except when an American edition precedes and, in some instances, differs from the first English edition. For further American material he refers his readers to the bibliography attached to J. G. Wilson's *Thackeray in the United States.*

The main body of Van Duzer's book is a list of "first editions in book form and first appearances in periodicals and newspapers, including posthumous publications." It is arranged alphabetically, so that major books, slight articles, and collected editions are lumped indiscriminately together. A chronological index is helpful for the student who is interested in Thackeray's development or his work at any particular period. A separate list of "Thackeray's Writings in *Fraser's, Punch,* and the *Cornhill"* must be used with caution, though Van Duzer intended it to be definitive. With regard to the contributions to *Fraser's* he said that "there is reason to believe that Thackeray wrote at this early date [before

1835] various book criticisms and other articles which I have included in the list, those not generally acknowledged to have been contributed by Thackeray I have enclosed in brackets." In the list of articles in *Punch* Van Duzer offered a few additions and corrections to Spielmann's volume of 1899. On these matters, however, his attributions have been superseded by the authoritative evidence given by Gordon Ray in *The Letters and Private Papers of William Makepeace Thackeray* (vol. IV) and in his list of forty-four hitherto unidentified pieces in *Punch* (*TLS*, 1949).

Other sections of the Van Duzer bibliography deal with "portraits, water colors, etchings, manuscripts, and drawings" (confined solely to items in his collection) and "Thackerayana," the latter being a list of biographical and critical articles which likewise records merely the books and periodicals in Van Duzer's library and is useful only in pointing out a few relatively early items which might not be easily traced through other bibliographical aids.

In spite of its shortcomings, Van Duzer will probably remain the standard bibliography. Little if anything of importance is added in M.L. Parrish's *Catalogue of an Exhibition of the Works of Thackeray* (1940) or in John D. Gordan's catalogue of Thackeray material in the Berg collection (*BNYPL*, 1947).

A useful work of reference is *A Thackeray Dictionary* (1910), by Isadore Gilbert Mudge and M. Earl Sears. This opens with synopses of the novels and then provides full references to all the characters, particularly valuable because of Thackeray's habit of introducing the same persons or their relations in various books. The concluding "Index to Originals" is of limited value since Ray and others have greatly increased the number of identified portraits in the novels.

II. *Editions*

The first collection of Thackeray's work that laid claim to completeness and editorial supervision was the thirteen-volume Biographical Edition of 1898–1899, with introductions by his daughter Anne Thackeray Ritchie. Immediately it became clear that a large quantity of Thackeray's ephemeral work had not been included. M. H. Spielmann's volume of *The Hitherto Unidentified Contributions of William Makepeace Thackeray to "Punch"* and Walter T. Spencer's *Mr. Thackeray's Writings in the "National Standard" and the "Constitutional"* both came out in 1899. Lewis Melville in 1901 issued a volume entitled *Stray Papers* in a format imitating that of the Biographical Edition. Later R. S. Garnett recognized eleven articles by Thackeray in the *Foreign Quarterly Review* and edited them as *The New Sketch Book* (1906). Much of this material was incorporated in a reissue of the Biographical Edition, enlarged to twenty-six volumes and renamed the Centenary Biographical Edition (1910–1911). Meanwhile another reasonably complete and conscientious set, the Oxford Edition, with introductions by George Saintsbury, had been issued in seventeen volumes in 1908. Saintsbury trusted to his literary intuition in deciding which of the anonymous items were good enough or well enough authenticated to be included. A useful feature is the appending of passages discarded in Thackeray's final revision of the novels.

The records published in Gordon Ray's edition of *The Letters and Private Papers* facilitated further identification of Thackeray's fugitive pieces. As well as printing in *TLS* his list of the unrecognized items in *Punch,* Ray has edited a volume of the book reviews that he found in another paper, *Thackeray's Contributions to the "Morning Chronicle"* (1955). The question of Thackeray's work for a short-lived New York journal, the *Republic,* is raised by W. C. Desmond Pacey in "A Probable Addition to the Thackeray Canon" (*PMLA,* 1945). In "Thackeray's Contributions to the *British and Foreign Review*" (*JEGP,* 1948), Lela Winegarner identifies two articles and tentatively attributes a third one. Obviously, a good deal of already identified material remains uncollected and must be sought in the files of the sometimes obscure journals that Thackeray wrote for; and probably there is further material yet to be discovered. One doubts, however, whether any of this is of sufficient importance to be accorded the dignity of reprinting in book form.

It is not surprising that questions of exclusion have arisen as well as questions of inclusion. R. H. Shepherd's unauthorized volume of 1887, *Sultan Stork and Other Stories and Sketches,* included "Elizabeth Brownrigge," a story from *Fraser's Magazine* of 1833, which, if written by Thackeray, would be his earliest extensive piece of fiction. Ernest Boll has argued zealously in favor of the attribution in "The Author of *Elizabeth Brownrigge*" (*SP,* 1942), but all other modern scholars regard the evidence as unconvincing.

Like the other Victorian novelists, Thackeray has been neglected in regard to textual study. Even more than most of them, he was a careless and hasty worker, submitting his manuscript to the printer at the last moment and evading the rigors of proof-reading. An egregious example is the misplaced paragraph in chapter lix of *Vanity Fair.* One of the letters published by Ray in 1945 made it clear that Thackeray was aware of this mechanical error, which occurred in the serial issue and persisted in all later editions; and indeed any intelligent reader ought to have recognized that the paragraph was absurdly irrelevant where it was placed. Yet the elementary correction was not made until George Ford's edition of *Vanity Fair* in Harper's Modern Classics, in 1958.

A pioneer textual study was David A. Randall's "Notes toward a Correct Collation of the First Edition of *Vanity Fair*" (*PBSA,* 1948), which includes a five-page list of variant readings between the serial parts and the first book edition of that novel. Since Randall's purpose was the strictly bibliographical one of establishing "points" for the first issues, he did not analyze the literary significance of the emendations and omissions that he recorded. An edition of *Vanity Fair,* by Geoffrey and Kathleen Tillotson (1963), based on collation of the manuscripts and the various editions, and fully annotated, at last provides a magisterial text. Similar analysis of existing manuscripts, serial issues, and subsequent editions in book form will unquestionably reveal misreadings, revisions, and omissions in Thackeray's other novels, shedding light on methods of work and leading to more accurate future printings.

A satisfactory edition of Thackeray's correspondence was long awaited. Several inaccurate and discreetly selective volumes of his letters to particular recipients came out during the half century after his death: *A Collection of Letters of William Makepeace Thackeray, 1847–55*, with an introduction by Jane Octavia Brookfield (1887); *Thackeray's Letters to an American Family*, with an introduction by Lucy W. Baxter (1904); *Some Family Letters of William Makepeace Thackeray, together with Recollections by His Kinswoman, Blanche Warre Cornish* (1911). Undependable though they were, these books indicated something of Thackeray's charm as a letter writer and supplied a few glimpses of his personality and his private life that were of use to biographers. The great mass of his papers, however, remained in the hands of his daughter Lady Ritchie and then of his granddaughter Mrs. Hester Ritchie Fuller, who withheld them from publication, originally for reasons of discretion and subsequently because Mrs. Fuller had thoughts of editing them herself. At an opportune moment, when she was beginning to realize the unlikelihood of her being able to carry through the monumental task, she was approached by Gordon N. Ray, who had recently written a dissertation on Thackeray for the doctorate at Harvard. Granted full rights to the correspondence, Ray was able to find large numbers of further letters elsewhere, and his diligent editorial work resulted in four massive volumes of *The Letters and Private Papers of William Makepeace Thackeray* (1945–1946).

Inevitably, such an ambitious work was susceptible to fault-finding. Some specialists pointed out occasional misreadings of Thackeray's handwriting and found inaccuracies in the annotations, others objected to the policy of completeness that has justified the inclusion of short and trivial letters such as replies to invitations. (See, for example, the correspondence by Humphry House, *et al.*, in *TLS*, 1947, and the hostile review article by Ernest Bernbaum in *JEGP*,

1947.) More serious is the fact that all existing letters of importance were not included. Ray was acquainted with many for which permission for printing could not be obtained, and others came to light later, so that enough material exists for at least another volume. In spite of slight cavils, however, there can be no question that Ray's work is not only the cornerstone for all recent and future research in Thackeray's life and writings but also one of the most important American contributions to Victorian scholarship.

III. *Biography*

Near the end of his life Thackeray was moved by his reading of a conscientious official biography to remark to his daughters, "When I drop, there is to be no life written of me." While piously observing this prohibition, his daughter Anne (later Lady Ritchie), herself an author, was subjected to increasing pressure to make available her personal knowledge and the family papers, in order to counteract various journalistic compilations and irresponsible reminiscences which were giving currency to inaccurate statements and distorted impressions. Neither Lady Ritchie nor Edward Fitz-Gerald (one of Thackeray's oldest surviving friends) consented to supply information even to so eminent an admirer as Trollope when he was commissioned to write the monograph on Thackeray for the prestigious English Men of Letters series.

Leslie Stephen's essay on "The Writings of W. M. Thackeray," appended to a collected edition in 1879, represented the family position, since Stephen's first wife was Thackeray's younger daughter: "I shall state no biographical facts which are not already public property, and draw no inferences as to character which are not to be justified from these facts and from the writings themselves." Twenty years later Lady Ritchie composed what amounted to a fairly full biography, broken up into the separate introductions to the thirteen volumes of the Biographical Edition. Though authoritative and pleasantly written, this information was far from complete, and was presented in an incoherent form because each introduction attempted to provide the data relevant to the background and the composition of the particular book to which it was appended. About the same time Leslie Stephen wrote a clear factual narrative of Thackeray's life for the *Dictionary of National Biography* (1898), which was given official status by being reprinted as an appendix to the final volume of the Biographical Edition, to serve as a thread upon which Lady Ritchie's scattered beads could be strung together.

In contrast with these well-informed contributions, the first extensive book on the author's life was ill-proportioned and undependable. *The Life of William Makepeace Thackeray* (1899) was by Lewis Melville, an assiduous compiler of literary data. A second edition (1909) was revised and considerably improved, but still fell far short of telling the whole story.

Meanwhile a great deal of tangential material about the Thackeray family and about incidents in the author's career had come into print. The earliest was a privately printed volume by Jane Townley Prime and Alicia Bayne, *Memorials of the Thackeray Family* (1879). Later came *The Thackerays in India* (1897) by Sir W. W. Hunter. Eyre Crowe, who had been Thackeray's secretary on his first tour of the United States, published a gossipy volume, *With Thackeray in America* (1893), and this was subsequently overshadowed by General James Grant Wilson's colossal two-volume opus, *Thackeray in the United States* (1904), an indiscriminate accumulation of everything Wilson could find about the novelist's two tours. Hence came the ironical fact that for the next half century a couple of brief interludes in Thackeray's life, totaling less than twelve months, had been recorded in far fuller detail than all the rest of his life put together.

In 1924, after the death of Lady Ritchie, her daughter Hester Fuller brought out a somewhat disjointed book, *Letters of Anne Thackeray Ritchie*, which provided some additional letters and anecdotes. Other glimpses of unexplored areas in Thackeray's life were being afforded in volumes of reminiscences and collections of correspondence, and many of these were utilized by Malcolm Elwin in *Thackeray: A Personality* (1932). This book was a great improvement over Melville in grace of style and clarity of arrangement, as well as in the validity of its information. In particular, Elwin undertook for the first time to deal with the baffling contradictions in Thackeray's behavior and with the interpretation of his psychological traits. Shortly afterwards, G. U. Ellis' short monograph in the Great Lives series (1933) made a similar attempt in a livelier style, with no burden of documentation to impede his remarks.

The great controversy over "debunking" was at its height in the thirties and both Elwin and Ellis were assailed as practitioners of the Stracheyan art. Their most startling new information had been Thackeray's falling in love with Mrs. Brookfield, which Ellis particularly emphasized. The two books evoked partial support from Simon Nowell Smith, "In Defence of Thackeray" (*Nineteenth Century*, 1933), and a rebuttal from Colonel C. B. Thackeray, "Thackeray and the Melancholy Humourist: The Gentle Art of 'De-bunking'" (*Cornhill*, 1935).

With the availability of fuller evidence, Thackeray's career was fully narrated for the first time by Lionel Stevenson in *The Showman of Vanity Fair* (1947). Although some of its factual details can no longer be accepted as accurate, this remains the only book that provides the essential biographical information within the compass of a single volume.

From the time when Gordon Ray's edition of the correspondence was published, it was known that he was at work upon a massive biography of Thackeray, which he was uniquely qualified to write, in view of his exhaustive knowledge of the family archives, enhanced by research in the papers of the East India Company and other unexplored sources. A sampling of this material was provided by Ray in his Lowell lectures at Harvard, published as *The Buried Life* (1952). Subtitled "A Study of the Relations between

Thackeray's Fiction and His Personal History," it is chiefly of value in study of the source material of the novels, but it reveals meticulous knowledge of Thackeray's family and touches upon some of the ambiguous questions of his feelings toward his wife, his mother, and other people who were close to him.

Ray's long awaited *Thackeray* appeared in two volumes, with differentiating subtitles, *The Uses of Adversity* (1955) and *The Age of Wisdom* (1958). Undoubtedly this will remain the basic source of information, for further revelations are unlikely to occur. The biography is admirably written, temperate in its judgments, and convincing in the discussion of psychological questions. It includes several chapters which are elaborate set pieces depicting the social and literary milieu in which Thackeray lived and worked. These are of such general value to any student of the period that they can be recommended as independent essays; but perhaps in their context they blur the focus of the biography by subordinating Thackeray to his environment. The relationship of the various experiences and influences in Thackeray's life is not easy to display, and Ray has not been altogether successful, not only because the static chapters impede the flow of the narrative but also because he treats separate elements in extensive blocks, so that the account of Thackeray's journalistic work, for example, is carried through a period of some five years, then comes analysis of the fiction he wrote during the same era, and then his personal activities. This is apt to be confusing, if not positively misleading, for readers who lack Ray's total familiarity with the chronological sequence.

There is a further reason why this major biography must be used with some discretion. Perhaps to allow space for his set pieces and for his prolonged initial study of the Thackeray family in its Indian setting, or perhaps to avoid the charge of repeating himself, Ray refrains from including some of the relevant material that he previously published in *The Buried Life* and in the elaborate prefatory sections and notes in *The Letters and Private Papers*. Accordingly, these sources must be consulted along with the biography if one is to be sure of obtaining all the information that Ray has so amply provided.

IV. *Criticism*

Because of the paucity of biographical material, most of the earlier books about Thackeray contained a large proportion of critical discussion. The treatise by Anthony Trollope in the English Men of Letters series (1879) is chiefly noteworthy as one eminent novelist's tribute to another, and so it is perhaps more important to students of Trollope than to students of Thackeray. Nevertheless, it includes a good many typically sensible remarks that are worth the attention of modern readers. In spite of Trollope's almost reverential discipleship of Thackeray, his innate caution restrains him from making extravagant claims about his master's stature, and he resorts repeatedly to such evasive statements as these: "As to the realism of Thackeray, I must rather appeal to my readers than attempt to prove it by quotation"; "let the reader ask himself what are the lessons which Thackeray has taught"; "as to the other question, whether Thackeray be amusing as well as salutary, I must leave it to public opinion." His strongest argument for the merit of Thackeray's books is "that their charm has been proved by their popularity."

Trollope is positive, however, that Thackeray contributed largely to the development of realism in the Victorian novel. He "was determined to run counter to the recognized taste of novel readers . . . With Thackeray it was essential that the representations made by him should be, to his own thinking, lifelike." Trollope's other principal assumption is that the chief business of great fiction is to "instruct in morals." Thackeray was "endeavouring to represent human nature as he saw it, so that his readers should learn to love what is good, and to hate what is evil." On this basis Trollope rates *Henry Esmond* as far the best of Thackeray's books. "The lesson taught in *Esmond* is salutary from beginning to end.

The sermon truly preached is that glory can only come from that which is truly glorious and that the results of meanness end always in the mean." Therefore Trollope tries to defend Thackeray from the then current charge of cynicism: "That Thackeray's nature was soft and kindly — gentle almost to a fault — has been shown elsewhere. But they who have called him a cynic have spoken of him merely as a writer — and as a writer he has certainly taken upon himself the special task of barking at the vices and follies of the world around him." The tolerant Trollope could not approve of Thackeray's persistent disillusionment: "It has to be confessed that Thackeray did allow his intellect to be too thoroughly saturated with the aspect of the ill side of things." Trollope has to fall back upon the paradox that he was "of all satirists the most humorous, and of all humorists the most satirical."

The decline in Thackeray's prestige during the next quarter century can be perceived in another book written for one of the once popular series of introductory studies — that by Charles Whibley in the Modern English Writers (1903). Whibley was an urbane and somewhat ruthless critic, and his appreciation of Thackeray's sarcastic wit is tempered by distaste for his sentimentality and prudery. He finds in the early fiction "a strange mixture of contemptuous irony and that peculiar kind of sentimentalism known as Early Victorian; he seems to snigger behind his sobs, and to weep under the secure cover of contemptuous irony. The worst is that he could not, either early or late, keep his two methods separate, so that while his pathos does not melt the wise to tears, his irony is seldom sustained at a perfect level." Or again, "Unto the end of his career, [Thackeray] delighted somewhat naïvely in the obvious emotions." Not surprisingly, Whibley regards *Barry Lyndon* as Thackeray's masterpiece, and allots disproportionate space to praise of this cynical novel, just as later he devotes no less than fourteen pages to a comparison of *Vanity Fair* and *Coningsby* on the trivial basis of the use of Lord Hertford as model for a character in both books, his conclusion being that Disraeli gives a truer portrait.

Even Thackeray's much admired style does not satisfy

Whibley: "He was the master of an easy style, more familiar than correct, more boisterous than energetic." Later the indictment is amplified: "The style must needs be at times inaccurate and undistinguished. The solecisms of which he is guilty, and they are not few, may readily be forgiven. It is more difficult to pardon the frequent lack of distinction." He grudgingly admits, however, that "despite its occasional inaccuracy, it has many shining qualities. It is graphic, various, and at times elegant."

After Whibley's book came a hiatus in Thackeray criticism, and the nadir of his reputation probably arrived in 1931 when Michael Sadleir in his biography of Bulwer-Lytton denigrated Thackeray both as a man and as a writer. In the same year, however, a turning point was marked by the publication of the best among the earlier critical studies, *A Consideration of Thackeray*, by George Saintsbury, a reprinting of the introductions contributed to the Oxford edition of Thackeray's works in 1908. With his affinity for the eighteenth century and his knowledge of French literature, Saintsbury was well qualified to discuss the major elements in Thackeray's work, and he knew even the most insignificant pieces more thoroughly than any other critic. Whibley had grumbled because "the demon of curiosity pursued Thackeray from *Fraser's* to *Punch*, so that it is our own fault if we do not know every line and scratch which he sent to our only comic paper. The archaeologist has devoted infinite research to the discovery of the unimportant." Saintsbury, in contrast, boasts that "I have read 'Cox's Diary' at least a score of times," and again, "In hardly any case, I think, often as I have read everything of Thackeray's, can I take up a piece of his, small or great, without reading it through. I have read 'The Ravenswing' through more than once or half a dozen times." Nor was the familiarity confined to the books in their final form: repeatedly Saintsbury mentions differences between the original periodical issues and the subsequent revised versions, a matter that no scholar has yet investigated in detail.

The book displays all Saintsbury's exasperating idiosyncracies in full bloom — the ferocious prejudices, the irrelevant anecdotes and literary allusions, the tortuous sentences; but it shows also his merits of enthusiastic appreciation, critical discrimination, and scholarly range. He has nothing but scorn for Thackeray's detractors, and he finds something to praise in most of the journalistic pieces; but, confident in his personal taste, he does not hesitate to go counter to some of the conventional judgments in Thackeray's favor, as for instance (and perhaps in intentional opposition to Whibley) in his low esteem of *Barry Lyndon*. Almost all the points made by recent fault-finders are observable in Saintsbury's book, but they are reduced to proper proportion by being intermingled with intimate appreciation of Thackeray's greatness.

Each book is seen in the context of its own time, and some of the incidental suggestions of literary antecedents, such as the connection between Thackeray's early fiction and that of Theodore Hook, still remain to be explored further. Many brief comments, such as the comparison of Thackeray's essays to Hazlitt's and of his "combination of romance with satire of romance" to Heine's, are brilliant. On Thackeray's style, on his humor, on his "eidola" (nowadays more often termed his "personae"), Saintsbury is unrivaled.

As a whole, the book is most valuable in its thorough discussion of the minor works. Since the chapters were originally attached to the respective volumes of a complete edition of Thackeray, the amount of space devoted to the major novels is relatively small: the chapter on *Vanity Fair* is no longer than that on "*The Paris Sketch Book* and Art Criticisms."

In contrast with the discursive books of Trollope, Whibley, and Saintsbury, the disciplined and intelligent procedures of modern French scholarship are represented by Raymond Las Vergnas's book *W. M. Thackeray: l'homme, le penseur, le romancier*, 1932. Las Vergnas abjures the "biocritical method": "To follow the life and genius of Thackeray in their development would have constrained us to model ourselves in an almost irksome fashion upon our predecessors . . . While the novels have often been analysed and their specific merits displayed in relation to Thackeray's evolution, the unity of the Thackerayan personality, thought, and fiction has remained obscure . . . This work is offered essentially as a *psychological and critical synthesis.*" Unlike Saintsbury, Las Vergnas concentrates upon the major novels: "The secondary aspects of his activity — articles, poetry, lectures, essays, drawings, have been considered only to the extent that they help in determining the Thackerayan unity."

The study is organized in such a highly analytical manner that the table of contents provides an admirable summary. Book I, "The Man," is in four parts: "Dickens and Thackeray," "Contradictions — the Thackerayan Dualism," "Cynic?" and "The True Thackeray." Each of these is subdivided into several chapters, those on "the Thackerayan Dualism," for instance, being "Sadness and Joviality," "Snobbery and Bohemianism," "The Problem of Knowledge," "Chauvinism and Lucidity," and "A 'Minor' Personality." Book II, "The Thinker," is even more elaborately categorized, under three main heads, "The Models — the Historian and the Eighteenth Century," "Social and Personal Satire," and "The Message of Thackeray." In Book III, "The Novelist," the principal divisions deal with "Realism," "The Concept of the Novel," and "The Art of Thackeray." The conclusion surveys Thackeray's literary position and the development of his reputation. In Las Vergnas's own estimation, the most significant themes of his study are "the minor tonality," "the two snobberies," "the historical incantation," "the message," and "the 'type' novel."

Appearing within a few months of the biographical studies by Elwin and Ellis, the Las Vergnas monograph can be regarded as further indicating a revival of serious attention to Thackeray. A decade elapsed, however, before the publication of a comparably important study by an American scholar. In the interim, the only general work published in English was H. N. Wethered's *On the Art of Thackeray* (1938), a vague and rambling discourse eked out with long quotations from Thackeray's writings and deriving most of its ideas from Trollope and Saintsbury.

Then in 1941 came *Thackeray: A Critical Portrait,* by John Wendell Dodds, which reverted to the "biocritical" method. Dodds describes the book as "criticism with some biographical infiltration — an attempt to trace the growth of a mind and at the same time to identify the quality of an art in fiction." He affirms that "Thackeray's writings are the reflection of a rich and intricate personality . . . It is because he reveals so much of himself that some people have found him baffling. Deep as the reach of his understanding is, he has no philosophical or sociological system to propound, nor does he turn to the world a carefully draped and judiciously spotlighted portrait of himself. By reason of his transparency he seems often paradoxical and inconsistent." Dodds explains that the purpose of his book is to trace the "symmetry" of Thackeray's "reading of life," and that he gives much attention to the writings antecedent to *Vanity Fair* "because in the early writings the development of his dominant ideas and the fixing of his artistic manner can best be seen. Incidentally, the quality of some of that early work is better than one who has never explored it might expect."

Dodds's bland manner precludes overt comment upon critics who condemn Thackeray for lack of a consistent intellectual base and for intrusive moralistic comments, but he praises the novelist on both those counts, holding that the clue to Thackeray's art is "the complete and covering irony through which his view of life is filtered . . . A philosophic irony, a sense of the irony of things, of the contrast between the real and the apparent." Dodds goes on to suggest that "connected with this large ironic treatment is the point of view from which Thackeray tells the story. It seems to me that Thackeray's interpolations add, in the long run, to the illusion of reality, certainly to our enjoyment of the story. In the dramatic novel they would be quite out of place, but in the discursive novel of manners they indicate the mood of the story and intensify the mellow, introspective manner which is the very tissue of a Thackeray novel."

Though Dodds admits that "occasionally the moralist defeats the artist and upon the characters are poured the vials of Thackeray's ethical indignation," his general opinion is that "few novelists can immerse the reader as completely in the satisfaction that comes from learning to know people so that he forgets to ask after plot." If not notably incisive, Dodds's book remains a dependable survey of Thackeray's achievement.

In diametrical antithesis to the appreciative tone and the respectful ideological emphasis of both Las Vergnas and Dodds, the next critical work is the most hostile that has yet appeared. The title of *Thackeray: A Reconsideration*, by J. Y. T. Greig (1950), implies that it is a rebuttal of Saintsbury's book. Basing his concept of the novel on E. M. Forster's dictum that "all literature tends towards a condition of anonymity, and that, so far as words are creative, a signature merely distracts us from their true significance," Greig condemns Thackeray for the personal element in his outlook and style, which, in the view of Saintsbury, Las Vergnas, Dodds, and many others, is one of his principal charms. Not content with the assumption that the presence of any novelist's personality in his work is an unwarranted intrusion, Greig insists that Thackeray's personality is peculiarly distasteful: that he lacked "a stable and undeviating mind" and "a systematic philosophy of human nature"; that his view of society is contradictory when it is not obvious; in short, that he did not possess "a well integrated personality."

In support of this hypothesis Greig cites adverse comments and anecdotes recorded by Thackeray's enemies, while rejecting the favorable evidence of his friends; he adduces passages from Thackeray's letters without making allowance for the whimsical self-mockery that was one of his traits; and he accepts the view presented in Sadleir's life of Bulwer-Lytton but ignores the recantation that Sadleir published in 1946 in a review of *The Letters and Private Papers*. In order to convict Thackeray of being deficient in psychological and social theory, Greig is obliged to approve the doctrinaire element in other Victorian novelists, even while arguing that an author's personal opinions ought not to obtrude. Thackeray is condemned for seeing several sides of any situation rather than rendering didactic judgments, and yet at the same time he is attacked for "sermonizing."

Greig lays strong emphasis upon sexual feelings as a factor in Thackeray's attitudes, and finds the treatment of sex relations particularly unsatisfactory in the novels. His book is organized according to the principal influences that affected the novelist: his ambivalent feelings toward his mother, the loss of his fortune, the difficulties with his wife and her mother, his involvement with Mrs. Brookfield. Greig's genuine admiration for Thackeray's gift in the creation of character is responsible for the exasperation with the "sentimentalizing, agonizing, and sermonizing" which assumes undue prominence throughout his study and leads him to the strange verdict that Thackeray was "a novelist *manqué*."

Eight years later Greig recapitulated his main idea in "Thackeray: A Novelist by Accident," contributed to *From Jane Austen to Joseph Conrad* (ed. R. C. Rathburn and M. Steinmann, Jr., 1958), though with the claim that "I count myself one" of Thackeray's "host of admirers." Greig reiterates at the outset, "my contention is that Thackeray was not a born novelist"; but the only reason adduced is the recurrent moralizing on the action of the stories; and at the end of the essay, after positively enthusiastic praise of *The Newcomes*, Greig temporizes: "Perhaps, after all, Thackeray *was* a novelist born. If so, why in the name of heaven did he overlay his supreme talent with so many fustian annotations?"

Published within a year of Greig's book, Lambert Ennis' *Thackeray, The Sentimental Cynic* (1951) covers some of the same topics, but in a less dynamic manner. Ennis seldom commits himself to positive literary judgments. He terms his book "a study of Thackeray's attitudes," its purpose being "to trace his conduct during the major crises of his life in terms of these attitudes." Again Thackeray's relationship with various women occupies a prominent place. The main thesis is Thackeray's "preoccupation with masks," not only the protective disguises for himself but also his penetration of them in others. Ennis makes some good comments on the early writings and tends to neglect the work of the final period. On the whole, the use of the epithet "the sentimental cynic" indicates that Ennis proposed little modification of the accepted view of Thackeray's character and outlook.

A more penetrating and militant defense of Thackeray's genius was offered by Geoffrey Tillotson in *Thackeray the Novelist* (1954). In agreement with Las Vergnas (whom he does not mention), Tillotson abandons biographical detail and pays little attention to the minor works. He rejects Greig's psychological explanations and feels that Ray indulges too much in identifying the originals of characters and thus obscures Thackeray's creative originality. Tillotson confronts the main objections raised by previous critics and undertakes to refute them. Predicating the unity of the world of Thackeray's novels, he defends the personal commentary as integral to the illusion of reality in these books, pointing out that "the authorial I" is not Thackeray himself but an individualized fictitious character. The sixth chapter, running to sixy pages, deals with "The Author's Truthfulness of Personage and Action," with emphasis on what is termed "the humane fulness of Thackeray's practice." Tillotson believes that the informality of Thackeray's techniques is one of his positive merits: his disregard of formal structure differentiates his world from that of other authors; the "lack of edged shape" and the "bufferless endings" contribute to the totality of his illusion. Tillotson emphasizes Thackeray's kinship with such approved realists as Eliot and James and even suggests that he was a pioneer in experimenting with "stream of consciousness." Careful attention is given to recurrent images and the subtle overtones of apparently casual words and phrases. A compendious final chapter on Thackeray's philosophy is classified into twenty sections, and concludes that "what we honour in Thackeray is our own mind at a finer pitch, working on our experience widened and deepened."

This matter of his philosophical outlook is perhaps the most glaring example of the bias against Thackeray among modern critics. On the one hand, the Victorian novelists as a group are decried for being didactic and doctrinaire, and then on the other hand Thackeray is singled out for condemnation because he did not display a consistent and explicit system of thought. He is usually dismissed as being either hopelessly inconsistent or else merely incapable of any sustained thinking whatsoever. A notable exception is Joseph E. Baker, who in *"Vanity Fair* and the Celestial City" (*NCF*, 1955) undertakes to align Thackeray with three great religious or philosophical figures, Bunyan, St. Augustine, and Plato. "Thackeray was a great thinker," say Baker, "but never wrote philosophy . . . His prose is ambivalent, or multivalent. He contemplated life with something of that poetic feeling which makes Platonism so charming, that love for the beauties it recognizes as transitory."

Baker can scarcely be expected to substantiate his impressive theory fully in a ten-page article, for the elusive and paradoxical character of Thackeray's attitude toward life and art has been a cause of critical controversy for more than a century. The earliest substantial study of his writings, that of Hermann Conrad (Berlin, 1887), bore the subtitle *Ein Pessimist als Dichter*; but few subsequent critics have been so positive about his views. The modern books have offered helpful but often mutually exclusive opinions, and a number of articles in periodicals have been of some value in isolating particular areas of the subject for closer scrutiny and yet have oversimplified it by the isolation.

The earliest of these attempts to resolve the paradoxes was "Thackeray's Romanticism," by Emerson Grant Sutcliffe (*SAQ,* 1922). Sutcliffe quotes from Cabell's *Beyond Life* the remark that Thackeray is a romantic because he "avoids many a logical outcome of circumstance . . . by killing off somebody and blinding the reader with a tear-drenched handkerchief"; but in Sutcliffe's opinion "his romanticism lies deeper than that . . . A fleering spirit of truth sat in his brain and refused to suppress its comment. But somehow his romanticism had to come out. So it took vent in the sentiment and didacticism which so oddly color his satires." An effort to define and differentiate the elements can be found in Hilda Hurst's *Ironischer und sentimentaler Realis-*

mus bei Thackeray (Hamburg, 1938). An unsympathetic
present-day critic, Russell A. Fraser, uses one of the major
novels as basis for a definition of what is distasteful in the
author's attitude in "Sentimentality in Thackeray's *The
Newcomes*" (*NCF*, 1949): "There seem to be three cardinal
qualities that make for Thackeray's own kind of sentimentality: (a) the delivery of commonplaces, either genial or sor-
rowful, by the author, (b) the use of stereotyped words and
word groupings that by their very nature have sentimental
connotations, (c) the deliberate evocation of the pathetic
image." Fraser returns to the attack in "Pernicious Casuis-
try: A Study of Character in *Vanity Fair*" (*NCF*, 1957), asserting categorically that "if Thackeray, like his master Fielding,
is to take upon himself the role of a Chorus, he must speak
with fixed purpose from a single point of view. It will not
do to deride a fool's piety one moment and to applaud it
sententiously the next."

An aspect of Thackeray's thought that has seldom been
examined is his equivocal view of religion. A minor point,
involving the question of anti-Catholicism, was illuminated
in a pair of articles in the *Revue anglo-américaine*, 1932:
"Sur un chapitre des *Newcomes*," by A. Digeon, and "Sur
un passage des *Newcomes*," by A. Barbeau. The accusation
of anti-Catholic bias, combined with that of injustice to
Ireland, was stated strongly by B. G. MacCarthy in "Thackeray in Ireland" (*Studies: An Irish Quarterly Review*, 1951).
The writer asserts that Thackeray visited Ireland burdened
not only with "prejudice, both political and religious, culpable and indurated ignorance, muddle-headed sentimentality," but also with a psychological fixation arising from his
wife's insanity, which had culminated in that country. "It
would be incorrect," MacCarthy concedes, "to ascribe to
Thackeray a clearly realized animosity to Ireland. No matter
what country might be concerned, Thackeray's ideas in the
political, religious, or sociological sphere were uniform only
in their confusion and consistent only in their inconsistency
. . . For independent thought he substitutes a set of clichés.
They are the clichés of his political, religious, and social background." One cannot help inferring that MacCarthy is an-

noyed because Thackeray did display "independent thought" on certain Irish problems but arrived at conclusions that do not confirm the clichés of MacCarthy's "political, religious, and social background."

Since Thackeray was essentially a social satirist, a persistent question concerns the theory of society that underlies his books. This is handled favorably though almost entirely negatively by Chauncey W. Wells in "Thackeray and the Victorian Compromise" (*University of California Publications in English*, I, 1929): "In his novels and minor writings there is but slight evidence of current politics; of the social movement not much more; of the spiritual ferment hardly a trace . . . This is not to say that Thackeray was indifferent to prevalent injustice — far from it; much of the poignancy of his writing is due to an uneasy social conscience; nor that he was indifferent to the proletariat . . . The Victorian Compromise as it laid a blight upon upper and middle class family life in the England of his maturity — this remained for Thackeray to show."

With a similar object in view, Robert S. Forsythe examined his political views in "Thackeray, Critic of His Times" (*University of North Dakota Quarterly Journal*, 1932), determining that "with some of the projects of his day Thackeray sympathized fully; others he opposed with all his might; still others he ignored virtually or wholly . . . Nominally in early and middle life, he was politically a Radical; in fact, he was nothing of the kind. The writer for the *Constitutional* was really as much a Liberal-Conservative as the candidate for parliament twenty years later." The same topics are included in a somewhat more general survey by John W. Dodds, "Thackeray in the Victorian Frame" (*Sewanee Review*, 1940). Dodds decides that "Thackeray is for the most part a supporter of policies rather than parties or even of men . . . In his attitude toward the proper function of the novelist Thackeray is both more and less than a typical Victorian, and here is seen something of his own divided mind. At times he seems to accept whole-heartedly the conventions of his age, and at other times to revolt helplessly against them."

A prominent element in Thackeray's social attitude was

his exaggerated concern over the attributes of a gentleman and his inveteracy toward snobs. A Bonn dissertation by Werner Behmenberg deals with *Der Snobbismus bei Thackeray* (Düsseldorf, 1933), and Margaret M. Goodell's Hamburg dissertation is on *Three Satirists of Snobbery: Thackeray, Meredith, Proust* (1939). A later Continental discussion is by Friederich Schübel, "Thackeray's Begriffe 'Gentleman' und 'Snob' " (*Festschrift für Walther Fischer*, Heidelberg, 1959). This problem is central also in one of the few studies devoted to any of the final novels, "Thackeray's Recantation," by Joseph E. Baker (*PMLA*, 1962). Oblivious to the complexity of Thackeray's irony, Baker works up to a high pitch of righteous indignation and querulous sarcasm over the snobbery, intolerance, and worldliness into which he believes that the novelist had lapsed by the time he wrote *The Adventures of Philip.*

The ambiguities of Thackeray's attitude can be observed with particular clarity in his portrayal of individual characters. Of these, of course, Becky Sharp is the most notorious, and Thackeray has incurred the accusation of becoming favorable toward his villain. It is remarkable that several of the critics who accept Becky as a sympathetic portrait are women. Catherine Beach Ely's amateurish and colloquial article "The Psychology of Becky Sharp" (*MLN*, 1920) defends Becky because, having "the artistic temperament . . . she did not understand in the least the pain she inflicted." A more persuasive assertion is by Mrs. Harold Sandwith, in "Becky Sharp and Emma Bovary: A Comparative Study" (*Nineteenth Century*, 1922): "As we close both *Vanity Fair* and *Madame Bovary* we involuntarily feel that here is the true life history of a woman, a history told without veil or varnish . . . Becky Sharp represents, we may almost say, a new type of woman — a woman until then not met with in fiction . . . Becky Sharp is the type of the complex, incomprehensible, mysterious woman, who is worse at once and better than her life." A similar view is expressed in "Enter Becky Sharp," a centennial article in *TLS*, 1947: "Mrs. Anna Jameson, who had decorously examined the characters of

Shakespeare's heroines, said with some loss of decorum — 'No woman resents Becky' . . . Audacious, indomitable Becky, with her flashes of mocking good will to dull virtue, her conscienceless, bright-plumed vitality! *Vanity Fair* must have lived immortally if only because she lived in it." The assumption of Becky's merit remained so endemic in modern critical studies of Thackeray that John E. Tilford, Jr., felt impelled to enter a protest with "The Degradation of Becky Sharp" (*SAQ*, 1959), in which he marshals the evidence that throughout the book Thackeray clearly indicated her viciousness.

A corollary to the problem of his depiction of Becky is that of Amelia, the ostensible heroine of the novel. In "A Note on Thackeray's Amelia" (*NCF*, 1955) Mark Spilka terms the portrayal "a dramatic fraud." She "is never vividly 'present' in her given role . . . We are given most of the facts about Amelia, but we are given them through strangely deceptive means . . . Thackeray's use of indirection was rooted in his own confusion, and it led to an unquestionable falsification of experience." Subsequently, however, the author's workmanship was defended by Myron Taube in "The Character of Amelia and the Meaning of *Vanity Fair*" (*VNL*, 1960), demonstrating that "while Amelia is a satiric comment on Victorian life and social mores, her character is more modern and complex than has hitherto been assumed."

The other character who has aroused most argument is Rachel Esmond. A judicious summary of the debate is given by Howard O. Brogan in "Rachel Esmond and the Dilemma of the Victorian Ideal of Womanhood" (*ELH*, 1946). His conclusion is that "with the waning of Victorian idealism the attitude of the critic shifts from outright moral disapproval of Rachel to discreet admiration of Thackeray's characterization of her . . . From one point of view she represents the Victorian ideal of womanhood . . . Where Thackeray departed from the ideal was in his clear-sighted perception that such virtues can easily be carried to excess. He saw into the heart of the dilemma, realizing that the intense concen-

tration upon domestic affections required by Victorian morality inevitably resulted in selfish possessiveness." The topic
was taken up by John E. Tilford, Jr., in two articles, "The
'Unsavory Plot' of *Henry Esmond*" (*NCF*, 1951) and "The
Love Theme of *Henry Esmond*" (*PMLA*, 1952), in which he
confirms Brogan's favorable opinion: "Those who are un-
hampered by presuppositions . . . will be rewarded by an
ironically perceptive interpretation of an uncommon human
relationship. They will also find one of the most provocative
and subtle portraits of a lady in nineteenth-century English
fiction." The discussion is carried further by William H.
Marshall in "Dramatic Irony in *Henry Esmond*" (*Revue
des langues vivantes,* 1961), his conclusion being that "in
order to exculpate himself [Esmond] suggests the sinfulness
(qualified, it is true, by the record of atonement) of a woman
who is otherwise pictured as lovable and explicitly described
as inspirational to him . . . If we do not read *Henry Esmond* completely within its structural frame, the memoirs
of an old man ordering his recollections so that they reveal
what is exemplary and in so doing trying to escape the trap
into which they necessarily lead him, the dilemma appears to
be merely an artistic flaw.'

More objective evidence can be offered in support of another sort of discussion relating to characterization — the
originals from whom the characters were derived. Thackeray
himself was unhappily aware that his powers of invention
were limited and that he drew his best material from his own
experience, and therefore scholars are not unjustified when
they search for his models, many of whom are to be found
in his own family. Lady Ritchie indicated some examples in
her introductions to the Biographical Edition. Among later
writers, Robert Sencourt offered a sketchy suggestion of
several originals in "Thackeray and his Anglo-Indians"
(*Hindustan Review*, 1923; reprinted in *Living Age*). Also
in the field of his Indian antecedents, P. R. Krishnaswami
contributed four articles on "Some Thackeray Originals" to
the *Cornhill Magazine*, 1927–1928, and reprinted these,
along with half-a-dozen others, as *In Thackeray's Workshop*,

1956. Family sources are suggested by Phillips George Davies for "the remarkable number of mulattoes and half-breeds which appear in Thackeray's novels and sketches, and his numerous references to miscegenation" ("The Miscegenation Theme in the Works of Thackeray," *MLN*, 1961). The fullest exploration among the family portraits was conducted by Gordon Ray in *The Buried Life*.

Originals outside the family circle have also been suggested. As a partial model for Becky Sharp, Lionel Stevenson proposed the Irish novelist Sydney Owenson, Lady Morgan ("*Vanity Fair* and Lady Morgan," *PMLA*, 1933). In *The Seamy Side* (1937) William Roughead pointed out resemblances between Becky and Mlle. Deluzy, a governess involved in a notorious scandal in the French household of the Duc de Praslin about the time the novel was written; and Violet Biddulph added confirmatory details in a letter to *TLS* (1938). Arthur Sherbo mentions Mary Cholmondeley, a sister of Peg Woffington, as a forerunner of Becky, and also nominates her grandnephew, the first Marquis of Cholmondeley, as model for Becky's husband ("A Suggestion for the Original of Thackeray's Rawdon Crawley," *NCF*, 1955). Resemblances between Becky and Mrs. Guy Flouncey in Disraeli's *Coningsby* are observed by D. J. Greene ("Becky Sharp and Lord Steyne — Thackeray or Disraeli," *NCF*, 1961).

Several short articles have pointed out originals for minor characters. Harold H. Scudder in "Thackeray and N. P. Willis" (*PMLA*, 1942) proposes the American journalist as the model for Paul John Jefferson Jones in *Vanity Fair*, and in "Thackeray and Sir Martin Archer Shee" (*PMLA*, 1946) identifies the President of the Royal Academy as the model for Mr. Smee in *Vanity Fair* and *The Newcomes*. Morchard Bishop's "Emily Fotheringay and Ellen Ternan" (*TLS*, 1956) suggests a model for the Irish actress in *Pendennis*.

For the same reason that Thackeray's novels of contemporary life drew so largely upon people he knew or read about, his historical fiction was based upon conscientious use of sources. The validity of his depiction of the Augustan

Age has been generally praised, though with qualification regarding his personal prejudices against certain individuals, notably Marlborough and Swift. In "Thackeray et la société anglaise du XVIIIe siècle" (*Revue anglo-américaine*, 1924) Marguerite Weill sets forth the deficiencies of *Henry Esmond* as a historical document: "We must recognize in him that the great constituted by far the most interesting group of the epoch. Nevertheless we may be surprised to find no trace of the political, philosophical, and religious transformations in England of that time. It is above all the underside of the history of the period of Anne and George II on which he insists . . . Certainly we find in him anachronisms, often intentional and due to the desire to condense into a narrow period the characteristics of the eighteenth century . . . Our author nevertheless inaugurated a genre: he painted society as a participant in the drama, which renders the representation of it as lively as authentic memoirs."

On the other hand, Jay B. Hubbell, an authority on Virginian literature, after examining the sources used for *The Virginians* ("Thackeray and Virginia," *VQR*, 1927), decided that "the picture of life in Virginia which Thackeray draws is surprisingly accurate . . . It seems clear that Thackeray took far more pains to make his picture of Virginia life accurate and vivid than anyone has supposed." And Colonel F. E. Whitton, writing on "Thackeray and the Army" (*Nineteenth Century*, 1931), exclaims: "Thackeray revelled in war, and he must certainly have made a close study of military history." The fullest study of his use of historical source material is Robert S. Forsythe's book *A Noble Rake* (1928), which narrates the life of Charles, fourth Lord Mohun, and compares it in detail with the fictional presentation in *Henry Esmond*.

There have been few special studies of Thackeray's literary technique. His addiction to making cross-references from one novel to another was discussed by W. A. Hirst in "The Chronology in Thackeray's Novels" (*Cornhill Magazine*, 1929). Hirst asserts that "one phase of this many-sided genius is his exquisite chronological accuracy . . . The dates of each character agree with those of his neighbours and ancestors, and, further, all the many historical events which occur in the novels are correct both in relation to themselves and the fictitious events." Nevertheless, Hirst cites a number of discrepancies, and John E. Tilford, Jr., adds a further instance in "The Untimely Death of Rachel Esmond" (*NCF*, 1957).

The most important article in this field is "Thackeray's Narrative Technique," by John A. Lester, Jr. (*PMLA*, 1954). Though admitting that "there are clear errors of chronology in all Thackeray's major novels," Lester is strongly favorable toward both his "handling of chronological sequence in the story and his variations in method between telling the story personally in his own words and presenting it dramatically in scenes . . . It soon proves futile to survey simply those two poles of author-presentation and dramatic enactment. A Thackeray novel displays not only the two poles but every shade and variety of narrative presentation in between . . . He invented an entire range of narrative devices."

"Time and Memory in Thackeray's *Henry Esmond*," by Henri-A. Talon (*RES*, 1962), is an interpretation of the narrative method based on the ideas of Bergson, Poulet, and Lukacs, including an effective contrast with Proust: "According to their temperament novelists see time as an inner dimension or an outer frame." Though there are a few good insights in the article, Talon tends to make fairly obvious features of the novel seem abstruse by his use of currently modish concepts. A less pretentious study, "The Unity of *Henry Esmond*," by George J. Worth (*NCF*, 1961), emphasizes that the whole novel is a deft and controlled interweaving of "the religious theme, the political theme, and the military theme" in the maturing of the central character. To the same issue of *NCF* John Hagan contributed "A Note on the Napoleonic Background of *Vanity Fair*," suggesting that Napoleon and his actions help to intensify the basic theme of the novel. The consensus of such articles is that Thackeray was aware of technical problems and solved them with unobtrusive skill.

Another aspect of Thackeray's technique has been dealt

with by G. Armour Craig, "On the Style of *Vanity Fair*" (*Style in Prose Fiction*, ed. Harold C. Martin, 1959). Stating that Trollope's praise of Thackeray's "lucidity" is true in only a superficial sense, and that the novelist's attitude of detachment is misleading, Craig explains: "The limits of this detachment — its very bankruptcy — can be shown only as we glimpse the howling wilderness outside, where the secrets of private feelings are violently confused with public forces of huge and mysterious dimensions, and where there is neither lucidity nor truth . . . To put us where we cannot know 'what *had* happened' and to face us with the bewildering irrelevance of our polite detachment, Thackeray was driven to an extreme that no style of his could control. He could not be clear without being untruthful, and he could not be truthful without being obscure." Hence Craig justifies Thackeray's omissions and ambiguities. "The narration here, clustered about with confidential comments and dismissive questions, sets before us a way of knowing the world. It is a way so inferential, so dependent upon unfinished implications, that it comes close to the character of gossip. And a good gossip, while its unfinished sentences and its discreet and indiscreet omissions may keep us from the exhilaration of indignation or rhapsody, can suggest values and insights superior to the vocabulary of the purveyor or the listener."

Discussion of Thackeray's methods of composition is likely to be facilitated by attention to what he said about other writers and about the writer's art. Edwin R. Clapp offered a rather general view of Thackeray's aesthetic pronouncements in "Critic on Horseback" (*Sewanee Review*, 1930), summing them up as "sober, flippant, prejudiced, kindly, in all shapes and guises, incredibly bad, extraordinarily good." The subject was pursued in greater detail by Philip Enzinger in the *University of North Dakota Quarterly Journal*, 1930–1931, in three articles on "Thackeray, Critic of Literature," a useful survey which is unhappily buried in a rather inaccessible periodical. Enzinger pays particular attention to Thackeray's views on prose fiction, and dwells upon "the essential unity of his opinions . . . To study Thackeray's criticism is to view the spectacle of a personality creeping into every corner of his product."

More extensive consideration has been given to some of the influences that may have shaped Thackeray's work, particularly those of the eighteenth-century novelists. The earliest important critical essay on Thackeray was Walter Bagehot's on "Sterne and Thackeray" in the *National Review* (1864), reprinted in Bagehot's *Literary Studies* (1879). Bagehot alleged "that there was one fundamental and ineradicable resemblance between the two. Thackeray, like Sterne, looked at everything — at nature, at life, at art — from a *sensitive* aspect. His mind was, to some considerable extent, like a woman's mind . . . Those who perceive that this irritable sensibility was the basis of Thackeray's artistic character . . . must have been vexed or amused . . . at the common criticism which associates him with Fielding. Fielding's essence was just the reverse; it was a bold spirit of bounding happiness." Another, but less important, early essay on the same subject was "Thackeray and Sterne," by William Mackay (*New Monthly Magazine*, 1869–1870), chiefly devoted to condemning Thackeray for the unfairness of his lecture on Sterne.

Contradicting Bagehot, Frederick S. Dickson, in "William Makepeace Thackeray and Henry Fielding" (*North American Review*, 1913), asserted roundly that "Thackeray owes more to [Fielding] than to any other person or thing, or to *all* other persons and things." A more scholarly consideration of the topic was undertaken by Eva Beach Touster, "The Literary Relationship of Thackeray and Fielding" (*JEGP*, 1947), her purpose being "to study Thackeray's views upon Fielding as shown by his theory and practice and to determine whether his practice in the novel is in accord with his judgment of Fielding's art." Mrs. Touster's conclusion is "that Thackeray's genuine admiration of Fielding as a painter of the manners and morals of his own day was tinctured by disapproval of that part of Fielding's character which he considered 'low' and which at times caused Fielding to violate the demands of art." The question was reopened in another article in *JEGP*, 1957, "Thackeray's Injustice to Fielding," by Ralph Wilson Rader, written in the light of the fuller biographical material that had become available. Rader declares that "sometime between 1840, when he wrote a review of Fielding's works for the *Times*, and 1851, when he lectured on the English Humourists, Thackeray had drastically revised his opinion of Fielding and his work . . . The feeling of personal guilt, which Thackeray developed after his wife's attempted suicide, accounts almost entirely for the much-altered attitude toward Fielding and his work . . . Thackeray's condemnation of Fielding is significant because it shows his consistently moral approach to literature to be a conscious or unconscious attempt to palliate a guilty conscience." E. D. H. Johnson's "*Vanity Fair* and *Amelia*: Thackeray in the Perspective of the Eighteenth Century" (*MP*, 1961) summarizes the resemblances and differences between the two novels.

Along with Fielding and Sterne, the literary influence most frequently studied is that of Balzac. Here again the earliest contribution goes back to the beginning. Abraham Hayward's review of *Vanity Fair* in the *Edinburgh Review* (1848), remarked that Balzac was Thackeray's only rival in understanding of feminine psychology. Philarète Chasles compared the two novelists in the *Revue des deux mondes* (1849), and Taine in 1867 pointed out the differences between them, as illustrated by the contrast between Becky Sharp and Valérie Marneffe. An anonymous essay on "The Style of Balzac and Thackeray" appeared in the *Dublin University Magazine* in 1864. *Entstehungsgeschichte von W. M. Thackeray's Vanity Fair* (1908), by Erwin Walter, accepts the influence of *La Cousine Bette* on Thackeray's novel, and suggests also a resemblance between César Birotteau and Barry Lyndon. The subject was resumed by Paul T. Lafleur, "Sainte-Beuve, Balzac, and Thackeray" (*MLR*, 1914). Lafleur points out a number of specific resemblances between *Henry Esmond* and *Le Lys dans la vallée* but hesitates to assert any influence because the general attitudes of the two novelists are so different and because Thackeray seldom mentions Balzac. Dissatisfied with this opinion, W. C. D. Pacey published an article on "Balzac and Thackeray" in the same journal in 1941, insisting that Thackeray refers to Balzac's books with casual familiarity, that his device of linking his tales by reintroducing known characters is indisputably from Balzac, and that the themes and characters in *Pendennis* and *The Newcomes* have many parallels in the French author's work.

E. Maitre, however, in "Balzac, Thackeray, et Charles de Bernard" (*Revue de littérature comparée*, 1950) argues that the critics who have not hesitated to make Thackeray a disciple of Balzac have been too much impressed by "strange coincidences, resemblances of detail, a certain parallelism of general effect"; the fact that the two authors deal with the same literary themes does not necessarily prove direct borrowing. "Other contemporary novelists were able to use them and to produce similar effects." Maitre decides that "Thackeray's hostility toward Balzac and toward his work, his ignorance of the great novels of *La Comédie humaine*, the dissimilarities of temperament and of works, finally the negative evidence provided by the publication of Thackeray's letters and private papers, incline us to believe rather in the combined effect of odd coincidences, of a certain simultaneity in the literary trends of the two countries, and of indirect influences." As the particular transmitter of influence Maitre proposes Charles de Bernard, "who occupies the paradoxical position of friend and disciple of Balzac and protégé of Thackeray, who first introduced him in England."

Maitre's thorough marshaling of evidence did not put an end to the controversy. "Balzac et Thackeray," by A. Carey Taylor (*Revue de littérature comparée*, 1960), marks a return to the position taken by Pacey. After having "demonstrated how much Thackeray's social diagnosis resembles Balzac's," he proceeds to inquire whether Thackeray's "new conception of the novel" owed anything to Balzac's influence. His conclusion is that "one can see how hard it is to *prove* that Thackeray had read more than two or three of Balzac's novels; but 'internal evidence' is not lacking, and numerous analogies have already been indicated in such-and-such novels of Thackeray and of Balzac."

There have been a few other scattered studies of literary antecedents. Edward P. Vandiver's "Thackeray and Shakespeare" (*Furman Studies*, 1951) shows that "a detailed analysis of the many Shakespearian references and criticisms in Thackeray's works indicates not only Thackeray's intimate acquaintance with Shakespeare's plays and his fondness for referring to them but also the Shakespearian situations, characters, and lines to which his mind most often reverted." With regard to the influence of Scott, both Andrew Lang and John Buchan believed that *Henry Esmond* was deeply indebted to *Woodstock*, though Saintsbury demurred. John Robert Moore, in "Scott and *Henry Esmond*" (*N&Q*, 1944), declares that "however much *Esmond* owed to the excellent plot of *Woodstock* . . . the central situation of Thackeray's story (which has no equivalent in *Woodstock*) was adapted from . . . *St. Ronan's Well*." Walter Kurrelmeyer pointed out a possible source for one of the early short stories, "Miss Shum's Husband," in "Thackeray and Friedrich von Heyden" (*MLN*, 1933). There is need for a more sustained and coherent investigation of Thackeray's literary ancestry.

It is clear also that much of the research on Thackeray has concentrated on only two novels, *Vanity Fair* and *Henry Esmond*. There is room for fuller criticism of the three other major novels and the fiction of his last years, and also for studies of his work in the short story, the essay, and other forms. A pioneer analysis of his early work was *Thackeray's Literary Apprenticeship* (1934), by Harold S. Gulliver, which is still of some value, though Gordon Ray's research has since added many items to the canon. John W. Dodds, in "Thackeray as a Satirist Previous to *Vanity Fair*" (*MLQ*, 1941), makes "an attempt to identify the quality and indicate something of the evolution of Thackeray's early satire." Otherwise, the only discussion of Thackeray's early writings is to be found in Ray's biography and in the general critical studies, particularly Saintsbury's and Ennis'.

Another desideratum is a good history of Thackeray's reputation. The sole published contribution covers a limited area, "American Criticism of Thackeray, 1848–1855," by Richard C. Tobias (*NCF*, 1953), which sought "to determine if there was a shift in the appreciation of Thackeray as a result of his first American lecture tour in 1852–53." In view of the acrimonious differences of opinion that have been expressed ever since the publication of *Vanity Fair,* a thorough survey of the whole debate would be not only helpful to students of Thackeray but also revealing as to critical trends and factions for more than a century.

Fuller study might well be given to the notion of Trollope and Tillotson that Thackeray did more than any other Victorian novelist to promote the cause of realism. Most necessary of all, however, is a perceptive analysis of Thackeray's multiple levels of irony, his double perspective and his elusive changes of tone, with all their implications about the relativity of truth.

5 ℬ≈

Anthony Trollope

Donald Smalley

F EW NOVELISTS appear, on the face of things, to
have written so plainly as Anthony Trollope, with so little
hint of anything intricate below the surface; few seem so
willing as the story goes along to share with the reader all
their confidences. In his *Autobiography*, too, Trollope seems
eager to show how really simple and routine the whole process
of making novels has been for him. It comes as something unexpected, then, to discover that scholars and critics have
found Trollope among the most difficult of Victorian novelists to explain and categorize. "Trollope's quality," wrote
Michael Sadleir, "remains intangible, baffles resolution."
How could one explain the mysterious potency and charm
of work "so featureless, so sober and so undemonstrative"?
At the close of the final chapter of his biography — after what
probably remains the best discussion of the subject to date —
Sadleir continues tentative, divided between calling the
manner of *Doctor Thorne* and the quite different manner
of *The Way We Live Now* Trollope's finest achievement.

No one since has come close to a statement of Trollope's
special quality and manner or to an estimate of his permanent rank in English fiction that has won anything like
general consent. Opinions expressed in responsible places
and by reputable critics have shown a remarkable lack of
agreement. In recent years Trollope has been pronounced

a significant artist and he has also been dismissed as a "minor writer" — a simple craftsman and no artist at all. Trollope's novels have been put aside as the "sedative of gossip" and, in other quarters, praised as vehicles for some of the subtlest character portrayal and most delicate handling of the nuances of dialogue in English. Trollope's manner of intruding his observations as author into the story he is telling has been condemned as the worst of blunders; it has also been pointed out as a sophisticated device nicely calculated for sustaining an ironic balance essential to his art. "But in truth I find it difficult to judge Trollope's novels by any ordinary standards or accepted rules," Chauncey Brewster Tinker writes in his preface to *The Duke's Children* (1954). And Bradford A. Booth aptly entitles the concluding chapter of his *Anthony Trollope: Aspects of His Life and Art* (1958) "The Chaos of [Trollope] Criticism."

In his life as in his writings, Trollope seems, for all his pretensions to simplicity in the *Autobiography* and elsewhere, to pose special problems that defy easy resolution. Sadleir's portrait of Trollope remains in its essentials the dominant view, especially since Booth's careful consideration and rejection of recent attempts to read into this writer a bitterer, more disturbed, more "profound" personality than is apparent in his memoirs or in his letters. The argument is likely to go on. It can be held (and recently has been) that Trollope the artist reveals himself only in his novels, showing to society, like the ambivalent character in James's *The Private Life*, only a public self that did not really matter.

In special studies of Trollope's writings — studies of his command of Latin or law or politics, for example — there is wider agreement, though in regard to his view of society there is very nearly as much disagreement as there is upon the degree and quality of his genius. Trollope has been blamed for lacking a coherent view of society and he has been commended for having one. Conflicting appraisals of his intent in particular novels have also flourished of late.

If, however, there is something like chaos in Trollope studies, rather than anything close to general agreement, it is a chaos not of inertia but of colliding forces; and it is strong evidence that the work of this prolific author, pronounced dead or dying at the end of the last century, is very much alive.

I. *Bibliography and Letters*

In bibliography the student of Trollope faces alternate feast and near famine. Michael Sadleir's *Trollope: A Bibliography* (1928) was frankly intended to be a volume so thorough in its method as to serve as a history of Victorian bookmaking in miniature: "Just as Trollope the man serves to illustrate the psychology of his period," Sadleir states in his preface, "so Trollope the maker of books may serve to illustrate the methods of book-writing, book-producing and book-distributing which were in vogue between . . . 1850 and 1880." Employing Trollope as his selected specimen, Sadleir traces the publishing history of this author with such completeness that the work continues a byword for excellence in the field of author bibliography. There is, however, no remotely comparable aid for the following of scholarship and criticism. Mary Leslie Irwin's *Anthony Trollope: A Bibliography* (1926), with its sections for portraits, photographs, maps, autographs, and so forth, is indiscriminate and overfull. Nevertheless Miss Irwin's book is helpful through the first quarter of this century, and especially so for her extensive listing of early book reviews. From 1945 onward the *Trollopian* and its successor *Nineteenth-Century Fiction* provide guidance both in reviews and in a helpful running column of comment on current books.

Morris L. Parrish's great Trollope collection is described by Carroll A. Wilson and Bradford A. Booth in articles in the first issue of the *Trollopian* (1945). Another valuable service of the *Trollopian* was a listing in September 1946 of the current location of twenty-nine Trollope manuscripts. Additions appeared in the issues of 1947–1948. Unfortunately, the manuscripts of the early novels continue missing; but the record from *Framley Parsonage* (1860) is relatively complete. A useful bibliography of Trollope criticism is appended to Rafael Helling, *A Century of Trollope Criticism* (Helsingfors, 1956). The Stebbins biography (discussed below) offers chapter-by-chapter listing of source material in lieu of a bibliography.

An invaluable aid in the study of Trollope, especially for its remarkably thorough indexing and identification of characters and place names in the novels, is Winifred Gregory Gerould and Jane Thayer Gerould's *A Guide to Trollope* (1948).

Publication of Bradford A. Booth's edition of *The Letters of Anthony Trollope* in 1951 was an event of prime importance. Of the 923 letters, 750 had been previously unpublished and many of these were little known. The letters go far to invalidate the strangely hostile sketch of Trollope presented by the Stebbinses; they corroborate and fill in valuably the general portrait of Trollope to be seen in the *Autobiography* and in Michael Sadleir's *Commentary*. Though Sadleir in the *Spectator* (Aug. 24, 1951), amid his praises for the best of the letters and the quality of Booth's editing, felt constrained to enter a complaint against the inclusion of occasional dull letters that affected him like the "monotony of water dripping from a tap," few serious students will be inclined to wish the collection less inclusive than it is. Letters of interest written by other members of the Trollope family can be found in Frances Eleanor Trollope, *Frances Trollope* (1894); A. G. K. L'Estrange, *The Friendships of Mary Russell Mitford* (1882); Thomas Adolphus Trollope, *What I Remember* (1888); and Robert H. Taylor, "The Trollopes Write to Bentley" (*Trollopian*, 1947).

II. *Editions*

Since, as Chauncey Brewster Tinker once pointed out, Trollope wrote more novels (forty-seven) than the combined output of Dickens, Thackeray, and George Eliot, it is not surprising that a complete edition of his work has never been published. The Barsetshire Novels, edited by Michael Sadleir, appeared in the attractive Shakespeare Head Edition in 1929. The Political Novels, edited by Michael Sadleir and Frederick Page, are available in the Crown Edition (1948–1954). Thirty of the novels, including both the Barsetshire and the Political Novels as well as nearly all works that are awarded one or more asterisks in Sadleir's lists at the back of his *Commentary,* are available in the Oxford University Press's World's Classics series. Notable exceptions are *Sir Harry Hotspur of Humblethwaite* and *Mr. Scarborough's Family.*

Surprisingly, in view of the extensive Trollope revival, two recent efforts to bring out collected editions have proved abortive. An American Trollope Society planned a series of handsome volumes but the only two which appeared before the war put an end to the project were *The Kellys and the O'Kellys,* with an introduction by Shane Leslie (1937), and *The American Senator,* with an introduction by Henry S. Drinker and a prolegomenon by A. Edward Newton (1940).

Subsequently, the Oxford Illustrated Trollope was begun under the editorship of Michael Sadleir and Frederick Page. Eight of the novels appeared, with appreciative introductions by such authorities as Sadleir, Sir Shane Leslie, Sir Edward Marsh, R. W. Chapman, R. A. Knox, and L. S. Amery; but in spite of such distinguished auspices the sales were so discouraging that the undertaking was abandoned, and the volumes are now falling out of print.

Trollope was extremely casual with proof, and the printed text, as R. W. Chapman has industriously pointed out in the *Trollopian* (1945), *NCF* (1949), and elsewhere, occasionally suffers for the author's carelessness. A full edition of Trollope's novels, brought into line with the existing manuscripts, is a long-term desideratum. Meanwhile Frederick Page has anticipated the event in his edition of *An Autobiography* (1950). Comparing the first edition, published posthumously in 1883, with the manuscript in the British Museum, Page found 544 errata, including serious misreadings and omissions.

Many of Trollope's multitudinous nonfictional writings

have been published in one form or another in the last four decades. In 1923 there was issued for the first time, with a notable foreword by Michael Sadleir, Trollope's *The Noble Jilt*, a play he had composed in 1850 that clearly anticipates the plot and characters of his novel *Can You Forgive Her?* Trollope's *North America* appeared for the first time in this century in 1951, edited with full introduction, annotation, and appendixes by Donald Smalley and Bradford A. Booth. A volume with significance for students of Anthony Trollope though not part of the canon, Frances Trollope's *Domestic Manners of the Americans,* edited by Donald Smalley with an introductory history of her life in America, full annotation, and appendixes, including many passages from Mrs. Trollope's notebooks and rough draft, was published in 1949 and reissued as a paperback in 1960.

In addition, several collections of Anthony Trollope's speeches and scattered contributions to the press have appeared. *London Tradesmen* (1927 and 1928), with an introduction by Michael Sadleir, contains a series of sketches written in 1880 for the *Pall Mall Gazette. Four Lectures*, edited by Morris L. Parrish (1938), reprints "The Present Condition of the Northern States" (Trollope predicts that the Union will never be restored), "The Civil Service as a Profession," "Higher Education for Women," and — most generally interesting of the four — "On English Prose Fiction as a Rational Amusement." *The Tireless Traveller,* edited by Bradford A. Booth (1941), reproduces twenty lengthy letters Trollope sent back during 1875 for the *Liverpool Mercury* describing his observations in Ceylon and Australia. The much admired *Hunting Sketches,* originally collected from the *Pall Mall Gazette* in 1865, have been republished several times in recent years.

Additional uncollected writings and various speeches appear dispersed through the numbers of the *Trollopian* and *NCF.* Notable among these are several articles presenting Trollope's marginal and flyleaf notations upon his reading in a variety of works ranging from Bacon's essays and the *Arcadia* through Jane Austen's *Emma* and Scott's novels up to Owen Meredith's poem *The Wanderer* and Froude's *Caesar*.

III. *Biography*

There is general agreement that Michael Sadleir's *Trollope: A Commentary* (1945) remains the best biography — this despite the fact that the revised edition is essentially the book Sadleir had first published in 1927. Certainly accounts that deviate from Sadleir's reading of Trollope's personality by probing for dark and sinister labyrinths behind the bluff façade have not proved very fortunate. Sadleir's masterful chapter "The Portrait of Anthony," based upon Trollope's self-portrait in the *Autobiography* but profoundly enhancing and modifying it, is likely to continue our best single means of seeing Trollope plain. For insight, tact, and judgment Sadleir's work as a whole remains indispensable. If one can hope that eventually still another, more inclusive biography will be written, the reason is that subsequent biographical scholarship (a phrase to make Sadleir shudder), though it has not greatly altered the outlines of Sadleir's portrait, has filled in a good deal since 1927; and Trollope criticism has also expanded profitably since that time.

In 1945 the American novelist Lucy Poate Stebbins and her historian son, Richard Poate Stebbins, published *The Trollopes: The Chronicle of a Writing Family.* This is an exciting book, and in the popular press it was widely hailed as a brilliant biography. From the scholar's view also the work is worth careful assessment. Making use of materials unearthed in the two decades since the first appearance of Sadleir's *Commentary* and adding impressively on its own part to the store, this volume presents a fuller account of many aspects of Trollope's career than Sadleir was able to provide in 1927 or had been inclined to provide, in line with his frank distaste for anything that could be called "Trollopian Studies" (*Spectator*, Aug. 24, 1951), in his second edition.

The work of the Stebbinses is especially valuable for its full and sympathetic account of Anthony's mother, Frances

Trollope, and of his writing brother, Thomas Adolphus Trollope. Unfortunately this book, with all its positive virtues, is marred by the authors' merging of the method of responsible biography as it is generally thought of with the method of fiction. With much resort to the more familiar patterns of Freudian analysis, they manage to weave about the person of Anthony a texture of familial tensions and conflicts that often seems a good deal more highly colored than a less creative view of the evidence would permit. It is no very drastic simplification to say that Anthony is here portrayed as the bad son who resents and competes with his novelist mother (after an earlier spell invested in hating his father). The elder brother Thomas Adolphus becomes by contrast (and this at least is not so far from an impartial view) the good and dutiful son who understands and waits in faithful attendance upon her. Anthony by degrees grows into a petty and cynical materialist who chooses to betray his artistic conscience by writing whatever will sell best and most. In the end he is paid for his sins by an embittered old age in which he entertains long thoughts of terminating it all in suicide. As the Stebbinses manage to see it, Trollope's *Autobiography*, written in his last years and designed to be published posthumously, represents a patent revelation of his "sad story," his polemical defense of a mean-minded and unhappy life. He had missed the good things life offers: "He had no pleasure in life except work, hunting, whist, and the society of his men friends." Here and often elsewhere in the book, one is fairly sure he is viewing a particularly feminine interpretation of a definitely masculine personality.

The deficiencies of the Stebbinses' biography are perhaps less important, once they are taken into account, than the considerable values. The amount of fresh factual material affords a useful supplement to Sadleir's work. The Stebbinses provide detailed chapter-by-chapter notation of their source materials and an elaborate genealogical chart.

Though both Sadleir and the Stebbinses draw upon them, two earlier accounts are still worth reading at first hand for their authors' personal acquaintance with the novelist. T. H.

S. Escott's *Anthony Trollope: His Work, Associates and Literary Originals* (1913) is frequently inaccurate in point of fact but contains a store of reminiscence from several years of friendship with Trollope and a good deal of information obtained from other of his surviving friends. Julian Hawthorne's chapter on Trollope in his *Confessions and Criticisms* (1887) presents a brilliant characterization of Anthony as he appeared in 1879.

A few biographical articles that have appeared since 1945 are worth mentioning. Bradford A. Booth in the *Trollopian* (1947) recounts further particulars of Trollope's quarrel with Charles Reade. Trollope's granddaughter Muriel Rose Trollope in the *Trollopian* (1948) provides fresh personal anecdotes. Drawing upon local newspapers and upon official documents, Lance O. Tingay in "Trollope and the Beverley Election" (*NCF*, 1950) fills in much detail of Trollope's frustrated effort to win a seat in Parliament. In the same journal in 1951 Tingay quotes a half-dozen reviews of Trollope's first novel, *The Macdermots of Ballycloran* (1847), which Trollope had remembered as having failed of any critical notice whatsoever. Though it is primarily a work of criticism, there is a good deal of well-documented evaluation of Trollope's personality and life in Booth's *Anthony Trollope: Aspects of His Life and Art* (1958).

Those who wish to follow out the history of Frances Trollope as fully as they can will find Frances Eleanor Trollope's *Frances Trollope* (1894) still of value; and Thomas Adolphus Trollope's *What I Remember* (1888) continues useful. Much fresh material upon Frances Trollope's life in the United States will be found in the introduction and notes of her *Domestic Manners of the Americans,* edited by Donald Smalley (1949).

IV. *General Criticism*

Though Trollope's special qualities, as was remarked at the outset of this chapter, continue to elude precise definition, there has been no dearth of attempts at defining them.

Nearly everyone who deals with a larger view of the Victorian novel has felt called upon to consider Trollope, if only, like F. R. Leavis, to deny that he is worth serious attention. From the many critical studies it is not easy to decide upon the items that, within a limited space, most require comment. It is unlikely that another student of Trollope would come up with identical decisions, and the best that can be urged for what follows is that it has some claims to reasonableness. A few of the older works are included mainly because they appear on lists of recommended readings and call for cursory description and assessment on that score.

If we are to proceed chronologically, the first choice, at least, is not hard to make. After seven decades Henry James's extended critical essay, first printed in the *Century* in 1883, a year after Trollope's death, and later collected in James's *Partial Portraits* (1888), remains very much alive. Although reviews of Trollope's novels written by James in earlier years had been supercilious, as a mature critic he is able to take a longer and broader view. Trollope's unconcern with the problems of technique, it is true, he views as regrettable, and Trollope's habit of intruding his own observations into the story he is telling, James feels, is nothing short of suicidal. James is acutely conscious of what he considers Trollope's faults, but — what is less often pointed out — he is at least equally conscious of Trollope's special virtues, and this at a time when Trollope's reputation was at its nadir. James's ambiguous praise of Trollope for his "complete appreciation of the usual" is often quoted. Another of his judgments is seldom mentioned: "In spite of his want of doctrinal richness I think that [Trollope] tells us, on the whole, more about life than the 'naturalists' in our sister republic . . . his perception of character was more just and more liberal than that of the naturalists." When one remembers that "telling about life" is a phrase with rich implications in James's critical writings, this becomes a statement worth reflecting upon. If the essay seems full of insights but curiously ambiguous in its final assessment of Trollope's attainments, the reason may well be that, like later critics, James found Trollope elusive when he tried to measure him by set rules. There was much that, on theory, should be bad in Trollope which actually had the sort of life that baffled classification. The essay is conveniently available in *The Future of the Novel,* a collection of James's essays on the art of fiction edited by Leon Edel (1956).

Another early essay, narrower in scope but fresh in point of view, should also be mentioned. Apparently composed, perhaps as a lecture, not long after 1906, W. P. Ker's "Anthony Trollope" may have first reached print only in the posthumous *On Modern Literature: Lectures and Addresses,* edited by Terence Spencer and James Sutherland (1955). The piece represents an early and discerning attempt to show Trollope, despite his modest disclaimers in the *Autobiography* and elsewhere, as an abler and subtler writer than the *fin de siècle* critics had been willing to suppose. Ker argues that Trollope's fiction is controlled by the author's well-considered theory of realism. The purpose is "allusion to real life" rather than anything closer to an attempt at reproducing real life on the page. Trollope's essential method, Ker maintains, is the method of comedy and entails comedy's reticences and objectivity. *The Last Chronicle of Barset,* the "best of Trollope's novels," could easily have gone the road of tragedy; but if Trollope had abandoned comic detachment for the "concentration of tragedy" he would have ended with a shallower and a poorer novel.

George Saintsbury's two studies of Trollope, the first in his *Corrected Impressions* (1895) and the second in *Essays and Studies by Members of the English Association* (1920), seem mainly noteworthy as convenient and dramatic representations of attitudes toward Trollope in two points of time a quarter of a century apart. In 1895, in the spirit of the nineties and conscious of Trollope's descriptions of his journeywork methods in the *Autobiography,* Saintsbury holds that though Trollope might once have seemed durable, it is now clear that he will not live. He is "doomed to pass — with everything that is of the day and the craftsman, not of eternity and art." Twenty-five years and a world war later,

Saintsbury has reread Trollope and has become convinced that he will remain one of the permanently significant novelists of the nineteenth century, a faithful recorder of his society and a satisfying means of insight into another age. Michael Sadleir was later to elaborate this theme in presenting Trollope in his *Commentary* as "the voice of an epoch."

The value of Spencer Van Bokkelen Nichols' little book *The Significance of Anthony Trollope* (1925), frequently recommended in Trollope reading lists, seems chiefly historical or recreational. It contains a general essay that is still pleasant if low-paced reading and an attractive map of Barsetshire, together with several pages of gloss. Readers who wish not so much to cope with Trollope as simply to enjoy him will find that the work successfully conveys Mr. Nichols' own frank pleasure in his author.

Though primarily a biography Michael Sadleir's *Trollope: A Commentary,* originally published in 1927, is also a critical study of major importance, and especially so for Sadleir's final chapter entitled "The Books." Though Sadleir finds the essence of Trollope's special quality ultimately elusive, he feels that it probably rests in Trollope's "acceptance and his profound understanding of ordinary life." Trollope is "the supreme novelist of acquiescence." He gives us the "illusion of ordinary life." *Doctor Thorne,* Sadleir feels, is Trollope's best exemplar of these virtues and his best novel. And yet Sadleir has an uneasy sense that Trollope's essential quality still evades him. He concludes his chapter with an admiring account of *The Way We Live Now* — that "sour and pitiless picture of a sordid scene" — and a question whether this may not, after all, be Trollope's greatest novel. If so, one would judge, "acquiescence" and "the illusion of ordinary life" are not terms that could well take care of all the attributes of Trollope's special power as a novelist. In the last sentence Sadleir grants the palm to *Doctor Thorne*; but it seems clear that he observed more in Trollope's novels than he could readily explain or easily codify.

Though in considerable part it travels ground already covered (and more brilliantly) in his *Commentary,* Sadleir's introduction to the Shakespeare Head Edition of the Barsetshire Series (1929), later reprinted in his collection of essays entitled *Things Past* (1944), contains a more thoroughgoing discussion of the world of Barsetshire, Trollope's treatment of clerics, and Trollope's religious opinions.

If the last-named essay has a hint of the perfunctory rather than the inspired about it, this tone is far stronger in Hugh Walpole's *Anthony Trollope* (1928), prepared for the English Men of Letters series. The book is unreliable in detail and less than stimulating in many of its discussions. A novelist cannot very well treat another novelist without moments of special understanding, however, and in presenting the attractions of *Rachel Ray,* a much-neglected classic of the comedy of manners, and its likeness to the temper and spirit of Jane Austen, Walpole is good reading. Of greater significance is Paul Elmer More's chapter on Trollope in *The Demon of the Absolute* (1929), especially for More's eloquent protest against Sadleir's playing down of the ethical element in the novels of Trollope. As a humanist More argues cogently for the vitality of moral purpose in Trollope's fiction.

Although the appearance of Sadleir's *Commentary* in 1927 is sometimes considered to mark a turning point, after which critics took Trollope more seriously than he had been taken earlier, two influential surveys of the Victorian novel published in the 1930's, though they discuss his work at length, persist in viewing the author as a relatively simple craftsman with a flair for creating delightful but essentially shallow and uncomplicated characters. His great quality as David Cecil interprets him in a chapter of *Early Victorian Novelists* (1935) is his humor. Cecil has penetrating things to say upon Trollope's absorption in the social order and the ability of the novels to evoke the Victorian social scene. In spite of his high praise for the "legacy of enjoyment" that Trollope has left us, however, the final effect of the essay is to place Trollope among the minor novelists of the period — weak in imagination, commonplace in point of view, and possessed of a style that is really no style at all. Ernest Baker, in *The History of the English Novel* (VIII, 1937), finds in

Trollope a sort of Rip Van Winkle among Victorian novelists: "He did not alter the fabric or change the content . . . he might have been a survivor of the eighteenth century." And again Trollope's virtues consist in his faithfully mirroring the social life of his day. "Though he had not the vision essential to great creative art, in the sphere marked out by his superlative craftsmanship this degree of artlessness was a positive asset."

Trollope's affinities with the eighteenth century are elaborated along other lines by C. J. Vincent in "Trollope: a Victorian Augustan" (*Queen's Quarterly*, 1945). Vincent feels that though Trollope wrote about the mid-Victorian era, the values that sustain his characters are essentially those of a "calmer, more peaceful world," a world that had survived fairly well in the rural south of England, remote from the industrial and commercial centers, since the eighteenth century. This is a modest and low-keyed essay, but valuable for its fresh view of Trollope's world.

By 1945 Trollope's remarkable popularity during the war years challenged explanation. Elizabeth Bowen's sensitive *Anthony Trollope: a New Judgment,* published as a booklet in 1946, after being presented as a radio broadcast, is cast in the form of a playlet. A young soldier on his way to the front talks first with his Edwardian uncle (who cannot abide Trollope) and then with the apparition of Anthony himself mulling the tantalizing question of why this mid-Victorian author exerts a peculiar attraction for a war-torn generation. The young soldier feels the answer may be that Trollope's men and women are stronger than circumstances: they make decisions; they offer a support for him against the "sort of *hopelessness*" that pervades his own time and generation. He wants to believe in people, and "in their power to live." In Trollope he has found ordinary people, neither heroes nor monsters. "And you see, we long for what's ordinary." Trollope's ghost takes up the statement: Trollope, too, had "yearned for the ordinary, like a lover," and had made of it his dream world, thrust out of it by the shabby finances of his family even as the young man of 1945 had been forced to view it from the outside by the circumstances of war. Had this golden world of the ordinary ever really existed as more than Trollope's own wistful "mirage-illusion"? The reader is left with the question.

The widespread enthusiasm for Trollope both in England and the United States did not, however, end with the war; and critical comment upon Trollope, much of it of only ephemeral value, became commonplace in the newspapers and periodicals of the time. Three essays from the periodicals of 1947 seem worth special comment. W. L. Burn in "Surtees and Trollope" (*Blackwood's*) makes profitable distinctions between the two novelists, both of them enjoying a new popularity with the public, showing how much deeper Trollope goes into the thoughts and feelings of his characters than does Surtees. In the same year D. M. Alexander in the *Trollopian* writes intelligently upon "Trollope's Cosmopolitanism," giving evidence for considering Trollope in a profound sense a citizen of the world though the Stebbinses had classified him in their biography as an insular Englishman who refused to learn from his travels.

The most impressive critical essay of 1947, however, is Chauncey Brewster Tinker's "Trollope" in the *Yale Review*. Trollope's intrusion of his own observations as author upon the characters and situations he is in process of developing — a practice which James in 1883 had considered nearly unforgivable and other critics since had often considered merely naïve or blundering — is not only defended by Tinker but presented as one of the chief attractions of Trollope's novels. This device enables us to associate with Trollope himself, "a man worldly-wise, yet kindly and, above all, fair minded." Trollope's own voice, impartial, untroubled, provides us with a sort of chorus for the action he sets before us, a humane commentary, charitable and broad-minded; "it is a privilege to be with him." The essay reappears in Tinker's *Essays in Retrospect* (1948).

If Beatrice Curtis Brown's *Anthony Trollope* in the English Novelists series (1950) is not one of the most exciting studies of this author, it is one of the most earnest and most admiring. Miss Brown finds Trollope remarkable for the "adultness" of his view: "He had an adult concern for and with the activities which exercise adult minds." Trollope saw life steadily and always with an eye to proper proportion. His was a peculiarly English mind. Miss Brown, indeed, seems to find in him something of a father figure for the nation: "Throughout the generations, English readers hearing Trollope's own voice in his writings will say, 'that was like my father.'" The style is on the heavy side, and one wonders whether Miss Brown, for all her sincere effort to catch the essential writer, has not missed some of Trollope's most important qualities, his finely developed sense of comedy among them. It is only fair to add that a number of serious reviewers have apparently found the book, despite its egregious errors in factual detail, a good deal more rewarding than I have found it.

Joseph E. Baker's essay "Trollope's Third Dimension" (*College English*, 1954) though brief, warrants special attention. It is notable for speaking unabashedly of Trollope's "great art" and his "richness and complexity." These are terms that do not sort well with the traditional view of Trollope (including, with some important qualification, James's and Sadleir's) as an honest and conscientious or even a superbly gifted craftsman, a faithful recorder of an epoch in social history, a tolerant or fatherly companion, but a writer lacking the complexity or high style or profundity of insight that would entitle him to be called an artist. However, Baker supports his judgment by a suggestive series of examples demonstrating how Trollope "enables us to understand . . . more about a social situation than he has yet put into words." By means of a peculiarly deft management of detail and action, Baker maintains, Trollope contrives to make us participants in the "excitement of a whole social group." Baker feels that it is only in the novels themselves that Trollope the subtle and resourceful artist can be observed. "It is almost as if this great novelist's *letters* were written by his business manager."

If a case can be made for holding that Sadleir and others

read too much of the biographical record into the art of the novels themselves, thereby finding a simpler writer than the novels judged alone might reveal, A. O. J. Cockshut in *Anthony Trollope: A Critical Study* (1955) may perhaps be indicted conversely for reading too much from what he finds in the later novels of Trollope back into the personal experience of the author. As Cockshut sees him, Trollope was a "gloomier, more introspective, more satirical, and more profound writer" than has generally been supposed. Indeed Trollope was, it develops, a sort of robust, middle-class Hamlet, who doubted his vitality so much that "he had to be proving it every hour of the day" by hunting, traveling about the world, arguing down his fellow members at his club, or writing. Trollope's zest for writing so much and so steadily is offered as a sign of something especially unhealthy in him; and the fact that after such labors Trollope could sleep nine solid hours without stirring, and prided himself on doing so, is presented as evidence that Trollope did not enjoy his waking hours. The shadow of the Stebbins biography hangs large over this volume. Nevertheless, Cockshut has read the novels thoroughly and with affection, and there is much in the later chapters, especially the stimulating analyses of *The Way We Live Now* and *Dr. Wortle's School,* that is worth reading.

In 1958 appeared what has been judged by fairly general agreement the most valuable book-length study of Trollope since Sadleir's *Commentary* in 1927. Bradford Allen Booth's *Anthony Trollope: Aspects of His Life and Art* carries the authority of this scholar's many years of intimacy with the novelist in the process of editing Trollope's letters and other of his writings and conducting the editorship of the *Trollopian* and *NCF.* Half of Booth's book is devoted to a thoroughgoing examination of Trollope's world — the scenes Trollope chooses and the affirmations and prejudices that underlie Trollope's treatment of them. The portrait that emerges is very like Sadleir's, though Booth, drawing upon three subsequent decades of scholarship and criticism, supplies us with much new detail and provides a fuller analysis of several of the novels. In the second half of his book Booth undertakes to assess, in terms of the highest attainments of the novel, what can be considered of lasting significance in the novels of Trollope. The attendant search through the Trollope canon is an intensive one and represents the most informative tour of that country on record. Booth proves, however, despite his obvious personal enthusiasm for Trollope, to be a rigorous guide, and his ultimate judgments are perhaps somewhat austere. Even in *The Last Chronicle*, which he considers Trollope's best novel, the author "falls short of the highest distinctions of art through faults of organization and taste." In the final analysis Trollope was "not a man of transcendent genius but of extraordinary talent." Booth's emphasis throughout is upon the long and judicious perspective. Though he has pointed things to say of the Stebbinses, Cockshut, and the *Scrutiny* critics, the tone is in general measured rather than polemic. His book affords carefully weighed judgments, a satisfying amount of mature informed insight into aspects of the novels, and a convincing and attractive view of the novelist as his contemporaries saw him.

In the same year — 1958 — there also appeared two significant essays on Trollope in the collection of critical studies entitled *From Jane Austen to Joseph Conrad*, edited by Robbert C. Rathburn and Martin Steinmann, Jr. Bradford Booth's essay *"Orley Farm*: Artistry *Manqué"* offers an analysis of *Orley Farm* and a comparison of this novel with *The Last Chronicle of Barset*. Though these are, in Booth's judgment, the two best novels of Trollope, each possesses a flaw that keeps it out of the highest company. The essay supplements Booth's treatment of the two novels in his own book. Arthur Mizener's "Anthony Trollope: the Palliser Novels" represents a striking divergence from orthodox views of Trollope in the same direction that Joseph E. Baker had taken briefly in his essay of 1954. Mizener, like Baker, feels that there is in Trollope a "kind of greatness" obscured by the fact that his weaknesses are of the very sort to lay him open to derogation when assessed in terms of the critical tenets now most in vogue. Trollope had "little interest in

the delicate cabinet-making which fascinates artificers of
the well-made novel." Trollope's own disclaimers of any
great pretensions to distinction have, Mizener feels, unduly
influenced our judgments of him. The fact is that Trollope
misled himself and others because "in those respects in which
he was a great novelist he was so easily and naturally one and
did so much of the work of the imagination when he was not
at his writing desk." In a penetrating analysis of the Political,
or Palliser, Novels Mizener illustrates what he means.
"Irony," "delicacy in ironic balance," are key terms in this
subtle study of Trollope's best manner. Mizener finds the intrusion of the author into his story a vital aspect of Trollope's
method. Like Jane Austen, Trollope is a master of the device.
This is an exciting essay, and it is perhaps ungrateful to ask
for a balanced appraisal within its limits. It is certain, however, that whereas Trollope could employ the novelist's intrusion for felicitous effects, as Mizener brilliantly points out,
he could also use it for less fortunate effects, or even (see
Booth's chapter V) for nearly incredible lapses.

One of the notable foreign doctoral dissertations upon English literature in recent years both in style and substance,
Rafael Helling's monograph *A Century of Trollope Criticism*
(Helsingfors, 1956) provides an ambitious history of criticism
of Trollope from the early periodical reviews to 1955. Covering much of the same territory though from a somewhat different perspective, I have found Helling's survey laudably
careful in its facts and responsible in its judgments. This is
a useful and informative work.

Elizabeth Bowen in her excellent introduction to *Doctor
Thorne* (1959), an extended essay that goes well beyond the
problems of the immediate novel, maintains, like Arthur
Mizener, that Trollope was at times greater than he professed or knew: "Yet there can, I believe, be an artistry which
is inadvertent — more than unconscious, all but unwilling.
To this Trollope was subject . . . An artist transmits more
than he knows: in that sense we find Trollope to be an artist."
For Miss Bowen, however, Trollope's highest artistic achievement is concerned with "something idyllic, if not poetic,"

that at times illumines his pages, or with moments of authority and inspiration in his handling of his stage at crises of emotion.

Hugh Sykes Davies, in "Trollope and His Style" (*Review of English Literature,* 1960), finds in Trollope a special "characteristic cadence . . . a quality of moral conception." The novels "tend to display [him] not so much as a great moralist, an explorer of the bases of right and wrong, but rather as a passionate casuist, an observer of the relation between principle and practice." Sykes Davies is also the author of the monograph on Trollope in the useful Writers and Their Work series (no. 118, 1960). Here he correlates the novels with the *Autobiography* to show how they emerged out of Trollope's years of daydreaming as an escape from his personal handicaps. Trollope became "the moral historian of men and women in the . . . usual run of humanity," exploring issues and cross-issues in their situations, letting his imagination play upon their "differing modes and degrees of moral sensibility."

Like Sykes Davies, Jerome Thale, in "The Problem of Structure in Trollope" (*NCF,* 1960), observes in the novels a minimum of conventional plot. Their artistic form derives rather from an intricate pattern of "parallels, contrasts, repetitions, and slight variations . . . In a Trollope novel, a large number of characters respond differently to the same situation, or do the same thing for different reasons . . . Thus the Trollope novel . . . is like a vast mural, one of those comprehensive images that cover walls, crammed with figures and united spatially."

Audrey L. Laski, in "Myths of Character: An Aspect of the Novel" (*NCF,* 1960), discovers still another dimension to Trollope's art. He employs effectively the "myth of the aristocrat," following the history of the two Dukes of Omnium through a sequence of novels culminating in the political group: "The simple statement [in *Wuthering Heights*] of this basically violent myth has far more power, but there is a subtle and serious pleasure to be derived from the contemplation of Trollope's elaborately evolved and hopeful modifications." Gerald Warner Brace, in "The World of Anthony

Trollope" (*Texas Quarterly,* 1961), argues moderately for Trollope's sense of pattern and "fertility of invention," his ability to create "an illusion of wholeness, of large interrelationships — often awkward and tenuous, but in the main sufficient for the aesthetic adventure that a long novel proposes."

John E. Dustin ("Thematic Alternation in Trollope," *PMLA,* 1962) is willing to concede Trollope "unsuspected profundities" in a few of the late novels; but his study otherwise makes strongly against the current of recent articles. Dustin presents Trollope through the greatest part of his career as an agile and industrious carpenter of plots who turns out fiction with the aid of two themes, varied ingeniously to suit the characters and settings: (1) "Within what is generally a rural setting two, sometimes three, families are discovered in a state of extreme mutual hostility. Conflicting interpretations of an inheritance, the complications of entail — especially concealed illegitimacy as it affects entail — and successive wills are the specific bases for this hostility." (2) Trollope also uses as a frequent theme "the career of a bright young man of the city who early in the novel commits an error in moral judgment. Generally he succumbs to some form of temptation while he is on a trip . . . The curve of his career following the mistake usually encompasses momentary regret, a temporary success, then financial troubles, involvement with money lenders, and a fall." Dustin's analysis, ably tracing the two themes and their many variations through the novels, is of value in its own right. So far as data bearing upon Trollope's special qualities as an artist are concerned, however, the essay establishes approximately what Trollope himself had made plain in the *Autobiography* and what Saintsbury had pronounced the sufficient case against Trollope in the *fin de siècle.* Dustin's analysis is challenged by William Cadbury in "Shape and Theme: Determinants of Trollope's Forms" (*PMLA,* 1963), on the ground that he "ignores the effective totality of each novel," which "is a function of the *importance* of origins of conflict to the development of the whole action: the number, complexity, and relatedness of the various plots; and the nature, significance, and extent of the world presented."

With "Mr. Harding's Church Music" as his particular focus, Sherman Hawkins (*ELH,* 1962) presents a suggestive study of Trollope's resources as a novelist: "Trollope states his theme through a variety of techniques ranging from the personal allusions, parodies, and mock-heroic of Augustan satire to the symbols, allegories, and myths so dear to contemporary novelists. Thus he finds a precise symbolic notation for his pattern of conflict and reconciliation in the pervasive imagery of music." Mr. Harding is seen as a means whereby opposites are reconciled: Dr. Grantly, the traditionalist, and John Bold, the reformer, are the opposites. Mr. Harding "represents a still deeper aspect of his maker's character: the tenderness, the need of affection, the shyness and melancholy which Trollope's bearish manner and aggressive practicality concealed."

It is likely we are due for further critical studies that hold for Trollope's being far less the craftsman and much more the intuitive artist than the main line of criticism up to the last few years has been willing to allow.

V. *Studies of Individual Novels*

Although there is no scarcity of general studies of Trollope's work, only a few significant analyses of individual novels have been made. The narrow focus can be a most profitable one, and it is to be hoped that such studies will soon be more plentiful.

Robert A. Donovan in "Trollope's 'Prentice Work" (*MP,* 1956) shows by analysis of *The Kellys and the O'Kellys* that Trollope's early Irish novels, despite their flaws, served him valuably as training and indeed anticipated his mature manner more closely than did *The Warden. The Warden* itself is analyzed by Maude Houston (*University of Texas Studies in English,* 1955), who argues that this novel, contrary to earlier opinion, is carefully plotted and well constructed. The administrative scandals that provided the raw material for the story are fully set forth in *The Whiston Matter,* by Ralph Arnold (1961), and "The Road to Hiram's Hospital," by G. F. A. Best (*VS,* 1961). Norris D. Hoyt in his study of *Can*

You Forgive Her? in the *Trollopian* (1947) traces the relation of plot structure and ideas in this novel to a variety of sources. Henry J. W. Milley in *SP* (1939) discusses reasonably the likelihood that the "detective element" of *The Eustace Diamonds* owes a debt to *The Moonstone* of Wilkie Collins. John Hazard Wildman deals with *The American Senator* in "Trollope Illustrates the Distinction" (*NCF*, 1949); and a year later in the same journal David Stryker writes knowledgeably upon the relation of that novel to the novelist's own experiences in the United States. Nevertheless, the full import of Trollope's portrayal of Senator Elias Gotobed probably awaits further exploration.

VI. *Studies of Special Subjects*

Compared to the impressive amount of careful scholarship that has been devoted in the last decades to close analysis of the novels of Dickens or Thackeray or George Eliot, studies of special aspects of the novels of Anthony Trollope make but a scant showing. If, as an increasing number of recent articles suggest, Trollope is capable of rewarding such analysis, then a great deal awaits doing.

In addition to materials remarked upon in earlier sections of this chapter, a modest number of studies of special aspects of Trollope's work require mention. Frank Pierce Jones in "Anthony Trollope and the Classics" (*Classical Weekly*, 1944) carefully examines the evidence for Trollope's slender knowledge of Greek but extensive command of Latin language and literature. Judged as a classicist by avocation only, Trollope is seen to have achieved impressive stature, doubly surprising in view of his inauspicious beginnings at Harrow and at Winchester. In "Trollope and the Bi-columned Shakespeare" (*NCF*, 1951) William Coyle makes a suggestive pilot study of Trollope's use of literary allusion. Lionel Stevenson's "Trollope as a Recorder of Verbal Usage" (*Trollopian*, 1948) shows how Trollope exploits divergent levels in grammatical usage to aid him in depicting characters of differing social strata. The detailed topography of Trollope's imaginary county is expounded by Lance O. Tingay in "Mapmaking in Barsetshire" (*NCF*, 1949).

A painstaking study by C. C. Koets, *Female Characters in the Works of Anthony Trollope,* a dissertation at Amsterdam, was published in 1933. The relation of Trollope's characters to actual personages, a topic touched upon in the biographies, receives fuller treatment in specific areas in R. W. Chapman, "Personal Names in Trollope's Political Novels" (*Essays Presented to Sir Humphrey Milford,* 1948), and Ruth M. Adams, "Miss Dunstable and Miss Coutts" (*NCF,* 1954). In "Anthony Trollope's Younger Characters" (*NCF,* 1951) Russell A. Fraser considers Trollope's characteristic refusal to heighten the attributes of either the most or least worthy of his dramatis personae so as to add drama to his stories by painting his heroes or villains larger than life. The subject is treated much more fully in the lengthy and admiring chapter on Trollope in Mario Praz, *The Hero in Eclipse* (1956). The chapter is suggestive but curiously inaccurate and, at times, even inept — on the whole a disappointing contribution from this eminent scholar.

Trollope's relation to other Victorian authors is a matter that comes frequently into the biographies. Special aspects of the subject are usefully elaborated in Carl Weber's "In Thomas Hardy's Workshop, Part I: Hardy and Trollope" (*Colby College Bulletin,* 1934); Ernest Boll's "The Infusion of Dickens in Trollope" (*Trollopian,* 1946); Lionel Stevenson's "Dickens and the Origin of 'The Warden' " (*Trollopian,* 1947); and Wilson B. Gragg's "Trollope and Carlyle" (*NCF,* 1958).

Trollope's handling of legal matters in *Orley Farm* was sharply attacked by Sir Francis Newbolt in the *Law Journal* (1923). Clement Franklin Robinson in "Trollope's Jury Trials" (*NCF,* 1952) replies, broadening the inquiry to other of Trollope's novels and granting Trollope a generally favorable verdict on the accuracy of his trial scenes. Francis Lyman Windolph's chapter ambitiously entitled "Trollope and the Law" in his *Reflections of the Law in Literature* (1956) is actually an entertaining but leisurely redaction of the story of *Phineas Redux* with some enlightening asides upon legal matters involved therein.

Trollope's position in politics as a cautious Victorian liberal with a trust in the good effects of hastening slowly is ably analyzed by W. L. Burn in "Anthony Trollope's Politics" *(Nineteenth Century and After,* 1948); but a still more valuable study is Asa Briggs's "Trollope, Bagehot and the English Constitution" *(Cambridge Journal,* 1952). The comparison with Bagehot proves a rewarding one, and the essay throws light not only upon Trollope's politics and his political novels but also upon his general view of the England in which he lived. The piece reappears in Briggs's *Victorian People* (1954).

Trollope's attitude toward and theory of the social world he depicts figure so largely in his novels that they have inevitably received much discussion and divergent interpretations. John Hazard Wildman in a conscientious monograph entitled *Anthony Trollope's England* (1940) classifies various aspects of Victorian society as they appear in the Barsetshire Novels though he does not go as deeply as one might wish into the ways in which Trollope's England is peculiarly his own and ordered by his creative purposes. Francis Hackett, writing on "The Trollope Problem" in the *New Republic* (1956), does what can be done to see in Trollope's work evidence of a reforming zeal in the manner of mid-twentieth-century liberalism. John Hagan's essay "The Divided Mind of Anthony Trollope" *(NCF,* 1959) offers some useful observations upon the problem of individual social advancement and the problem of the marriage of convenience as these appear in Trollope's novels but somewhat blurs the issues by scolding Trollope for "vagueness and ambiguity" in his attitudes toward the aristocracy, apparently confusing the aims and obligations of the novelist with those of the political scientist or social historian.

From the strenuous overall tone and point of view of the collection, one would expect Seymour Betsky's chapter "Society in Thackeray and Trollope" in *From Dickens to Hardy,* edited by Boris Ford (1958), to be severely censorious of

Trollope's ambiguous social attitudes and easygoing accept-ances; but the essay offers instead a sympathetic and able analysis of Trollope's special view of society, the best thing outside the broader treatments of the subject in the volumes of Sadleir and Booth, and distinctly valuable in its own right because of its limited and precise focus — the sort of special study of Trollope's novels it is to be hoped will multiply and flourish in the next decade.

All in all, Trollope's particular qualities both as a writer and as a personality continue to evade definition, perhaps more so than with any other Victorian novelist of note. Dis-tinguished work has already been done. But this prolific author, often dismissed in his own time as a writer for Mudie's and *jeunes filles*, gradually accepted as a creator of adult books for adult minds, is now increasingly viewed as an artist offering profound challenges for the scholar and critic. He seems still in process of being discovered.

6 🐦

The Brontës

Mildred G. Christian

WHEN ONE SPEAKS of studying the Brontës, he may mean four gifted children of a Yorkshire clergyman. Their parents' writings, didactic in purpose, have also been assiduously read by those seeking the roots of genius. But genius is hard to find in Maria Brontë (nee Branwell) as author of *The Advantages of Poverty in Religious Concerns,* or in the more ambitious output of her husband, the Reverend Patrick Brontë. His *Cottage Poems* (1811), *The Rural Minstrel* (1813), *The Cottage in the Wood* (1815), *The Maid of Killarney* (1818), and miscellaneous short works collected for publication by J. Horsfall Turner in *Brontëana: The Rev. Patrick Brontë, His Collected Works and Life* (1898) show chiefly Mr. Brontë's piety and his interest in certain local happenings and national events discussed by him in regional papers. Of the caliber of his known work the just estimate that Annette B. Hopkins has made in *The Father of the Brontës* (1958) is not likely to be affected by any later discoveries of his fugitive pieces.

Study of Maria's and Patrick's four children who survived to maturity requires no justification. Writing about Charlotte, her sisters, and her brother has been prolific since the appearance of *Jane Eyre* (1847); and it has now concerned itself with not only the mature work of the four, but also the juvenilia; with the biography of the family group and its members singly; with their portraits, their friends, their reading, their village and shire, and indeed with many related or side issues. It has ranged in tone from the adulatory — a Brontë "cult" has become well rooted — to the acrimonious. Objective writing about the Brontës is scanty, and scholarly examination of them rare. The advent of Fannie E. Ratchford in the field with her penetrating book *The Brontës' Web of Childhood* (1941) accelerated serious study of this gifted family, for she broke virtually new ground; her *Gondal's Queen* (1955) has spurred re-examination of Emily Brontë in particular. Today scholars in Europe, the Far East, and the western hemisphere are investigating the Brontës carefully, critically, and in growing numbers.

I. *Bibliography and Manuscripts*

Despite the title *A Bibliography of the Writings in Prose and Verse of the Members of the Brontë Family* (parents and four children) published by Thomas James Wise (1917), no complete bibliography of Brontë works yet exists. Wise himself was to add to this publication by another, also incomplete: *A Brontë Library. A Catalogue of Printed Books, Manuscripts and Autograph Letters by the Members of the Brontë Family* (1929); and he permitted his name to appear with that of J. Alex Symington as coeditor of the Shakespeare Head Brontë (1931–1938), of which the twentieth and final volume was to have been a bibliography of the complete writings of the Brontës. The volume never appeared. Few, if any, of the publications carrying Wise's name are strictly reliable; for example, his *Ashley Library Catalogue* (1922–1936) attributes to Emily a composition by Branwell, *The Wanderer*. The authoritative air of the publications by Wise continues to mislead students who do not go directly to the Brontë manuscripts.

Yet Wise has contributed to knowledge of the Brontës, as in his *A Reference Catalogue of British and Foreign Autographs and Manuscripts*, part I (1893), for the Society of Archivists; and in the steady succession of pamphlets, such as

Letters Recounting the Deaths of Emily, Anne and Branwell Brontë by Charlotte Brontë (1913) and *Letters on Charlotte Brontë by Mrs. Gaskell* (1914), each devoted to publishing one or more unpublished brief manuscripts by or about one of the Brontës.

Wise's prominence in any bibliographical study of the Brontës is due to his having once owned the bulk of the Brontë manuscripts by purchase chiefly from: the Reverend A. B. Nicholls (husband of Charlotte), through the agency of Clement K. Shorter; Miss Ellen Nussey (Charlotte's closest friend); and the family of William Smith Williams (reader for Charlotte's publishers, Smith, Elder and Company). Though Wise sought to buy *all* Brontë manuscripts, he failed to secure a number. Among them are two significant private collections in England, both begun just after Charlotte Brontë died; and because one is still withheld from the free use of students, it is as yet impossible to prepare a complete bibliography of the Brontës' works. Much more can, however, be done toward that end than T. J. Wise accomplished.

Should a student assume such an undertaking his chief additional aids would be various bibliographies produced, largely by acknowledged amateurs, since the mid-1890's, when the Brontë Society was founded, the *Transactions of the Brontë Society* (hereafter cited as *BST*) began, and a Brontë Museum was set up in Haworth, Yorkshire, the home of the Brontës. Some bibliographies having no connection with the society or museum were made from private collections or for sales catalogues; but *A Bibliography of the Works of the Brontë Family* (1895) by Butler Wood, bibliographical secretary of the new Brontë Society, formed part I of the first (1898) volume of *Transactions and Other Publications of the Brontë Society*. It is a serious, careful, and organized record of published works by and about the Brontës, including a list of magazine articles on them, their residence, and their village. Wood's *Supplement* to it appeared in *BST* for 1897, and his "Some Bibliographical Notes on the Brontë Literature" in *BST* for 1910. An 1896 *Descriptive Catalogue of*

Objects [including manuscripts] in the Brontë Museum was prepared and published by F. C. Galloway. "Catalogue of the Objects in the Museum of the Brontë Society" (*BST,* 1908), compiled by W. T. Field, was the first "official" catalogue. It opens with a section called "Paintings, Drawings, Letters and Manuscripts by Members of the Brontë Family." "The Early Manuscripts of Charlotte Brontë: A Bibliography" in three parts (*BST,* 1922, 1923, and 1924) is by C. W. Hatfield. Sotheby catalogues from 1886 on give a detailed description of each Brontë item offered for sale by that firm. Another *Catalogue of the Brontë Museum and Library* (1927), by J. Alex Symington, then curator of the museum, is the least helpful of any, since its numerical listing bears no relation to the actual identifying number to be found on any item in the museum but is simply sequential in the compiler's recording.

The large and valuable gift to the Brontë Museum by Mrs. Henry H. Bonnell in memory of her husband, the chief American collector of Brontë items to the time of his death in 1926, led to a *Catalogue of the Bonnell Collection in the Brontë Parsonage Museum* (1932). The most informative catalogue of museum holdings to that date, it carries numerous facsimiles. Its compiler, C. W. Hatfield, remains one of the most accurate of all students of the Brontës.

An unpublished *Catalogue of the General Collection of Manuscripts, Drawings, Paintings, and Manuscript Association Material in the Brontë Museum* (1958), prepared by Mildred G. Christian, was designed to supersede all earlier museum catalogues of the General (that is, non-Bonnell) Collection of primary material, and to make each item easily available through its acquisition number. The catalogue is in the hands of the Brontë Council and Museum.

"A Census of Brontë Manuscripts in the United States" (in five parts, 1947–1948, in *The Trollopian*), by Mildred G. Christian, takes account of public and private holdings ranging from single items to large collections. A "Corrigenda and Addenda" section in part V comments upon incorrect information sent in by some libraries. Leslie A. Marchand's

"An Addition to the Census of Brontë Manuscripts" (*NCF*, 1949) records the then just acquired Symington Collection of Rutgers University. That collection is more generally described by Marchand in *Journal of Rutgers University Library* (1948). A few Brontë manuscripts and association pieces not previously accounted for (especially those in the Elizabeth C. Gaskell and the George Henry Lewes papers) may be found catalogued in the British Museum Students' Room. Included are the items presented to the museum in 1933 by the heirs of George Smith of Smith, Elder and Company.

A British Museum staff member, J. P. Anderson, prepared for Augustine Birrell's *Charlotte Brontë* (1887) the excellent first bibliography. It is divided into sections: "Works" (that is, editions of); "Biography, Criticism, etc."; and "Magazine Articles" (British, American, Canadian, French, and German). *A Catalogue of the Gleave Brontë Collection at the Moss Side Free Library, Manchester,* by John Albert Green (and later compilers), in successive revisions with additions from 1905 to 1916 (possibly later), records much useful and curious information about the Brontës, including early and later periodical comment on them. British periodical matter is also recorded (to about 1930) in the Symington Collection of typed and secondary matter in the Library of the University of Texas.

The chief repositories of Brontë manuscripts are the two Bonnell Collections (Philadelphia and Haworth); the General Collection, Brontë Museum; the Brotherton Library, Leeds University; and the British Museum. The extant Brontë manuscripts relevant to a study of the fiction alone are comprised of: juvenilia; the Angrian continuation of these into the authors' early maturity; foul and fair drafts of novels and sections of novels, sometimes in notebooks; and the devoirs produced by Charlotte and Emily at the Pensionnat Heger [1] in Brussels. The Gondal story I arbitrarily exclude since it survives in poetry only.

---

[1] This name (of Central European, not French, origin) should, according to the family, never carry an accent.

The juvenile tales include four groups: *The Young Men's Play, Our Fellows, The Play of the Islanders,* and *Legends of Angria* — titles assigned chiefly by editors, for convenience. The Angrian tales were the concern of Charlotte and Branwell, who wrote them, in the main, in microscopic handprint and who usually hand-bound them.

Charlotte's novels are *The Professor* (in manuscript in the Pierpont Morgan Library, New York) and *Jane Eyre, Shirley,* and *Villette* (all in holograph in the British Museum). Novelistic fragments by Charlotte (for example *The Moores, Emma,* and *The Story of Willie Ellin*) exist in manuscripts listed in Christian's *Census* and in the catalogues of the Bonnell and the General Collections in the Brontë Museum. Manuscripts of Emily's *Wuthering Heights* and Anne's *Agnes Grey* and *The Tenant of Wildfell Hall* have disappeared, possibly along with the firm of Newby, which accepted them for publication. The devoirs, widely scattered, exist sometimes in two forms — draft corrected by M. Heger, and final.

II. *Editions*

The term "fiction" will, for the purposes of this chapter, be confined to the novels and such other prose narratives — non-Angrian juvenile tales and Angrian tales of earlier and later date — as were the products of imagination.

The most complete edition of writing by all members of the family is the Shakespeare Head Brontë (19 vols., 1931–1938), ed. T. J. Wise and J. A. Symington. This edition is neither letter perfect nor complete. Nonetheless, it is for several reasons the indispensable tool for research in the Brontës. No other collection contains so full a representation of their juvenilia, so much previously unpublished material by them, so many additions to and corrections of Shorter's edition of their letters in *The Brontës: Life and Letters* (2 vols., 1908), so large a benefit from Hatfield's knowledge of Brontë literature, and so much connective and associational matter. Reluctance to accept Hatfield's decision on what was or was not by Branwell, in particular, led the editors to resort to use of facsimiles from holograph, with a minimum of editorial comment. Since the facsimiles reproduce poorly, the usefulness of these volumes is much reduced.

Limited editions of selected short prose pieces have been prepared by Wise and by C. K. Shorter in imitation of him. Among these editions are: for Wise, P. B. Brontë's *And the Weary Are at Rest* (1924); and for Shorter, Charlotte Brontë's tales *The Four Wishes* (1918), *Napoleon and the Spectre* (1919), and *The Twelve Adventurers and Other Stories* (1925).

Single tales by Charlotte have appeared in various publications: *The Adventures of Ernest Alembert, A Fairy Tale* in W. Robertson Nicoll and T. J. Wise, *Literary Anecdotes of the Nineteenth Century,* vol. II (1896), where a page of facsimile reveals some inaccuracies in their transcription of the tale; *The Spell,* with introduction by George Edwin MacLean (1931); and *A Leaf from an Unopened Volume* (with a facsimile) in A. Edward Newton's *Derby Day and Other Adventures* (1934). *BST* has from time to time printed most of the known shorter prose of the Brontës.

Collected prose juvenilia may be found in: Fannie E. Ratchford and William Clyde DeVane's edition of five tales, *Legends of Angria* (1933); Phyllis Bentley's edition of eight tales, *Stories from Angria* (1949); and *The Complete Works of Emily Brontë* — a misnomer — vol. II: *Prose* (1911), with an introduction by C. K. Shorter and many facsimiles of Emily's handwriting.

Smith, Elder published the first collection of all the Brontë novels (1872–1873), reprinting without editorial comment. A textual edition of the novels is in preparation by the Oxford Press. The first critical edition, the Temple Edition (12 vols., 1893), ed. F. J. S. (still unidentified), pales by comparison with the next: the Haworth Edition (1899–1903), *Life and Works of the Sisters Brontë* — "works" meaning "novels" — with prefaces by Mrs. Humphry Ward and annotations to Mrs. Gaskell's *Life of Charlotte Brontë* by C. K. Shorter. The edition is still the best, even without the benefit of twentieth-century scholarship. Mrs. Ward proves herself a penetrating, just, original, and widely read critic, drawing with equally telling effect on English, French, and German literature for comparison.

The Temple Edition was reprinted in 1901 and again in 1905 under a new editor, May Sinclair (reprinted, 1938). Miss Sinclair, not confining herself to biographical comment, writes with vigor, sound judgment, and discrimination.

The Thornton Edition (12 vols., 1901), ed. Temple Scott, is heavily indebted to C. K. Shorter's *Charlotte Brontë and Her Circle* and fairly unoriginal in all respects until B. W. Willett takes over the editorship of the final volume, Mrs. Gaskell's *Life of Charlotte Brontë*. Willett examines Shorter's annotations of the work in the Haworth Edition, points out the essentially journalistic quality of Shorter's comment and his errors in fact, and proves the need for careful re-examination of his conclusions.

Phyllis Bentley has edited the six novels (and selected poems and Angrian tales) for both the Heather Edition (1949) and the Collins New Classics series (1947–1954). Her introduction for the one is biographical in stress; those for the other are compactly analytical of structure.

The 1901–1907 World's Classics series was edited by Theodore Watts-Dunton; its *Wuthering Heights* (1930; reprinted, 1950) was edited by H. W. Garrod, who uses the text of the first edition of the novel. The introductions by Rose Macaulay of the Everyman Library editions of *Wuthering Heights* (1907) and *Jane Eyre* (1908) are dependent upon earlier comment. The recent Everyman editions of all the novels by Charlotte (1953–1957) carry brief and refreshingly unhackneyed introductions by Margaret Lane.

Singly, the Brontë novels have had many editions. That of *Jane Eyre* by Shorter for the Camelot Series (1889) has a long, predominantly biographical introduction strongly colored by the views and reminiscences of Ellen Nussey. *Jane Eyre and The Moores* (1902), ed. W. Robertson Nicoll, first publishes one of the trial pieces for *The Professor*. The bibliographical introduction reports the views of those critics whom Nicoll trusts. Rose Macaulay did a second edition of

Wuthering Heights, this time for the Travellers' Library (1926), but without much change in her position. Paul M. Fulcher's introduction to the Modern Readers' series edition (1929) is more valuable. The handsome Heritage Press Edition (1940) is prepared by J. T. Winterich.

III. *Biography*

Basic to all later biographical studies of the Brontës and to most literary criticism devoted to them is *The Life of Charlotte Brontë* (2 vols., 3 editions, 1857), by Elizabeth Cleghorn Gaskell, the biographer selected and assisted by Charlotte's father, husband, and best friend (Ellen Nussey). The first two editions are almost identical; the third was altered under two threats of suit against Mrs. Gaskell for statements that she believed true concerning the Cowan Bridge School and Mrs. Edmund Robinson (by then Lady Scott). The suppressed passages, along with results of a collation of the first three editions, may be read in *BST* (1921).

This work, because of the thoroughness with which Mrs. Gaskell searched for information and the art with which she presented it, held its place of absolute authority until the appearance of T. Wemyss Reid's articles in *Macmillan's Magazine* (1876), which were considerably expanded into his *Charlotte Brontë: a Monograph* (1877), a work drawing upon about 100 letters by Charlotte Brontë to Ellen Nussey and not shown by the latter to Mrs. Gaskell. Reid in this volume hinted that Charlotte had fallen in love with her Belgian schoolmaster, M. Constantin Heger. These hints deeply offended Miss Nussey, as did A. Mary F. Robinson's extended treatment in *Emily Brontë* (1883) of Branwell's degeneration; and as did J. B. Leyland's implication, in his answering defense of his brother's friend Branwell (*The Brontë Family, With Special Reference to Patrick Branwell Brontë,* 1886), that Miss Nussey had supplied Miss Robinson with material on Branwell's misbehavior. Partly as a result of this indignation Miss Nussey searched for a biographer to set the record straight and vindicate her. Eventually she found Clement K. Shorter. Her generous supply of information and material to him put him in position to become a Brontë authority, write many books on the Brontës, and become holder of the copyright on Brontë manuscripts. His *Charlotte Brontë and Her Circle* (1896), *Charlotte Brontë and Her Sisters* (1905), and *The Brontës: Life and Letters* (1908) prepared the way for the Wise-Symington *The Brontës: Their Lives, Friendships and Correspondence* (4 vols.) in the Shakespeare Head Brontë. Shorter's *The Brontës and Their Circle* (1914) is a slight reworking of his 1905 volume.

Shorter's 1896 volume incorporated part, and his 1908 volume the whole, of J. Horsfall Turner's printing of Charlotte's nearly 500 letters to Miss Nuusey — a printing that Shorter required Turner to destroy. He benefited also from the personal assistance of A. B. Nicholls, and Nicholls' and Miss Nussey's sale of manuscripts to T. J. Wise. Shorter, by now ranked next after Mrs. Gaskell, edited her *Life of Charlotte Brontë* for the Haworth Edition of the novels (1900). He supplied it with an introduction and copious notes based on materials not available to her.

In 1913 in the *Sphere* Shorter disagreed with M. H. Spielmann, who, in the *Times,* had published, translated, and interpreted as love letters four letters in French written by Charlotte Brontë to M. Heger. Biographers and literary critics have ever since divided over the significance of the letters. Only Mrs. E. H. Chadwick, a Haworthian who sought vainly to better Mrs. Gaskell, argued in her book *In the Footsteps of the Brontës* (1914) that it was Emily who loved M. Heger — a view overlooking Charlotte's specific witness to Emily's dislike of him. *The Secret of Charlotte Brontë* (1914) by Fredericka Macdonald, herself a product of the Pensionnat Heger, is a gossipy expansion into book form of her more factual article, "The Brontës at Brussels" (*Woman at Home,* 1894). Mrs. Macdonald sides with Spielmann. After a seemingly objective opening to his *Charlotte Brontë* (1932), so does E. F. Benson, one of the bitterest condemners of Charlotte's attitude toward Branwell's infatuation for Mrs. Robinson. Benson sees her as pharisaical, and has inspired numerous denigrators of her character.

Psychological analysis first impinged upon Brontë biography in Lucille Dooley's "Psycho-Analysis of Charlotte Brontë as a Type of the Woman of Genius" (*American Journal of Psychology*, 1920). Romer Wilson's *All Alone* (1928) assumes a "Dark Hero" who "occupies" the seven-year-old Emily and compels her henceforward to a "double life." This imaginative proposal still has considerable vogue, variations of it appearing in otherwise serious Brontë criticism. Other ventures into psychology are Rosamond Langbridge's sensational *Charlotte Brontë: a Psychological Study* (1929), full of repeatedly disproved "facts," and Virginia Moore's *The Life and Eager Death of Emily Brontë* (1936), first enunciating the theory that Emily willed her own death, and supplying her with a nonexistent lover, Louis Parensell (a misreading of Emily's hand in the title of her poem "Love's Farewell"). Somerset Maugham's biographical comment in *Great Novelists and Their Novels* (1948) charges Emily with Lesbianism, her object Anne — a comment showing vast ignorance of the Brontës. Muriel Spark's part in her and Derek Stanford's *Emily Brontë: Her Life and Work* (1953) presents an Emily moving toward a mental imbalance completed by about 1847. Such idle theories survive only by discounting abundant contrary witness in the correspondence of Charlotte, her father, and Ellen Nussey. Norma Crandall's *Emily Brontë* (1957) also belongs to the theoretical, unreliable accounts. The only biography of Emily to stand test is the healthy, sensitive one by Charles Simpson, *Emily Brontë* (1929). Further, its author has uncovered facts about Law Hill that bear on the sources of *Wuthering Heights*.

E. E. Kinsley's *Pattern for Genius: a Story of Branwell Brontë and His Three Sisters* (1939) develops the thesis of their fascinated study, in their novels, of their brother's degeneration. Branwell has been the chief subject not only of Leyland's defense of him but of F. H. Grundy's *Pictures of the Past* (1879), an untrustworthy record written years after the events in which he and Branwell shared. Alice Law's *Patrick Branwell Brontë* (1925) argues unconvincingly that Branwell had a large and influential part in *Wuthering Heights*. Daphne du Maurier's *The Infernal World of Bran-*

well Brontë (1960) and Winifred Gérin's *Branwell Brontë* (1961) invite comparison by their completely opposite reading of the same evidence concerning Mrs. Robinson. Miss du Maurier exonerates her, Miss Gérin does not. The Robinson papers support Miss du Maurier and reveal that Miss Gérin has ignored a mass of evidence against her and has misread handwriting, reading "him" for "wine" in one passage, with amazing consequences. Though Miss du Maurier sins by using pseudo-Freudian speculations to fill gaps in information about Branwell's childhood, the bulk of her book abundantly supplies solid new evidence bearing on the whole Brontë family. Among Miss Gérin's faults is her pervasive use of Branwell's fictional tales as if they were autobiography.

Not inspiring the emotional response that the other Brontës have evoked, Anne Brontë for a long time lacked separate biographical treatment. Will T. Hale's "Anne Brontë: Her Life and Writings" (*Indiana University Studies,* 1929), a sensible, thorough, unexaggerated piece of writing, covers most of what is said in two recent studies of Anne: Ada Harrison and Derek Stanford, *Anne Brontë: Her Life and Work* (1959); and Winifred Gérin, *Anne Brontë: a Biography* (1959). Miss Harrison's biographical essay is superior to Miss Gérin's book though both show a strong bias toward Anne and against Charlotte, and repose confidence in an unprovable assumption of Anne's love for William Weightman. In the light of this assumption, they interpret all Anne's writings in maturity. Miss Gérin's claim to scholarliness is invalidated by her practice of burying source references so far from their use in her book as to imply her original discovery of data unearthed by others before her. Her real contribution is an effective re-creation of Anne's milieu, through a detailed study of topography and local history. Lawrence and E. M. Hanson's *The Four Brontës* (1949) calls attention to the long neglect of Anne and seeks to repair it. These biographers are in the Benson tradition as regards Charlotte.

The defamation of Charlotte Brontë is, indeed, the work of the last thirty years. E. C. Gaskell, C. K. Shorter, C. W. Hatfield, May Sinclair (in *The Three Brontës,* 1912), F. E.

Ratchford, and Kathleen Tillotson (in *Novels of the Eighteen-Forties*, 1954), to mention only selected critics, have taken a quite different view of her. So did her contemporaries and immediate successors; see memoirs of her in R. H. Horne's "Portraits and Memoirs" (*Macmillan's Magazine*, 1870), "Miss Nussey's 'Reminiscences' " (*Scribner's Monthly*, 1871; reprinted in *BST*, 1899), George Smith's "Charlotte Brontë" (*Cornhill Magazine*, 1900), and E. M. Delafield's *The Brontës: Their Lives Recorded by Their Contemporaries* (1935). See also *Charlotte Brontë; 1816–1916; a Centennial Memorial* with foreword by Mrs. Humphry Ward, ed. Butler Wood (1918).

Several compact biographies of the family — *The Brontës* (1933) by Irene Cooper Willis, and *The Brontës* (1948) and *The Brontë Sisters* (1950) by Phyllis Bentley — all manifest sanity, a strict regard for truth, and excellent judgment. Miss Bentley, a Yorkshirewoman, best reveals the significance of the economic history of her shire, and the social and geographical factors there that impinged on Brontë minds.

Probably the most permanent contribution made recently to biography of the Brontë family as such is *The Brontë Story: a Reconsideration of Mrs. Gaskell's Life of Charlotte Brontë* (1948) by Margaret Lane (the Countess of Huntington). She achieves a far more effective revision of Mrs. Gaskell's book than did Shorter in that it is better organized and has the advantage of a half century more of Brontë study behind it. Miss Lane takes account of the growing tendency to describe Emily as a "mystic" and handles with sensitiveness and common sense the attempts at psychoanalyzing the Brontës. Her study, delightfully written, is companion to, not substitute for, the original work.

Search for the origins of the racial strains that contributed to the Brontë genius has led to many articles on their Irish and Cornish heritage; for example, *BST* has had several on this subject. A book that purported to be the first serious investigation of Mr. Brontë's genealogy was the Reverend Dr. William Wright's largely fictional and often ludicrously credulous work, *The Brontës in Ireland* (1893). Yet it did

open the way for two other biographers: the Reverend Angus
M. Mackay, in *The Brontës: Fact and Fiction* (1897), correcting more than Dr. Wright's book; and J. Horsfall Turner,
whose *Brontëana* (1898) took the author to Ireland to go over
the same ground as Dr. Wright. Both books manifest a de-
termination to adhere to fact. One other biography in the
period was W. W. Yates's *The Father of the Brontës* (1897),
giving special attention to Mr. Brontë's work at Dewsbury
and Hartshead and, in a final chapter, to Charlotte at Roe
Head.

Mrs. Gaskell's essentially unsympathetic treatment of Mr.
Brontë has for many years contributed to a distorted view
of him only recently effectively opposed by Annette B. Hopkins in *The Father of the Brontës* (1958), though in the mean-
time a few quiet defenders of him have spoken briefly. Miss
Hopkins' evaluation, the result of careful, impartial study of
the materials concerning every phase of his life, his views and
the influences that helped create them, is the most reliable account of Mr. Brontë. It serves as a corrective to the witty,
readable, but highly prejudiced, even gleefully malicious,
attack on him in G. Elsie Harrison's *The Clue to the Brontës*
(1948). The clue is Wesleyan Methodism, to which Mr.
Brontë was early exposed and by which he certainly remained
influenced even after becoming an Anglican clergyman.

The files of *BST* reveal many biographical contributions
to Brontë history. Among these are accounts of Mrs. Brontë,
and of A. B. Nicholls (three times). Nicholls has been studied
twice in the *Cornhill Magazine*: by Harriette K. Bell, his
niece (1927), and by Margaret Lane (1950). No book has
been devoted to him.

A useful tool for students of Brontë biography is J. J.
Stead's "A Chronology of the Principal Events in the Lives
of the Brontës" (*BST*, 1897).

The effort to preserve the record of fact as a sure footing
in the swirling current of theories and errors that have pervaded Brontë biography was behind K. A. R. Sugden's *Short
History of the Brontës* (1929). But theory begets theory and
hence Ernest Raymond was justified in writing "The Brontë

Legend, Its Cause and Treatment" (*Essays by Divers Hands*, XXVI, 1953). Mr. Raymond offers a defense for Mr. Brontë, "Aunt Branwell," and M. and Mme. Heger. Three compact and cogent essays by G. F. Bradby are especially effective in exposing untenable stories about the Brontës, in particular Miss Robinson's, to the light of plain logic. The essays open *The Brontës and Other Essays* (1937), and are entitled "Charlotte Brontë and Mr. Nicholls," "Emily Brontë," and "Brontë Legends."

This chapter makes no pretense of having mentioned all biographical studies of the Brontës, or even all that have virtues. It does supply an account of all the major contributors to the subject, and of the works marking new departures.

IV. *Criticism*

To cabin within this portion of a chapter an evaluative survey of the prolific literary criticism devoted to the Brontës in the last thirty years is to be forced at times to listing of examples.

Modern criticism of the Brontës is markedly indebted to the past, especially to Mrs. Gaskell's *Life of Charlotte Brontë*, which initiated the biographical reading of the Brontës' works, through stress on heredity, environment, and education. Precisely these factors are scrutinized by Sir Herbert Read in "Charlotte and Emily Brontë" (*Yale Review*, 1925; reprinted in *Reason and Romanticism*, 1926). His emphasis on the literary product of the two sisters is, nonetheless, not Gaskellian, nor is his addition of Jungian interpretations; however valuable his insights as literary critic — and they are many — his amateur psychoanalysis attributing to Charlotte "a longing for the lost mother" and to Emily "psychical hermaphroditism" has contributed to much absurdity in later comment on the Brontës, particularly in Richard Chase's "The Brontës: A Centennial Observance (Reconsiderations VIII)" (*Kenyon Review*, 1947; reprinted as "The Brontës, or Myth Domesticated," *Forms of Modern Fiction*, ed. William Van O'Connor, 1948). Chase uncritically accepts Rosamond

Langbridge's theories as if proved facts, and combines with them some Jung and some Toynbee with extravagant results. His essay has been overacclaimed.

Virginia Woolf, in *"Jane Eyre* and *Wuthering Heights"* (*The Common Reader,* 1925), brought a characteristically fresh and distinguished point of view to bear on her subject, recognizing in Charlotte an ardent love of nature equal to Emily's, and finding in power of personality and narrowness of vision strong similarities between Charlotte and Hardy. Mrs. Woolf speculates that Emily's poetry may outlive her novel, an uncommon belief.

Another member of the Bloomsbury group, C. P. Sanger, in *The Structure of "Wuthering Heights"* (1926), accorded the novel the sort of close analysis it had never been given, thus exposing the shallowness of judgment of those earlier critics who charged it with inexpertness and "crudity." He demonstrated beyond question Emily's attention to minute details of chronology and the remarkable accuracy of her treatment of the British laws governing inheritance. Though Ernest A. Baker in his *History of the English Novel* (1937) does not share certainty about Emily's knowledge of British law, Charles Travis Clay, in "Notes on the Chronology of *Wuthering Heights"* (*BST,* 1952), has added details to Sanger's evidence. In fact, Sanger's study has proved a landmark in the reassessment of Emily, a process hastening the modern reversal of judgment upon the comparative merits of Emily and Charlotte as writers. (Compare, for example, the remark by Edith C. Batho and Bonamy Dobrée, *The Victorians and After,* 1950: "Charlotte was a very considerable artist, Emily a supreme one.")

Those reluctant to see Emily alone credited with *Wuthering Heights* found a spokesman in Alice Law, whose *Emily Jane Brontë and the Authorship of "Wuthering Heights"* (1928) revives the contention of F. A. Leyland and of Francis Grundy that Branwell shared in the writing of the novel. This argument was not effectually answered until Irene Cooper Willis' *The Authorship of "Wuthering Heights"* (1936; summarized in *The Trollopian,* 1947). Miss Willis' brilliant, compact analysis of the style of Branwell and that of Emily demolishes the case of the Branwellians and is itself a fine contribution to the literary appreciation of Emily. With the turn of the tide toward Emily came simultaneously a condemnation of Charlotte as artist, in Lord David Cecil's *Early Victorian Novelists* (1935). An analysis as close as his had never been granted Charlotte's novels, and, while a rereading of his essay proves it to be less destructive than it appears initially, his effect has been to give her reputation as artist a blow from which it has never fully recovered. His essay on Emily in the same book pays the warmest tribute to her structural skill, her poetic power, and the grandeur of her vision. Ernest A. Baker in his *History of the English Novel* picks up these ideas as well as Swinburne's recognition of Emily's sense of the value of the individual soul.

The reprint of H. E. Wroot's *Sources of Charlotte Brontë's Novels: Persons and Places* (supplement to *BST*, 1935) strikingly points up, by its old-fashioned method and emphasis upon the "actual" behind her novels, differences between earlier and recent techniques of literary criticism. Yet two modern critics have made significant contributions to knowledge of Charlotte's and Emily's materials by producing studies of the same general class as Wroot's: Gustave Charlier in "La Vie bruxelloise dans *Villette*" (*Passages*, 1947; translated in *BST*, 1955); and Hilda Marsden in "The Scenic Background of *Wuthering Heights*" (*BST*, 1957).

Of the earlier style of criticism is Florence S. Dry's *Brontë Sources* (1937). Though citing some parallels to Shakespeare and Tennyson in the stories of Charlotte and Emily, Mrs. Dry finds their novels pervaded by the influence of Scott, a thesis that she rides too hard. Lew Girdler's "Charlotte Brontë's *Shirley* and Scott's *The Black Dwarf*" (*MLN*, 1956) is a more convincing study of Scott's influence. The chief value of G. P. Insh's "Haworth Pilgrimage" (*BST*, 1944) is its identification of two borrowings from *Lear* and *Macbeth* in *Wuthering Heights*, chapter II, and in the choice of ingratitude as the theme of the novel as well as of these two plays. Arnold P. Drew's "Emily Brontë and *Hamlet*" (*N&Q*,

1954) is one of a number of articles picking up the influence of Shakespeare on specific details in Brontë stories; see Drew's illuminating comment on Catherine's wild speech about the feathers in her pillow as variously indebted to *Hamlet*, IV, i.

V. Dupont's "Trois notes sur les Brontës" (*Etudes anglaises*, 1953) results from examination of files of the *Leeds Mercury* and *Leeds Intelligencer* during the formative years of the Brontë children. His purpose is to show the possible effect on the fiction by Charlotte and Emily of those papers' treatment of religious hypocrisy, exploitation of child labor, and education, and the opinion of the *Leeds Mercury* that a novel should have a serious purpose. Ann Lapraik Livermore's "Byron and Emily Brontë" (*Quarterly Review*, 1962) reopens the whole question of Byron's (and Shelley's) profound influence on all the Brontës. In a sense, Grace E. Harrison's *Haworth Parsonage: A Study of Wesley and the Brontës* (1937) and *The Clue to the Brontës* (1948) are both source studies, as well as studies in mental attitudes. Expressing a certain malice toward Mr. Brontë, she writes with vitality. Through cumulative evidence she proves what a strong hold Methodism had upon the thinking of every member of the Brontë family, affecting their writing in subtle ways.

Charles Morgan in "Emily Brontë" (*Great Victorians*, ed. H. J. Massingham, 1932) conveniently brings together certain convictions about Emily that had been expressed before by various persons, and that became recurrent themes in later critical interpretation of her. For example, he argues for her experience of love, of a mystical vision, and of a readiness for death; he stresses the oneness of her poetry, and hence objects to the division of it into (a) personal and (b) Gondal; he credits her with the authorship of *Wuthering Heights*, and finds unity of tone and vision in both her poetry and her novel.

This last point had received some development by May Sinclair in *The Three Brontës* (1912), a fact recognized by Leicester Bradner in "The Growth of *Wuthering Heights*" (*PMLA*, 1933). Bradner re-examines Emily's poetry to weigh its relation to the novel, concluding that certain Gondal characters and events "may account for the emotions in the novel, but not for the plot and persons." For plot and characters he finds a source in *The Bridegroom of Barna*, available to Emily in *Blackwood's Magazine*. His argument carries weight. It bears too on the date of composition of *Wuthering Heights*, and upon the deliberate design of the book.

In 1941 Fannie E. Ratchford's *The Brontës' Web of Childhood* pointed Brontë criticism in a completely new direction. The primary accomplishment of this study was to reveal the extensive and thorough laboratory experience in writing that the four young Brontës gave themselves, individually and as a group, from 1829 to 1845. Mrs. Gaskell had alluded to but not analyzed the writing of this period, a lacuna that Miss Ratchford expertly fills by study of all available Brontë manuscripts. She defines the nature and content of the juvenilia, differentiates the characteristics of the individual writers of them, studies the interaction of the four contributors and their alliances among themselves, judges the value of their bulky product, and draws conclusions about the bearing of this practice work on the mature writing of each sister. She shows why Branwell can command no serious attention as writer, contends for the nonautobiographical nature of the mature works of Charlotte and Emily, and argues against the description of Emily as a mystic. Further, she expands and modifies the schemes proposed by earlier students of Emily's poems so as to reconstruct the full lost prose "epic" of Gondal.

Laura L. Hinkley's *Charlotte and Emily* (1945) is a reaction to *The Brontës' Web of Childhood*, restudying the same materials (through secondary sources only). Discursive and loosely designed but pleasantly written, its somewhat different reconstruction of the Gondaliand has been given thoughtful attention, for example by Jacques Blondel (*Emily Brontë: expérience spirituelle et création poétique*, 1956) and Mary Visick in *The Genesis of "Wuthering Heights"* (1958).

Much modern criticism is concerned with Emily's sense of values as it determines the meaning of her novel. Study of her own nature is thus considered pertinent, as in Victoria Ocampo's *Emily Brontë: Terra Incognita* (Buenos Aires, 1938); Lucienne Escombe's *Emily Brontë et ses démons* (1941) — the demons being family ones, and neither mysterious nor requiring a Freudian interpretation; and Peter D. Lucas' *An Introduction to the Psychology of "Wuthering Heights"* (1943), where symbolism and psychiatry "explain" the novel's thesis, "on the supposition" — certainly foreign to Emily — "that all the characters . . . are parts of the personality of one central figure," Catherine the first, and that her moor home "represents the unconscious." Edmond Jaloux's "Le Mystère d'Emily Brontë" (*D'Eschyle à Giraudoux*, 1946) is less extreme. Margiad Evans' "Byron and Emily Brontë" (*Life and Letters Today*, 1949) sees both writers as mystics in that each singled out "*the* self among the Selves" and, in "a perfectly lucid, sensible state of mind," detached himself from life and chose death as a means of reunion with the Absolute. (Emily's supposed will to die is a recurrent theme in recent comment.) The third section of Evans' essay is marked by brilliant insights not dependent on her untenable central thesis. In Jacques Debû-Bridel's *Le Secret d'Emily Brontë* (1950) the secret imagined for her is a beloved childhood playmate whom Emily rejected out of pride when he turned farm servant; *Wuthering Heights* later became her self-denunciation for that pride. Georges Bataille's "Emily Brontë et le mal" (*Critiques*, 1957; reprinted in *La Littérature et le mal*, 1957) treats her "illness" as the pathology of genius. Felix Carrère's "Les Hauts de hurlevant d'Emily Brontë, histoire d'amour?" (unpubl. diss., University of Aix-Marseille, 1958) is, like Debû-Bridel's book, pure fantasy. Thomas Moser's "What is the Matter with Emily Jane? Conflicting Impulses in *Wuthering Heights*" (*NCF*, 1962) is the study of a lay psychologist. Moser is sympathetic to Mrs. Van Ghent for her recognition of window imagery in the novel, and to Richard Chase because of his stress on its sex symbolism. Moser points out "that only a few novels will respond to this kind of examination — those in which unconscious creation plays a large part and in which sex is a central subject." He admits that his interpre-

tation of some of the window or door imagery is "second
guessing." At times it is distortion, yet the cumulative effect
of examples he cites has force. Moser's mind "inevitably
wanders away from the work of art to its creator" whose
"careful arrangement of symmetrical sets of characters" in
the two generations, "rather than signifying her continual
involvement with her subject, denotes simply that she has
abandoned it."

Bruce McCullough's level-headed analysis of *Wuthering
Heights* in *Representative English Novelists* (1946) is ex-
cellent antidote to extravagances of criticism of the book.
V. S. Pritchett's "Implacable, Belligerent People in Emily
Brontë's Novel, *Wuthering Heights*" (*New Statesman and
Nation*, 1946) is one of the strongest personal witnesses to
the accuracy and power of her observation of Yorkshire
people.

In the centennial year, 1947, Edith M. Weir's "Contemporary Reviews of the First Brontë Novels" appeared
in *BST*, an essay designed to defend Emily, and to attack
Charlotte for stressing unfavorable comment on *Wuthering Heights* while minimizing the favorable. This study
anticipates several other such reviews of critical history.
Derek Traversi's objective "*Wuthering Heights* after a
Hundred Years" (*Dublin Review*, 1949) is sensitive to
Emily's remarkable concreteness, her poetic effect, the
personal and social themes of her novel, her "profound
sense of the finite and dependent nature of man," and
her "desire to make contact with a reality . . . beyond
the self." He conceives the meaning of the novel as a moral,
though not a Christian, one. Melvin R. Watson's "*Wuthering
Heights* and the Critics" (*Trollopian*, 1949) passes the time
limits Mrs. Weir set herself, as does Joseph H. Dugas' "The
Literary Reputation of the Brontës, 1846–1951" (*Dissertation Abstracts*, 1952). Watson's article, otherwise reliable, is
marred by a curious blindness to the skill of Mrs. Humphry
Ward as critic. Allan R. Brick's "Lewes's [1850] Review of
Wuthering Heights" (*NCF*, 1960) expands Watson's article.
Brick studies Lewes's "divided effect" in recognizing "an

error in art [in the novel] — the excessive predominance of shadows" equivalent to a reduction in humaneness — while he praises the undeniable truth of its characterizations. That instincts "insubordinate to law" would in fact operate as they do in the novel he calls "the moral of the book." Emily's depiction of Cathy's defiance of the world through love of Heathcliff expresses, he says, "real mastery," evidencing "genius in the highest sense of the word." Brick condemns Charlotte's reaction to this and other reviews of *Wuthering Heights*.

Centennial criticism centered on *Wuthering Heights* often adopts such adjectives as "Aeschylean" (for example, see Chase, "The Brontës") and "Elizabethan" (as in Peter Quennell's introduction to *Novels of the Brontë Sisters*, 1947). The highest order of such criticism may be found in D. G. Klingopulos' essay "*Wuthering Heights*: The Novel as Dramatic Poem, II" (*Scrutiny*, 1947). Klingopulos tests the novel by a measure of an Elizabethan play: "by the quality of the poetry at its crises of meaning." He judges it by the quality of its style, by its concern with man's place in the universe, by its symbolism, and by the ambiguity of its statement, especially in characterization. He concludes that it has been overpraised, though he sees in Emily the first to employ the novel "for that kind of statement . . . contained in the finest of English dramatic poetry." Melvin R. Watson, in "'Tempest in the Soul: The Theme and Structure of *Wuthering Heights*" (*NCF*, 1949) also sees the novel as drama: a five-act arrangement with prologue, the whole the "product of a mature artist." Heathcliff is, for him, a Hamlet without irresolution. Watson's analysis in effect rejects Lord David Cecil's interpretation.

B. G. MacCarthy's "Emily Brontë" (*Studies: An Irish Quarterly Review*, 1950), a long, six-sectioned comment, is a concentration of errors and prejudices; an "appreciation," not an analysis.

Though minor errors in handling biographical facts mar Royal A. Gettmann's introduction to *Wuthering Heights* (1950) it makes excellent points on the function of Nelly

Dean ("to control passions, to bring out their meaning, and to make them beautiful"), the change in Heathcliff, and the use of Hareton to effect harmony. Bonamy Dobrée's introduction to a 1952 edition of *Wuthering Heights* printed in Holland, the edition prefaced by an inaccurate biographical note by "H.d.R." (nowhere identified), recalls attention to Charlotte's marking out, in 1850, the channels criticism of *Wuthering Heights* was to pursue for many years. Dobrée contrasts present-day emphasis on symbolism in this novel, on its concern with technique, and on its "metaphysical" considerations. He too compares the novel to *Lear*. Yet this essay, chiefly an examination of Emily's narrative method, declares itself uncertain of the book's meaning.

By contrast, Arnold Kettle in *An Introduction to the English Novel*, vol. I (1952), is confident that "There is nothing vague about this novel"; its meaning is unsentimental and positive. For Emily is an unromantic realist, harsh, uncompromising, and powerfully moral in effect through subtle study of changing attitudes and through attacks on the reader's complacency, as in respect to social (that is, class) assumptions. Kettle finds the novel in its symbolic nature an advance over the moral fable.

The concentration of literary criticism on Emily to the neglect of Charlotte through much of the 1940's began to be corrected by prefaces to new editions of the novels, and by M. H. Scargill's "All Passion Spent: a Revaluation of *Jane Eyre*" (*UTQ*, 1950). Scargill's title refers to that moment in the novel, at the end, when the conflict between flesh and spirit being resolved, the novel "speaks for all humanity," recording a spiritual experience "as powerful in its way as King Lear's ordeal of purgation." Such exaggeration does Charlotte disservice. Scargill's conviction that she enlarges the uses of fiction by employing the novel "as a poet does," through use of symbols, is better supported.

Bonamy Dobrée's introduction to the Collins edition (1952) of *Jane Eyre* rates the work as not supremely great but a "very good" novel, manifesting technical skill, an extraordinarily strong pictorial sense, and the power to make us

become Jane, "an amazing feat" on Charlotte's part. Dobrée's essay has some virtues but lacks originality and force.
Edgar F. Shannon, Jr., in "The Present Tense in *Jane Eyre*"
(*NCF*, 1955), finds art in Charlotte's control of tension, effect
of immediacy, handling of pace, and marking or foreshadowing of structural divisions in the novel, all through manipulation of tenses. Wayne Burns's "Critical Relevance of
Freudianism" (*Western Review*, 1956) applies his test to
Jane Eyre. But the importance of psychological analysis is
more convincingly demonstrated in two important studies
by Robert B. Heilman. "Charlotte Brontë's 'New' Gothic"
(in *From Jane Austen to Joseph Conrad*, ed. R. C. Rathburn
and Martin Steinmann, Jr., 1958), sees Charlotte behind
every first-person speaker in her works, sometimes grace-
lessly wooing herself. Charlotte's version of Gothic occurs,
Heilman says, in her "new sense of the dark side of feeling
and personality," *Villette* drawing heavily on "the psychic
darkness." But Charlotte is anti-Gothic also, he finds, in use
of symbolic dreams, thus escaping "the bondage of the trite."
Heilman's "Charlotte Brontë, Reason, and the Moon" (*NCF*,
1960) penetrates into the conflict in her between reason and
intuition. He develops his argument entirely through the
prevalent moon imagery in her writings. The Freudian emphasis is strong also in Joseph Prescott's "*Jane Eyre*: a Romantic Exemplum with a Difference" (*Twelve Original
Essays on Great English Novels*, ed. Charles Shapiro, 1960).
Prescott's argument is that Charlotte's suppressed sexual
passions are revealed in her unintentionally erotic imagery.
This essay treats the book's melodrama and didacticism ruth-
lessly. A more tolerant essay is William H. Marshall's "The
Self, the World, and the Structure of *Jane Eyre*" (*Revue
des langues vivantes*, 1961). Marshall argues that "the essential but overlooked structural fact of the novel remains that
it assumes the form of an autobiography of a naive and
superstitious woman [Charlotte's persona] who . . . wishes
to vindicate publicly the course of her action . . . in an
essentially simple but meaningful universe." Charles Burkhart, following Heilman's method, proposes, in "Another

Key Word for *Jane Eyre*" (*NCF*, 1961), the word "nature," "equally handy [with 'moon'] as a guide to 'conflict between reason-judgment[*sic*].'" Charlotte's style, "rich with the mythic, natural, unconscious strength of an earlier literature," is "unwilled art."

"*Villette* and the Life of the Mind" (*PMLA*, 1960), by Robert A. Colby, approaches the novel "as Charlotte Brontë's literary, not her literal, autobiography," "an analogue" of her "creative life." His thesis requires him to review all her novels, and he thus arrives at a number of new and well-documented judgments on her accomplishment and stature as artist. The article is an important one, the most significant piece of strictly literary criticism devoted to *Villette*. Georgia S. Dunbar's "Proper Names in *Villette*" (*NCF*, 1960) throws valuable sidelights on the intent of the novel; one recalls Charlier's evidence on this novel in "La Vie bruxelloise dans *Villette*" (previously mentioned), though Charlier's purpose and emphasis differ from Miss Dunbar's. Charles Burkhart's "Brontë's *Villette*" (*Explicator*, 1962) continues analysis of moon imagery, choosing to interpret it as "organic poetic metaphor" in a "largely autobiographical book" wholly concerned with "frustrated sexual love." He believes that sun imagery in the novel reinforces his interpretation.

Four analytical studies of *Shirley* have appeared; Girdler's "Charlotte Brontë's *Shirley* and Scott's *The Black Dwarf*" (already considered), Jacob Korg's "The Problem of Unity in *Shirley*" (*NCF*, 1957), Asa Briggs's "Private and Social Themes in *Shirley*" (*BST*, 1958), and J. M. S. Tompkins' "Caroline Helstone's Eyes" (*BST*, 1961). Korg effectively shows that the novel is unified through numerous episodes and conversations deliberately designed to contrast attitudes ("Essentially, *Shirley* is a philosophical novel") so as to form "a gradually unfolding romantic criticism of conventional ideas." "Revelation rather than narration is, in fact, the method of *Shirley*" and pulls it "into a single fabric." Briggs calls the novel "a complete work of art," though recognizing its many weaknesses. A native Yorkshireman, he finds Charlotte absolutely accurate in depicting Yorkshire character and scene, so that *Shirley* is "perhaps the first impressive regional novel in the English language." He concentrates on three themes in the novel, bringing in evidence a large body of hitherto unexamined records on the Luddite riots. His final tribute to the novel as readable, interesting, and "full of imaginative vitality" implies a lesser claim for it than his initial one. Concern with the author's purpose in *Shirley* leads J. M. S. Tompkins to regard the change in color of Caroline's brown eyes to blue as clue to a redirection of the book, its composition having been interrupted by Anne Brontë's death. The spinisterish solitude and even death designed for Caroline now became, for Charlotte, a reminder of the blue-eyed Anne's sorrows. Caroline's fate, like her eyes, therefore changes color. "There was nothing in Charlotte's attitude to her art to oppose this imperious necessity to comfort herself," Tompkins argues.

Though Anne's sole appearance in recent criticism is in Lewis M. McKneely's "Anne Brontë: Novelist of Reform" (*Dissertation Abstracts*, 1959), Emily has continued to receive exhaustive study. For example, William E. Buckler's "Chapter VII of *Wuthering Heights*: a Key to Interpretation" (*NCF*, 1952) considers the chapter as revelation of Emily's view of life and of art, for here she brings the chief characters "into proper relation with one another; Heathcliff becomes determined in his 'sin'; and the trustworthiness of the narrator is established." Another study of detail, Dorothy Van Ghent's "The Window Figure and the Two-Children Figure in *Wuthering Heights*" (*NCF*, 1952; reprinted in *The English Novel: Form and Function*, 1953) points up the significance of the two devices, unnoticed by any previous critic. In 1954 Rebecca West in "The Role of Fantasy in the Work of the Brontës" (*BST*) first condemned Charlotte out of hand on the ground that she indulged in fantasy (daydreaming, the suppression of truth) rather than in imagination; then judged *Wuthering Heights* great because it is a work of powerful, honest imagination, a fantasy "set in relation to reality and exposed as fiction." Further, "it presents an interpretation of the universe." The theme ("the conflict between love and hatred in the heart of man") is "made visible," by Lintons versus Earnshaws. Miss West anticipates Kettle's view that Emily criticized ill-bred privileged classes in the Lintons. The incest motif that Miss West sees in the Catherine-Heathcliff love she believes to be a reflection of the Emily-Branwell relationship, nonsexual in character. Perhaps Eric Solomon took suggestion from this essay for "The Incest Theme in *Wuthering Heights*" (*NCF*, 1959), but in his view Heathcliff is the illegitimate son of Mr. Earnshaw and hence actual brother of Catherine.

C. Day-Lewis's *Notable Images of Virtue* (1954) presents an Emily quite other than that implied by Solomon. Her imagery, Day-Lewis believes, moves in both her poetry and *Wuthering Heights,* as all poetry does, from the particular to the general, and always under the inspiration of a pure and passionate search for liberty.

Entering an unaccustomed field, Daphne du Maurier in her uneven introduction to *Wuthering Heights* (1955) recurs to a topic long ignored: the date of composition of the novel. On grounds of Emily's subject matter, style, and known habits of composition Miss du Maurier argues very persuasively for a date as far back as 1841; and she offers strong evidence for sources of Emily's names "Earnshaw" and "Lockwood," and for the relevance of the Heaton family records to the plot of the novel.

In 1955 Miss Ratchford proposed, in *Gondal's Queen,* a more detailed reconstruction than formerly suggested for the "novel in verse" that Emily created around Gondal. Miss Ratchford fully documents her argument, and herself calls attention to material "left over" from the Gondaliand as here reconstructed. Were the lost Gondal prose found, it would, she believes, substantiate her thesis that this residue was once part of the whole "epic." Her Emily is marked by clarity of moral judgment — indeed, nobility of soul.

Emily Brontë: expérience spirituelle et création poétique, by Jacques Blondel (1956), mentioned earlier, is a thorough exploration of known fact about Emily, and of every theory about her that an exhaustive bibliography represents. His own analysis of her uncovers a "fundamental dualism" arising in large degree from the unlike religious influences on her youth, assimilated by her to nondogmatic uses so that she could simultaneously regard actual life as a spectacle of cold brutality (and so feel "a need to play with torturing the nerves") and envision perfection in the afterlife (and therefore hold faith in the beauty of righteousness). For Blondel, her artistic creation is a special kind of self-love (*l'amour de soi*), serving her as a means to test her own nature through its response to imagined experience.

B. H. Lehman's "Of Material, Subject, and Form: *Wuthering Heights*" (in *The Image and the Work*, 1955) demonstrates "the exacting task of the critical reader": to "raise the whole work of literature in the remembering mind" by a very close reading of the text. Much recent procedure, however, has been just the opposite: to concentrate on some limited aspect of the book, for example, its narrators. John K. Mathison's searching article "Nelly Dean and the Power of *Wuthering Heights*" (*NCF*, 1956) finds subtlety in Emily's use of Nelly to rouse respect and liking for her admirable character yet distrust of her judgment, so that eventually the reader's sympathies are entirely with the unconventional emotions and behavior of Catherine and Heathcliff. This manipulation of the reader is "an important cause of the power of the novel." Naturally associated with this essay are Carl Woodring's "The Narrators of *Wuthering Heights*" (*NCF*, 1957), James Hafley's "The Villain in *Wuthering Heights*" (*NCF*, 1958), and George J. Worth's "Emily Brontë's Mr. Lockwood" (*NCF*, 1958). Woodring observes that Emily's handling of the narrators makes of them a "transformed convention." Lockwood, the stranger, balances Nelly Dean, the intimate; he reacts for the reader, while Nelly serves as judge, interpreter, chorus, attorney, and actor in her own right. Is Lockwood prig, ironist, reticent or gregarious man? Is he inane? Woodring judges him consistently the sentimentalist. Hafley's "villain" is Nelly Dean. Mrs. Humphry Ward (though Hafley does not mention her) had put forward a somewhat similar suggestion in 1899; she did not suggest as he does that "surely we are meant to recognize the tragic innocence of Heathcliff and Cathy" and to read the final lines of the novel in the same wondering spirit as Lockwood, who, till now, has been subjected to the traitorous Mrs. Dean's "viciousness." Hafley's essay requires a rereading of the novel. Worth's examination of Mr. Lockwood, reviewing the various earlier interpretations of him, proposes the thesis that Emily Brontë intended him to be a clearly self-defined figure revealed simultaneously as other than he thinks himself. Emily thus employs "considerable irony." Lockwood is actually gregarious, garrulous, and sentimental, wearing a veneer of misanthropy (in contrast to the genuine misanthrope, Heathcliff), but reacting conventionally to the complexities beyond his understanding. He is thus a character "with comic overtones."

Edgar F. Shannon, Jr., in "Lockwood's Dreams and the Exegesis of *Wuthering Heights*" (*NCF*, 1959), becomes a defender of Lockwood against the charge of "milksop," showing him, too, capable of brutality. Shannon further argues that these two dreams "alert the reader to the ethical eye of the storm" in the plot, and bear on "the thematic problem of the novel — the nature of Catherine's offense." This essay also effectively demolishes Ruth M. Adams' identification, in her "*Wuthering Heights*: the Land East of Eden" (*NCF*, 1958), of Genesis 4:24 as source of the text of the Reverend Jabes Branderham's sermon in *Wuthering Heights*. Shannon proves that both the title and substance of the sermon "derive from Matt. 18:21–22." He provides also sound correction to Dorothy Van Ghent's explication of the novel "in terms of the nightmare alone," and rejects her view that *Wuthering Heights* is a work in which "perverse values . . . prevail." He reads it as a "search for a definition of evil — a quest that results in a paradigm of love." The essay rouses Vereen M. Bell, in "*Wuthering Heights* and the Unforgivable Sin" (*NCF*, 1962), to take issue with Shannon on his overlooking aspects of Lockwood's first dream where the unforgivable sin, defined within the action of the dream itself, emerges as "the absence of forgiveness, of forbearance, of mercy" — a sin that infects almost every character. Bell thus clears Catherine of Shannon's implication of sole guilt.

Earlier, in "*Wuthering Heights*: the Rejection of Heathcliff" (*EC*, 1958), Miriam Allott undertook a comprehensive interpretation of Emily's philosophy and artistic design in the novel by correcting Cecil's notion of her "peculiar metaphysics": "Her 'philosophy' is less extraordinary than he supposes: less daemonic and inherently more probable." Mrs. Allott suggests the design of the novel as two "arcs" representing Emily's "effort . . . to modify the 'storm-calm' opposition" (proposed by Cecil) so as to "eliminate the most violent and troubling elements that give the first generation story its peculiar intensity." The simple, devout nature of Emily produced, Mrs. Allott argues, a novel in equilibrium, its harmony at the end not the reconciliation of opposites, but a new combination. Mrs. Allott's review (*EC*, 1959) of Mrs. Visick's *The Genesis of "Wuthering Heights"* (1958) develops new questions out of her careful summary of previous critics' views on the relation between Emily's poems and novel.

Robert C. McKibben's "The Image of the Book in *Wuthering Heights*" (*NCF*, 1960) returns to a study of detail. He concludes that Emily's respect for books colors her frequent use of them in the novel to evoke, in her characters, attitudes toward books that expose the nature of these persons. Christopher Dean examines Emily's use of dialect in the novel; his article entitled "Joseph's Speech in *Wuthering Heights*" (*N&Q*, 1960) is a corrective to much careless assumption about the language of the novel. He also shows that Emily attempted a kind of phonetic spelling. Miriam Allott's argument in "Mrs. Gaskell's 'The Old Nurse's Story': a Link between *Wuthering Heights* and *The Turn of the Screw*" (*N&Q*, 1961) is persuasive to recognizing Emily's influence in this sequence. Keith Conrad Odom's "The Brontës and Romantic Views of Personality" (*Dissertation Abstracts*, 1961) reads their characterizations in terms of their Romantic "attitudes toward childhood and the reflection of personality in nature." Odom relates these attitudes to their concept of goodness, and to their preference for country over city. Another study in imagery is William H. Marshall's "Hareton Earnshaw: Natural Theology on the Moors" (*VN*, 1962), the animal analogies producing, he argues, a sort of Caliban theology. The argument is unconvincing.

Probably the most compelling study of evil in Emily's novel is Wade Thompson's "Infanticide and Sadism in *Wuthering Heights*" (*PMLA*, 1963), an exceedingly well-documented analysis. Its final sentence is a sardonic "tribute to Emily Brontë's uncanny poetic powers that she has deceived generations of readers into believing that they were reading a beautiful, romantic and indeed glorious love story."

The contradictory judgments on *Wuthering Heights* are the most striking fact in its critical history. A sufficient ambiguity resides in the novel to require continual rereading of it. The late discovery that more subtleties reside in Charlotte than had long been assumed is another development of critical history. A comparison of the resemblances between Charlotte and Emily would be instructive, acting as corrective of bias and contributing to just assessment of their product. Indeed some reassessment has already emerged from the renewed and detailed consideration of four manifestations of art as they bear on the Brontë novels: imagery, symbolism, structural design, and meaning.

Elizabeth Cleghorn Gaskell
Charles Kingsley

James D. Barry

MRS. GASKELL

E LIZABETH GASKELL'S fiction has given rise in recent decades to a body of commentary which has both intrinsic interest and value for its reflection of the taste and critical outlook of modern times. It is true that the revival of interest in Mrs. Gaskell is markedly less than that in Dickens or in Eliot, but the attention given her in recent times is short of what her contemporary fame would lead us to expect. The available material leads to speculation on some useful and exciting investigations that remain to be launched. It is too soon to aver that history has proved Henry James wrong; rather we should look anew at Mrs. Gaskell as a person and as a writer to search out the causes of James's high esteem for her (*Nation*, 1866).

I. *Bibliography*

The three major guides to the writing of Mrs. Gaskell are John Albert Green's *A Bibliographical Guide to the Gaskell Collection in the Moss Side Library* (1911), Morris L. Parrish's *Victorian Lady Novelists: George Eliot, Mrs. Gaskell, The Brontë Sisters, First Editions in the Library of Dormy House* (1933), and Michael Sadleir's *Excursions in Victorian*

Bibliography (1933). The two most comprehensive bibliographies (those which contain many more references to works *about* Mrs. Gaskell) appeared in 1929 and must be supplemented by annual bibliographies, since later studies present only selected references. The wide availability of both of these makes it unnecessary to list here items which they contain. The lesser of the two appears in A. Stanton Whitfield's *Mrs. Gaskell: Her Life and Work*; the best single source was compiled by Clark S. Northup for Gerald DeWitt Sanders' *Elizabeth Gaskell* in the Cornell Studies in English. Its more than one hundred pages are indexed, and its chronologically arranged divisions are bibliographies, collective editions, single works, undated editions, and biography and criticism. An article covering the thirty-four years since Northup's and Whitfield's compilations would be helpful.

II. *Editions*

The two major collected editions of Mrs. Gaskell, the Knutsford edition and the World's Classics edition, are valuable for different reasons. The Knutsford edition in eight volumes, ed. A. W. Ward (1906), includes an extensive and useful introduction to each volume. It contains close to fifty (almost all) of Mrs. Gaskell's titles. Ward accounts for his exclusion of the *Life of Charlotte Brontë* by its availability in collections of Miss Brontë's writings. His reason for excluding other, smaller pieces is less convincing: he states that he has printed "all those which she would have desired to see included in a 'definitive' edition of her writings." Ward's introductions are almost invariably helpful in leading the reader into the fiction as well as in providing bibliographical data on such points as periodical appearances and serializations. His biographical essay includes two important poems seldom reprinted.

The World's Classics edition prepared by Clement Shorter (1906–1919) is the most complete collection of her works. Its fifty-five titles include the *Life of Charlotte Brontë*, a sequel to *Cranford*, and various prefaces. Not included is a ghost story which A. B. Hopkins describes in *Elizabeth Gaskell: Her Life and Work* (1952). A brief introduction to each volume provides adequate background information.

The extensive publishing history of Mrs. Gaskell's most popular work, *Cranford*, would be important to a study of her literary reputation. A. B. Hopkins reported over 170 editions and reprints between its serial appearance in *Household Words* and 1947 (*Elizabeth Gaskell: Her Life and Work*). Many of these editions have no introductions; others are high-school text editions replete with introductions, notes, and questions — some of them provocative, for example, Albert Elmer Hancock's 1910 edition for the Lake English Classics. Other outstanding reprints are the Methuen's Standard Library edition (1906), introduced by E. V. Lucas, and the 1891 edition introduced by Anne Thackeray Ritchie and illustrated by Hugh Thomson. Two modern reprints deserve attention: the Chiltern Library edition (1947), which includes *Cousin Phillis* and is introduced by Elizabeth Jenkins, and the Collins New Classics edition (1952), which includes a brief account of Mrs. Gaskell's life, a useful introduction by David Ascoli, and a short bibliography.

Four other reprints of Mrs. Gaskell's writings merit notice. *Mary Barton* (1947), *Wives and Daughters* (1948), and *North and South* (1951) are in the Chiltern Library, whose publisher, John Lehmann, has championed her works. They are introduced by Lettice Cooper, Rosamond Lehmann, and Elizabeth Bowen respectively. The fourth, *Mary Barton* in the Norton Library, (1958), is introduced by Myron F. Brightfield.

Mrs. Gaskell's other works have not appeared in new formats in recent years. And A. Stanton Whitfield's 1929 plea remains unanswered: "It is high time that someone prepared an edition of the novelist's best short tales."

III. *Letters*

A short time before her death in 1913 Mrs. Gaskell's last surviving daughter, Meta, destroyed many letters and papers relating to her mother. There remains, however, a considerable body of correspondence to be collected and ordered. Recently, Arthur Pollard and A. J. V. Chapple announced (*TLS*, Aug. 26, 1960) that they are preparing an edition of Mrs. Gaskell's letters. This undertaking will not be easy, since the letters were often written — to use Henry James's word — "undatedly" and since they are scattered throughout England and the United States. Among the major manuscript depositories are the Brotherton Library of the University of Leeds, the Arts Library of the University of Manchester, the John Rylands Library, the Manchester Central Library, the archives of John Murray (50 Albemarle St., London), the Parrish Collection at Princeton University, the Symington Collection at Rutgers University, and the Berg Collection at the New York Public Library.

Two biographies, Elizabeth Haldane's *Mrs. Gaskell and Her Friends* and A. B. Hopkins' *Elizabeth Gaskell: Her Life and Work*, contain excellent selections of Mrs. Gaskell's letters. There are, in addition, two rather extensive collections. The earlier, *Letters of Mrs. Gaskell and Charles Eliot Norton, 1855–1865* (ed. Jane Whitehill, 1932), contains an informative introduction and forty-two letters, many of them lengthy. A charming series, it is of almost no help from a strictly literary point of view: "To show the quality of that attachment, to call back to life momentarily the two friends as they thought and spoke, here and there to catch the flavour of the time — such ends only will these letters serve." The second collection, this edited by Ross D. Waller in the *Bulletin of the John Rylands Library* (1935), is made up of "Letters Addressed to Mrs. Gaskell by Celebrated Contemporaries." They contain surprisingly few critical comments on her fiction, although there is one long discussion of *Mary Barton* from Maria Edgeworth. Also, Clement Shorter privately printed Mrs. Gaskell's "My Diary" (1923), a document subtitled "The Early Years of My Daughter Marianne" and containing entries from March 10, 1835, to October 28, 1838. An article by Annette B. Hopkins in the *PULC* (1954) reproduces a fascinating letter in which Mrs. Gaskell reveals the conflict between her literary work and the duties of her state in life.

IV. *Biography*

Mrs. Gaskell had a personal dislike of bringing her life before the public. The tentative, sketchy method and the errors of early biographers can be traced to a family feeling that she did not wish a biography undertaken. A remark to her daughters that she hoped that there would be no biography was interpreted by them as a charge to keep out prying eyes.

The Reverend George A. Payne (*Mrs. Gaskell and Knutsford,* 1900) respects the family wish but brings together information which he thinks Mrs. Gaskell's admirers will find valuable. Her self-confessed champion, he provides background on Knutsford, a brief biographical account containing comments on her works, and a sketch of William Gaskell. The same author's rather disjointed book *Mrs. Gaskell: A Brief Biography* (1929) is another version of that part of its predecessor which deals with Mrs. Gaskell's life together with a new chapter on "Mrs. Gaskell and Religion." This moral biographer embraces his "labour of love" convinced that "the pure fiction of Mrs. Gaskell will produce a beneficent influence upon all who read."

Mrs. Ellis H. Chadwick's *Mrs. Gaskell: Haunts, Homes, and Stories* (1910; rev. ed., 1913) is customarily classified as a biography, but it focuses on descriptions of places associated with Mrs. Gaskell's life and identifications of the originals of her scenes and characters. The tone of the book communicates Mrs. Chadwick's high confidence in her ability to trace almost any page of Mrs. Gaskell's fiction to a biographical equivalent. Mrs. Chadwick's errors in fact and the effusive and endless detail on such matters as the architecture of Mrs. Gaskell's haunts and homes make her unconvincing.

A. Stanton Whitfield (*Mrs. Gaskell: Her Life and Work,* 1929) had at his disposal private sources, for example, letters not available to previous writers and the privately printed "My Diary." He provides interesting detail on Mrs. Gaskell's friends and travel and on the circumstances of composition. Over half of the book concerns itself with her fiction. Summaries of the action, judicious quotation, and comment on her literary development make this section a readable introduction to Mrs. Gaskell. Although Whitfield's expression is sentimental ("And if a writer's voice is in harmony with the vibrations of the human heart, then he or she takes a place in our literature"), his esteem for Mrs. Gaskell is based on a standard of realism: his conviction that most of the time she was capable of recording her careful observations with great fidelity and art. When she observed well, she did her best work; when she observed poorly, for example, in her account of the absurdly naïve Ruth, her work faltered. Her fiction has preserved for us a part of the Victorian age: its domestic spirit in *Wives and Daughters*, its petty provincial life in *Cranford*, its problems with industrialization in *North and South* and *Mary Barton*.

Although Gerald DeWitt Sanders (*Elizabeth Gaskell*, Cornell Studies in English, 1929) presents some new biographical material and corrects some hitherto unchallenged errors in past studies, he labels his work a study of Mrs. Gaskell's works, not a Life. His chronological treatment gives some deserved notice to her shorter works. This study is strong in historical background (for instance, on the press gang in *Sylvia's Lovers*), which Sanders presents always for the light that it throws on the fiction. Also mindful of the development of Mrs. Gaskell's art, he makes comparative judgments on such matters as motivation, the development of action, and theme — notably the last. Thus, in addition to the detailed analysis of *Ruth*, which includes both censure for its lack of unity and praise for the characterization of Sally, Bradshaw, and Ruth, there is his view that in *Ruth* Mrs. Gaskell "demonstrates fully her creed and her religion."

Sanders' work is valuable in many respects: in its provision of the details surrounding the time of composition and of Mrs. Gaskell's dealings with publishers and correspondents;

in its accurate and full data on the periodical appearances of her work; in providing the most thorough chronology available; in illustrating her rich and precise use of the speech of Lancashire and Yorkshire. Sanders declares the probability that Mrs. Gaskell's fiction and the studies of her husband were instrumental in effecting the proper use of dialect in realistic fiction.

Elizabeth Haldane's *Mrs. Gaskell and Her Friends* (1931) is chiefly concerned with presenting her "in relation to the friends who were intertwined with her life." All accounts of Mrs. Gaskell give some attention to her friendship with Charlotte Brontë and her writing of Miss Brontë's biography; Miss Haldane, in accordance with her purpose, devotes almost a quarter of her book to this relationship. The chief remaining friends of Miss Haldane's title are Florence Nightingale, Madame Mohl, and the Winkworth sisters. Miss Haldane attends, especially in discussing Mrs. Gaskell's early works, to the climate of opinion when her books first appeared and synthesizes their contemporary reception. Her account is laced with letters, some appearing here for the first time, almost all of them quoted extensively or printed in their entirety. In the absence of an edition of Mrs. Gaskell's correspondence one must overlook the folksiness of this portrait and accept it as the most readily available source for many letters. Aina Rubenius, however, points out in *The Woman Question in Mrs. Gaskell's Life and Works* that Miss Haldane's versions of the letters "often differ considerably from the originals."

The best brief survey of Mrs. Gaskell's life and works comes in the English Novelists series, Yvonne ffrench's *Mrs. Gaskell* (1949). Written in a chatty, feminine style, it is interested in more than the person of Mrs. Gaskell and the originals of her characters. Miss ffrench's comments on structure, theme, and tone — if not always penetrating and sufficiently detailed — are sane and thought-provoking. She praises, for example, the employment of the objective narrator as the "most effective of all her devices for veiled irony." Miss ffrench objects to viewing Mrs. Gaskell primarily as a social reformer, stressing that her true mission was "promoting understanding." Again, she sees Mrs. Gaskell's work as largely controlled by two dominant personality traits; thus there exists "a constant attempt at reconciliation between her natural escapism and the sense of moral obligation forced upon her by period, circumstances, and upbringing." Miss ffrench's preference for the stories in the tradition of *My Lady Ludlow, Cousin Phillis,* and *Cranford* and her dissatisfaction with *Mary Barton* and *North and South* demonstrate her feeling that Mrs. Gaskell's fiction profited greatly when its creator could escape the demands of the times. The same critic's authoritative essay in *From Jane Austen to Joseph Conrad* (ed. Robert C. Rathburn and Martin Steinmann, Jr., 1958) centers on this fortunate escape from the "missionary zeal" of her early writing to a charming and artistic preoccupation with the English life and spirit.

The most recent full-scale biography of Mrs. Gaskell (Annette B. Hopkins, *Elizabeth Gaskell: Her Life and Work,* 1952) is also the most scholarly. If it is not quite the definitive study, it is one to which all future students must give homage. More interested in Mrs. Gaskell's many-sided character than in her writing, Miss Hopkins achieves real insight into Mrs. Gaskell the person — partially by judicious quotation from her correspondence, for example, the passages reflecting her friendship with George Smith (much of this never before published) and those which show her contentment in Rome after the completion of the *Life of Charlotte Brontë.*[1] Yet Miss Hopkins does not restrict herself to a consideration of the works only insofar as they reflect Mrs. Gaskell's character. In her discussion of *Ruth,* to choose perhaps the best example,[2] she admits its faults (the unreality of the young

---

[1] Mrs. Gaskell's role as a biographer, not the concern of this essay, forms a fascinating chapter in her life. Despite discoveries about the Brontë family made in this century, her *Life of Charlotte Brontë* remains a substantially reliable and absolutely indispensable contribution. For an authoritative account of this phase of Mrs. Gaskell's life, see the Hopkins biography, pp. 158–199. A longer and popular rendering is Margaret Lane's *The Brontë Story: A Reconsideration of Mrs. Gaskell's Life of Charlotte Brontë* (1953).

[2] The chapter on *Mary Barton* is essentially the same as Miss Hopkins'

boy and the failure to make the reader see some of Belling-ham's enchantment for Ruth) and demonstrates how this single book raised the artistic level of the English problem novel "by virtue of its character drawing, its descriptive power, the clear presentation of the problem, and the reason-ableness with which it is handled." The heroine, much as she has her creator's sympathy, is shown to have some serious faults; the novel bravely censures the Victorian attitude of ostracizing sex offenders and of looking upon marriage as a social salvation; the novelist presents her theme by the drama of the story rather than by exposition and preachment. Miss Hopkins calls for an assessment of Mrs. Gaskell's fiction in the Victorian panorama; this important study still awaits its writer.

Miss Hopkins directs her vision at one especially fascinat-ing aspect of Mrs. Gaskell's personality — the conflict, often hidden, between her social self and her inner self. As a social being she was aware of the suffering of the world and of her duties as wife, mother, and Christian; from her inner self came the desire to escape conscience, to revel in beauty and convenience. Miss Hopkins feels that Mrs. Gaskell's early death was in large part due to the presence of this con-flict in her soul rather than the often noted serenity. One wishes that Miss Hopkins had made connections between these qualities and the fiction.

There are shortcomings in this work: Miss Hopkins lacks complete objectivity because of her great admiration for her subject; she is occasionally slow-moving and banal ("But honeymoons, like all good things, have a way of coming to an end"); she fails to clarify or strengthen certain critical comments ("How could Mr. Gibson, a man of intelligence, commonsense, honour, integrity, fall for such a woman? . . . The answer may be found in observing the countless mis-mated couples in real life"). Yet critics who would cavil over these defects run the danger of losing sight of Miss Hopkins'

---

earlier essay in the *Trollopian* (1948). There are in the periodical, however, some informative notes that do not reappear in the biography. Miss Hopkins' discussion of Dickens and Mrs. Gaskell is treated below.

major accomplishment: a thorough, well-balanced, carefully documented account that makes maximum use of widely scattered primary sources and stands as a corrective of past studies.

The most recent study of Mrs. Gaskell, Miriam Allott's pamphlet for the Writers and Their Work series (1960), is a thoroughly serviceable introduction which communicates ably — despite its brevity — the flavor of each of the novels. In *Cranford, Cousin Phillis,* and *Wives and Daughters,* Miss Allott finds Mrs. Gaskell's best work — work which unites her warm personal sympathy, quiet humor, and expert observation of social intercourse. The novelist's defects are traceable, especially in the social novels, to her going beyond her range. There is an excellent, partially annotated selected bibliography.

V. *Other Studies*

A. W. Ward's introductory essays in the Knutsford edition are strongest when the material at hand calls for historical or cultural background, notably in the cases of *Mary Barton* and *Sylvia's Lovers.* The introduction to the former, to illustrate a very full treatment, concerns itself with material on the circumstances of composition, the historical background on the "hungry forties," the contemporary response, and Mrs. Gaskell's literary qualities. Ward does not divide Mrs. Gaskell's writings into periods, though he does note her literary preoccupations. Without detailing his conviction, he sees a constant theme playing through all her writings, one which he summarizes in his final words on *Wives and Daughters*: "The book of contrasts . . . tells us, as everything that Mrs. Gaskell has written tells us, by what power such contrasts are effaced, the troubles which they helped to create removed, and human wrongs set right. Love is enough."

The purpose of Aina Rubenius in *The Woman Question in Mrs. Gaskell's Life and Works* (1951) is to examine in detail this hitherto neglected area, with special attention to the influence of the times and of Mrs. Gaskell's personal experience and reading. Miss Rubenius' study is perhaps best when it presents, as a result of a methodical scrutiny of the works, Mrs. Gaskell's attitude toward a given problem, for example, factory work for women; it is weakest when it engages in the dangerous effort of detecting the cause for such an attitude, for example, in attributing her developing indignation toward employers of dressmakers' apprentices chiefly to Henry Mayhew's 1849 articles in the *Morning Chronicle*. Again, the literary judgment that Mrs. Gaskell's fictional wives change is used to assault the traditionally idyllic picture of the Gaskell marriage; the result is some interesting, though probably not sufficiently cautious, writing on the shortcomings of the marriage.

Miss Rubenius' treatment of fallen women is representative of her method. Having provided the historical background, she takes up the instances in Mrs. Gaskell's fiction which deal with seduced women, noting a development from her conformity to contemporary literary handling in her early writings to the challenge to Victorian beliefs in *Ruth*. Miss Rubenius is tempted, despite the admitted absence of proof, to trace the ideas for *Ruth* to an 1850 *Westminster* article on prostitution. In both the article and the novel certain common points arise: the Victorian attitude that insists on a girl's absolute ignorance of sex while expecting instinctive knowledge of danger to her virtue is attacked as a cause of prostitution; the double standard is assaulted; the solution of having the seduced woman marry her seducer is questioned. The critic might be wrong in contending that Mrs. Gaskell went to this source, but her precise examination of the writer's attitude toward the fallen woman was as needful as it is detailed. Miss Rubenius' other topics include domestic servants, needlewomen, and problems of wives and of girls engaged to be married. She continually documents the accuracy with which Mrs. Gaskell presents the social ills of the time.

Three appendixes deal with "Factory Work for Women," "Literary Influences in Mrs. Gaskell's Works," and "Mrs. Gaskell's Quotations from and References to Other Writers and Works." The second includes a demonstration of the arresting similarity between *North and South* and Henry F. Chorley's *Pomfret*. Miss Rubenius also sees in *Wives and Daughters* a strong, though not necessarily a conscious, dependence on novels of Fredrika Bremer.

Lord David Cecil's essay on Mrs. Gaskell in *Early Victorian Novelists* (1934) — balanced, perceptive, full of insights — opens with a consideration of the effects of her femininity on her writing, a lack of virile qualities such as intellectual structure and an absence of intense vision. He quickly points out, however, that these are limitations and not defects, limitations which have corresponding merits. Among these merits are a taste that allows the novelist to produce a simple pathos unmarred by the wish to exploit the audience, a feminine command of detail and subtlety which is psychological as well as visual, and a freshness of outlook. It is true that only "the home life of the professional classes and the country gentry" shows the facility of her creative vision; it is true that all of her fiction is — in the words of *Cranford* — "in possession of the amazons"; but it is also true that her pictures of this limited world are marked by a perceptive reality of social structure, notably in *Wives and Daughters*, and by unforgettable characters, chiefly Cynthia.

Yet Cecil admits that despite these and other merits Mrs. Gaskell's reputation is not great. The reason is that, like her contemporaries, she wrote outside her range. Nothing could be farther beyond her proper areas of the domestic and the pastoral than *Mary Barton* and *North and South*. Thus, like the majority of Mrs. Gaskell's readers, though with considerably greater critical finesse, Cecil finds the richness of her outstanding qualities in *Sylvia's Lovers, Cousin Phillis, Cranford,* and *Wives and Daughters*. Elizabeth Jenkins, in her introduction to *Cranford* and *Cousin Phillis*, feels with Cecil that these two novels artistically mirror the times.

One of the comments elicited by Lord David's essay was V. S. Pritchett's defense of *North and South* (*New Statesman and Nation*, 1941). Pritchett agrees that Mrs. Gaskell's range did not include economics but insists that she is an effective social historian who succeeds here where she always succeeds, in skillful observation and deft satire. The enthusiastic appreciation of *Wives and Daughters* (1948) by Rosamond Lehmann is an attempt to win readers for this "neglected Victorian classic" as well as an answer to some of Cecil's strictures, notably to that which pronounces Mrs. Gaskell's portrayal of elderly men as not so bad and young men as terrible. In words reminiscent of Henry James's salute to Mrs. Gaskell's last novel (*Nation*, 1866), Miss Lehmann puzzles over the comparative neglect of this book: "surely, in its breadth and generosity of scope, in its fun, its compassion, its quiet irony and uncorrupted pathos, in the fineness and subtlety of its character drawing, it constitutes a world of irresistible comfort and pleasure for any reader, no matter of what sex." (This Chiltern Library introduction also appeared in *Penguin New Writing*, no. 32, 1948.)

The only real correspondence between Cecil's essay and the apparently similar study by Marjory A. Bald (*Women-Writers of the Nineteenth Century*, 1923) is one of length. Miss Bald's essay, with sections devoted to various aspects of Mrs. Gaskell, for example, atmosphere and setting, humor, and pathos, is an undistinguished chronological meandering through Mrs. Gaskell's fiction, a mere exercise in illustrating these characteristics.

Recent biographical and critical essays on Mrs. Gaskell are marked by a great variety of scope, method, and worth. Perhaps because of her often noted charm, she seems peculiarly capable of prompting appreciative essays. From Arthur Quiller-Couch's quiet advocacy of her nostalgic "sunset softness" (*Charles Dickens and Other Victorians*, 1925), through the syrupy adulation of James Brockbank (*Papers of the Manchester Literary Club*, 1932), to Clarice Short's somewhat more sophisticated explanation of her esteem for *Cranford* (*Western Humanities Review*, 1957), there is little progress in the analysis of Mrs. Gaskell's appeal. Superior to these three is a recent and authoritative introductory survey of Mrs. Gaskell's life and work by Arthur Pollard (*Bulle-*

tin of the John Rylands Library, 1961). Another excellent essay, Naomi Lewis' in *A Visit to Mrs. Wilcox* (1957), points to *Wives and Daughters* and especially to *Cranford* to suggest that Mrs. Gaskell's most distinctive gift was comic, the witty display of a social group in action. Mrs. Gaskell's humor has never been formally studied.

Perhaps the chief value of Lucy Poate Stebbins' appreciative essay in *A Victorian Album* (1946) rests in her comments on the theme of the lie as it reveals itself in various narratives. Sanders pauses over this point briefly in his *Elizabeth Gaskell,* and an unpublished doctoral dissertation by Clara Schnurer ("Mrs. Gaskell's Fiction," University of Pittsburgh, 1932) treats deception as one of Mrs. Gaskell's central ideas. The themes of her fiction and the degree of artistry with which they are set forth are deserving of study.

Two worthwhile studies of biographical and historical interest are D. S. Bland's "Mary Barton and Historical Accuracy" (*RES,* 1950) and David Shusterman's "William Rathbone Greg and Mrs. Gaskell" (*PQ,* 1957). The first illustrates Mrs. Gaskell's remarkably accurate picture of Manchester as a means of demonstrating "the value of literary evidence to the social historian." Shusterman, convinced that *North and South* was designed partially "to assuage the feelings" of Greg, censorious reviewer of *Mary Barton,* and other leading Manchester men, proposes that the chief model for John Thornton was not James Nasmyth, as Mrs. Chadwick had suggested, but Greg himself.

A biographical study of great interest is Annette B. Hopkins' thoroughly documented account of the relationship between Dickens as editor and Mrs. Gaskell as contributor to *Household Words* and *All the Year Round (HLQ,* 1946). Dickens' attitude seems to move from beginning adulation to dissatisfaction with her cooperation, especially with regard to serialization, to a continuing desire to obtain her contributions. Mrs. Gaskell shifts from beginning docility to refusal to make suggested alterations and on to the decision to leave Dickens in favor of George Smith and the *Cornhill.* This material is incorporated in Miss Hopkins' biography.

The distinctions among various versions of Mrs. Gaskell's narratives have never been analyzed. Miss Hopkins' purpose, in her discussion of *North and South*, is not to characterize the artistry of the serial version and the final version but only to outline the differences. Such an analysis would be useful. In addition, there is at the University of Leeds a rough draft of *Mary Barton*, which would form the basis for a study of this book from germ to fulfillment. (We know also that Mrs. Gaskell's publishers required her, over her protests, to add about twenty-four pages toward the end of her story.) A third area for this kind of investigation is *Cranford*. It might be studied in terms of (1) the minor changes between serial and book, (2) the earliest use of this material in "The Last Generation in England" (*Sartain's Magazine*, 1849), and (3) the sequel, "The Cage at Cranford" (*All the Year Round*, 1863). Miss Hopkins has treated this last in her biography. A further instance would involve a comparison between "Martha Preston" (*Sartain's Magazine*, 1850) and its revision into "Half a Lifetime Ago."

Although several essays united by their interest in Mrs. Gaskell's industrial novels may be summarized here, notice must be taken of the pioneering of Louis Cazamian in *Le Roman social en Angleterre, 1830–1850* (1903).[3] Focusing on *Mary Barton* and *North and South*, Cazamian sees them as products of a religious sentiment reacting against an evil industrial system. His extensive and appropriate quoting from the novels has a twofold end: the analysis of the social phenomena illustrated by various actions and characters and the demonstration of his conviction that "la thèse vaut surtout par l'illustration, l'idée abstraite par le détail vivant" (thesis is especially valuable by illustration, abstract idea by living detail).

Annette B. Hopkins' "Liberalism in the Social Teachings of Mrs. Gaskell" (*Social Service Review*, 1931) sees in Mrs. Gaskell's reliable portrayals of industrial problems an expression of liberal thought in the mid-nineteenth century,

[3] The "nouvelle édition" of this work (1934) is in no sense a revision of the 1903 printing.

especially for social and religious tolerance. In another socio-logical journal (*Social Forces*, 1928), Josephine Johnston writes that Mrs. Gaskell's works demonstrate her advocacy of reforms in three areas of social work: case work, institu-tions, and industry.

Lettice Cooper focuses her introduction to *Mary Barton* on the idea that the book grew out of a new problem, how to attain a happy life in this world "conditioned by the machine." She observes that the nostalgia for country life, in Mrs. Gaskell's case no doubt influenced by Knutsford, was a symptom of a generation that longed for the life ante-dating rapid urban expansion. Kathleen Tillotson (*Novels of the Eighteen-Forties*, 1954) objects to the derogatory label-ing of *Mary Barton* as a thesis novel and perceptively com-ments on various aspects of the book which contribute to its artistic unity — for example, the author's central and knowl-edgeable concentration on John Barton and her use of Job Legh as a contrast to him. This study stands as an admirable model for an analytical consideration of theme and its rela-tionship to other aspects of the work. Writing chiefly from a viewpoint that sees literature as a product of economic forces, Arnold Kettle ("The Early Victorian Social-Problem Novel," in *From Dickens to Hardy*, ed. Boris Ford, 1958) treats Mrs. Gaskell's involvement in the condition-of-England question, especially in *Mary Barton*. According to Kettle, be-cause her emotions involved her in the life of the people, Mrs. Gaskell succeeded nobly in an accurate portrayal of the time and, more importantly, in her forceful and dis-tinguished understanding of John Barton, "apart from Heath-cliff . . . the nearest approach to a tragic hero which the early Victorian novel permitted itself." Myron F. Bright-field's introduction to *Mary Barton* also views John Barton as a tragic figure, one whose fate has been well prepared for by Mrs. Gaskell's skillful integration of the social and artistic aspects of fiction. Raymond Williams' essay "The Industrial Novels" (*Culture and Society: 1780–1950*, 1958) directs a penetrating eye on "the structure of feeling" in *Mary Barton*. The novel, which in the beginning reflects Mrs. Gaskell's identification with the plight of the working man, falters, in Williams' view, as attention is diverted from John to Mary Barton. What started as a representative book changes to one dealing with a special case, a murder of a singular kind. John Barton evolves into an allegorical figure representing a widely felt fear in the upper and middle classes, the fear of violence.

Elizabeth Bowen's distinguished introduction to *North and South* admits that the novel is outdated as a social document but insists on its pre-eminence as a presentation of feeling — the feelings of Margaret Hale and John Thornton chiefly, who reflect the opposition between the world of action and that of escape. The conflict is resolved in the heroine by her realization that there is no escape from change, that the South itself is unstable, that change is good. And underlying this conflict is, Miss Bowen suggests, the North and South in Mrs. Gaskell, who — unlike Margaret — "was either spared from feeling or did not permit herself to feel" the impact of moving from the South to the North. It is regrettable that Miss Bowen did not expand her analysis.

Two article-length reviews in *TLS* contribute to the revival of interest in Mrs. Gaskell. The first, Aug. 30, 1947, reviews the Chiltern Library edition of *Mary Barton*. The second, March 28, 1952, reviews this edition of *North and South* and the Hopkins biography. Another review of this edition of *North and South* and Miss Hopkins' biography develops into a full-length essay: H. P. Collins (*EC*, 1953) sees Mrs. Gaskell's cardinal characteristic as a "naked sensibility," one that did not possess the power to transmute experience into a self-contained and objective fictional world, as did Eliot in *Middlemarch*; Mrs. Gaskell's fiction always reveals her own feminine sympathies. Consequently, according to Collins, a full-scale revival of her popularity is undesirable.

An entirely different problem concerns Richard D. Altick in his scholarly comparison of Boucicault's *The Long Strike* with *Mary Barton*, on which it was based (*NCF*, 1959). He concludes that the skillfully constructed melodrama is more satisfying in showing the special effects of the sensation play than is *Mary Barton* in fulfilling the function of serious fiction. In Boucicault's acquisition of these dramatic effects, however, he loses qualities more appropriate to fiction, most noticeably the complexity of Mary's feelings for her two admirers. A similarly instructive study might be undertaken on the stage adaptations of *Cranford*.

There has been only one formal study of Mrs. Gaskell's reputation, Annette B. Hopkins' thoroughly documented "Mrs. Gaskell in France, 1849–1890" (*PMLA*, 1938). Miss Hopkins finds as the underlying reason for French admiration of Mrs. Gaskell the protest of French literary conservatism against the rise of naturalism. In her fiction the French found embodied a Christian love of humanity. The remaining areas of Mrs. Gaskell's reputation, despite scattered references in biographies to the initial reception of her books, await analysis.

Another important sector of investigation concerns influences upon Mrs. Gaskell and her influence upon other writers. In Ward's introductions to the Knutsford edition and in various other studies, we read scattered remarks on writers who may have influenced her. Among these are Crabbe, Gray, Maurice, Carlyle, George Sand, Kingsley, Harriet Martineau, and Jane Austen. Similarly, Mrs. Gaskell's influence on other writers remains to be investigated. Among those mentioned as perhaps influenced by her are George Eliot, Tennyson, Stevenson, Barrie, Moore, and Dostoyevsky. Mrs. Gaskell's influence on Dostoyevsky is taken up by Leonid Grossman in *Voprosi Literaturi* (1959) and *Anglo-Soviet Journal* (1960). And Miriam Allott points to Mrs. Gaskell's "The Old Nurse's Story" as a link between *Wuthering Heights* and "The Turn of the Screw" (*N&Q*, 1961).

It has been the custom of historians of English fiction to give Mrs. Gaskell very little notice — sometimes none at all. The obvious exception is Ernest A. Baker (*The History of the English Novel*, vol. VIII, 1937). His typically thorough survey, though marked by a few statements since disproved, is characterized by judicious quoting and urbane comments on her worth in relation to her contemporaries. Other exceptions are Edward Wagenknecht (*Cavalcade of the English Novel*, 1943), Walter Allen (*The English Novel*, 1954), and Lionel Stevenson (*The English Novel*, 1960). There is need for an overall critical study of Mrs. Gaskell's fiction and a reassessment of her position both within Victorian fiction and within English fiction as a whole.

KINGSLEY

The fiction of Charles Kingsley has attracted little critical attention during recent decades. It is as if the commonplace that he was a writer for boys has been taken to heart. Such disregard has not, however, been the lot of Kingsley the man. The enigma of this many-sided and controversial Victorian has continued to fascinate twentieth-century scholars, and the last word on him is yet to be spoken.

I. *Bibliography*

There are two major bibliographies of Kingsley's writings, each excellent in its way. M. L. Parrish's *Charles Kingsley and Thomas Hughes* (1936) provides thorough detail on the "First Editions (with a few exceptions) in the Library at Dormy House." This collection, one of Parrish's finest, serves as a virtually complete bibliography. Descriptions of and additions to it are recorded in three articles in *PULC* by Margaret F. Thorp (1946), Verna E. Bayles (1947), and Alexander D. Wainwright (1956). The best guide to Kingsley's writings, Margaret F. Thorp's bibliography in *Charles Kingsley: 1819–1875* (1937), is a chronological list of Kingsley's works which includes many unsigned and uncollected items formally attributed to him by Mrs. Thorp. Ruth E. Matthews (*Stanford Studies in Language and Literature,* 1941) has discovered and reproduced three essays by Kingsley which he wrote for a little-known American periodical *Out West* in 1872.

The only extensive bibliography about Kingsley and his works is in Stanley E. Baldwin's *Charles Kingsley* (1934).

Robert B. Martin's *The Dust of Combat* (1959) provides a selected list of authorities used in this biography.

II. *Editions*

Of the many collected editions of Kingsley's writings, the first published is the most complete: a twenty-eight-volume edition of *The Works of Charles Kingsley* (1880–1885) in which fewer than half of the volumes were needed for his fiction, the remainder being composed chiefly of sermons and lectures. The few omissions in this collection can be located with the aid of Mrs. Thorp's bibliography. Other less complete but more available editions include the seven-volume *Works of Charles Kingsley* (1898–1899), with introductions by Maurice Kingsley; the fourteen-volume *Novels, Poems, and Memories of Charles Kingsley* (1899); and the nineteen-volume *Life and Works of Charles Kingsley* (1901–1903). All of these are completely adequate for a study of Kingsley's fiction.

In 1916 there appeared for the first time *The Tutor's Story*, a novel begun by Kingsley and completed by his daughter Lucas Malet (Mrs. Mary St. Leger Harrison). A first edition in the Parrish Collection at Princeton University has pencil notations in Mrs. Harrison's hand which indicate which parts of the novel are hers, which her father's.

Eric V. Sandin's edition of "The Nun's Pool" *(Charles Kingsley's Only Short Story*, 1937) is an abstract of a University of Illinois dissertation. This story, which appeared originally in *The Christian Socialist* (1851) but is not in the collected editions, is commonly referred to as the basis for *Yeast*. There are, however, no parallel passages; the similarities are in setting and the references to a curse.

In recent years Kingsley's fiction has not been honored by many reprints with significant introductions. The earliest of note is an edition of *Westward Ho!* for the Limited Editions Club (1947), illustrated by Edward A. Wilson and introduced by John T. Winterich. L. A. G. Strong has written introductions for the Collins New Classics editions of both *West-

ward Ho! (1953) and *Hereward the Wake* (1954). Each has a brief biographical sketch of the author and a selected bibliography. In 1955 James A. Williamson wrote a new introduction for the Everyman edition of *Westward Ho!* It has a select, but hardly up-to-date, bibliography.

III. *Letters*

The primary source of printed material on Kingsley is his wife's official biography, *Charles Kingsley: His Letters and Memories of His Life* (1877),[4] which has been reprinted and edited many times. Many of the later editions contain material not in the original one: for example, the 1879 popular edition prepared by Mrs. Kingsley abridges the earlier material but also adds a dozen new areas of discussion; and it, in turn, differs from an abridgment copyrighted by Scribner, Armstrong and Company in 1877 and prepared by one identified as the "Editor of the Abridgment." Mrs. Kingsley, who wished to show only the most admirable facets of her husband's character, deleted most personal references. And she did not always attend to such matters as dating. Until someone edits the Kingsley correspondence, scholars will have to exercise care in using Mrs. Kingsley's work.[5]

In *Charles Kingsley's American Notes: Letters from a Lecture Tour, 1874* (1958) Robert B. Martin presents twenty-four letters, many of which had been published in part by Kingsley's wife, in "an attempt to record an eminent Victorian's reactions to his trip to North America, complete with the unflattering remarks which his wife thought unsuitable for publication." There are detailed — sometimes painfully detailed — explanatory notes for each letter and an introduc-

---

[4] Robert B. Martin (*The Dust of Combat*) points out that, though the title page gives the date as 1877, this work first appeared in 1876. Mr. Martin's own book is dated 1959 on its title page but did not appear until 1960.

[5] Robert B. Martin, who announced his editing of Kingsley's correspondence in 1949 (*TLS*, June 24), made use of his findings in *Charles Kingsley's American Notes* and in *The Dust of Combat*, but has deemed the correspondence unworthy of publication in its entirety and has discontinued the project.

tion treating Kingsley's reputation, his travels, and the un-kind reception given him by the American press. The three recent biographers — Margaret F. Thorp, Una Pope-Hennessy, and Robert B. Martin — make use of unpub-lished manuscript materials. Information on the location and character of some manuscript letters is available in Robert B. Martin (*PULC*, 1952), Carey S. Bliss (*HLQ*, 1953), and Alex-ander P. Clark (*PULC*, 1958).

IV. *Biography*

Stanley E. Baldwin's *Charles Kingsley* (1934) provides "an account of the social, economic, and religious problems that Kingsley faced, and an appreciation of his work in meeting those problems, especially as an author." It is the only study that systematically addresses itself to each of Kingsley's major novels. Convinced that an introduction to Kingsley's life and work and a consideration of the influence of Car-lyle and Maurice are essential for an understanding of his writing, Baldwin gives us three chapters on these matters before his six essays on the major fiction. (An earlier study of Carlyle's influence is Maria Meyer's *Carlyles Einfluss auf Kingsley in sozial-politischer und religiös-ethischer Hinsicht*, 1914.) Baldwin's survey of the religious, social, and industrial background of Kingsley's novels is highly informative. That such a chapter is so valuable — even essential — for a proper reading of Kingsley's fiction is perhaps symbolic of the utter dependence of his writings on the times from which they rose.

In a representative discussion of a Kingsley novel, Baldwin reviews the plot and characters and treats purpose, theme, and the use of characters and plot to exemplify theme. In his list of a novel's virtues one always finds approving mention of Kingsley's skill in description, and among the defects one regularly reads some remark on the lack of plausibility. Fully aware that *Yeast* is a social treatise rather than a novel, Bald-win notes that the plot is "so thin as scarcely to cast a shadow," that the characters begin preaching as soon as they are introduced, and that the theme scatters itself in attacks on the many evils of the day. Basically, Baldwin analyzes *Yeast* as a kind of morality play, examining each character to determine what he represents and noting the use of various themes. In treating *Alton Locke,* Baldwin emphasizes the accuracy of Kingsley's information on the hungry forties and the consequent historical value of his presentation. This is accomplished by a documentation of Kingsley's association with the historical Thomas Cooper and of the astonishing resemblance between the activities of the man Cooper and the character Locke. This identification is also detailed in Louis Cazamian's *Kingsley et Thomas Cooper, étude sur une source d'Alton Locke* (1903), and W. Henry Brown's *Charles Kingsley: The Work and Influence of Parson Lot* (1924).

Baldwin's overall view can be expressed in this way: although Kingsley is clearly open to charges of intolerance, an understanding of the man and of his noble purpose helps us to make allowances for his excesses; although his fiction has been attacked as mere propaganda, a more judicious view is to accept as justifiable much of the criticism of *Yeast* and *Alton Locke* but to point out that the historical novels are artistic creations in the sense that the polemics are skillfully blended with the characterization and setting. Kingsley's faults are many and obvious; yet all his writings evidence "enough of true vision and undeniable beauty . . . to cause confusion among critics as to whether they are great books or merely books with a large element of greatness in them."

Margaret Farrand Thorp's *Charles Kingsley: 1819–1875* (1937) skillfully and economically presents the significance of Kingsley's life and work both for his own time and for succeeding generations. As Queen Victoria is the typical Victorian woman, so Kingsley — Mrs. Thorp maintains — is the embodiment of the typical Victorian man: "He believed in England, in the Empire, in the Established Church; in the ennobling influence of womanhood and the sanctity of the home; in a good God guiding the universe and each of its individual inhabitants; in the spiritual brotherhood of men within a benevolent aristocracy; in evolutionary progress

and the compatibility of science and religion. Most of the
great literary figures of the nineteenth century were rebels
against or thinkers in advance of their time. Kingsley's influence was due in large part to his not being a thinker at all."
Mrs. Thorp emphasizes throughout her study the particular
ways in which Kingsley is representative of his era. In treating *Two Years Ago*, for instance, she demonstrates Kingsley's attitudes on science, sanitation, the doctrine of eternal
damnation, Dissent, extreme High Churchmen, and the
nature of the artist.

Mrs. Thorp's expert use of Kingsley's letters and memoirs
is praiseworthy. Her chapters are readable, and it is a tribute
to the interest she arouses that we sometimes desire more
expansive treatment in some areas. A more precise explanation of how *Hypatia* reveals Kingsley's conviction that Christianity, not "Emersonian Anythingarianism," contains the
answer for nineteenth-century man's search for individuality
would be interesting.

A special feature of Mrs. Thorp's study is a chapter on
Kingsley's literary criticism gathered from a wide variety
of sources. Here and elsewhere the biographer makes use of
private collections of material which she enumerates in her
preface and which she is the first biographer to obtain.

Una Pope-Hennessy's *Canon Charles Kingsley* (1948) excellently exemplifies the approach to Kingsley prevalent in
recent decades: concerned with literary criticism in only the
most marginal way, the book directs its attention to the
events, people, and books that influenced the enigmatic personality that is its subject. Dame Una demonstrates that
Kingsley's life was governed largely by feeling instead of
principle or intellectual development, but she does not explain his motivation. Although a personality in the end cannot be grasped, can only be sensed, we will profit, she says,
from examining Kingsley's responses to the stimuli of his
life. The result is a book rich in fascinating background
of the age, especially in religious matters such as the ferment
caused by *Essays and Reviews* but also in such social and
familial concerns as Kingsley's reaction to the Rajah Brooke

affair and to his brother's writing, which the biographer thinks "made him feel that he simply could not compete." Constantly aware of the shortcomings of Fanny Kingsley's idealistic biography, Dame Una frequently notes her frustrations over the reticence of the novelist's wife, especially with regard to other members of the Kingsley family. She makes commendable use of unpublished materials and contemporary records, for example, on the status and conduct of the clergy, though she provides no bibliography and few footnotes. Her book is also a helpful source for information on Kingsley's minor writings as well as for more commonly treated material such as the Newman controversy. This, then, is an anecdotal biography of a fascinating figure who happened to write novels; it is not concerned with Kingsley qua novelist.[6]

The most recent biography of Kingsley, Robert B. Martin's *The Dust of Combat* (1959), is the fullest treatment to date. Martin enriches the material of Mrs. Thorp's biography in many areas, introducing new documents and presenting more detailed accounts. His habit of detailing produces particularly helpful insights in the chapter on "The World of Letters," which reports Kingsley's opinions of several literary contemporaries, and in the discussion of his capacity for friendship and of the friends themselves. The detail becomes excessively minute at times, particularly in the account of the American tour. On the other hand, there are areas that require more analytical treatment than they are accorded, notably Kingsley's theological place in the Church of England and his response to the scientific developments of the day. The almost total absence of documentation is sometimes disturbing.

Other features of this biography include Martin's view of Kingsley as a typical — though also highly individual — Victorian; brief discussions of the novels and their contemporary

[6] In Arthur A. Adrian's expansion of Dame Una's account of Kingsley's visit to Boston (*HLQ*, 1956), we hear about certain literary facets of Kingsley's character — his respect for Longfellow and admiration for the poetry of William Collins and Spenser, for example.

reception (this is a biography, not a critical study); a focus on Kingsley's life as divided into two periods, the phase of Parson Lot and the phase of the eminent Victorian; and a treatment of the origin of Kingsley's hatred of Roman Catholicism in his attitude toward sex and love and his consequent inability to conceive of a reason for respecting celibacy. *The Dust of Combat* is the best single source for Kingsley's life; the definitive biography, however, has not yet been written.

The discussion of *Two Years Ago,* although too brief, is illustrative of Martin's method. He first comments on its descriptive power, the originals of characters, and the use of recurring types of characters. He then turns to its open mirroring of Kingsley's doctrines, notably his anti-intellectualism, his views on the function of art, and his belief that works were more important than faith. Martin concludes that in these attitudes lies the reason for Kingsley's failure as a writer: his attempt "to combine the emotional drive of the artist with the intellect of the Philistine; Pegasus and the plough-horse seldom pull together in harness."

V. *Other Studies*

If perceptive critical writing is largely dependent on the perception of the creative artist under study, we should not be surprised at the small body of criticism concerned with Kingsley's fiction. Much evaluation of Kingsley relates to his connection with the contemporary scene, notably with movements for social reform. Charles William Stubbs (*Charles Kingsley and the Christian Social Movement*, 1899) focuses on what can still be learned from Kingsley's teaching, emphasizing the novelist's support of cooperative associations, improved sanitation, and the like. His book carries the authority of a writer intimate with the problems of the time and acquires interest from its extensive references to seldom used primary sources.

Several other studies follow the lead of Stubbs: although they refer to the novels with some frequency, they concentrate on Kingsley's teaching. Colwyn E. Vulliamy (*Charles*

Kingsley and Christian Socialism, 1914) sees the social movement in the churches as originating in the work of the Christian Socialists. He stresses Kingsley's desire to reform men individually and his insistence that class differentiation remain. W. Henry Brown's *Charles Kingsley: The Work and Influence of Parson Lot* (1924) treats with admiration the leading role played by Kingsley in the fight for improved cooperative associations. Brown's friendship with J. M. Ludlow and his access to contemporary records contribute to the authoritativeness of his discussion. More recent considerations of the question include Crane Brinton's *English Political Thought in the Nineteenth Century* (1933) and Bernard N. Schilling's *Human Dignity and the Great Victorians* (1946). Brinton accomplishes his purpose, a descriptive definition of Christian Socialism, by culling Kingsley's writings. Schilling studies Kingsley's response to the condition-of-England question in terms of his attacks on certain evils, chiefly poor sanitation and the working conditions of tailors, and his proposals for a reformed England, notably his insistence that individual reform must precede social reform.

The only full-length consideration of Kingsley's thought is Guy Kendall's *Charles Kingsley and His Ideas* (1947). Kendall feels that Kingsley's fame should and probably will rest not on his fiction but on his qualities as a man, a man seen through his ideas. In addition to those topics treated by every critic of Kingsley, for example, Chartism and the Newman controversy,[7] Kendall discusses in some detail the cooperative movement of the forties and fifties, the significance of theme in *The Saint's Tragedy* and *The Water Babies,* the controversy over the existence of eternal punishment, the novelist's attitude toward Darwinism, and his philosophy of history.

[7] Thorp, Pope-Hennessy, and Martin provide able résumés of the events, characters, and documents involved in the Newman-Kingsley controversy. The written exchange is readily available in Charles F. Harrold's edition of Newman's *Apologia Pro Vita Sua* (1947). Other analyses include those of Noel Annan (*New Statesman and Nation,* March 25, 1944, and March 8, 1947), T. L. Robertson, Jr. (*MLN,* 1954), and Walter E. Houghton (*Theology Today,* 1947). Houghton views the controversy as one between Protestant liberalism and Christian orthodoxy, and penetratingly analyzes its relevance for modern Protestant theology.

The reader is a little uncomfortable through all of this as he recalls from the preface that the war prevented Kendall from consulting important documents. Although Kingsley's ideas in various areas are sympathetically detailed, there is little of the expert use of contemporary records and manuscript material that we find in Thorp, Pope-Hennessy, and Martin. We are perhaps most forcibly aware of this when Kendall, unwilling to accept the customary approach to Kingsley as a man of inconsistent opinions, attempts to see a pattern in his development, for example, in his change from democratic to aristocratic leanings.

Four German writers treat phases of Kingsley's intellectual outlook. Fritz Köhler (*Charles Kingsley als Religiöser Tendenz-Schriftsteller,* 1912) analyzes each of the novels for Kingsley's views of the Anglican Church, Calvinist sects, and the Roman Catholic Church and for his concept of the ideal Christian. Anna Jacobson (*Charles Kingsleys Beziehungen zu Deutschland,* 1917) examines his life and works to demonstrate his connection with and reflection of all aspects of German life. The major chapter deals with his indebtedness to German literature, notably Goethe. Hilda Welte (*Das heroische Element bei Charles Kingsley,* 1934) discusses his concept of heroism, of which the chief quality is self-sacrifice, the sources for his ideas on the heroic, and the effect of these ideas on his thinking and writing. Finally, Willy Karl Marcard's *Charles Kingsley's Stellung zum Sport und zur Erziehung durch Leibesübungen in Leben und Dichtung* (1927) is valuable for its discussion of the importance that Kingsley attached to sports and physical exercise.

Several studies can be grouped here as treatments of Kingsley's relation to various phenomena of his century. George H. Ford (*UTQ,* 1948) places Kingsley among his contemporaries as he analyzes the response in England to the Governor Eyre case. Constance L. Beach treats *Hereward the Wake* in her dissertation on "The Use of Anglo-Saxon Material by Scott, Bulwer-Lytton, Kingsley, and Tennyson in Relation to the Anglo-Saxon Revival in England" (*University of Chicago Abstracts of Theses, Humanistic Series, 1930–*

1932). Arthur Johnston (*English,* 1959) briefly examines *The Water Babies* as a book which deals with three controversial topics of 1862: the employment of children, elementary education and the examination system, and Darwinism — especially the last. Mary W. Hanawalt's thoroughly documented exposition of the effect of science on Kingsley's life and writing (*SP,* 1937) wishes to clear up a misunderstanding of Kingsley's philosophy and art brought about by the disregard of his interest in science. She accomplishes this objective "first, by showing Kingsley's lifelong interest in science; secondly, by considering the relation of this study and research to his theory of art as revealed in his novels and poetry; thirdly, by presenting . . . further evidence of his realization of the importance of science in man's existence; and fourthly, by showing the influence of science upon such a philosophy as he held." In the second part of her study Miss Hanawalt documents the influence of science on the novelist's selection of characters, his use of scientific terminology, stress on environment, and realistic description of disease. Charles S. Blinderman (*VNL,* 1961), in discussing Kingsley's relationship with Huxley, also treats his response to science.

Three studies on Kingsley and history merit notice here. Ludwig Dicke (*Charles Kingsleys Hereward the Wake: eine Quellenuntersuchung,* 1906) compares the historical material from such sources as the *Anglo-Saxon Chronicle* with Kingsley's novel. He also discusses the contemporary reception of *Hereward* and other treatments of the Hereward story. Bernardus Merker's *Die historischen Quellen zu Kingsleys Roman Hypatia* (1908) investigates the use of historical sources both in the principal occurrences of this novel and in the description of the institutions and customs of the time. Albert Nicol's *Charles Kingsley und die Geschicte* (1936) speaks of such matters as Kingsley's use of history in his narrative technique and his place in the development of the novel, but its emphasis is on the novelist's formal philosophy of history.

Any consideration of Kingsley as a social novelist, as contrasted with Kingsley as a social theorist, must refer to the pioneering of Louis Cazamian in *Le Roman social en Angle-terre, 1830–1850* (1903). Cazamian treats Kingsley's part in Christian Socialism and his indebtedness to Maurice and Carlyle. More importantly, he studies in depth *Yeast* and *Alton Locke,* chiefly by scrutinizing each character and analyzing his function. Further, "Chez Kingsley, la vie et la précision du détail ne se nuisent pas l'une à l'autre; la condition des paysans et celle d'un certain prolétariat urbain n'ont jamais été décrites avec plus de vigueur saisissante," (In the works of Kingsley, life and precision of detail do not conflict; the conditions of the peasantry and of a specific urban proletariat have never been described with more striking vigor.) Although Macario Marmo (*The Social Novel of Charles Kingsley,* 1937) sees evidence of "vivid artistic intensity" in Kingsley's social writings, he focuses on Kingsley the teacher. In discussing *Alton Locke,* for instance, Marmo is concerned to present Kingsley's beliefs that industrial and agricultural development, not revolution, should be the basis for social change and that the social fabric will be mended only when men embrace their personal duties. Also, Marmo points out that Kingsley's leading characters often follow a pattern of conversion: they move to an interest in their fellow men as a result of love for a woman, but they idolize this love to the virtual exclusion of God. When the love is taken from them, they awake to a clearer and more religiously oriented vision of their social duties.

Kingsley's social novels also receive attention from Raymond Williams (*Culture and Society: 1780–1950,* 1958) and Arnold Kettle ("The Early Victorian Social-Problem Novel," in *From Dickens to Hardy,* ed. Boris Ford, 1958); neither, however, attends to Kingsley as much as to Mrs. Gaskell. A Washington University dissertation, Richard E. Allen's "Charles Kingsley and the Industrial Revolution" (1956), analyzes Kingsley's social creed by comparing it with the principles of Maurice and Carlyle. N. C. Peyrouton (*Dickensian,* 1962) disproves the assertion that Kingsley's Christian Socialism was influenced by and similar to the social teachings of Dickens. Kingsley's use of the novel for propaganda is treated in William J. Hyde's Wisconsin dissertation, "The English Peasantry in Contemporary Novels, 1815–1900" (1954).

A recent — and rather lonely — champion of Kingsley the novelist, L. A. G. Strong calls for a revaluation of Kingsley's writings in his introduction to *Westward Ho!* He admits the impossibility of separating the imaginative writer from the strangely prejudiced propagandist, but he still includes Kingsley within the great tradition of the English novel as a writer who thrived on moral purposes, who had "an imaginative vitality that could animate the most unpromising material and transform propaganda into art." Strong finds an ally in James A. Williamson, who in *his* introduction to *Westward Ho!* views Kingsley as a portrayer of societies. Moreover, this novel provides us with "not one historical novel but two, a living portrait of the Victorians and an animated picture of the events and setting of Elizabethan England." In Strong's introduction to *Hereward the Wake* we read that here more than in any of Kingsley's other novels we have the damaging intrusion of Kingsley the man — now as historian, again as theologian. Yet the resulting deficiencies are overpowered: *Hereward* becomes a great book because — fortunately — "Kingsley, the historian in Holy Orders, setting out with the deliberate design he had proclaimed at the book's beginning, was elbowed aside by Kingsley the storyteller, pouring out from the depths of his spirit the living flood of his tale." Two other voices which praise Kingsley as novelist — these less analytical, more appreciative — are W. M. Conacher (*Queen's Quarterly,* 1938) and J. B. Price (*Contemporary Review,* 1953).

Like Mrs. Gaskell, Kingsley receives little or no notice from most historians of the novel. Ernest A. Baker (*The History of the English Novel,* vol. VIII, 1937) provides an able introduction to Kingsley, placing him — along with Hughes, G. A. Lawrence, and others — in the reaction against the quiet domestic novel typified by Trollope. Discussions by Edward Wagenknecht (*Cavalcade of the English Novel,* 1943) and Lionel Stevenson (*The English Novel,* 1960) complete the list of those who honor Kingsley with expert analytical comment. Other areas for study may be seen. Various commentators note in passing Kingsley's interest in Spenser, Malory, Shelley, Scandinavian saga literature, and Henry Brooke. Similarly, it is said that Kingsley influenced Kipling and Noyes. These questions of influence on and by Kingsley await scholarly investigation. In the field of intellectual history several areas need further study. One of these, a minor one, is Kingsley's ethnological outlook, evidence of which is scattered throughout his writings. Also, Kingsley's children's stories merit analysis as a reflection of the man and his age. More importantly, the definitive word on religion in Victorian England cannot be written until Kingsley's sermons have been analyzed. In this connection, although most commentators advert to the presence in *Hypatia* of Kingsley's attitude toward contemporary religion, the details of his allusions need attention. Such a study would no doubt involve itself in the novelist's use of sources. A study of the contemporary reception of Kingsley's activities and books would be of interest for an understanding of the period. Many of these studies relate to placing Kingsley in the intellectual currents of the nineteenth century. This has been done in various areas, but the great diversity of Kingsley's activities and interests make an attempt at an overall study seem eminently worthwhile. Somewhat peripherally, the periodicals *Politics for the People* and *The Christian Socialist* deserve formal study; however, Kingsley's part in each is reported on by his recent biographers.

8 ಕ⊷

Wilkie Collins
Robert Ashley

Charles Reade
Wayne Burns

As it has long been customary to consider Wilkie
Collins and Charles Reade together in discussions of the Victorian novel, and as there has not been a great bulk of research devoted to either one, they are here dealt with in a
single chapter, though each is treated by a separate scholar.
Reade was the elder of the two authors, but Collins began to
write novels earlier, and so he is placed first.

After a long period of neglect as a cheap "sensation novelist" Collins regained critical approval when several distinguished modern intellectuals developed an interest in the
detective story. Reade has not been so widely acclaimed, but
his work has now begun to receive scholarly attention.

COLLINS

I. *Bibliography and Editions*

The standard, though occasionally inaccurate, bibliography is M. L. Parrish's *Wilkie Collins and Charles Reade*
(1940), which in addition to a descriptive bibliography of
Collins' published works contains a number of his letters as
well as posters and programs of his plays. The only other des-

criptive bibliography appears in Michael Sadleir's *Excursions in Victorian Bibliography* (1922). Dorothy Sayers' contribution to *CBEL*, vol. III (1941), has the advantage over Parrish and Sadleir of including a partial roster of Collins' articles and stories not reprinted in book form; this bibliography was brought up to date in the 1957 supplement. A study of Collins' unreprinted contributions to periodicals was announced some years ago as in progress by M. J. Cooke at St. Anne's College, Oxford. In 1949 Francesco Cordasco and Kenneth Scott published *Wilkie Collins and Charles Reade: A Bibliography of Critical Notices and Studies,* one of a series of annotated bibliographical pamphlets issued by the Long Island University Press; and in 1960 A. W. Andrew prepared "A Wilkie Collins Check-List" for *English Studies in Africa.* Each of the three biographies of Collins and each of the doctoral dissertations include bibliographies of works by and about Collins. But none contains an exhaustive list, and the Collins researcher must consult them all in order to miss nothing.

No Collins bibliography would be complete without mention of the Parrish Collection at Princeton; the highlights of this invaluable collection are described in *PULC,* 1956 and 1957.

The standard British collected works of Collins was published by Chatto and Windus, his regular publishers after 1875. By the early 1900's, when all the copyrights held by other publishers had expired, this "library edition" contained all of Collins' work published in book form except the biography of his father *Memoirs of the Life of William Collins* (1848), his travelogue *Rambles beyond Railways* (1851), the early novelette *Mr. Wray's Cash-Box* (1852), and the late novelette *The Guilty River* (1886). The complete works were apparently kept in print until 1925, with separate titles available after that date. In the United States, Harper and Brothers issued a seventeen-volume "library edition," which remained in print at least until 1912, some volumes remaining available later. The most nearly complete American collected edition was printed by Collier in 1900; like Chatto and Windus, Collier omitted only the *Memoirs, Rambles beyond Railways, Mr. Wray's Cash-Box,* and *The Guilty River.* A cheap edition apparently issued for distribution to readers of the Collier periodicals, this series is not reliable textually. *The Moonstone* and to a lesser extent *The Woman in White* are included in the standard reprint series. Two brief selections of Collins' stories have been published in recent years: *Tales of Suspense* (New York, 1954) and *Short Stories of Wilkie Collins* (Emmaus, Pa., 1950; reissued, New York, 1960).

Of Collins' plays, eleven were published, one (*The Frozen Deep*) was privately printed, and four (*The Lighthouse, The Red Vial, Rank and Riches,* and *The Evil Genius*) exist only in manuscript, which can be found, respectively, in the Forster Collection at the Victoria and Albert Museum in London, the privately held Dorothy B. Sayers Collection, the Lord Chamberlain's Office in London, and the Harvard Theatre Collection in the Houghton Library. All of Collins' dramas are available in the Widener Library at Harvard, either in print, in manuscript, or on microfilm. There has never been a selected or collected edition of the plays, but Nuel P. Davis, author of the most recent Collins biography, is preparing an edition for publication by the University of Illinois Press.

Collins' letters have never been collected. By far his most valuable letters went up in smoke when Dickens, irritated at the invasion of his privacy by the press, consigned the whole of his correspondence to a bonfire at Gad's Hill. Neither side of an apparently frequent correspondence with Reade has survived. What has survived, except for some early letters to his family, is largely correspondence with various publishers. The most notable collections of Collins letters are listed in the Robinson, Davis, and Ashley biographies and in the Cordasco-Scott bibliography. One omission is the Dorothy Sayers Collection, which contains letters, first editions, and Miss Sayers' notes for a projected, but never-written, biography; this collection has not been available to Collins scholars, but is now for sale and may be accessible soon. In 1956 David

Shusterman of the University of Kansas announced a collection of Collins letters, but has since abandoned the project.

II. *Biography*

Until recently the irregular nature of Collins' private life threw insuperable obstacles in the way of a biographer. The facts were unquestionably known to his friends — especially since Collins was quite frank in his correspondence — but were never allowed to become public. An authorized biography was out of the question. Therefore, for many years Collins enthusiasts had to content themselves with scattered references in the reminiscences of the novelist's contemporaries in the world of art, literature, and the theater. Such works as Holman Hunt's *Pre-Raphaelitism and the Pre-Raphaelite Brotherhood,* Mrs. E. M. Ward's *Memories of Ninety Years,* Hall Caine's *My Story,* J. Henry Harper's *The House of Harper,* Harry Quilter's *Preferences in Life, Literature and Art,* William Winter's *Old Friends,* Edmund Yates' *Celebrities at Home,* R. C. Lehmann's *Memories of Half a Century,* Forster's *The Life of Charles Dickens,* Percy Fitzgerald's *Memoirs of an Author* and *Memories of Charles Dickens,* Nat Beard's "Some Recollections of Yesterday" (*Temple Bar,* 1894), Frank Archer's *An Actor's Notebooks,* Squire and Marie Bancroft's *The Bancrofts,* Wybert Reeve's "Recollections of Wilkie Collins" (*Chambers's Journal,* 1906), and the various collections of Dickens letters, especially Walter Dexter's *Mr. and Mrs. Dickens* and Laurence Hutton's *Letters of Charles Dickens to Wilkie Collins,* gave some indication of the kind of man Collins was without ever penetrating the mystery of what the *DNB* coyly called his "intimacies." Until the 1950's the only biographies were two inaccessible and unrewarding German works: Ernst von Wolzogen's *Wilkie Collins: Ein Biographisch-Kritischer Versuch* (Leipzig, 1885) and Hans Sehlbach's *Untersuchungen über die Romanskunst von Wilkie Collins* (Jena, 1931).

As for Collins' private life, J. G. Millais (*The Life of John Everett Millais,* 1899) ended his account of the dramatic meeting of Collins and "the woman in white" with the tantalizing sentence, "Her subsequent history, interesting as it is, is not for these pages." Late in her life Dickens' daughter Kate, who married Wilkie's brother Charles, told Gladys Storey that Wilkie had a mistress named Caroline, that she was the original of "the woman in white," and that after living with Collins for several years she left him to marry another man (Gladys Storey, *Dickens and Daughter*, 1939). It remained for Clyde K. Hyder to identify Caroline as Caroline Elizabeth Graves, widow of an army officer, and to establish the fact of her residence for a number of years at the same address as Collins. Hyder also discovered Wilkie's second "intimacy," Martha Rudd Dawson, who bore him three illegitimate children and, with Mrs. Graves, was the major beneficiary in his will (Clyde K. Hyder, "Wilkie Collins and *The Woman in White*," *PMLA*, 1939). The final piece was fitted into the puzzle by Kenneth Robinson in his 1952 biography of Collins. Robinson corroborated Kate Dickens' story by discovering the record of Caroline's marriage to Joseph Clow, a plumber, whom, however, she left very shortly to return to Wilkie.

Robinson's was the first and best of the three biographies which appeared in the 1950's, a straightforward piece of work with sound literary criticism and biographical details as complete as the available material allows. Robert Ashley's *Wilkie Collins*, which followed Robinson's by only a few months, is a shorter work tailored to fit the English Novelists series. Nuel P. Davis' *The Life of Wilkie Collins* (1956) adds nothing to the known facts about Collins. Instead, Davis imaginatively and inferentially reconstructs Wilkie's life by searching out autobiographical details in his fictional and nonfictional writings. The job is brilliantly done, yet the reader must constantly remind himself that Davis' method is conjectural rather than factual and substitutes clairvoyance for scholarship.

III. *Criticism*

After sympathetic essays in the 1890's by Andrew Lang (*Contemporary Review*, 1890) and Swinburne (*Studies in*

Prose and Poetry, 1894), critics paid little attention to Collins
for over thirty years. Collins undoubtedly suffered from the
general neglect of Victorian fiction, but he also suffered from
the particular dislike of such Dickensians as Forster, Fitzgerald, and J. W. T. Ley (see the latter's *The Dickens Circle,*
for instance), whose resentment of the intimacy between their
master and Collins expressed itself in a jealous disparagement
of Collins' achievement. The rebirth of interest was signalized
by S. M. Ellis' *Wilkie Collins, Le Fanu and Others* (1927) and
by T. S. Eliot's article in *TLS,* Aug. 4, 1927 (reprinted in
Eliot's *Selected Essays, 1917–1932* and, somewhat revised, as
the introduction to The World's Classics edition of *The
Moonstone*). Eliot praised Collins as a master melodramatist,
emphasized the influence of Collins on Dickens, and labeled
The Moonstone "the first, the longest, and the best of modern
English detective novels." When this praise of *The Moonstone* was echoed by Dorothy Sayers in the Everyman's edition
and by Alexander Woollcott in the Modern Library Giant,
which also included *The Woman in White,* the revival was
on. Just as Collins had earlier suffered from the general
Victorian oblivion and the particular animus of professional
Dickens-lovers, now he profited from the general Victorian
renaissance and the particular vogue of detective fiction.

The best of the brief British studies of Collins were Walter
de la Mare's in *The Eighteen Sixties,* edited by John Drinkwater; Malcolm Elwin's in *Victorian Wallflowers*; Michael
Sadleir's in *Excursions in Victorian Bibliography*; and Dorothy Sayers' in *The Omnibus of Crime.*

In the United States, writings on Collins took a more
scholarly turn. As early as 1919 Walter Phillips published his
thesis-like *Dickens, Reade, and Collins, Sensation Novelists.*
Four unpublished doctoral dissertations were written in the
1940's and 1950's. The first of these, H. J. W. Milley's "The
Achievement of Wilkie Collins" (Yale, 1941), is notable for a
penetrating analysis of Collins' favorite character types and
plot motifs. Dougald MacEachen's "Wilkie Collins: Victorian
Crusader" (Cincinnati, 1948), as its title implies, is a study
of Collins as a social critic. Robert Ashley's "The Career of

Wilkie Collins" (Harvard, 1948) is a chronological survey of Wilkie's fictional, nonfictional, and dramatic writings; the composition, sources, contemporary reception, and publishing and stage history of each work are given. Nuel P. Davis' "The Early Life and Literary Career of Wilkie Collins" (Illinois, 1955) emphasizes the influence of Collins on Dickens and Collins' development of a new type of fiction, "the narrative drama." Two dissertations have been listed as in progress: an examination of the literary relationships of Collins and Dickens by Robert Brannan at Cornell and a study of Collins' novels by Lowell Stratton at Stanford.

The American scholarly interest in Collins also bore fruit in a number of monographs. In *"The Eustace Diamonds* and *The Moonstone" (SP,* 1939) H. J. W. Milley advanced the thesis that the Trollope novel was a mischievous, comic, and satiric rewriting of the Collins novel; and in "Wilkie Collins and *A Tale of Two Cities" (MLR,* 1939), the thesis that Wilkie's novelette *Sister Rose,* not Carlyle's *French Revolution,* inspired Dickens' choice of a French Revolutionary background.

Among other treatments of the Dicken-Collins relationship, Earle Davis' "Charles Dickens and Wilkie Collins" *(Municipal University of Wichita Studies,* 1945) extends Eliot's examination of Collins' influence on Dickens; Arthur Adrian's "A Note on the Dicken-Collins Friendship" *(HLQ,* 1953) points out a possible cause for the estrangement of the two novelists; and Robert Ashley's "Wilkie Collins and the Dickensians" *(Dickensian,* 1953) discusses the curious antipathy of certain Dickens idolators toward Collins. A rebuttal to Ashley by K. J. Fielding appeared in the following number of the *Dickensian.* This running battle between Dickensians and Collinsians may perhaps be given its authoritative treatment in the Brannan dissertation mentioned above.

Beatrice Corrigan's "Antonio Fogazzaro and Wilkie Collins" *(Comparative Literature,* 1961) points out the debt of the Italian novelist to the English. Collins in America is the subject of C. K. Hyder's "Wilkie Collins in America" *(University of Kansas Humanistic Studies,* 1940) and Robert

Ashley's "Wilkie Collins and the American Theater" (*NCF*, 1954). In "Wilkie Collins' First Short Story" (*More Books: The Bulletin of the Boston Public Library*, 1948) Ashley analyzes "The Twin Sisters," Collins' previously unidentified earliest published story; in "Wilkie Collins and a Famous Vermont Murder Trial" (*New England Quarterly*, 1948) he discusses the relationship between Collins' novelette *The Dead Alive* and the trial of the Boorn brothers for the murder of Russell Colvin at Manchester, Vermont, in 1819; and in "Wilkie Collins and the Detective Story" (*NCF*, 1951) he points out that Wilkie's contributions to the development of detective fiction were not limited to *The Moonstone*. Lewis A. Lawson, in "Wilkie Collins and *The Moonstone*" (*American Imago*, 1963), offers a Freudian interpretation of Collins' most famous novel. Dougald MacEachen's "Wilkie Collins and British Law" (*NCF*, 1950) is another specialized study, whereas both Bradford Booth's "Wilkie Collins and the Art of Fiction" (*NCF*, 1951) and Robert Ashley's "Wilkie Collins Reconsidered" (*NCF*, 1950) are more general in content.

Despite a late start, scholars have pretty well covered the Collins material. Re-evaluation and reinterpretation are always in order; but, as of the moment, the only notable omission is a selection of the plays, which we may hope Nuel P. Davis will provide. Since the most interesting and valuable portion of Collins' correspondence has disappeared, it is doubtful that a worthwhile collection of letters can be assembled.

READE

I. *Bibliography*

Robert Ashley's foregoing remarks on M. L. Parrish's *Wilkie Collins and Charles Reade* and Michael Sadleir's *Excursions in Victorian Bibliography* apply to Reade as well as Collins. And in Reade's case as in Collins' the various unpublished theses contain useful bibliographies. But the bibliography compiled by Francesco Cordasco and Kenneth

Scott, *Wilkie Collins and Charles Reade,* is grossly inaccurate
and incomplete in its treatment of Reade. For example, the
compiler's list of "all critical notices and studies" of Reade
and Collins includes a grand total of one hundred and four
items, whereas Léone Rives, in her *Charles Reade: sa vie,
ses romans* (published eight years earlier), lists some two hundred "critical notices and studies" devoted to Reade alone.

Rives's study also contains a complete bibliography of
Reade's works. For each novel she includes what would appear to be each of its various editions; for each play she en-
deavors to list the place and date of its first production, the
name of the printer or publisher, the date of printing or publication, plus any further information on the play that she
deems necessary or pertinent. Rives also explains, in a note
appended to her bibliography, that she has corrected Michael
Sadleir's dating of the first performances of certain of Reade's
plays.

Presumably, therefore, Rives's bibliography of Reade's
plays would also correct the "List of London Theatrical Pro-
ductions and Revivals" (based, in part, on Sadleir) that Malcolm Elwin includes in his *Charles Reade* (1931). But the
contradictory evidence Bradford A. Booth encounters, in his
efforts to trace a presumed revival of *Shilly-Shally* in Liverpool ("Trollope, Reade, and *Shilly-Shally*," part II, *Trollopian,* 1947), shows that the bibliography of Reade's plays is in
many respects still as "obscure and confused" as Michael
Sadleir left it in 1922. Nor have a number of other bibliographical questions raised by Sadleir and Elwin been satisfactorily answered. For instance there is still no positive evidence that a pamphlet Sadleir mentions (*Excursions in
Victorian Bibliography,* p. 161) actually appeared in print.
In this and other instances much bibliographical work remains to be done.

II. *Biography*

In his *Charles Reade* Malcolm Elwin accurately characterizes John Coleman's *Charles Reade as I Knew Him* (1903) as
the work of a man "whose elastic notions of a biographer's

conscience allowed him to paraphrase Compton Reade's *Memoir* and call it Charles Reade's 'autobiography' as recounted to himself." As for the *Memoir* (Charles L. Reade and the Reverend Compton Reade, *Charles Reade, A Memoir,* 2 vols., 1887) it "is itself a treacherous authority," Elwin points out, "wherever it strays from the quotation of documents." And Elwin might, with justice, have called attention to the fact that the documents quoted in the *Memoir* represent a compilation "selected by Mr. Charles L. Reade, the deceased author's executor and residuary legatee" on the basis of "what he believes to have been the wishes of Charles Reade and the reverence due his memory." So much Compton Reade himself acknowledges in the preface to the *Memoir*. What he fails to acknowledge is that Charles L. Reade, Reade's executor and residuary legatee, was also Reade's natural son.

Nevertheless the *Memoir* does reproduce significant letters, diaries, and manuscripts, and so long as these documents are not otherwise available the *Memoir* itself can never be wholly superseded — although Elwin's *Charles Reade* has long since come to be regarded as the standard biography. And rightfully so, for it offers a scholarly and perceptive reinterpretation of the biographical materials that Compton Reade and Coleman had sacrificed to their Victorian notions of reverence and rhetoric, together with a useful and reliable account of Reade's career as dramatist, journalist, novelist, and social crusader.

Léone Rives devotes the first one hundred and eighty-six pages of her *Charles Reade: sa vie, ses romans* (Toulouse, 1940) to Reade's life. Drawing upon family papers inaccessible to Elwin, she presents facts which explain key aspects of Reade's life that Elwin had been obliged to treat conjecturally. But her biographical pages merely supplement Elwin's biography, they by no means supplant it. The present need, therefore, is for a full-scale biography, based not only on the manuscript materials available to Rives and her predecessors but also on the huge collections of Readiana now available in American libraries, including, of course, the new acquisitions in the Parrish Collection of the Princeton University Library described by Robert B. Martin in his "Manuscripts and Correspondence of Charles Reade" (*PULC*, 1958). In a personal letter Thomas D. Clareson of The College of Wooster has explained that he is beginning work on such a biography, and that he has "met and been in correspondence with members of the Reade family who have promised their cooperation and will make available . . . family letters and papers hitherto uncollected."

III. *General*

Emerson Grant Sutcliffe's study of Reade's Notebooks (*SP*, 1930) may be said to mark the beginnings of modern Readian scholarship in America. In this study he describes the thirty-two Notebooks that have come to be known as the London Library Notebooks; and in his succeeding articles he has drawn upon these Notebooks in exploring many significant aspects of Reade's life and writings. In "The Stage in Reade's Novels" (*SP*, 1930) Sutcliffe shows how Reade's "instinct to write plays, and his close association with the stage, affected the technique of his novels"; in "*Foemina Vera* in Charles Reade's Novels" (*PMLA*, 1931) Sutcliffe traces the principal types among Reade's female characters to their factual counterparts in the Notebooks. In "Plotting in Reade's Novels" (*PMLA*, 1932) Sutcliffe considers the demands of the three-volume format; then goes on to discuss "Inceptions," "Two Lines of Action," "Intervention," "Links," "Inset Stories," "Suspense" (with a number of subdivisions), and "Endings: Retribution." Reade's handling of character Sutcliffe analyzes in "Psychological Presentation in Reade's Novels" (*SP*, 1941); Reade's ethical principles, in "Fact, Realism, and Morality in Reade's Fiction" (*SP*, 1944); Reade's plot-formulas, in "Unique and Repeated Situations and Themes in Reade's Fiction" (*PMLA*, 1945); Reade's self-portraiture, in "Charles Reade in His Heroes" (*Trollopian*, 1946).

The value of these articles can hardly be overestimated — although they too may, in certain instances, be supplemented or corrected. Since 1930, when Sutcliffe published his study of the Notebooks, some fifty-five additional Notebooks have been made available to scholars (in the London Library and the Princeton University Library), and of these fifty-five only four have been described at length (Wayne Burns, "More Reade Notebooks," *SP*, 1945). Moreover there are some one hundred and eighty Notecards (the huge cards which Reade used directly in writing certain of his novels) now in the Princeton University Library, and of this number only those devoted to *Hard Cash* have been edited and analyzed (in Douglas Bankson's doctoral dissertation "Charles Reade's Manuscript Notecards for *Hard Cash*," University of Washington, 1954). The remaining Notecards including those devoted to *The Cloister and the Hearth* have yet to be described in full. Wayne Burns, in *Charles Reade: A Study in Victorian Authorship* (1961), has quoted entries and passages from a number of the Notecards (as well as from a number of the Notebooks not described in previous works on Reade), yet thousands upon thousands of entries still remain buried in the imposing mass of the Notecards and Notebooks.

And that, it may be argued, is where the great majority of these entries should remain. But what about the Notecards devoted to *The Cloister and the Hearth*? Or the Notebook in the Parrish Collection labeled "Old Notes Cloister and the Hearth"? Quite possibly the entries in this Notebook and on these Notecards might at the very least supplement Albert Morton Turner's wonderfully thorough study of Reade's sources and documentary techniques in the writing of this novel (*The Making of "The Cloister and the Hearth,"* 1938). Certainly Bankson's study of the Notecards for *Hard Cash* (mentioned above) contributes to a full understanding not only of the making of *Hard Cash* but of the making of Reade's other matter-of-fact romances, and studies of the Notecards devoted to other novels might prove equally revealing. Moreover the Notecards, and more especially the Notebooks, constitute unique collections of Victoriana that, intelligently edited, should throw new light on almost every phase of Victorian life and art.

In an effort to explain the rationale of the Note-books Lewis F. Haines ("Reade, Mill and Zola: A Study of the Character and Intention of Charles Reade's Realistic Method," *SP*, 1943) stresses Reade's indebtedness to John Stuart Mill. Wayne Burns, on the other hand, has argued (in *Charles Reade*) that Reade's prime debt (insofar as he was indebted to philosophy for his method) was not to Mill but to Bacon, that Reade's specific intention was to de-velop the Notebooks, not merely into a storehouse of literary materials, but into a nineteenth-century *Novum Organum*. Nevertheless Burns's discussion of these and related points is not, by his own admission, exhaustive.

Nor have the many studies of Reade's realism exhausted either the facts or the implications of his indebtedness to the fiction, theater, and painting of his own and earlier times. Edmund Ahlers, in *Charles Reades Romane und ihr Ver-hältnis zu ihren Literarischen Vorbildern* (Münster, 1914), traces in Reade's work the influence of novelists from Rich-ardson to William Godwin to Harriet Beecher Stowe; W. C. Phillips, ranging more widely in *Dickens, Reade and Col-lins: Sensation Novelists* (1919), traces the development of "sensation fiction" from its earliest beginnings to its cul-mination in these three writers. Yet if Phillips' study is in many respects brilliant, especially in contrast with Ahlers' pedestrian source hunting, it nevertheless tends to over-simplify and distort Reade's fictional theories and practices, which were not quite so close to those of Dickens and Col-lins as Phillips implies. In an effort to correct and supple-ment these and similar studies, Burns (in *Charles Reade*) has also discussed in some detail (but again, not exhaustively) Reade's awareness of and possible indebtedness to the real-istic theories and practices of playwrights, stage managers, and painters, more especially the theories and practices of Charles Kean and the Pre-Raphaelites.

Of the studies of Reade's realism that treat specific phases of one or more novels or plays Carl R. Woodring's "Charles Reade's Debt to William Howitt" (*NCF*, 1950) is notable for its close analysis of Reade's stylistic borrowings in the Australian section of *It Is Never Too Late To Mend*. Sheila

M. Smith, in "Realism in the Drama of Charles Reade" (*English*, 1958), combines a close analysis of one play, "It's Never Too Late To Mend," with a more comprehensive study of Reade's other social dramas; and in "Propaganda and Hard Facts in Charles Reade's Didactic Novels" (*Renaissance and Modern Studies*, University of Nottingham, 1960) Miss Smith relates the novel *It Is Never Too Late To Mend* to *Hard Cash*.

Apart from their intrinsic value these articles open or re-open neglected areas of scholarship — as does Bradford A. Booth's "Trollope, Reade, and *Shilly-Shally*" (*Trollopian*, 1947), J. B. Price's "Charles Reade and Charles Kingsley" (*Contemporary Review*, 1953), and Royal A. Gettman's "The Serialization of Reade's 'A Good Fight' " (*NCF*, 1951). But perhaps the most neglected area is that which R. H. Bowers describes in the opening paragraphs of "The Cancelled 'Song of Solomon' Passage in Reade's *Hard Cash*" (*NCF*, 1952): "We possess the rough drafts and corrected proof, the note-books, the relevant letters and private papers — the scaffolding and carpenter's waste lumber, so to speak — of many Victorian novels. A good deal of this material is still unpublished, and, much more important, still unstudied . . . Hence one imposing task for students of nineteenth-century fiction in the decades to come will be to make this unpublished material available; and I do not consider it rash to predict that many of our critical views will be altered, or at least modified, when this imposing task is completed." These predictions have already been fulfilled in such works as John Butt and Kathleen Tillotson, *Dickens at Work* (1957), and Jerome Beaty, *Middlemarch: From Notebook to Novel* (1960); and these works, along with Bower's essay, might serve as models for studies of the manuscripts of Reade's plays and novels.

IV. *Criticism*

Of critical studies in the generally accepted sense, that is, studies devoted primarily to the explication and evaluation of Reade's work, there have been very few of any consequence since Reade's death. Elwin's biography offers, in passing, general critical estimates of the novels and plays that are uniformly intelligent, although he reserved his most impassioned and in some respects his most telling criticism for *Old Gods Falling* (1939), in which he maintains that *Griffith Gaunt* is not only Reade's best novel but a masterpiece in its own right, "far exceeding anything ever achieved by Dickens in loftiness of artistic design and unflagging dramatic fervor." Nor is this praise wholly extravagant when viewed in relation to that of earlier critics. Swinburne, W. D. Howells, Henry James — these and numerous lesser known writers and critics from Hain Friswell to Hugh Walpole had proclaimed Reade a great novelist, *Griffith Gaunt* one of his greatest novels; and Elwin, in seconding their judgment, restates the case for the novel with considerable acumen.

The criticism in Rives' study, on the other hand, can hardly be taken seriously. At its best it reads like a modernized French version of Compton Reade's opinions in the *Memoir*; at its worst it is of a piece with Rives's "Preface" to her own edition of "It's Never Too Late To Mend" (Toulouse, 1940), which reads (in part) as follows.

Reade deserves to have the front rank in the history of the English stage, as the father of the modern theatre. After the decadent Restoration drama, and the poor attempts made by Colley Cibber, after Goldsmith and Sheridan, the English stage production was on the wane. Charles Reade gave it a new twist, by resuming the old conception of Aristophanes and Æschylus, who looked upon the theatre as a school of teaching. Together with Ibsen, he guided the dramatists of the twentieth century towards the realistic tendencies, nurtured and fostered by Arnold Bennett, Gilbert Cannan and Granville Barker. To him, first of all (see his play *Free Labour* dealing with the Trade-Union problems), we owe the drama "with a purpose" which revealed its highest pitch with Galsworthy and Bernard Shaw.

Donald Hutchins MacMahon's "Charles Reade as a Dramatist" (unpubl. diss., Cornell University, 1935) deserves special mention at this point, since it provides an intelligent critical survey of Reade's plays. And Edmund Morrison's "Charles Reade and His Novels" (unpubl. diss., University of California, 1940), provides an equally intelligent critical survey of Reade's novels — a survey that merits serious consideration by students of Reade and of Victorian fiction in general.

The most challenging and in some respects the most incisive piece of modern criticism, however, is George Orwell's reappraisal of Reade's work in *New Statesman and Nation* (1940). In this essay Orwell first of all attempts to account for "the attraction of Reade." "At bottom," he declares, "it is the same charm as one finds in R. Austin Freeman's detective stories or Lieutenant Commander Gould's collection of curiosities — the charm of useless knowledge . . . If you have the sort of mind that takes pleasure in dates, lists, categories, concrete details, descriptions of processes . . . the sort of mind that likes knowing exactly how a medieval catapult worked or just what objects a prison cell of the eighteen-forties contained you can hardly help enjoying Reade." Then, speaking for himself, Orwell acknowledges that "Reade wrote several dull books, and the *Cloister and the Hearth* is one of them. But he also wrote three novels that I personally would back to outlive the entire works of Meredith and George Eliot," the three being *Foul Play, Hard Cash,* and *It Is Never Too Late To Mend.*

Where this judgment leaves Meredith and George Eliot it is difficult to surmise, since Orwell, after praising Reade's three novels so highly, goes on to classify them as "desert-island stories" and then proceeds to dismiss them from serious literary consideration on much the same grounds that E. M. Forster, in *Aspects of the Novel,* dismisses *The Antiquary,* along with the rest of Scott's fiction. "Reade was," Orwell concludes,

simply a middle-class gentleman with a little more conscience than most, a scholar who happened to prefer popular science to the classics. Just for that reason he is one of the best "escape" novelists we have, *Foul Play* and *Hard Cash* would be good books to send to a soldier enduring the miseries of trench warfare, for instance. There are no problems in them, no genuine "message," merely the fascination of a gifted mind functioning within very narrow limits . . . What he lacked was one notion that the early railway age, with the special scheme of values appropriate to it, was not going to last forever . . . Of all the nineteenth-century novelists who have remained readable, he is perhaps the only one who is completely in tune with his own age. For all his unconventionality, his "purpose," his eagerness to expose abuses, he never makes a fundamental criticism . . . He sees nothing wrong in an acquisitive society, with its equation of money and virtue, its pious millionaires and erastian clergymen.

Taking direct issue with Orwell (without denying the validity of many of his critical observations), Wayne Burns has attempted, in the concluding chapters of his *Charles Reade*, a full-scale revaluation of Reade's novels in relation to those of his greater and lesser contemporaries, and more specifically in relation to those of Dickens and Thackeray and George Eliot. But whatever the merits of Burns' critical chapters they cannot in themselves repair the critical neglect of more than half a century. *Griffith Gaunt*, for example, can hardly gain the recognition it deserves until it has received at least some critical attention — as much, say, as has in recent years been devoted to any one of a half dozen of Anthony Trollope's novels.

9 ࣷ

George Eliot

W. J. Harvey

THE BODY of published work on George Eliot may fairly be represented by the figure of a globe densely populated at its poles, yet at its equator but sparsely inhabited. On this analogy one pole represents the period beginning with the first reviews of *Scenes of Clerical Life*, reaching its point of greatest density in 1885 with Cross's official *Life and Letters* and ending roughly with Leslie Stephen's *George Eliot* (1902). The other pole essentially represents a post-1945 phenomenon. Between lies a long desert of neglect.

Such an analogy is not entirely valid when applied to biography and intellectual history, but within the narrower field of literary criticism G. S. Haight was certainly correct when he remarked in a review (*NCF*, 1948) of Gerald Bullett's *George Eliot* that the 1930's marked the lowest ebb of her reputation. Since then the ebb tide has turned to full flood. The period when Lord David Cecil could say in his *Early Victorian Novelists* (1934) that "her reputation has suffered a more catastrophic slump than any of her contemporaries" now seems remote indeed; today, many of George Eliot's admirers must rather be uneasily wondering whether in fact she is not in danger of being overrated.

To guide our way through this perplexing geography of taste we may at the outset chart abstractly the main problems discussed and the main attitudes adopted by writers on George Eliot. This will provide us with a sufficiently defined body of terms with which to characterize particular studies, thus avoiding much tedious repetition. It should be pointed out that most of these problems and attitudes are to be found in Victorian critics and commentators. No student can afford to neglect, for example, Leslie Stephen's *George Eliot* or the impressive, intelligent, and insufficiently known array of Victorian reviewers. Of these perhaps the most important is Henry James, whose many essays and reviews of George Eliot are detailed in Leon Edel and Dan H. Laurence, *Bibliography of Henry James* (1957).

Most views of George Eliot's life and personality derive from the opposition and interaction of two stereotyped attitudes. At one extreme there is pictured the earnest, brooding figure of later life, the oracle of the Priory so frequently to be encountered in Victorian biographies and memoirs; this image we may call George Eliot the sibyl. At the other extreme is opposed the picture of George Eliot the woman, deriving from a much greater emphasis on her childhood and life up to her union with Lewes. The image now is not of a majestic, self-sufficient intellect but of a shy, diffident girl, rebelling and renouncing, with a great capacity for affection and a great need of reassurance. The stress is not on serenity and sobriety but rather on turmoil, distress, emotional involvement. Historically the sibylline George Eliot dominates at first but in the period with which we are concerned there is a strikingly uniform stress on George Eliot the woman. The reasons for this change are complex, deriving in part from a much greater knowledge of her early life, in part from a natural reaction against Victorian hagiography, and in part from the biographer's desire to find the maximum of drama and "human interest" in his subject.

These tensions in biographical treatment have their critical correlatives. From the sibylline George Eliot stems the idea of her as a novelist-philosopher, whose works are seen as disguised tracts, the narrative gilding the didactic pill and the characters incarnating idealized moral states or conflicts. One variant of this view implies a progressive degeneration of George Eliot's creative talent; that is to say, her early work is seen as embodying a nostalgic picture of her childhood which gradually gives way before a more cerebral, abstract, and austere treatment of ideological interests. Her work is thus seen as a conflict between recollected emotion and mature intellect, *Romola* generally being taken to mark the point at which mind begins to dominate heart.

From the stress on George Eliot the woman derives the idea that her novels, for better or worse, are simply dramatizations of her personal conflicts and dilemmas, that she intrudes overtly or obliquely into her fiction, which thus becomes a form of creative therapy. At its crudest, this view takes one of two forms; the first we may call the atonement theory, the idea being that the sufferings and frustrations of her characters, particularly her heroines, are a form of fictional self-punishment for her own moral shortcomings. The second form, by contrast, we may call the compensation theory, the idea here being that George Eliot frequently indulges in sentimental daydreaming, that her novels are often colored by a kind of reverie and wish fulfillment in which the ugly duckling turns into a beautiful swan, in which a Dorothea finally attains union with a Ladislaw. Both these theories, which might seem to be incompatible, are often held by the same critic; both are maintained sometimes with extreme crudity, sometimes with critical acuteness and relevance. Certainly, the sense of some kind of personal intrusion, whether of undue sympathy or undue animus, is a feature of her fiction with which most critics have felt it necessary to deal.

These very different critical approaches often have similar aesthetic consequences; both tend to stress the obsessive concern with a limited number of human situations so dealt with as frequently to involve extensive omniscient intrusion, faulty structure, and turgid style. The recent concern with imagery and symbolism has generally been related to George Eliot's personal dilemmas or to her typical moral concerns. No critic, so far as I know, has denied her a central moral seriousness; the main debate has been on the adequacy or inadequacy of an aesthetic correlative. Is she a novelist-philosopher or — a very different thing — a philosophic novelist? How often, to use her own terms, does she lapse from the picture to the diagram?

Clearly related to both biography and criticism are the problems of intellectual history. Again, both George Eliot's strength and her weakness have been seen as stemming from a conflict between province and metropolis, Warwickshire and London, her childhood roots and her adult milieu. In particular, great stress has been laid on her religious crises, the point usually being made that she retained a strong religious or ethical sense despite her rejection of formal doctrinal allegiance. All intellectual studies see the decisive ideological dramas as played out before the period of creation begins.

Such are the main outlines of modern inquiry and discussion. Clearly, many shades of opinion are possible and no classification can do justice to the complex permutations of interpretation and comment. The adequacy of such interpretation and comment has largely depended on the synthesis the writer has achieved of these complex and often apparently contradictory elements; the fact that they *are* complex and contradictory is, one may suppose, the basis of George Eliot's sustained interest and increased reputation for a generation of readers and critics who can, once again, see the Victorians as human beings like themselves.

I. *Bibliography, Editions, Letters*

No complete bibliography of George Eliot exists, though a cooperative venture by scholars from several countries is in progress. The fullest description of first editions is to be found in M. L. Parrish's *Victorian Lady Novelists* (1933), which also contains a description of one of the manuscript notebooks or quarries for *Romola*. Against this may be checked P. H. Muir's "A Bibliography of First Editions of the Books of George Eliot" (*Bookman's Journal*, Supplement, 1927–1928). The best checklist of early literature about her is still that of J. P. Anderson, appended to Oscar

Browning's *Life of George Eliot* (1890). The bibliographies by G. W. Cooke in his *George Eliot* (1883) and by F. Waldo and G. A. Turkington, appended to Mathilde Blind's *George Eliot* (new ed., 1904), may also be found useful. These have been greatly extended by J. D. Barry's "The Literary Reputation of George Eliot's Fiction" (*Bulletin of Bibliography*, 1959). Many of the works subsequently to be mentioned contain bibliographies which will be noted if of particular interest or value.

There is a general note by G. S. Haight on the main manuscript locations of George Eliot material (*VNL*, 1958); for further details of the most important of these — the collection of the Yale University Library — see R. L. Purdy, "Journals and Letters of George Eliot" (*YULG*, 1932), and G. S. Haight, "The Tinker Collection of George Eliot Manuscripts" (*YULG*, 1955) and "The George Eliot and George Henry Lewes Collection" (*YULG*, 1961). The recent discovery of two new *Middlemarch* notebooks in the Folger Shakespeare Library has been reported by B. R. Jerman (*VNL*, 1962).

There is no complete or critical edition of George Eliot's work. Several more or less "complete" editions were published by Blackwoods; besides the novels, these will generally be found to contain the poems and most of the nonfictional prose. They do not contain the translations of Strauss and Feuerbach; there is a recent paperback edition of *The Essence of Christianity* (1957), but no recent edition of Strauss. The last edition of George Eliot's works to be published in her lifetime was the Cabinet Edition (1877–1880; Cross's *Life and Letters* was subsequently added). In addition one should note the *Early Essays* (1919) reprinted not from manuscript as the preface claims, but from cuttings of George Eliot's contributions to the Coventry *Herald* exhibited in 1919, and J. Beaty's "George Eliot's Notebook for an Unwritten Novel" (*PULC*, 1957).

George Eliot often revised the text of her novels after the first edition had appeared; the only editions to note the most interesting of these textual variants are by G. S. Haight of *Middlemarch* (1956) and *The Mill on The Floss* (1961).

One of the major tasks of George Eliot scholarship still to be undertaken is a complete and critical edition of her work. A critical edition of her novels under the general editorship of J. Beaty is in progress. Many of her reviews have never been collected and there remain many interesting problems of attribution. Thus one must return a verdict of "unproved" on J. D. Rust's attribution in his "George Eliot and *The Blithedale Romance*" (*Boston Public Library Quarterly*, 1955).

If work on George Eliot's text leaves much to be desired students will be grateful for Gordon S. Haight's edition of *The George Eliot Letters* (1954–1955), which supersedes all previous collections. This is a truly monumental piece of scholarship. The introduction identifying George Eliot's correspondents is in itself a major item of biography; the text is impeccably edited; the footnotes are always adequate and never prolix or pedantic; there are valuable appendixes concerning the literary activities of George Eliot and G. H. Lewes. The most interesting sections of George Eliot's journals are reprinted and there are many interesting letters to or about her as well as by her. This edition must make a deep impression on future works of scholarship or criticism.

Two immediately important consequences may be noted here. Like Cross's *Life and Letters,* this edition provoked a flood of reviews and comment too great to notice in this survey. Much of the comment was in itself of great interest and value. Secondly, it is one of the valuable paradoxes of scholarship that such an edition creates the conditions for a still more complete text by calling forth odd letters that have hitherto been hidden or withheld. A few letters by or to George Eliot have recently come to light; it is much to be hoped that enough will be forthcoming for Haight to publish a supplementary volume. So masterly has his work been, however, that the fascinating picture of George Eliot is complete in its main outlines. Haight's edition corrects the distorting reticence of Cross's *Life and Letters*; it will stand as a permanent tribute to scholarship at its most devoted, thorough and impeccable.

II. *Biography*

At the risk of a distorted chronology we may first single out four biographical studies of substantial interest, upon which much work of secondary importance has been based. Although it is itself based on secondary materials, we may begin with M. H. Deakin's *The Early Life of George Eliot* (1913), since it probably became, as much as Cross's *Life and Letters,* the source of many later biographies. It is a good deal better than most of them. Modest and generally accurate, it aims to show "how the sensitive, passionate child, with so eager a longing for love, grew into the pious, intro-spective maiden" and "how for a time her habits of life and thought numbed and cramped the artist within her." The book is relatively weak in its depiction of George Eliot's intellectual milieu, tending to overemphasize Comte as an isolated influence. On the other hand George Eliot's fiction is related to her early life with more than usual sensitivity.

About G. H. Lewes, the most important figure in George Eliot's life, Miss Deakin could say little that was new. The first major advance in biographical studies from this crucial point of view was Anna T. Kitchel's *George Lewes and George Eliot* (1933). The author was the first to make detailed use of Lewes's manuscripts in the interests of "the following as intimately as possible of Lewes's life with George Eliot." She wisely avoids the danger of reading into the young Marian Evans the attributes of the mature George Eliot; consequently one of the main virtues of the book is her keen sense of emotional and intellectual development. Although some details need correction, this is the standard work on Lewes; it is a piece of original research which has permanent value.

One crucial period of George Eliot's life — her entry into the intellectual world of the metropolis — is fully studied in

G. S. Haight's *George Eliot and John Chapman* (1940), which includes transcripts of Chapman's diaries for 1851 and 1860. Haight takes a firmly anti-sibylline view of George Eliot; he finds the "key to an understanding of her extraordinary life" in Bray's remark that "she was not fitted to stand alone." One issue arising from Haight's presentation of new evidence is the question of whether or not George Eliot was Chapman's mistress. This assertion was made, among others, by Anthony West in a review of Haight's edition of the *Letters* (*New Yorker*, Oct. 2, 1954; reprinted in West's *Principles and Persuasions*, 1958), which relates George Eliot's work to her life in an extraordinarily crude and hostile manner. West's charges were vigorously rebutted by Haight (*New Yorker*, Nov. 6, 1954); the evidence for such a relationship does not, to say the least, seem conclusive.

The sibylline view of George Eliot was greatly enhanced by the many reminiscences of her, generally in her Priory days, which appeared in Victorian memoirs. K. A. McKenzie's *Edith Simcox and George Eliot* (1961), which draws heavily on Edith Simcox's manuscript journal, presents a fresh view of George Eliot's later life in which the apparent calm of the Priory is disturbed by the passionate devotion of one of her most intense admirers. The journal is at once detailed and fragmentary but it creates an intimate picture of this chapter in George Eliot's life. In few other documents is the human scene so vividly displayed; the emotional climate thus re-created is an exciting, perhaps suffocating, blend of near hysteria and sober good sense.

These books, together with the *Letters*, should be the main concern of students of George Eliot's life. There are a large number of lesser works which may be briefly mentioned. Biographies of George Eliot were frequent when good criticism was scarce. We may list E. S. Haldane, *George Eliot and Her Times* (1927); J. L. May, *George Eliot* (1930); E. and G. Romieu, *The Life of George Eliot* (trans. B. W. Downs, 1932; originally published in French in 1930); A. Fremantle, *George Eliot* (1933); and S. Dewes, *Marian* (1939). Of these, the books by Dewes and the Romieux are vulgar dramatizations, frequently inaccurate and generally worthless. E. S. Haldane's study is rambling, diffuse, and secondhand but does make some attempt to relate George Eliot to her milieu; J. L. May's book is honest and well intentioned but often inaccurate and not worth serious study. A. Fremantle's book is very brief but more accurate and balanced than most; she is, I think, the first to make any use of Chapman's diaries.

The best general biography of this period is B. C. Williams' *George Eliot* (1936). It is a substantial piece of work, inadequately documented and somewhat overwritten but containing a certain amount of new material. Passion broadening into compassion is taken as the keynote of George Eliot's life and as the motive behind her work. The author is modest and tentative in relating biography to creative achievement; she inclines, if anything, to the compensation rather than to the atonement theory.

A mixture of compensation and atonement theories is to be found in *Marian Evans and George Eliot* (1952) by L. and E. Hanson. This is the fullest general biography to appear and hovers, a little uneasily, between the popular and the scholarly. The documentation, though apparently impressive, is in some ways unsatisfactory (see letter by Humphry House, *TLS*, Nov. 7, 1952). The book is a little pedestrian, as is Margaret Crompton's *George Eliot; The Woman* (1960), an unpretentious and sensible study which, although the first biography to take advantage of the *Letters*, adds little to our understanding of George Eliot.

The title of Margaret Crompton's book is typical of the kind of stress to be found in most modern biographies; nearly all the works mentioned in this section lay great emphasis on George Eliot the woman. In doing so, most of them have perhaps understressed some of the actual and substantial features of the sibylline portrait; most of them fail to treat satisfactorily the breadth and intensity of George Eliot's intellectual life and few of them include an adequate critical treatment of her novels. The definitive biography remains to be written; for that we must await the outcome of G. S. Haight's labors.

III. *Intellectual and Cultural Milieu*

Much of the published work on this aspect of George Eliot is the result of French scholarship. We may begin with M. L. Cazamian's *Le Roman et les idées en Angleterre* (1923) which contains useful background material as well as a long chapter on George Eliot. Although Mme. Cazamian tends to oversimplify the causal connections between external influences and George Eliot's mind and sensibility, her work is substantial and is more likely to be found useful than E. J. Pond's *Les Idées morales et religieuses de George Eliot* (1927). Pond deals faithfully with a number of formative influences but does not explore in any depth the connections between philosophic outlook and artistic achievement. Instead we are offered lengthy and pedestrian paraphrases of the novels before reaching the disputable conclusion that "le tempérament intellectuel domine le tempérament artistique chez George Eliot, que la pensée didactique est antérieure à la création d'art." ("In George Eliot the intellectual temper dominates the artistic temper so that the didactic thought is prior to the creation of art.") The most valuable chapter of this book is its last, which outlines the critical reception of George Eliot's work in France; there is a useful bibliography.

The standard work on the subject is still P. Bourl'honne's *George Eliot: Essai de biographie intellectuelle et morale, 1819–1854* (1933). This book, which contains valuable sections on the influence of Spencer, Comte, Lewes, Spinoza, and above all Feuerbach, is marred by the author's attempt to pack the complex and often contradictory facts into the Procrustean bed of a particular psychological theory. His general thesis is that after the early religious crises, in which George Eliot was characterized by a hunger for ideas, "a lyrical pantheism," and a passion for renunciation, she achieved, under the influence of Spinoza and Feuerbach, a momentary and precarious resolution of the conflict between soul and body, between things spiritual and things material. It was in accord with this mood of philosophic calm and exaltation that she justified her union with Lewes. This very union, however, destroyed her intellectual equipoise and left her with a permanent sense of guilt which she obsessively dramatized in her novels. As Bourl'honne himself recognizes, his psychological theories create many difficulties: "Il y a, entre le jugement que nous avons été amené à porter sur le caractère de Miss Evans et la philosophie exprimé dans les romans de George Eliot, une antinomie apparente que nous ne pouvons laisser sans explanation." ("There is, between the judgment which we have been led to propose on the character of Miss Evans and the philosophy expressed in the novels of George Eliot, an apparent antinomy which we cannot leave unexplained.") His attempt to reconcile these contradictions is not, however, very convincing; his study, therefore, though valuable should be treated with caution. Certainly it has retained more of its value than M. Toyoda's *Studies in the Mental Development of George Eliot* (1931), which, though painstaking, is naïve.

Bourl'honne's analysis of the central antinomy in George Eliot's work is in terms of a conflict between an optimistic belief in the power of the will to work toward the good and a pessimistic sense of the powerlessness of man determined by circumstances largely beyond his control. This diagnosis has been accepted by Basil Willey in his *Nineteenth-Century Studies* (1949). Willey suggests that a " 'conservative-reforming' impulse was the leading *motif* of her life; that her lifelong quest, as it was Comte's and the century's, was for a reconcilement between these opposites, a synthesis (as Comte would say) between the Static and the Dynamic principles, between Order and Progress, Tradition and Enlightenment, the heart and the head."

Willey's study, though relatively brief, is in itself perhaps the best synthesis between a wide knowledge of the intellectual background and a sensitively critical appreciation of her novels. Where he puts the main stress on European influences, Humphry House's essay "Qualities of George Eliot's Unbelief" (*All In Due Time*, 1955) is a compact and sensible relation of George Eliot to English traditions of rationalism and skepticism. H. R. Murphy's "The Ethical Revolt against Christian Orthodoxy in Early Victorian England" (*American Historical Review*, 1955) contains an excellent analysis of George Eliot's early religious crises, sustaining the point that her rejection of dogma was due to moral revulsion rather than to the influence of the "higher criticism." For a general survey of her social milieu during her Coventry period readers should consult J. M. Prest, *The Industrial Revolution in Coventry* (1960).

The title of the most recent study of George Eliot's intellectual background is misleadingly general; P. G. Maheu's *La Pensée religieuse et morale de George Eliot* (1959) is in fact mainly concerned with tracing parallels between her thought and Defoe's *History of the Devil*, one of her favorite childhood books. Maheu is careful not to assert too crude a causal connection but his work does sometimes seem a case of special pleading. Many of the ideas he traces were commonplaces and their presence in George Eliot's work cannot be assigned to the influence of any specific author.

One aspect of George Eliot's intellectual life has received increasing attention. This is the body of critical ideas and theories outlined in her essays and reviews and their relation to her fiction. Readers may profitably consult W. Casey, "George Eliot's Theory of Fiction" (*West Virginia University Bulletin*, 1953); J. D. Rust, "The Art of Fiction in George Eliot's Reviews" (*RES*, 1956); W. J. Hyde, "George Eliot and the Climate of Realism" (*PMLA*, 1957); and R. Stang, "The Literary Criticism of George Eliot" (*PMLA*, 1957). The particular influence of G. H. Lewes is a major issue; that he was a decisive critical influence has been argued by A. R. Kaminsky, "George Eliot, George Henry Lewes and the Novel" (*PMLA*, 1955), but she does not, I think, prove her case. A useful outline of Lewes's critical position is to be found in M. Greenhut, "George Henry Lewes as a Critic of the Novel" (*SP*, 1948). G. S. Haight has commented on some of these articles in "George Eliot's Theory of Fiction" (*VNL*, 1956).

George Eliot's intellectual outlook and development are frequently dealt with in primarily critical studies which will be mentioned later. Three general points need stressing here. First, her mind was so powerful that she is unlikely to have been, as so many scholars assume, a kind of intellectual aeolian harp, passively echoing external influences. Second, the transmutation of ideology into fiction is a complex process; intellectual historians need to be good critics as well. This point may be illustrated by contrasting George Levine's "Determinism and Responsibility in the Works of George Eliot" (*PMLA*, 1962) with "George Eliot's Religion of Humanity," by Bernard J. Paris (*ELH*, 1962). Paris considers George Eliot's treatment of the problem of "how can man lead a meaningful, morally satisfying life in an absurd universe" and lucidly outlines her efforts to compensate for the lack of a metaphysically sanctioned ethic. But in attempting to present "a systematic and condensed account of Eliot's quest for values" he does not try "to show how her beliefs are dramatized in her novels." Levine, however, blends a wide-ranging interest in intellectual history with a sensitivity to the way ideas function within a work of art. He demonstrates how George Eliot's theories of causality are never to be seen as an excuse for avoiding moral responsibility and his conclusion is unexceptionable: "George Eliot's handling of the problem was artistic rather than theoretical. Determinism was for her not a rigid and depressing system but an aspect of the world which she saw and dramatized." This is an important essay.

Another welcome recognition of the complex interaction between ideas and art is to be found in Miriam Allott's "George Eliot in the 1860's" (*VS*, 1961). While she grants that "George Eliot's imagination, then, is from the first most at home in a region where the sense of tragic entanglement is acute and her meliorism . . . faces its stiffest challenge," she finds the period between *Silas Marner* and *Middlemarch* one of "ebbing creative vitality." There are many reasons for this, she argues, but most important is the fact that George Eliot "was now facing for the first time the more sombre implications of her own doctrines." Mrs. Allott's essay is an exception to the third general point that needs to be made. Nearly all the other studies mentioned have assumed, for better or worse, that George Eliot's intellectual development was virtually complete by the time she began writing fiction. This seems a large assumption. Granted that there are no intellectual upheavals after 1857 comparable with those before, nevertheless it is doubtful whether a mind as capacious as George Eliot's ever stood still. Her later development is a field well worth exploring; such a study might modify the relations which are generally, and often crudely, asserted between her intellectual powers and her creative achievement.

IV. *General Criticism*

The central critical debate on George Eliot's creative achievement is dramatically represented by juxtaposing Lord David Cecil's *Early Victorian Novelists* (1934) and F. R. Leavis' *The Great Tradition* (1948). It is essentially a debate on what is meant by moral seriousness in a work of art. For Cecil the sibylline George Eliot predominates; she is heavy, ponderous, highbrow; her works are built around ideas; she works from abstract themes to dramatic life; it was "analysis that started her creative imagination working." While her intellectual power results in many artistic virtues and makes her, for Cecil, the first modern novelist, in the last analysis she lacks creative imagination. Moreover, "an exclusively moral point of view is, at any time, a bleak and unsatisfying affair." This is especially true of "Victorian ethical rationalism" which "is the least inspiriting of creeds." Her characters are consequently creatures for dissection; behind the puppets we all too often see the puppet master.

Leavis will have none of this. The "bare bones of Puritan ethics" from which, for Cecil, "George Eliot's imagination had to scrape what nourishment it could" are seen by Leavis as a serious, subtle and adult view of the moral life, intimately related to George Eliot's distinctive aesthetic strength. When she fails it is due rather to an inability to separate the woman who suffers from the artist who creates; we feel "an urgency, a resonance, a personal vibration, adverting us of the poignantly immediate presence of the author." The novels are consequently marred by an occasional immaturity of treatment which results in the idealization of such characters as Maggie and Dorothea.

It is fair to say that Leavis rather than Cecil has provided the main stimulus to modern criticism of George Eliot. He is characteristically blunt and forthright in his appraisal of individual novels and his criticism has the Johnsonian quality of provoking valuable disagreement on relevant and important issues.

Occupying a roughly intermediate position between Cecil and Leavis is Gerald Bullett's *George Eliot* (1947). Part of the book consists of a sympathetic biographical study; the same quality is found in the critical section. Bullett rejects the atonement theory and lays a welcome emphasis on George Eliot's humor; his criticism is sane and balanced but not really incisive or penetrating. Many of the same strengths and limitations may be found in the substantial chapter on George Eliot in E. A. Baker's *History of the English Novel* (vol. VIII, 1937) and in Robert Speaight's brief study *George Eliot* (1954).

A more important and ambitious work than those mentioned in the last paragraph is Joan Bennett's *George Eliot; Her Mind and Art* (1948). The first part of this book, a biographical and intellectual study, is of much less consequence than the second, purely critical section. Mrs. Bennett finds many structural flaws; in particular, the frequency and extent of omniscient intervention distresses her but she valuably insists on the organic form of George Eliot's novels. Perhaps the best chapters in her book are those on *Middlemarch* and on "Vision and Design," a transitional section in which she stresses the important formal function in the novels of the relation between individual and society.

Lettice Cooper's *George Eliot* (1951) is brief and very slight; the bibliography may be found useful. The section on George Eliot in John Holloway's *The Victorian Sage* (1953) relates her philosophy of life to her methods as a novelist in a sensible and sensitive manner. If he does not reach any strikingly original conclusions he is at least aware of the delicate problems involved in such a relation. His concept of the "Victorian Sage" is an interesting and challenging one; the whole book should be consulted as providing for George Eliot a general Victorian context of intellectual concern and literary method. Mario Praz's *The Hero In Eclipse* (1956) adds little that is new, and though George Eliot's work might seem to illustrate exactly his central theme — the predominance of the "unheroic hero" in the nineteenth century — his reading of the novels occasionally seems strained to fit the demands of his general thesis.

The last few years have been productive ones for critical studies of George Eliot. They include Barbara Hardy, *The Novels of George Eliot* (1959); Reva Stump, *Movement and Vision in George Eliot's Novels* (1959); Jerome Thale, *The Novels of George Eliot* (1959); and W. J. Harvey, *The Art of George Eliot* (1961).

Of these Mrs. Hardy's book is probably the best. Indeed, it is probably the best single critical study of George Eliot yet published. While dealing particularly with the problems of using the novel as a vehicle for tragedy, she is mainly concerned to stress the formal properties of George Eliot's art, observed as these have been both by the realistic surface of her novels and by a limited critical concept of "form" deriving from the precept and practice of Henry James. She has substantial chapters on plot, character, and imagery but perhaps the most original and profound section is that entitled "Possibilities." In this she demonstrates how the strongly deterministic nature of George Eliot's novels is subtly qualified by "something very like the actual appearance of alternative destiny within the 'irrevocable' and finished book. There is a strong and deliberate suggestion of the possible lives her characters might have lived." Mrs. Hardy's book is compact, closely argued and dense with specific and relevant reference.

Reva Stump's book is an extremely detailed study of image patterns in *Adam Bede, The Mill on The Floss,* and *Middlemarch.* A little pedestrian in style and occasionally obscured by its very profusion of detail, it is nevertheless a valuable and substantial work. Miss Stump avoids the prevailing vices of such studies — mere ingenuity and mechanical cataloguing — because she is always concerned to relate George Eliot's use of imagery to the main moral issues of her novels. Thale's book is a chronological study of the novels. Again, he is primarily concerned to relate aesthetic properties to moral concerns; perhaps the most valuable chapter is that on *Daniel Deronda* in which he demonstrates "a new and direct confrontation of certain kinds of evil, and perversity, hitherto unacknowledged." The concluding general chapter is also very stimulating. Although Thale's book is made up of disparate essays it is unified by his recurring analysis of certain key themes, such as "George Eliot's reduction of theology to psychology" and her "analysis of Puritan individualism." Though she deals with the interaction of character and society, he argues that "society as object is never the main concern" of her work, "still less was she concerned with the disintegration of society . . . with shifts and erosions in public values." Her main stress is on the moral process within individual characters as they develop toward crucial moments of decision. Thale's analysis of the relation of character to society is debatable but he has written a valuable book. W. J. Harvey's book is a general study of the formal properties of George Eliot's art; he digresses frequently into general critical theory and reaches much the same conclusions as Mrs. Hardy.

Oddly enough, the critical books on George Eliot outnumber the general critical essays. Readers should not forget Virginia Woolf's pioneer and surprisingly sympathetic essay "George Eliot" (*TLS*, 1919; reprinted in *The Common Reader*, 1925) in which she anticipates much modern criticism by singling out *Middlemarch* as George Eliot's masterpiece, a judgment which would have surprised most Victorian critics. Just how much George Eliot suffered from a lack of serious critical attention is indicated by the date of the next critical essay worthy of notice, S. L. Bethell's "The Novels of George Eliot" (*Criterion*, 1938). Bethell sounds the theme of the novelist-philosopher with the consequent view of her fiction as torn by the conflicting claims of intellect and imagination. According to him, the fault lies not so much in George Eliot as in the naturalistic and positivistic climate of her age.

Graham Hough takes a different position in his "Novelist-Philosopher; George Eliot" (*Horizon*, 1948). In his view her intellectual life "seemed to set her emotions in focus, to put them at a right distance . . . It is this tough, matured intelligence that makes her return to her childhood so successful." This is a short and general essay but always sensible and frequently penetrating.

W. Nauman in "The Architecture of George Eliot's Novels" (*MLQ*, 1948) tries to relate the structure of her novels to her philosophy of life. This is a somewhat confused essay, as is John Arthos' "George Eliot: The Art of Vision" (*Rivista di Letterature Moderne e Comparate*, 1952), since Arthos never gives his central concept of "visionary passion" adequate definition in relation to particular novels. Kate O'Brien's "George Eliot: A Moralizing Fabulist" (*Essays by Divers Hands*, 1955) is very slight and rambling. Equally disappointing is the essay of another contemporary novelist, Louis Auchincloss, contained in his *Reflections of a Jacobite* (1961). He takes a heavily sibylline view of George Eliot; she was "woefully preoccupied with duty . . . she shares with the Victorian public an admiration for what we consider pointless sacrifice." Only *Middlemarch* is exempted from his general censure.

Most studies of George Eliot's use of imagery have subsequently been reprinted in works already mentioned or to be mentioned later; there remains D. R. Carroll's "An Image of Disenchantment in the Novels of George Eliot" (*RES*, 1960). Carroll argues that in order to articulate the moral and psychological progress of her characters from egoism through disenchantment to regeneration, George Eliot sometimes uses Christian symbols but more often creates her own. Thus disenchantment is often conveyed by images of ruins which, because they also figure literally in her novels, allow George Eliot "to combine utmost verisimilitude of incident with a symbolic interpretation."

An increasingly prevailing theme in these general studies is the defense of George Eliot's art, the concern to point out that her novels do not fall into James's category of the "loose, baggy monster." This vindication of George Eliot's literary conventions and fictional strategies is the most important single advance toward a proper critical understanding and appreciation of her art. One consequence of her increased popularity has been that general essays of this kind have given way to more detailed critical treatment of particular novels or particular themes; it is to these that we must now turn.

V. *Studies of Particular Topics*

Though several theses have been completed on the topic, there is no published equivalent on George Eliot of G. H. Ford's *Dickens and His Readers*. M. Parlett's "The Influence of Contemporary Criticism on George Eliot" (*SP*, 1933) contains some valuable information though the author does not sustain her thesis that contemporary reviews vitally affected George Eliot's work. This is a more useful essay than the same author's "George Eliot and Humanism" (*SP*, 1930) which is a somewhat confused study of George Eliot's views on classical learning and Victorian methods of education.

W. F. Wright's "George Eliot as Industrial Reformer" (*PMLA*, 1941) is a rather thin essay outlining her views on social order, the class system, and reform. Dealing mainly with *Felix Holt*, the author maintains that the superior perspective of her philosophic background compensates for a lack in historical detail. A different picture of her treatment of society is contained in C. T. Bissell's "Social Analysis in the Novels of George Eliot" (*ELH*, 1951). This is an excellent essay which demonstrates how the artist in George Eliot is never swamped by the sociologist; the kind of society she depicts is seen as vitally relevant to the central themes of her work.

M. J. Svaglic's "Religion in the Novels of George Eliot" (*JEGP*, 1954) concentrates mainly on her treatment of Dissent in order to show that the inconsistencies in her philosophic outlook are more apparent than real. She is seen as reacting against dogma but retaining the ethical idealism of Christianity, a traditional view of her which is hardly refreshed by this essay.

The most authoritative treatment of the relation of her characters to historical originals is to be found in G. S. Haight's "George Eliot's Originals" (in *From Jane Austen to Joseph Conrad*, ed. R. C. Rathburn and M. Steinmann, 1958).

Finally a small group of essays and notes on George Eliot's relation to other writers may be mentioned here. These include L. A. Bisson, "Proust, Bergson and George Eliot" (*MLR*, 1945 — Proust's own brief notes on George Eliot may be found in *Contre Sainte-Beuve*, trans. S. Townsend Warner, 1958); M. Allott, "*Romola* and *The Golden Bowl*" (*N&Q*, 1953); Q. D. Leavis, "A Note on Literary Indebtedness; Dickens, George Eliot, Henry James" (*Hudson Review*, 1955); W. H. Stone, "Hale White and George Eliot" (*UTQ*, 1956); Robert L. Selig, "The Red-Haired Lady Orator: Parallel Passages in *The Bostonians* and *Adam Bede*" (*NCF*, 1961); C. Knoepflmacher, "Daniel Deronda and William Shakespeare" (*VNL*, 1961); and S. Lainoff, "James and Eliot: The Two Gwendolens" (*VNL*, 1962). Vernon Rendall has four valuable articles on "George Eliot and the Classics" (*N&Q*, 1947–1948).

Since it does not fit easily into any category, *A George*

Eliot Dictionary (1924), by I. G. Mudge and M. E. Sears, may be mentioned here; though incomplete it is still very useful as a work of reference.

VI. *Criticism of Individual Works*

Apart from *Middlemarch, Adam Bede* has received more detailed critical attention than any of George Eliot's other novels. J. S. Diekhoff's "The Happy Ending of *Adam Bede*" (*ELH*, 1936) analyzes a contradiction between the conclusion of the novel and its main moral bias. V. S. Pritchett, "Books in General" (*New Statesman and Nation*, 1944; revised and reprinted in *The Living Novel*, 1947), also takes exception to the moral vision of the novel; for him George Eliot is "the first of the simplifiers, one of the first to cut moral paths through the picturesque maze of human nature." The same note persists in A. J. Fyfe's "The Interpretation of *Adam Bede*" (*NCF*, 1954), which in rebutting the atonement theory and relating the novel to contemporary philosophy still sees the narrative as sugaring a didactic pill. Dorothy van Ghent's chapter on the novel in *The English Novel; Form and Function* (1953) is more sympathetic, although the author dislikes the frequent omniscient intervention. She is the first to sound two distinctive notes in much modern criticism of this novel, the concern with time and the concern with imagery. Both are also dealt with in M. Hussey's perceptive essay "Structure and Imagery in *Adam Bede*" (*NCF*, 1955). For him the imagery enacts the novel's substance, "an intimate dissection of modes of living, a study of psychology in contrasting environments and of the perpetual cycle of the seasons." Various inconsistencies in the novel's time structure have been analyzed by D. P. Deneau, "Inconsistencies and Inaccuracies in *Adam Bede*" (*NCF*, 1959). G. R. Creeger's "An Intepretation of *Adam Bede*" (*ELH*, 1956) again stresses the novel's symbolism, especially the contrast between the worlds of Loamshire and Stonyshire. W. M. Jones, "From Abstract to Concrete in *Adam Bede*" (*College English*,

1955), emphasizes the thematic significance of Dinah's sermon.

Many of these critics have approached from different angles the central problem of the novel's unity, discussing whether, in the words of Leavis, "the book is too much the sum of its specifiable attractions to be among the great novels." In particular, the relation of a morally serious theme to a pastoral mode, the treatment of Hetty and the concluding marriage of Adam and Dinah have proved recurring issues of debate. Thus R. A. Foakes in *"Adam Bede* Reconsidered" (*English,* 1959) stresses the pastoral element as "central to the whole action in establishing the values operative in the Hayslope community." In these terms he defends the marriage of Adam and Dinah "which fits richly into the pattern of pseudo-pastoral, the image of a harmonious way of life broken and made whole again." I. W. Adam in "A New Look at Hetty Sorrel" (*VNL,* 1962) considers Hetty as an early example of a recurrent character type in George Eliot's fiction, the egoist who is restored to "the human family" by "direct, unequivocal appeals to the sympathetic feelings." (Readers curious to trace changes in the criticism of fiction should compare this essay with the high-spirited defense of Hetty in the old-fashioned but vigorous study of *Adam Bede* by Orlo Williams in *Some Great English Novels,* 1926). Most of these issues are rehearsed in Ian Gregor's "The Two Worlds of *Adam Bede"* (in *The Moral and the Story* by Ian Gregor and Brian Nicholas, 1962). This intelligent and sensitive essay is one of the best introductions to the novel; whether the reader agrees with Gregor's conclusion that the novel fails to unify its disparate elements will depend on whether he regards George Eliot as placing the main stress on the individual or on society — a problem central to the reading of all the novels.

Even more than with *Adam Bede,* the ending of *The Mill on the Floss* has been a major critical problem. B. J. Paris, "Towards a Revaluation of George Eliot's *The Mill on the Floss"* (*NCF,* 1956), attempts to refute the criticism that "the last two books reveal an inconsistency in the ideological structure that results in a disappointment of the expectations which have been aroused in the reader up to that point." A similar aim, but a different method, is to be found in W. R. Steinhoff's "Intention and Fulfillment in the ending of *The Mill on the Floss*" (in *The Image of the Work,* by B. H. Lehman and others, 1955). This essay attempts to defend the final catastrophe by establishing a symbolic relationship between the flood and George Eliot's treatment of the river earlier in the novel. On the other hand, A. Welsh in "George Eliot and the Romance" (*NCF,* 1959) finds in *The Mill on the Floss* "the typical situation and plot of romance" concealed by a surface realism. If we fail to appreciate the ending this is because "we are no longer experienced readers of the highly stylized genre with which this novel engages." This is a highly ingenious but ultimately implausible essay.

Little has been published on *Silas Marner* (Thale's book contains a good chapter earlier published in essay form); but readers may profitably consult R. B. Heilman's "Return To Raveloe" (*English Journal,* 1957).

Biagi's edition of *Romola* (1906) has a useful introduction on George Eliot's use of source material. This has been amplified and in part corrected by M. Tosello's *Le Fonti Italiane della Romola di George Eliot* (1956) which concentrates on George Eliot's debt to Italian historians; the author has not consulted the *Romola* quarries. Readers should also consult J. A. Huzzard's "The Treatment of Florence and Florentine Characters in George Eliot's *Romola*" (*Italica,* 1958). Much the best essay on this novel is Carole Robinson's "*Romola*: A Reading of the Novel" (*VS,* 1962). For her, "philosophic uncertainty is the keynote of the novel, and the source of *Romola's* failure is to be sought not in its moral intentions or its didacticism, but in doubt, and in the novelist's uncertain faith in the affirmations she proposes in her effort to satisfy doubt."

There is a very slight section on *Felix Holt* in M. E. Speare's *The Political Novel* (1924). Far more substantial is the chapter in Raymond Williams' *Culture and Society* (1958). A most useful essay on this novel is F. C. Thomson's "The Genesis of *Felix Holt*" (*PMLA*, 1959), in which he argues that the Transome-Jermyn story is the genesis of the novel and that the political theme is an afterthought. Thomson has used the quarry for *Felix Holt* in the Tinker Collection at Yale and though one must suspend judgment on his main thesis, his essay is full of interesting material. Thomson has also considered "*Felix Holt* as Classic Tragedy" (*NCF*, 1961). He relates the story of the Transomes to George Eliot's "Notes on *The Spanish Gipsy* and Tragedy in General," but argues that in *Felix Holt* "Nemesis is converted from the utterly implacable Greek concept to a rather positivistic form — a severe but ultimately compassionate moral determinism." The novel fails for him because this theme is "too much diluted by the politics and law" present in the book. By contrast D. R. Carroll in "*Felix Holt*: Society as Protagonist" (*NCF*, 1962) stresses George Eliot's vision of society as the unifying factor in the novel. Felix Holt, in trying to reform both Esther and the working class, is simultaneously involved in the private and the public worlds of the book. This thesis issues in a sensitive and penetrating analysis of the novel.

The increasing acknowledgment of *Middlemarch* as George Eliot's masterpiece accounts for the very full critical treatment accorded it. Pride of place must be given to two considerable pieces of scholarship. The first is A. T. Kitchel's edition of the "Quarry for *Middlemarch*" (*NCF*, Supplement, 1950). The Quarry contains detailed notes on medical and political information, part of which forms the background to the novel, and also on time-schemes and character relationships. The editor has provided full notes and a substantial introduction of value to those whose interest in *Middlemarch* may not extend to a close scrutiny of the Quarry itself. While she does not discuss the full critical implications of the notebook, her introduction raises a number of important critical questions. "Outline, elaborate, analyze" — these, for

Miss Kitchel, are George Eliot's creative imperatives, while the notebook shows a double "process of clarification and of fusion."

The second major work is J. Beaty's *Middlemarch from Notebook to Novel* (1960), the closest study yet made of George Eliot's creative processes. It is based on a minute examination of all available evidence: letters and journals, the Quarry, and the manuscript of the novel. Beaty traces in detail the gradual fusion of the main narrative streams; he is scrupulous in indicating where he passes from fact to speculation and entirely plausible in his hypothetical reconstruction of events. He discusses the effect on the book of its mode of publication and conclusively demolishes the view of George Eliot as a "spontaneous" and "inspired" genius by analyzing her processes of revision. This study provides much essential information and provokes many questions for any future critic of the novel, who will ignore it at his peril.

Apart from this major contribution, Beaty has commented briefly on the background of the novel in "History by Indirection: The Era of Reform in *Middlemarch*" (*VS*, 1957) and has conjectured in "The Forgotten Past of Will Ladislaw" (*NCF*, 1958) that the Jewish interests explored in *Daniel Deronda* may originally have been meant to form part of Ladislaw's character. This argument has been amply rebutted by Robert A. Greenberg's "The Heritage of Will Ladislaw" (*NCF*, 1961) and T. Pinney's "Another Note on the Forgotten Past of Will Ladislaw" (*NCF*, 1962), both critics arguing that references to Will's Jewish ancestry belong only to Middlemarch gossip.

At a time when critical interest was dormant, several brief but lively essays on *Middlemarch* appeared in the *New Statesman and Nation*. Those by Edward Sackville-West (1940) and Noel Annan (1943) stress George Eliot as the novelist-philosopher with a consequent "underlying conflict between feeling and intellect." By contrast, V. S. Pritchett (1942; revised and reprinted in *The Living Novel*, 1947) sees a more intimate connection between philosophy and creative achievement: "Her philosophy is valid because it enlarges and generalizes

the human issue . . . the great scenes of *Middlemarch* are
exquisite, living transpositions of real moral dilemmas."

F. G. Steiner in "A Preface To *Middlemarch*" (*NCF*, 1955)
approaches the novel from the viewpoint of a Jamesian concept of form and finds it defective in construction, being an
ill-organized collection of tales of provincial life. In particular
he objects to the omniscient mode of narration. Something of
the same bias may be detected in Sumner J. Ferris, "*Middlemarch*: George Eliot's Masterpiece" (in *From Jane Austen to
Joseph Conrad,* ed. R. C. Rathburn and M. Steinmann, 1958).
The unity of the novel is more sympathetically explored in
Quentin Anderson's "George Eliot in *Middlemarch*" (in
From Dickens to Hardy, ed. B. Ford, vol. 6 of the *Pelican
History of English Literature,* 1958). Anderson stresses George
Eliot's conception of the interdependence of things as ex-
pressed in the metaphor of the web; readers interested in
George Eliot's use of imagery in this novel should also con-
sult Mark Schorer's "Fiction and the 'Matrix of Analogy'"
(*Kenyon Review,* 1949) and D. R. Carroll's perceptive essay
"Unity Through Analogy: An Interpretation of *Middlemarch*" (*VS,* 1959). S. Monod's "George Eliot et les personnages de *Middlemarch*" (*Etudes anglaises,* 1959), discusses the
balance of sympathy and criticism in George Eliot's attitude
to her characters; the same blend of qualities forms the subject of L. D. Lerner's "The Cool Gaze and the Warm Heart"
(*Listener,* 1960). Arnold Kettle's *An Introduction to the
English Novel* (vol. I, 1951) has a stimulating chapter on the
novel which tends perhaps to lay too heavy a stress on the
quality of George Eliot's determinism. By contrast, Newton
P. Stallknecht's "Resolution and Independence: A Reading
of *Middlemarch*" (in *Twelve Original Essays on Great English Novels,* ed. C. Shapiro, 1960) sees the novel as "a genetic
study of a single human decision," Dorothea's marriage to
Will Ladislaw. "Since George Eliot is hardly an out and out
determinist, we are to see Dorothea make the decision. Thus
we must come to discern the shape of the ideals and the al-
ternatives that confronted her as she made up her mind." J.
Hagan in "*Middlemarch*: Narrative Unity in the Story of

Dorothea Brooke" (*NCF*, 1961) also begins by isolating Dorothea's role in the novel and "traces a process of initiation, education, growth, whereby the heroine makes decisive discoveries about her own nature and the reality around her." This leads him, like Stallknecht, to a wider analysis of the world of *Middlemarch* in which he traces with sympathy and perception the many parallels created in the novel between personal and social relations.

Most of the critical problems relevant to *Middlemarch* — the question of its unity; the relation of individual characters to social pressures; the degree of control in George Eliot's attitude to her characters, especially to Dorothea and Will — are discussed by David Daiches in his *George Eliot: Middlemarch* (1963). This long and unassuming essay has the great virtue of taking the reader patiently and sequentially through the novel. Book by book, sometimes chapter by chapter, Daiches traces the development of the characters and the unfolding of the design with sympathy and insight; unlike so many critics, he creates a sense of the novel as an artifact moving massively forward in time. The result is one of the best general introductions to the novel for the nonspecialist to have appeared so far.

Finally, we may isolate two essays on *Middlemarch* because they raise a question of general interest. Asa Briggs in "*Middlemarch* and the Doctors" (*Cambridge Journal*, 1948) relates Lydgate's career to the medical background of the period and to Victorian concern with issues of public health. The light thrown on this subject does not extend much further than that shed by Miss Kitchel's introduction to the "Quarry for *Middlemarch*" but the essay is interesting for its underlying assumption that George Eliot projects contemporary problems back into the period of her novel: "the problem she sets Lydgate and Dorothea is in its essence a mid-Victorian problem. Their vision and their struggle are the same as her own." The same assumption is implicit in Lloyd Fernando's "George Eliot, Feminism and Dorothea Brooke" (*Review of English Literature*, 1963), which relates George Eliot's treatment of her heroine to her general views

on the nature and status of women, as revealed in her letters
and essays. The idea that George Eliot used earlier generations to reflect contemporary problems is interesting and has
been relatively little explored (Carole Robinson's essay on
Romola, mentioned earlier, is a notable exception). If she
did, then it was certainly not in the sharply topical way to be
found, for example, in many of Dickens' novels. The problem
is well worth further consideration.

F. R. Leavis' discussion of *Daniel Deronda,* in which he
attempts a sharp distinction between the Gwendolen Harleth
story and the Zionist theme, has proved one of the most controversial parts of *The Great Tradition.* Leavis has considerably modified his view of the novel in his introduction
to a recent paperback edition of *Daniel Deronda* (1960) but
his original view has been the starting point of much subsequent criticism. M. Beebe, " 'Visions are Creators': The
Unity of *Daniel Deronda*" (*BUSE,* 1955), maintains that the
main theme of the novel — the need to lose one's life in
order to find it — is expressed in symbols that unite the two
parts of the book. D. R. Carroll in "The Unity of *Daniel
Deronda*" (*EC,* 1959) argues that "the organic unity of the
novel springs from Deronda's psychological condition." J.
Beaty has discussed various critical views on this subject in
"*Daniel Deronda* and the Question of Unity in Fiction"
(*VNL,* 1959). Robert Preyer's "Beyond the Liberal Imagination; Vision and Unreality in *Daniel Deronda*" (*VS,* 1960)
views the novel as breaking "new ground in an effort to per-
suade readers of the novel of the need for moral awareness
and the significance of individual endeavor for the general
good." Edgar Rosenberg's *From Shylock to Svengali* (1960)
has a chapter discussing the novel in the context of "the
whole pattern of apology and retraction that made the virtu-
ous Jew possible, and condemned him to be dull."

Little critical attention has been paid to George Eliot's
poetry. B. J. Paris, "George Eliot's Unpublished Poetry" (*SP,*
1959), includes some new material. There is also very little
on George Eliot's shorter fiction. Elliot L. Rubinstein's "A
Forgotten Tale by George Eliot" (*NCF,* 1962) briefly con-

siders *The Lifted Veil*, seeing it as unique in dealing with the supernatural and in being steeped in gloom; its subject is "the waste land of a diseased mind," while the hero embodies "the most extreme treatment in George Eliot's work of the theme of unfulfillment."

Finally, attention should be drawn to R. Stang's *Discussions of George Eliot* (1960), a useful anthology of critical essays and excerpts, ranging chronologically from Henry James to Jerome Thale.

The quantity and quality of literary criticism is not necessarily a true index of any author's permanent value, but even if we were to regard modern comment as no more than the manifestation of a generation's taste, we could not but conclude that George Eliot has regained the status she held for her contemporaries. This critical revival has been accompanied, as we have seen, by a revolution in biographical interest. R. L. Purdy's prophecy in 1932 that "it will be well for her when the Olympian meliorist is forgotten and the tragically human author of *Adam Bede* and *Middlemarch* is rediscovered" has been amply fulfilled.

In many ways criticism has outrun scholarship. We still need a proper text; a critical edition of the novels under the general editorship of Jerome Beaty is currently projected. In particular, a full edition of her critical writings is a desideratum, a gap happily to be filled before the appearance of this survey. The project for a full bibliography goes slowly but surely; for a biography to place beside the *Letters* we must hope that Gordon Haight will soon put us deeper in his debt. Historians of thought will find many gaps to be filled in — George Eliot's translation of Spinoza, for example, still awaits publication — and we may echo Haight's opinion "that the valuable contributions to scholarship will come now from a closer study of her works, from the manuscripts through the various revised editions." Such work will in its turn have important critical consequences.

For those who agree that much remains to be done we may fittingly borrow a conclusion from George Eliot herself, a conclusion perhaps particularly appropriate for the readers —

and the writer — of a survey such as this: "The habit of expressing borrowed judgments stupefies the sensibilities, which are the only foundation of genuine judgments, just as the constant reading and retailing of results from other men's observations through the microscope, without ever looking through the lens one's self, is an instruction in some truths and some prejudices, but is no instruction in observant susceptibility; on the contrary, it breeds a habit of inward seeing according to verbal statements, which dulls the power of outward seeing according to visual evidence."

George Meredith

C. L. Cline

As C. P. SNOW recalls, G. H. Hardy told him that "at Trinity in the 90's, in one of the most brilliant critical groups that England has ever thrown up, it was possible to argue that Tolstoi might be within touching distance of George Meredith, but that no one else possibly could be." In our own time F. R. Leavis has condemned Meredith to limbo, and E. M. Forster has pronounced most of his social values to be "faked." Though ardent Meredithians remain, it can hardly be disputed that time has badly tarnished Meredith's great reputation. Thus the pendulum swing of taste.

Perhaps we should not be surprised. The way of life depicted in his novels has disappeared, the types he described no longer exist, what never pretended to strict realism now seems artificial, the battles he fought were won long ago, and the complexities and mannerisms of his style repel impatient readers. Further, the novel itself has undergone change and is no longer the medium in which he worked.

Even so, there has been a fairly widespread feeling in recent years that the time is ripe for a rehabilitation of Meredith's reputation. Sir Osbert Sitwell was among the first to express it, in his Presidential Address before the English Association in 1947, when he predicted that "before long we shall be given more than one life of Meredith, together with many briefer comments on his achievement." This modest prophecy has been more than fulfilled, though judging by the number of Meredith's novels in print, there has been no corresponding increase in his popular audience, as Sir Osbert predicted there would be.

I. *Bibliography*

Older bibliographies by John Lane (1890; revised 1900) and Arundell Esdaile (1907), as well as the bibliographies by Esdaile in the Memorial and De Luxe editions, have been superseded by Maurice Buxton Forman's *A Bibliography of the Writings in Prose and Verse of George Meredith* (1922) and *Meredithiana* (1924). The *Bibliography* is both accurate and complete. *Meredithiana* is less complete than it is usually thought to be: an unpublished doctoral dissertation (University of London, 1960) by L. T. Hergenhan contains many reviews and articles, mostly in newspapers and minor journals, not included in it. H. Lewis Sawin lists the secondary material of the years 1920–1953 in *Bulletin of Bibliography*, 1956.

II. *Editions*

The standard edition of Meredith's works is the Memorial Edition (1909–1911), in twenty-seven volumes, to which the second edition of *Letters*, edited by his son and slightly revised, was added in 1912. Equally authoritative is the limited De Luxe Edition (1898–1910), in thirty-seven volumes, to which the first edition of *Letters* was added in 1912.

Except for *Beauchamp's Career*, listed in the World's Classics but not dependably in print, separate editions of the novels are limited to *The Ordeal of Richard Feverel* (Everyman, edited by Robert Sencourt; Modern Library, edited by Lionel Stevenson; Signet, edited by Norman Kelvin; and Rinehart, edited by Charles J. Hill) and *The Egoist* (Modern Library, edited by E. Aubert Mooney, Jr.; Riverside Editions, edited by Lionel Stevenson; World's Classics, edited by Lord Dunsany; and Dolphin). There are two different textual forms of *Feverel*: the original version of 1859 (Modern Library, for example, with a good critical introduction) and the

revised version of 1878 (Signet, for example, with a perceptive afterword). Opinion differs on the merits of the two. The
revision unquestionably tightened the structure but at some
cost to clarity. Meredithians are apt to prefer the original version; others are supported by the mature Meredith.

III. *Letters*

Letters of George Meredith (1912), edited by W. M. Meredith, aimed at a broad selection rather than completeness. It
has held the field for half a century, during which scholars
have become aware of its deficiencies. Inaccuracies of text,
misdatings, ellipses, deletions, incompleteness, and hap-
hazard editing make it an unsatisfactory work. Other letters
are to be found in four privately printed pamphlets: *Letters
from George Meredith to Edward Clodd and Clement K.
Shorter* (1913); *Letters from George Meredith to Richard
Henry Horne* (1919); *Letters from George Meredith to A. C.
Swinburne and T. Watts-Dunton* (1922); and *Letters from
George Meredith to Various Correspondents* (1924). All were
supposedly limited to thirty copies, but the number is suspect. *Memories of George Meredith* (1919), by Lady Butcher,
with many of Meredith's letters; various letters in the suppressed edition of S. M. Ellis' *George Meredith* (1919); *Letters from George Meredith to Alice Meynell* (1923); and
numerous letters in *A Catalogue of the Altschul Collection*
(1931), edited by Bertha Coolidge, complete the general list.

There is great need, obviously, for a collected edition of
Meredith's letters, with accurate texts and proper editorial
apparatus. It is to be hoped that this need will be met by my
edition, which will be published by the Clarendon Press,
probably in 1965. It will increase the number of letters from
the approximately 760 of *Letters* (plus the others listed
above) to some 2400 or 2500.

IV. *Biography and Literary Reputation*

J. A. Hammerton's *George Meredith in Anecdote and
Criticism* (1909), reissued in 1911 as *George Meredith: His*

Life and Art in Anecdote and Criticism, is a patchwork of personal anecdotes and critical writings about Meredith up to the time of his death and has little value today. The first serious full-length biography was S. M. Ellis' *George Meredith: His Life and Friends in Relation to His Work* (1918, 1920). Ellis, a cousin of Meredith's, was unduly anxious to correct aspersions he fancied cast on the family by *Evan Harrington* and *The Egoist,* in consequence of which his treatment of the subject is out of proportion to its importance. He is usually accurate and rather dull, but there are large gaps in his knowledge of Meredith and appreciation of the works. The first edition of the book had to be withdrawn because of wholesale infringement of copyright; the second edition contains the essential facts of the first stripped of much of the copyright material. In 1919 Lady Butcher published *Memories of George Meredith,* a record of forty-one years of friendship.

R. E. Sencourt might reasonably have been expected to produce a better biography than his *Life of George Meredith* (1929). Despite access to the Altschul Collection and letters in the possession of many of Meredith's surviving friends, his principal contribution is a narration of the previously unknown Hilda de Longueuil episode and an extension of our knowledge of the friendships of Meredith's later life. There are many factual errors in the book.

Siegfried Sassoon's *Meredith* (1948), of which much was expected, proved to be disappointing. Probably the chief reason is that his unfamiliarity with scholarly method caused him to overlook published materials of consequence and to make too little use of accessible unpublished materials. The substantive work necessary for definitive biography was thus lacking. Sassoon's intuitive approach to Meredith's works, however, is usually interesting and often marked by flashes of insight.

It is surprising to find that *The Year's Work in English Studies* for 1953 does not list Lionel Stevenson's *The Ordeal of George Meredith* and that the 1956 issue remarks that there has never been an authoritative life of Meredith. For it is precisely this previous gap in Meredith studies that Stevenson's biography fills. To the known facts of Meredith's life he adds many new ones based upon his own researches, deftly selects those passages from the letters in which Meredith speaks best for himself, and gives sympathetic and understanding consideration to the works as literature and as reflections upon the author's life. Stevenson belongs to the school of biographers who eschew footnotes, and in this respect only may scholars have cause for regret.

For the study of Meredith's literary reputation there are Maurice Buxton Forman's *George Meredith: Some Early Appreciations* (1909), a reprint of twenty-three representative reviews between 1851 and 1883; René Galland's more comprehensive *George Meredith and British Criticism: 1851–1909* (1923), which prints only excerpts but offers judgments of the reviews; and two unpublished doctoral dissertations: Dorothy Dee Bailey's "American Literary Criticism of George Meredith, 1860–1917" (University of Wisconsin, 1950), and H. B. Staples' "English Literary Criticism of George Meredith's Works, 1886–1951" (University of California, 1954).

V. *General Criticism*

As might be expected, the earliest books on Meredith's works were mainly appreciative. So Richard Le Gallienne's *George Meredith: Some Characteristics* (1890; 5th ed., with a postscript by Le Gallienne, 1900) is concerned chiefly with those things that the author liked best. The chapter on "Style and Aim" is brief but still worth reading. In between a chapter on style and influence and another on men and women characters, Hannah Lynch (*George Meredith,* 1891) sandwiches little more than summaries of the action of the novels. Walter Jerrold's *George Meredith* (1902) bears the subtitle "An Essay towards Appreciation," an accurate description of the book. In 1907, however, two books more thoughtful than any of the foregoing appeared. Elmer James Bailey's *The Novels of George Meredith: A Study* is critical rather than appreciative and gains depth of focus from the author's knowledge of Victorian literature in general. Mary

Sturge Henderson undertook, in *George Meredith* (1907), a complete examination of all the novels. (The book was revised and reissued as *The Writings and Life of George Meredith,* by Mary Sturge Gretton, in 1926.) The biographical sections have been superseded, but the analytical are those of a discerning reader and intelligent critic. Her thesis is that Meredith is primarily moralist and teacher, that his novels are glossaries of his reading of life, and that narrative is but the vehicle of his philosophy. Hence he is only intermittently a great artist. This view is echoed by various later critics.

To Richard H. P. Curle (*Aspects of George Meredith,* 1908) Meredith is a great philosophical and psychological novelist with a powerful imagination which he throws into all that he writes. The "aspects" of Curle's book are Meredith's philosophy, his insight into character, his concepts of comedy and tragedy, of love, egoism, and sentimentality, and his sense of humor. For the beginning student of Meredith, James Moffatt's *George Meredith: A Primer to the Novels* (1909) is a useful guide. It gives a clear, though not always accurate, summary of the plots, commentary on the characters and high points, occasional elucidation of obscure points, and various affinities of the novels. Following a visit to Meredith in 1908 Constantin Photiadès wrote *George Meredith: sa vie, son imagination, sa doctrine* (1910), translated by Arthur Price as *George Meredith: His Life, Genius, and Teaching* (1913). Only chapters IV and V, on art and teaching, will repay reading.

René Galland's *George Meredith, Les cinquante premières années: 1828–1878* (1923) remains an indispensable book. To it he brought the erudition, intelligence, and clarity of the best type of French scholarship. As a study of the influences on and affinities of Meredith, his friendships and complex personality, his literary purposes and accomplishments, it is still a book of great value. It is regrettable that it stops with the year 1878 and that there has never been an English translation of it.

J. B. Priestley's *George Meredith* (1926) has probably reached a wider audience than any of the preceding works.

Looking back from the vantage point of 1926, Priestley found that Meredith had created a new kind of novel, romantic comedy, and enlarged the scope of fiction. The modern novel begins with *Richard Feverel,* and the supreme example of romantic comedy is *The Egoist.* Meredith, theorizes Priestley, is the prime target of his own comic perception: failing to achieve harmony of blood, brain, and spirit in his own life, he had himself always as a model of incongruity before him. As Meredith said, his method was to prepare his readers "for a crucial exhibition of the personae, and then to give the scene in the fullest of their blood and brain under stress of a fiery situation." Comedy therefore exists in his novels not to produce a narrative but to produce a scene. This explains why he is pre-eminently the novelist of scenes and why he is often a weak and faulty narrator. He lacked the talents of an ordinary novelist, yet he did the most difficult things magnificently and easily (an echo of Henry James's pronouncement). Priestley maintains that only the lack of the universal quality of humanity bars him from the ranks of the greatest — Homer, Cervantes, Shakespeare.

In *Art and Substance in George Meredith* (1953) Walter F. Wright approaches Meredith's fiction from each of four major perspectives — the comic, the romantic, the tragic, and the tragicomic. Wright's method is to devote a chapter to the manifestations of each as they appear in various novels and to follow up with a chapter devoted to a single novel as illustration. The disadvantage of this method is that none of the novels is limited to a single perspective. But Wright acutely perceives that certain of Meredith's "truths" appear in his first novel and reappear in variant forms in the later novels with remarkable consistency. He finds Meredith most at ease in romance and comedy, least at ease in tragedy. In consequence tragic themes tend to be left undeveloped or shifted to tragicomedy, which is Meredith's most original and most influential contribution to the novel.

The biographical portions of Jack Lindsay's *George Meredith: His Life and Work* (1956) are marred by an incredible number of errors of fact. Lindsay's real interest is in Meredith's works, which he has read from a Marxist viewpoint. For him Meredith is a political novelist, the focus of whose works "implies a considered judgment, based in political economy, of the fundamental forces determining the general movement of society" toward the ultimate Communist ideal. "His work . . . from first to last is concerned with concretely grasping the ways in which the society of the cash-nexus distorts the human essence." Living at a time before the workers of the world had learned to unite, he was not always clear as to the means of achieving the goals of freedom and brotherhood. Nevertheless, he sees the resistance or submission of the people "to the alienating processes of capitalism as a political issue . . . sees it steadily and sees it whole" and is therefore a great novelist with a secure place in literature. This is criticism written astride a Marxist hobbyhorse, and as one would expect it omits or soft-pedals whatever does not contribute to its thesis.

The controlling themes in Meredith's works, believes Norman Kelvin (*A Troubled Eden: Nature and Society in the Works of George Meredith,* 1961), are nature and society, alternating in ascendancy. Kelvin sees a progression in these themes from *Feverel* up to the last three novels, in which Meredith was attempting to clarify his ideas about them and to reconcile their opposing claims. That the pattern of themes and the progression is perhaps too neat is suggested by the omission of a number of novels from consideration and the dismissal of *Shagpat* and *Farina* despite their germinal importance to the later novels. Except when writing of *Beauchamp,* for which a dubious hypothesis is advanced, Kelvin is a thoughtful critic whose analyses of individual novels rise above the limitations of his thesis.

Curiously, in view of the early German influence on Meredith and his interest in German culture, German scholars discovered him only in the twentieth century. The extent of his knowledge of German art and culture as reflected in his works has been assessed by Ernst Dick in "Deutschland und die Deutschen bei Meredith" (*Germanisch-Romanische Monatsschrift,* 1914) and by John Lees in *MLR,* 1917. Dick's study is summarized and interpreted in Guy B. Petter's *George Meredith and His German Critics* (1939), along with the work of more than a dozen German scholars. Petter's book is valuable but confusing in organization: some of the best chapters are original contributions by Petter and have nothing to do with German critics at all. So with an important chapter on Meredith and Richter, and so also with an even more interesting chapter on the influence of *Orlando Furioso* on Meredith.

Lucien Wolff's *George Meredith, poète et romancier: introduction à son oeuvre* (1924) devotes three chapters to the novels and a final chapter, "L'art," to both poetry and the novels. Such a book serves very well its purpose of introducing Meredith to a French audience unacquainted with his work. Laura Torretta's *George Meredith, Romanziere, Poeta-Pensatore* (1918) serves a similar purpose for an Italian audience. In spite of evidences of extensive research, however, it contains numerous errors. In *Meredith et la France* (1937) Mona Mackay shows the early German influence on Meredith being replaced in the sixties by stronger French influences. Miss Mackay's chapter on the Vulliamy family had been anticipated in part by Galland's work, just as her general subject was anticipated by him in briefer form. A large part of her book is devoted to a detailed study of the French elements in Meredith's novels (and poetry).

Much of the best work on Meredith lies in the field of criticism rather than research, and in surveying it, one must be highly selective. A good place to begin is with Percy Lubbock's analysis of the artistry of Meredith in his review of the collected works (*Quarterly Review*, 1910). Influenced by Henry James, Lubbock concludes that Meredith was not an artist and that his failure lies in the matter of representation. Instead of being interested in his characters as human beings, he was interested in their relationship to his philosophy, and in the later novels the action is too often a point of departure for a searching exploration into the recesses of the mind of the character concerned. The author, never far absent, surveys, comments, disposes, but never *tells*. (One would expect

the word *shows*.) All the same, he has given us women characters rivaled only by those of Shakespeare. Further, the novels
are "somehow or other deeply embedded in life," bearing to
actuality "a uniform and consistent relation," and we never
doubt "that something living and genuine is going forward."

If Meredith was not a great literary artist, what was he?
Stuart P. Sherman, in "The Humanism of George Meredith"
(*On Contemporary Literature*, 1917), answers, "a great humanist." His criticism of life, his message to his contemporaries and his successors, comprise his humanism, and his claim
to genius lies in his studying and solving in some measure
"the basic problems of our contemporary literature half a
century before it existed." These basic problems can be
reduced to a single essence: "How to present a view of life
both wise and brave, answering to experience as well as to
desire, serviceable in art or in the daily walk."

Ramon Fernandez asks if the spiritual experience of the
nineteenth century can furnish "some precise intellectual
principles which would make human life work better." In
attempting an answer in his book *Messages* (1927), he employs
what he calls philosophical criticism, in which the influence
of Bergson is obvious in its heavy reliance on intuition. What
has attracted Fernandez to Meredith is that the "artistic success of his work renders possible an infinitely fecund interpretation of life," thanks to a harmonious combination of intellectual and intuitive powers in him. His work is therefore
the direct, poetical transcription of a life lived and meditated
without reference to preconceptions or abstract theories,
a life of which the characters are allegorical representations.
His characters "come to life in him all at once, fully created,
with all their possibles and impossibles, the products of an
inner chemistry of which he is aware" intuitively.

Sir Osbert Sitwell's Presidential Address before the English
Association in 1947 has already been alluded to. In it he rejects the charge that Meredith's concern with country houses
constitutes snobbery; the country houses, he says, are simply
conventions, like miners' cottages in D. H. Lawrence. Because
of the change in manners and morals, however, it may take

the present-day reader a little time to get into Meredith's novels and be taken captive by them. But once into them he is transported to "a land bathed in the golden light and mist produced by his style — a prospect at once recognizable, spacious, with great stretches of undulating country, broken up by moral boundaries solid as stone walls and plain for all to see." Apparent improbabilities and the obsolescence of the types portrayed, Sitwell feels, in no wise mar the authenticity of the novels, which exist on their own plane as works of art. Their beauty and wisdom reside in their style and atmosphere exactly as in a great painting.

Briefer notice must be given the remaining articles of general critical nature. In "Mr. George Meredith" (*Modern Studies,* 1907) Oliver Elton writes sympathetically of him as a novelist who tested "human nature with his finger, like a glass, to see if it rings clear and right." Meredith's special power is that of "one of the masters of the spiritual life: — not the life of the lonely mystic or thinker . . . but the life of men and women in contact, snared by instinct or egoism, but capable of emerging with made souls, marked and scarred but ready to begin afresh." Frederick P. Mayer argues in "George Meredith: An Obscure Comedian" (*VQR,* 1925) that Meredith's greatness lies in his unreality and obscurity. His fictional view of life is a kind of pastoral vision, which requires "a reshaping of events from their real dimensions into those of the art world" and which, within its conventions, "has its own reality." Osbert Burdett ("George Meredith," *Critical Essays,* 1926) is excellent on Meredith's means of producing the illusions of wit and conversation, his theory of Nature, his concern with the manners, ideas, and intellectual atmosphere of a leisure class, his dualism, and his characters. For Anna Kimball Tuell ("George Meredith," *A Victorian at Bay,* 1932) Meredith is more than the "priest of sanity"; he is a novelist whose fiction "was one long contribution to the human intelligence which was his light" and whose characters were created to bear witness to that light.

Virginia Woolf ("The Novels of George Meredith," *The Second Common Reader,* 1932) thinks Meredith an imperfect novelist not because he could not do the sort of thing his predecessors had done but because, after *Pride and Prejudice* and *The Small House at Allington,* there was nothing for him and George Eliot and Hardy to do but launch out in new directions. They saved the novel from certain death and thus are due certain allowances for their imperfections. Yet to read Meredith "is to be conscious of a packed and muscular mind; of a voice booming and reverberating with its own unmistakable accent," and to "feel that we are in the presence of a Greek god . . . who talks brilliantly" and "who is marvellously alive and on the alert." The reasons for the present neglect of Meredith, thinks Edward Sackville-West (*Inclinations,* 1949), are that his view of life and his kind of wit became unfashionable. It is time now, however, to "assume again that belief in the self-renovating power of the soul which was the foundation of Meredith's muscular agnosticism." He lacked a professional sense of his own scope and relied on inspiration, but as a born improviser worked "his way towards the unknown center of his genius," which he reached in *The Egoist.* V. S. Pritchett, in "Meredith" (*Books in General,* 1953), absolves Meredith of being a snob but thinks that snobbery as a literary subject was peculiarly his own: "no other writer has so richly and so ironically conveyed the sheer pleasure the Victorians had in social position." He also has a fine sense of comedy and the great novelist's gift for generalizing character, by which "he moves with a brilliance that catches the breath and excites the mind."

Louis Auchincloss, in "Meredith Reassailed" (*Reflections of a Jacobite,* 1961), concludes, largely on the basis of narrative skill, that *Diana* and *The Egoist* are superb, the rest of Meredith unreadable. In "The Novels of George Meredith" (*Review of English Literature,* 1962) Phyllis Bartlett offers a spirited defense of Meredith against charges of cleverness, editorial intrusiveness, and lack of a tragic view of life. She finds him a tonic writer who saw into things with a deep power of joy and who has given us memorable characters and great variety. Except for the device of the intrusive novelist, his novels are the least rather than the most Victorian. Again, in *George Meredith* ("Writers and Their Work," no. 161, 1963), Miss Bartlett examines the novels in greater detail and — as always in her writings — with much good sense. The trouble with Meredith's novels, observes Donald S. Fanger in a thoughtful article on "George Meredith as Novelist" (*NCF*, 1962), is that he vacillated between poetry and prose, straining to synthesize the two. Hence his works do not conform to a conscious theory and lack discipline. Fanger contends that Meredith's view of life was not a philosophy but only Victorian optimism which finds expression in recurring themes. Botched in the handling, these themes are reduced to motifs, fragments of themes which are not accounted for in terms of the book.

VI. *Special Studies*

Nothing in Meredith has received so much study as have comedy and the Comic Spirit. Joseph Warren Beach's *The Comic Spirit in George Meredith* (1911; reissued, 1963) is still the standard work on the subject. Despite occasional omissions, for example, "The Procession of the Cake" in *Feverel,* it is on the whole a safe guide. The probability that Meredith knew and was influenced by Jean Paul Richter's *Vorschule der Aesthetic* is raised to near certainty by Edward V. Brewer in "The Influence of Jean Paul Richter on George Meredith's Conception of the Comic" (*JEGP*, 1930). There are striking parallels in imagery, in the discussions of irony, satire, and humor, in phraseology, and in the importance of freedom in the cultivation of the comic in both the *Vorschule* and the *Essay on Comedy*; in addition both men approached the subject from the viewpoint of the effect of the comic upon an observer. In "Meredith's Literary Theory and Science: Realism versus the Comic Spirit" (*PMLA*, 1938) E. Arthur Robinson correlates Meredith's theory of literature with his philosophy of evolution. Not that the Comic Spirit evolved from the doctrine of evolution; its sources lay rather in Meredith's temperament and literary interests. But in shaping it into an adjunct of Earth, he made his evolutionary doctrine the core and touchstone of his reflection upon the complexities of the universe and the life developed within it.

Despite his lecture on comedy and the prelude to *The Egoist,* Meredith never defined the limits of his comedy, thinks Frank D. Curtin ("Adrian Harley: The Limits of Meredith's Comedy," *NCF,* 1953). Nevertheless, they are more or less clear in the novels, especially *Feverel,* where Adrian Harley represents the Comic Spirit; he functions only when it presides, and his presence is a clue to the limits of the comedy. J. Gordon Eaker, in "Meredith's Human Comedy" (*NCF,* 1951), says that comedy offers the best approach to Meredith's work since such a view of it coincides with his own. The limitation of the method, however, is implicit in the omission of those novels which require a different approach. Gladys Turquet-Milnes ("Meredith and the Cosmic Spirit," *Contemporary Review,* 1927) sees Meredith as a pre-Bergson Bergsonian who produces "in us the sensation of that great wave of duration in which we live and which sets us in harmony with the infinite" and who regards laughter as a philosophy ordained by Nature "to correct our tendency toward inertia and excess and set us in the heart of reality." Since the lover of universal life "is in his essence a lover of Nature and laughter," the *Comic* Spirit is the *Cosmic* Spirit. Donald S. Fanger, in "George Meredith as Novelist" (*NCF,* 1962), disagrees with all who regard Meredith as an original theorist of comedy whose theories are embodied in his work. The Comic Spirit is rather an Ironic Spirit which expresses Meredith's attitude toward life.

Almost everyone who has written about Meredith has had something to say about his women characters. Of the several books and articles that deal specifically with the subject, Herbert Bedford's *The Heroines of George Meredith* (n.d.) has little value. The analysis by Garnet Smith, in "The Women of George Meredith (*Fortnightly Review,* 1896), on the other hand, is excellent. Erna Bierig's more extensive treatment, in *Frauengestalten bei George Meredith* (1936), is a work of intelligence and understanding. Petter calls it "a penetrating study." In *George Meredith as Champion of Women and of Progressive Education* (1937) Alice Woods combines Meredith's views of education with a discussion of some of his heroines. Meredith once told Foster Watson that he had two underlying aims before him in writing novels: education and the emancipation of women. Watson's subsequent article, "George Meredith and Education" (*Nineteenth Century*, 1910), is concerned only with the educational views and does not go much beyond those expressed toward the end of *Lord Ormont*. A thorough treatment of the subject, however, may be found in Reinhard Becker's *Die Erziehung bei George Meredith* (1928), the thesis of which is that education is the prevailing theme in Meredith's novels and that all of his heroes and heroines are subjected to the educative forces of Earth in their struggle with illusion.

Meredith's philosophy has been the subject of frequent study, most often in connection with the poetry. G. K. Chesterton, in "The Moral Philosophy of Meredith" (*Contemporary Review*, 1909), attempts to define the difference between the morality of Meredith and other writers. He believes that it approaches most nearly that of pre-Christian paganism but that it is nevertheless a religious paganism, with Meredith's symbols as its sacraments. James Vertner Fletcher, in an excellent dissertation, "The Background and Development of George Meredith's Ethics" (University of Washington, 1937), finds that the background of Meredith's ethical philosophy was Romantic, deriving from Wordsworth, Goethe, Carlyle, and Mazzini. A later influence was Darwinian evolution, which operated as a catalytic agent enabling Meredith to justify intellectually the Romantic ideas of earth worship imbibed earlier. The philosophy which has attracted some readers to Meredith nevertheless exacted its price, suggests O. J. Campbell in an important article, "Some Influences of Meredith's Philosophy upon His Fiction" (*Wisconsin Studies in Language and Literature*, II, 1918). Such women characters as Diana and Carinthia were created to illustrate Meredith's conception of Nature, rather than human nature, and such a character as Sir Willoughby was created to keep alive a French spirit of comedy. They were important to Meredith for their place in his philosophical system rather than for their individuality, and in place of "warm human blood" he filled their veins with "a much less vital ichor brewed in his metaphysical laboratory." In time these characters "have hardened into fixed philosophical concepts."

Allied to the topic of Meredith's philosophy is that of his religion. In "Mr. Meredith on Religion" (*Hibbert Journal,* 1905) the Reverend James Moffatt finds the essence of Meredith's religion rooted in his use of the word "Nature": "from all sides of his work the echo comes: *first that which is natural, then that which is spiritual.*" Moffatt understandably finds Meredith's "spiritual" indefinite. In any event it did not comprehend notions of personal immortality, as is emphasized by G. W. Foote in "George Meredith: Freethinker" (*English Review,* 1913). Robert Peel's *The Creed of a Victorian Pagan* (1931) is less an analysis of Meredith's creed than of his practice in the light of the philosophy of blood, brain, and spirit.

The title of Charles Dewey Tenney's " 'Rose Pink and Dirty Drab': George Meredith as Critic" (*Sewanee Review,* 1931) alludes to Meredith's view of sentimentality and naturalism in fiction. The article shows that Meredith disapproved of both extremes in the writings of others and that in his own writings he had a philosophical center firmly rooted in Earth. Irene M. Sturges, in "George Meredith: A Study in Theory and Practice" (unpub. diss., University of Utah, 1961), has examined Meredith's critical theories of the novel and applied them to *Feverel, The Egoist,* and *One of Our Conquerors* as a test of their validity.

Studies of Meredith's technique, style, and use of figurative language abound. The most thorough treatment of technique is Adam Brendel's *Die Technik des Romans bei George Meredith* (1912), in which Meredith's philosophy, themes, style, characters, and epic-dramatic structure are examined. In "Journey, Ordeal, Recovery: Metaphoric Patterns in Meredith's Early Prose and Poetry, 1849–1859" (unpub. diss.,

Duke University, 1961) Carolyn Herbert Smith points out that when financial necessity drove Meredith to fiction he compensated by using the techniques of poetry in the structure and imagery of his early prose.

So much has been written about Meredith and the Comic Spirit that few have stopped to ask whether he was a satirist or not. Nevertheless, he was one, though not in the traditional sense, says James Sutherland (*English Satire,* 1958). His satire is so delicate "that the traditional techniques of exaggeration and distortion have . . . almost given way to one of dispassionate exposure." Sir Willoughby's soul "is like a drop of water examined under the microscope, which is found to be swarming with amoebas and parameciums and other uncertain animalcula." This could only occur in a novel in which the dramatic method of self-revelation is supplemented by a commentary that matches the dialogue in delicacy. Meredith's penchant for breaking into his novels as narrator has often been observed and as often condemned, but into none of the early novels does he break more frequently than in *Sandra Belloni,* says Robert W. Watson ("George Meredith's *Sandra Belloni*: The 'Philosopher' on the Sentimentalists," *ELH,* 1957). Though Meredith knew that the Philosopher's interruptions destroyed illusion, he felt that the dramatic method alone did not sufficiently convey his meaning.

Others besides Sir Osbert Sitwell have been interested in Meredith's style. It is the style of a poet — "metaphorical, fearless and allusive," says Desmond MacCarthy in "Meredith's Method" (*Remnants,* 1918). If we realize his characters unforgettably, the reason is not that we have known them intimately but that he has this poetic gift. With much of this presumably Lionel Stevenson would agree. But examining Meredith's style against the background of style in the novel in general ("Meredith and the Problem of Style in the Novel," *Zeitschrift für Anglistik und Amerikanistik,* 1958), he points to another element — Meredith's conversational manner. In the words of Virginia Woolf it was "highly wrought, artificial conversation, with its crystallized phrases and its high-

piled metaphors, moved and tossed on a current of laughter."
Hence Meredith wrote, like Sterne, "in a style that has all
the traits of witty, cultivated conversation." Seen in the light
of his purpose, his style is not "an elaborate excrescence, but
has a functional relationship with the particular kind of fiction that he intended to create." A. W. Verrall (*Collected
Literary Essays*, 1913) proposes dexterity in the manipulation
of language as the touchstone by which one may judge
whether he cares for Meredith or not. But, objects G. M.
Trevelyan (*Clio, A Muse and Other Essays*, 1913), this leaves
out the other half of Meredith's prose, "the poetry of it."
For Trevelyan the drawing-room scenes pall quickly; it is
when the characters "stand in direct contact with Nature"
that they "put on their full grandeur or charm," as Vernon
Whitford asleep under the wild cherry tree, Lucy by the weir,
Carinthia Jane going out to "call the morning," and so forth.
By contrast with these articles, Frieda Gamper's *Die Sprache
George Merediths* (1927) is a pedantic treatment of its subject under the principal headings of sentence structure, syn-
tactic and stylistic problems, and artistic style.

Deborah S. Austin ("Meredith on the Nature of Metaphor," *UTQ*, 1957) has collected Meredith's pronouncements
on metaphor to show his belief "that the image-making capac-
ities of the poet had a valid use in the novel" in spite of
his awareness of their inherent dangers. His perception of
their special power is "conclusive evidence from the nineteenth century of serious experimentation with functions of
the novel which have not received adequate consideration until our time." Barbara Hardy and Bernard A. Brunner reach
similar conclusions. In " 'A Way to Your Hearts through
Fire and Water': The Structure of Imagery in *Harry Richmond*" (*EC*, 1960) Mrs. Hardy says that Meredith employs
imagery more freely, in a "greater degree of discordance and
casualness," than his contemporaries, and nowhere more
strikingly than in *Richmond*. Her examination of the
imagery demonstrates that it moves out of "its apparently
fixed pattern in many places and for many reasons" and warrants her conclusion that such displacements reveal the need

for revision of the concept of organic and total relevance. Brunner, in "Meredith's Symbolism: *Lord Ormont and His Aminta*" (*NCF,* 1953), finds that Meredith was a conscious and often highly successful artist in the use of symbolism before it became distinguished in fiction. Brunner singles out *Lord Ormont* as the novel in which it reached its "full flowering."

Meredith is usually regarded as a highly original novelist, owing little to his predecessors. Various works prove this to be overstated. The influence of Peacock has been observed by Galland and others, but the most thorough study has been made by Augustus Henry Able, III, in *George Meredith and Thomas Love Peacock: A Study in Literary Influence* (1933). Able finds remarkable likenesses in the two authors in theme and scene, character and incident, thought and style. Most striking of all is the close agreement between them regarding woman and the desirability of her intellectual and emotional emancipation. Richard Lionel Hillier, in "Traces of Dickens's Caricatures in the Early Novels of George Meredith" (unpub. diss., University of Colorado, 1932), finds the culmination of Dickens' influence in *Evan Harrington*; and the Reverend James Moffatt points out, in "Dickens and Meredith" (*Hibbert Journal,* 1922), a number of personal and literary resemblances not mentioned elsewhere. The influence of Richter and of *Orlando Furioso* has been noticed above. Of major influences, "the noble Goethe" was on Meredith's own testimony "the most enduring" of all. In "Der Einfluss Goethes auf George Meredith" (*Englische Studien,* 1925) Marie Krusemeyer justifies the statement on the basis of evidence in Meredith's letters and works.

What of Meredith's influence on other writers? Donald S. Fanger argues persuasively, in "Joyce and Meredith: A Question of Influence and Tradition" (*Modern Fiction Studies,* 1960), that the change in taste in the literate public during the last half century owes something to Meredith through his influence on Joyce. The influence is observable in the lyricism of the two, in the use of the interior monologue, and in a dislike for well-ordered plots. But what was undisciplined in Meredith was disciplined by Joyce.

Other special studies that may be mentioned include Barbara Alberts-Arndt's *Die Englische Gesellschaft im Spiegel der Romane von George Meredith* (1931), an analysis of the social structure of Meredith's time, his attitude toward it, and in particular its manifestations of egoism and sentimentality and their consequences as seen in his novels. Greta Grimsehl's *Das Verhältnis der Geschlechter in den Romanen George Merediths* (1919; translated by Petter, *George Meredith and His German Critics*, pp. 197–282) is a thorough treatment of Meredith's ideas about the sexes. A kindred work is that of Marie Moll, *Das Eheproblem bei George Meredith* (1933), in which the view is taken that Meredith's feminism has been exaggerated and that the freedom he demanded for women was to enable them to become suitable wives and comrades for men.

Meredith's interest in boys has been noted by Rowland Grey in "Certain Boys of Meredith" (*Fortnightly Review,* 1918), while Albert Santee Kerr has studied the conflict between the generations in "Victorian Parents and Children; Family Conflict in the Novels of Lytton, Trollope, Meredith, and Butler" (unpub. diss., Columbia University, 1951). And finally, two articles, W. G. Hartog's "George Meredith, France and the French" (*Fortnightly Review,* 1914) and Amy Foster Watson's "Meredith and Italy" (*ibid.,* 1919), are devoted to Meredith's relationships with France and Italy respectively and the French and Italian elements in his works.

VII. *Studies of Individual Novels*

The Shaving of Shagpat is to many readers a bewildering novel, and the temptation to regard it as allegorical has been irresistible despite a warning note by Meredith in the second edition. In 1906 the Reverend James McKechnie published *Meredith's Allegory, "The Shaving of Shagpat,"* on which Meredith placed an ambiguous stamp of approval. For McKechnie, Shagpat is any established evil, superstition, or tyranny which must be removed, and Shibli Bagarag a reformer who employs common sense to effect the reform. This interpretation, which has been generally accepted, is broad

344   *VICTORIAN FICTION*

enough to admit of variants and individual specifications. W. F. Mainland, in "A German Source for *The Shaving of Shagpat*" (*MLR*, 1936), notices several similarities between the novel and Hoffmann's *Klein Zaches, genannt Zinnober* and possible parallels between it and Hoffmann's *Der goldene Topf*. But Milton Millhauser (*N&Q*, 1937) suggests equally strong resemblances to the *Mabinogion* story "Kilhweh and Olwen." In both Hoffmann and the *Mabinogion* the hair motif is prominent.

An excellent survey of the qualities that make *Feverel* a favorite among the novels is to be found in John Erskine's "The Ordeal of Richard Feverel" (*The Delight of Great Books*, 1928), though even Erskine is misled by Meredith's subtlety into saying that Clare dies of a broken heart. In "*The Ordeal of Richard Feverel* as Tragedy" (*College English*, 1946) Gladys W. Ekeberg views the novel as tragedy and states that Meredith used contrast as a powerful means of achieving tragic effect. The novel opens in sunshine, as it were, with only faint but ominous rumblings of thunder overhead. The tragic conclusion is foreshadowed from the beginning, however, and as the novel progresses the tone changes from the comic to the tragic spirit.

Sir Austin's System has naturally attracted a good deal of attention. William R. Mueller, in "Theological Dualism and the 'System' in *Richard Feverel*" (*ELH*, 1951), treats the problem of the failure of the System in terms of the ethical dualism which runs throughout the novel and is the basis of the System itself. The System has as its premise the belief that each individual is a prize for which God and the Devil are struggling. The System does not fail; rather, at the pinnacle of its success, Sir Austin is false to it and abandons it. Mueller thinks that this explains the shift of the novel from comedy to tragedy. William H. Marshall ("Richard Feverel, 'The Original Man,'" *VNL*, 1960) agrees with Mueller on the importance of the theological implications, but whereas Mueller thinks that Sir Austin's attitude toward his System caused the tragedy, Marshall argues that the System produced it. System and Originator are one because the System embodies the ideas of Good derived from the Originator's image of Deity (a projection of himself). Therefore Sir Austin is wrong in believing that the failure of the System lies in an unworthy object; it lies in himself, as the novel makes clear. In "The Artistic Unity of *Richard Feverel*: Chapter XXXIII" (*NCF*, 1952) William E. Buckler goes over much of the same ground as Mueller in order to establish the unity of the novel. He accepts Meredith's statement in a letter to Samuel Lucas (*Altschul Catalogue*, p. 79) that the System "had its origin not so much in love for his son, as in wrath at his wife, and so carries its own Nemesis." Chapter XXXIII, "Nursing the Devil," is most pertinent to this interpretation because it is the direct result of Chapter I, as the last chapter is its inevitable consequence. Even so, Meredith perceived that he had not made this completely apparent.

In "Fiction and Philosophy in the Education of Tom Jones, Tristram Shandy, and Richard Feverel" (*College English*, 1952) Howard O. Brogan places *Feverel* in "a continuing tradition of educational theory" deriving from Locke and Herbert Spencer. All three novelists learned much from the speculative thinkers, but they were critical of the ideas received and placed much greater insistence upon the realities of the body than did the speculative thinkers. The knightly theme and its implications in Meredith's own life are considered by Phyllis Bartlett in "Richard Feverel, Knight Errant" (*BNYPL*, 1959), and Irving H. Buchen suggests, in "The Importance of the Minor Characters in *The Ordeal of Richard Feverel*" (*BUSE*, 1961), that the minor characters are exempla enabling us to see that the tragedies of the book are man-made, not immanent in the nature of Meredith's world.

Evan Harrington, except in its exhibition of the Comic Spirit, has not attracted much special attention. Royal A. Gettman, however, in "Serialization and *Evan Harrington*" (*PMLA*, 1949) has made an excellent study of the circumstances under which it was written as a serial for *Once a Week* and the effect of this mode of publication upon the novel.

Charles J. Hill thinks that *Rhoda Fleming* has received

less attention than its due and has devoted two articles to it. In "George Meredith and Thomas Hardy" (*N&Q*, 1953) he traces the personal relationship between the two men and points out that *Tess* and *Rhoda* have the same theme and that there is a "striking resemblance between the openings of the two stories." In "George Meredith's 'Plain Story' " (*NCF*, 1952) he traces the novel through its various stages to its final form. The development of this novel from an early short story is traced by Lionel Stevenson in "Meredith's Atypical Novel" (*The Image of the Work*, by B. H. Lehman and others, 1955).

Among the missing works of Meredith listed in the preface of Forman's *Bibliography* is an autobiography mentioned in Meredith's letters of 1864. The mystery of this "missing" work is resolved by Richard B. Hudson in "Meredith's Autobiography and *The Adventures of Harry Richmond*" (*NCF*, 1954). He shows that the reference was actually to *Richmond* and prints a fragmentary sketch in the Altschul Collection to show that the novel as finally published was vastly improved over its original conception. Barbara Hardy's study of the imagery of the novel (*EC*, 1960) has been noted above.

That Meredith's friend Captain Maxse served as the original of the hero in *Beauchamp's Career* and that Meredith used in the novel his own canvassing experience in the election of 1868 is well known. Charles J. Hill, in "The Portrait of the Author in *Beauchamp's Career*" (*JEGP*, 1953), offers evidence to support his theory that Meredith has included a disguised intellectual portrait of himself, as well, in the person of Dr. Shrapnel, who "can [often] be shown . . . to be speaking for the novelist." That these ideas derived from Carlyle, however, seems amply proved by John W. Morris in "*Beauchamp's Career*: Meredith's Acknowledgment of His Debt to Carlyle" (*Tennessee Studies in Honor of John C. Hodges and Alwin Thayer*, 1961). Morris calls *Beauchamp* "an astonishing double tribute to Carlyle" since it appropriates "his theory of biography-history for the novel" and pictures "his ideas as the principal creative forces of his age." Morris would have us accept this theory of biography-history as governing "the Meredithian novel in general," but it would surely apply more specifically to those novels having a basis in real people and real events than to the others. Frederick R. Karl, in *"Beauchamp's Career*: An English Ordeal" (*NCF*, 1961), rightly singles out *Beauchamp* as one of the novels "that can compete artistically with the finest of Victorian fiction," and his analysis of the qualities that justify the statement is to be recommended.

The Egoist, with *Feverel,* has been a favorite object of study among the novels. The comic tone of the novel, warns Richard B. Hudson, in "The Meaning of Egoism in George Meredith's *The Egoist"* (*Trollopian*, 1948), may cause it to be taken as little more than polite comedy. To establish a more serious purpose, he analyzes the meaning of egoism in Meredith's philosophy as expressed in his poetry. From Hudson's examination Sir Willoughby stands revealed as a "gross original," a flesh-and-blood representative of man's brutish past employing all of his abilities to enhance his own ego. In "Theme and Image in *The Egoist"* (*University of Kansas City Review,* 1954) Charles J. Hill shows the close relationship of the imagery of the novel to its theme. He notices numerous parallels between the novel and J. S. Mill's "The Subjection of Women" and concludes that "what Meredith has done . . . is to dramatize the ideas of Mill." Robert D. Mayo has written two interesting articles, "Sir Willoughby's Pattern" (*N&Q*, 1942) and *"The Egoist* and the Willow Pattern" (*ELH*, 1942), to demonstrate that the legend of the common willowware provided Meredith with the ground plan of the novel and that he presupposed familiarity of his readers with it. In the second of the articles Mayo pursues in detail the symbolism of the "porcelain-idea," which, among other things, explains the enigmatic designation of Clara as "a dainty rogue in porcelain." Mayo is overmodest in regarding all of this as merely "a superfluous piece of ingenuity."

Fabian Gudas' "George Meredith's *One of Our Conquerors"* (*From Jane Austen to Joseph Conrad,* 1958) is an attempt to clarify the meaning of an admittedly difficult novel by interpreting the character and destiny of Victor Radnor in terms of the key word "scheme." The novel, as the history of the failure of one of his grandest schemes, "may be read as a study of the effects which scheming has on the schemer and on those around him." Fred C. Thomson, in "Stylistic Revisions in *One of Our Conquerors*" (*YULG*, 1961), reports on his examination of two manuscript drafts of the novel; "from these one can learn something of Meredith's original design, trace its modifications, and see how deliberately in fact Meredith invited criticism of his style. They show fairly conclusively that . . . the stylistic obscurities of Meredith were frequently the result of tampering with material initially simple and clear." Perhaps none of these obscurities has been more often criticized than the opening sentence of the novel, which Phyllis Bartlett analyzes brilliantly in "The Novels of George Meredith" (*Review of English Literature*, 1962).

It may properly be asked, in conclusion, where do all of these riches in scholarship and criticism leave us? Biographers and historical scholars would seem to have done most of their work with Meredith. Though new facts will surely continue to be discovered, they will be predictably minor in importance. What has not been done extensively is to re-examine Meredith's novels in the light of contemporary standards of criticism. Only when this has been done can Meredith take his rightful place in the literary canon.

11 ⁊&

Thomas Hardy

George S. Fayen, Jr.

I. *Bibliography*

LITTLE NEEDS to be done in Hardy bibliography except to continue recording annually the increasing number of essays on his fiction. Richard L. Purdy's *Thomas Hardy: A Bibliographical Study* (1954), including both the prose and poetry and superseding the partial lists by A. P. Webb (1916), H. Danielson (1916), and John Lane (in Lionel Johnson's *The Art of Thomas Hardy,* 1894; revised, 1923), stands as the definitive work. It is more a biography in bibliographical form than an attempt simply to collate first editions and point out every significant printing. This it does with care and completeness, but it also locates and describes original manuscripts (almost all preserved in public or private collections), discusses the circumstances of composition and publication (serial installments and the demands of bowdlerizing for "family" magazines), traces the development of texts through subsequent editions and impressions, and indicates Hardy's uncollected contributions to periodicals and newspapers. Stage adaptations and performances of his novels and stories are noted; appendixes deal with a variety of biographical matters.

Literature about Hardy and his fiction, immensely diverse and vast in extent, can be surveyed and traversed with some ease by student and specialist alike. *Bibliographies of Twelve*

Victorian Authors (1936) by T. G. Ehrsam, R. H. Deily, and R. M. Smith offers a preliminary census, but the most comprehensive assemblage is contained in Carl J. Weber's *The First Hundred Years of Thomas Hardy: 1840–1940* (1942), which tries to tabulate "everything that had ever been written about Hardy anywhere during his first hundred years" or during the centenary itself. If such a purpose confuses the proper distinction between the rare and the routine or even trivial, this mass of material — over 3000 entries — nevertheless is rich in prospects. Alphabetically listed (according to author or periodical, but not cross-indexed under titles of novels) are works devoted entirely to Hardy or his writings and others with chapters or passages (critical, commemorative, or reminiscent) as well as numerous contemporary reviews and a smattering of foreign books.

For Hardy references after 1940, in *Modern Fiction Studies,* 1960, there appears the first-rate "Criticism of Thomas Hardy: A Selected Checklist" compiled by M. Beebe, B. Culotta, and E. Marcus, who — though including the most important items from Weber's *The First Hundred Years* — have emphasized the post-1940 materials. Scarcely anything of value has been excluded from this bibliography; its organization is especially helpful. Under "Studies of Individual Works of Fiction" (the third part; the first and second cover general studies and Hardy's poetry) the entry for each work is broken down into four sections: (A) the volume in the standard Wessex edition and, in the case of a short story, also the title of the volume where it was first collected; (B) a list of the modern editions containing introductions and notes, but omitting some paperbacks and at least one annotated set;[1] (C) an index to the page numbers of relevant passages in the general studies; (D) special studies not previously cited.

---

[1] Five of the novels and some stories are provided with rudimentary, somewhat school-masterish notes in the Scholar's Library (London, 1934–1936), all recently reprinted: *Far from the Madding Crowd,* ed. with intro. C. Aldred; *The Return of the Native,* ed. C. Aldred, intro. S. Lynd; *The Trumpet-Major,* ed. Mrs. F. S. Boas; *The Mayor of Casterbridge,* ed. with intro. V. de Sola Pinto; *The Woodlanders,* ed. with intro. C. Aldred; *Stories and Poems,* ed. N. V. Meeres.

This survey should answer all but the most unusual requirements.

II. *Editions and Texts*

There is no scholarly and authoritative text other than the Wessex Edition (1912–1931), available in print today in the Library Edition and incorporating final corrections that may date even from notes left at Hardy's death. Besides the extremely valuable prefaces Hardy put much rewriting and revising into the "first uniform and complete edition" (the "Wessex Novels," 1895–1896) for Osgood, McIlvaine and Co., whose plates have since become the source for many editions now generally read. But in 1912, ten years after he had transferred all his publishing agreements to Macmillan and Co., Hardy undertook still further, if less extensive, revisions for Macmillan's Wessex Edition. Its first twenty-one volumes were later issued by Harper and Brothers in editions called "Autograph" (1915) and "Anniversary" (1920), but seldom has its text been the standard for editions more readily available in the United States.[2] Though most of the discrepancies are not serious, commentaries based on anything but the Wessex text can meet error unwittingly — like the change of "milchers" (cows) to "milkers," which caused one critic to see Tess Durbeyfield, seated in the Talbothays barnyard, "exhibiting herself at the present moment to the eye in the rear as a circle on two stalks, down the center of which a switch moved pendulum-wise": hardly chivalrous or, in Wessex, correct.[3]

None of the collected editions of Hardy's prose can lay claim to completeness. Some pieces of fiction must be sought separately. *An Indiscretion in the Life of an Heiress,* the later version (1878) of his earliest and now lost novel, *The Poor Man and the Lady* (1868), has been privately printed (1934)

[2] See Purdy, *A Bibliographical Study,* pp. 281–282, 285–286. Some of the piracies and errors in American editions are presented by C. J. Weber in "Thomas Hardy in America" (*Colophon,* 1938) and in "The Tragedy at Little Hintock" (*Booker Memorial Studies,* ed. Hill Shine, 1950).

[3] See H. M. Reichard, *Explicator* (1956).

and also edited (by C. J. Weber, 1935). *Our Exploits at West Poley*, his boys' story completed in 1883 and forgotten after publication (1892–1893), was reissued with an introduction by R. L. Purdy (1952). And then there are the pieces of Hardy's nonfictional prose, the occasional writings gathered (without Hardy's consent) by Ernest Brennecke in *Life and Art* (1925). These essays — among them "The Dorsetshire Labourer," "The Profitable Reading of Fiction," "Candour in English Fiction," "The Science of Fiction," and "Memories of Church Restoration" — have yet to be read fully in conjunction with related concerns and mannerisms in the novels. *Thomas Hardy's Notebooks* (1955), through the editing of Evelyn Hardy (not a relative), have been inaccurately transcribed and foolishly annotated. There are additions and omissions which are not presented as such; the text cannot be trusted. *"The First Notebook* (1867–1920) together with some excerpts from *'The Trumpet Major' Notebook* [*sic*] (1878–1880)" is a compilation from older notebooks now destroyed. *"The Second Notebook* (1921–1928)" was used in assembling *Later Years*. These two contain the same assorted jottings and recollections to be found in *Early Life* and *Later Years*.

Textual studies represent one of the relatively untouched and most promising fields of research in Hardy. Although, or perhaps because, Hardy regarded his novels as mere "trade" and "journeywork," wishing to become only a "good hand at a serial," he complied briskly with both the advice and demands of editors [4] and assiduously rectified the misprints and mistakes cited by reviewers. At each step of the way from manuscript to serial, then on to published book, first "uniform" edition, and standard Wessex edition Hardy made many and varied changes in the text, often affecting considerably the tone and direction of his narrative. Some of

---

[4] See J. W. Beach, "Bowdlerized Versions of Hardy" (*PMLA*, 1921) and for chapters in Hardy's publishing ventures: J. Henry Harper, *I Remember* (1934) and *The House of Harper* (1912); Charles Morgan, *The House of Macmillan* (1943); C. J. Weber, *The Rise and Fall of James Ripley Osgood* (1959); Leonard Huxley, *The House of Smith Elder* (1923); and William Tinsley, *Random Recollections of an Old Publisher* (1900).

these are explored in Mary Ellen Chase's *Thomas Hardy from Serial to Novel* (1927), which summarizes the "results of a complete and minute comparison" between the English serial versions and the American Harper's editions of *The Mayor of Casterbridge, Tess of the d'Urbervilles,* and *Jude the Obscure.* It points to alterations in incident, characterization, setting and, to a lesser degree, in phrasing and diction; it does not, however, go back to manuscript sources.

This early study indicates what could be done with the textual history of all Hardy novels; one of them has now been examined extensively. Otis B. Wheeler, having collated the seven printed texts, concludes in "Four Versions of *The Return of the Native*" (*NCF,* 1959) that the "whole problem of Hardy's early critical reception" needs to be reconsidered, since the "versions of the novels by which he attained his reputation may be materially different from those we know." In *The Making of "The Return of the Native"* (1960), a model of precision and discernment, John Paterson has followed the how and why of each phase of textual development from the "equivalent of a rough draft" to the Wessex Edition — including a hypothetical "Ur-novel" embedded in the original manuscript. Hardy's reshaping of the main outlines of plot (the mother-son motif), setting (the widening of pastoral Wessex), and character (Eustacia altered from Egdon witch to a Byronic Promethean, Diggory Venn promoted socially and made "Mephistophelian" before being domesticated, Damon Wildeve reduced from adult philanderer to youthful victim of quixotic passions, and Clym never fully resolved) proves that the finished novel is "quite as much the product of revision as the product of vision."

In the absence of preliminary sketches or an elaborate quarry for any of Hardy's novels we cannot watch him at work as we can, for instance, Dickens or George Eliot. But the processes traced by Paterson do compel us to discard, finally, the common belief that Hardy usually worked from some mechanical blueprint, some "calculatedly rehearsed" symmetrical arrangement.[5] All Hardy's revisions in *The Re-*

[5] Evelyn Hardy's "Thomas Hardy: Plots for Five Unpublished Short

turn of the Native show rather that he felt his way imaginatively into the quadrilateral ironies of plot and became increasingly concerned with the poetics of language: his diction blending the Latinate and Anglo-Saxon (with effects
both gawky and sublime) and his sense of metaphor making
objects into "something less than symbol" but also "something more than sign." Any future revaluation of Hardy as
novelist must depend on a textual scholarship which at its
best supplies the deftest sort of critical reading.

Only a few of the texts of Hardy's later novels have been
analyzed in the main phases of their development. W. G.
Bebbington's *The Original Manuscript of Thomas Hardy's
"The Trumpet-Major"* (1948) seldom goes beyond description, and C. J. Weber's "The Manuscript of Hardy's *Two
on a Tower"* (*PBSA*, 1946) reproduces only four facsimile
pages. One solution to the whole muddled problem of borrowings and self-plagiarism is implicit in R. L. Purdy's
letter (Nov. 20, 1943) to the *TLS*. Some differences between
the English and American editions of *The Woodlanders* are
cited in C. J. Weber's "The Tragedy in Little Hintock"
(*Booker Memorial Studies,* ed. H. Shine, 1950). Hardy's
sensitivity to the "textual quibbles" of reviewers is shown by
Robert Hurley's "A Note on Some Emendations in *Jude
the Obscure"* (*VNL*, 1959). The public outcry against its
immorality, W. J. Hyde says in "Hardy's Response to the
Critics of *Jude"* (*VNL*, 1961), may not have been all that
shrill. Changes in the printed versions are discussed by Robert
C. Slack (whose variorum edition, an unpublished dissertation, is in the University of Pittsburgh Library) in "The Text
of Hardy's *Jude the Obscure"* (*NCF*, 1957). The original
manuscript discloses, according to J. Paterson's "The Genesis
of *Jude the Obscure"* (*SP*, 1960), that Sue Bridehead and her
precocious brilliance, not Phillotson, first attracted Jude to

---

Stories" in the *London Magazine* (1958) contains five skeletal outlines which,
she says, illustrate Hardy's typical method of "delineating the bare bones of
facts and characters first, later covering them with emotion, imagery, incident,
colour." It is equally possible that some of these notes were primarily for
poems.

Christminster. What had "its genesis in a short story conception involving the failure of a young man of the lower classes to satisfy his academic ambitions" became eventually an "attack on the stringency of the marriage laws and on the narrow Christianity responsible for their stringency."

III. *Biography*

Most needed, but not foreseeable in the immediate future, is a fuller biography of Hardy not subject to the limitations of *The Early Life, 1840–1891* (1928) and *The Later Years, 1892–1928* (1930). Though these were ostensibly written by his widow, Florence Emily Hardy (the subtitle has them "Compiled largely from contemporary notes, letters, diaries, and biographical memoranda, as well as from oral information in conversations extending over many years"), all but the last four chapters of the second volume were composed by Hardy from materials then destroyed.[6]

This autobiography is interspersed with social jottings and extracts from random books or newspapers, circumspect remarks about friends or notable contemporaries, much evidence about his main interests (music, painting, architecture, local Dorset customs, the funereal and the psychic), and every so often some fragmentary, vivid perception to remind us that things sensuously experienced precede and prompt Hardy's "ideas." The final effect is curious, at once more detached and impersonal than one would expect of autobiography, and yet strangely revealing for so reticent an author. This blend could well be compared to Hardy's special way with narrative fiction: its surface is thickly set with matter-of-fact and commonplace detail, but moving above and recording its depths are sudden glimpses of an extraordinarily active inner life of mind. Such moments, preserved in portions of diaries and notebooks available only in the autobiography, bring us closer to the man than could chronicle or social agenda; they indicate the substance from which the sensibilities of the

[6] Little remains among the Max Gate papers which Hardy himself did not wish to survive. Purdy, *A Bibliographical Study*, pp. 263–273.

novels were to take form and provide approaches not yet explored. Among these observations are comments on fiction which, according to so formidable a critic as Q. D. Leavis in "Hardy and Criticism" (*Scrutiny*, 1943), show that he "had a remarkably acute grasp of literary theory and a most intelligent response to its practice."

Whatever their oblique or direct value, *Early Life* and *Later Years* are silent on many important matters. We are not told much about Hardy's relationships with his parents, brother, and sisters, or about the difficulties of his education and professional training, or anything, really, about those months in Weymouth or the vital early years in London. How was he changing all this while? Did he gain anything, for example, from Dickens' public readings at the Hanover Square Rooms in the early sixties? What was the influence on him of Leslie Stephen, or Morley's advice to read George Sand? Whom did he know then? Why was the engagement to his cousin, revealed in Lois Deacon's *Tryphena and Thomas Hardy* (1962), suddenly broken in 1872 or shortly afterwards? No signs of this romance are included, nor is there any visible mark left by the deepening sorrow of his first marriage. Emma Lavinia's recollections in *Early Life* (reprinted *in toto* as *Some Recollections,* ed. E. Hardy and R. Gittings, 1961) show one kind of incompatibility, as do her *Alleys* (1911) and *Spaces* (1912), poetic and prose meditations of a mystical cast. Yet despite many gaps and unevennesses *Early Life* and *Later Years* are indispensable.

The prose of these two volumes has good cause for being guarded and reluctant. Hardy never wanted a biography; his hand was forced by F. A. Hedgcock's *Thomas Hardy: penseur et artiste* (1911) and E. Brennecke's *The Life of Thomas Hardy* (1925), both of which annoyed him by their intrusiveness and inaccuracy. Hedgcock managed to slight Hardy's family background, and except for scraps of reputed conversations Brennecke supplied little data and too many pointed queries. William Rutland in *Thomas Hardy* (Order of Merit series, 1938) succeeds in his aim of relating the "essential facts . . . more succinctly than has yet been done" and rightly brings Horace Moule and William Barnes to the fore. C. J. Weber's very readable *Hardy of Wessex* (1940) leans unsteadily on the fiction for biographical evidence. His appendixes listing Hardy's literary allusions are useful, particularly those to Shakespeare and Browning, but few are located by novel and chapter. Edmund Blunden in his *Thomas Hardy* (1942), drawing on personal acquaintance, indicates the position of Hardy's family in the Dorset village community. He includes many pertinent and relatively inaccessible contemporary reviews and comments. Though she is the only biographer to use any unpublished letters or manuscript sources, Evelyn Hardy in *Thomas Hardy: A Critical Biography* (1954) does not display a discriminating judgment or command of factual detail. She does have, however, a happy facility for tracing strands of imagery back and forth between the novels and poetry; these ought to be drawn toward some central significance.

Outside these biographies, and extending in every conceivable direction, lies an abundance of Hardiana: recollections of the man and brief evaluations of his work, numerous walks, talks, and bicycle rides at Max Gate, visits and endless interviews, all the mass of remembrance that gathers around a reputation. Anecdotes and oddities still are being recorded — from the gardener and the parlormaid at Max Gate and even from Hardy's barber (B. N. Stephens' *Thomas Hardy in His Garden*, E. E. T[itterington's] *The Domestic Life of Thomas Hardy, 1921–1928,* and W. G. Mills's *Thomas Hardy at the Barber's,* all 1963), with other monographs forthcoming. Most of the important items are listed in the bibliographies of secondary materials or in the latest periodical indexes; they vary in worth from the suspect, like Cyril Clemens' *My Chat with Thomas Hardy, 1925* (1944), to the reliable and revealing, for example, William Archer's *Real Conversations, 1901* (1904) and V. H. Collins' *Talks with Thomas Hardy at Max Gate, 1920–22* (1928). The reactions of American literati and common readers [7] are put forward, among

[7] One of Hardy's uncommon readers, Rebekah Owen, who became a persistent pilgrim and eventually a painful nuisance at Max Gate, clarifies a

other things, in C. J. Weber's *Hardy in America* (1946), which proposes to examine en route "his qualifications as guide or adviser, as we consult about the future."

Hardy's use of the landscape and folklore of southwestern England has been attentively surveyed. Among the countless topographical handbooks, many with a robust charm sounding the call to rucksack and hiking staff, only *Thomas Hardy's Wessex* (1913) by Hermann Lea (who also took photographs for the Wessex Edition) can be regarded as authoritative. It is clear from Lea's papers that Hardy quietly supervised — even to the details of phrasing — the descriptions and identifications of particular locales, landmarks, and buildings. F. O. Saxelby's *A Thomas Hardy Dictionary* (1911), in addition to specifying scenes, provides summaries of plot and character. The superstitions and customs of the Wessex country are fascinatingly reconnoitred by Ruth A. Firor in *Folkways in Thomas Hardy* (1931).

Other kinds of Hardiana offer diverse vantage points. Eva M. Grew audits his songs and melodic imagery in "Thomas Hardy as Musician" in *Music and Letters* (1940), which also contains Elna Sherman's discussion of three manuscript music notebooks belonging to the Hardy family ("Thomas Hardy: Lyricist, Symphonist"). Sherman's "Music in Thomas Hardy's Life and Work" in the *Musical Quarterly* (1940) looks more closely into the influence of Hardy's musical heritage on the novels. A partial checklist of music written about his settings and Wessex moods is to be had in C. J. Weber's *Hardy Music at Colby* (1945). The style of Hardy's drawings, whether informal sketch or architectural design, offers a subtle angle for seeing how persons and places are perceived in his fictional world.[8] Günther Wilmsen in *Thomas Hardy als impressionistischer Landschaftsmaler*

---

minor point or two in the novels: see C. J. Weber's *Hardy and the Lady from Madison Square* (1952).

[8] See Purdy, *A Bibliographical Study*, pp. 25–26; Hardy's illustrations for *Wessex Poems* (1898) and *The Queen of Cornwall* (1923); and the children's sketches reproduced in *TLS* (July 19, 1957). "Twenty Architectural Drawings" are described as Lot 70 in Sotheby's auction catalogue for May 29, 1961.

(Düsseldorf, 1934) links Hardy's viewpoint with theories of the Impressionists and connects visual features of his *Wessex Poems* illustrations (silhouettes, the lone figure, bursts of light) with similar effects in the novels. Hardy's two professions are joined in Josef Hartmann's *Architektur in den Romanen Thomas Hardy's* (Münster, 1934) and in sections of W. H. Smith's *Architecture in English Fiction* (1934).

Hardy's correspondence is so widely dispersed among private and public collections that the research and census alone would be an enormous undertaking, and furthermore it is doubtful whether a complete edition, even if feasible, would be very valuable. Hardy was not one to bare his soul in the public post or leave himself open to the quizzing of posterity. Most of his personal papers were long ago destroyed; few letters remain to his family, certainly nothing very intimate, and they are frequently of slight worth. Any edition of correspondence would have to be rigorously selective and edited in a fullness of knowledge which may not exist now.

Such a selection might be built up from the main blocks of surviving correspondence (such as Hardy to Sir Sydney Cockerell, Sir George Douglas, Sir Edmund Gosse, Lady Grove, and Mrs. Henniker) and from the segments diversely available in major university and municipal libraries. C. J. Weber's *The Letters of Thomas Hardy* (1954), a miscellany of items drawn from the Colby College Library, makes good browsing but contains little that is really useful.[9] Somewhat more important, especially for the fading of Hardy's first marriage and the extent of his London socializing, is Weber's *'Dearest Emmie': Thomas Hardy's Letters to His First Wife* (1963), which covers the period from 1885 to 1911. Further Hardy letters may be traced in the reminiscences or "Life and Letters" of his contemporaries.[10] Others

[9] Some measure of Colby's voluminous Hardiana, much of it significant only for special purposes, can be had by consulting Weber's *The First Hundred Years* and the index to the *Colby Library Quarterly* and the now defunct *Colby Mercury*.

[10] Among those with letters from Hardy (and some to him) are C. Archer's *William Archer* (1931); *Friends of a Lifetime: Letters to Sydney*

unpublished are listed or described in notes about recent acquisitions, the catalogues of exhibitions and personal collections, or the sales catalogues of auction firms.[11] What we can infer from Hardy's correspondence might better contribute to a good biography.

IV. General Criticism

Critical writing about Hardy's prose fiction has been changing gradually in emphasis and evaluation since his death in 1928. One recent study, Albert Guerard's *Thomas Hardy: the Novels and Stories* (1949), opens by distinguishing acutely between the "post-Victorian" generation of critics and the moderns, a difference more of attitude than of age. What the earlier generation approved or praised in the Hardy novels (a fascination with the picturesque details of architecture, field, and farm; an obvious craft in symmetrical plots and characters in counterpoint; and the author's tender sympathy for the afflicted and unhappy) now can evoke, says

---

Carlyle Cockerell, ed. Viola Meynell (1940); H. V. Marrot's *The Life and Letters of John Galsworthy* (1935); S. F. Damon's *Amy Lowell* (1935); Lilla McCarthy's *Myself and My Friends* (1933); C. Morgan's *The House of Macmillan* (1943); Alfred Noyes's *Two Worlds for Memory* (1953); and *The Swinburne Letters,* mainly vols. 5 and 6, 1883–1909 (1961), ed. Cecil Y. Lang. Some letters to Hardy of biographical interest are in *The Letters of J. M. Barrie* (1942), ed. Viola Meynell; Evan Charteris' *The Life and Letters of Sir Edmund Gosse* (1931); the letters of Julia Augusta Martin included in *Thomas Hardy's Notebooks* (1955), ed. E. Hardy; *The Letters of George Meredith* (2 vols., 1912); and F. W. Maitland's *The Life and Letters of Sir Leslie Stephen* (1906).

[11] See, for instance, R. L. Purdy's *Thomas Hardy, O.M. (1840–1928): Catalogue of a Memorial Exhibition* (1928) at Yale; Carroll A. Wilson's *A Descriptive Catalogue of the Grolier Club Centenary Exhibition* (1940); Wilson's *Thirteen Author Collections of the Nineteenth Century* (2 vols., 1950), ed. J. C. S. Wilson and D. A. Randall; and the recent acquisitions described in Ann Bowden's "The Thomas Hardy Collection," *The Library Chronicle* (University of Texas, 1962). Also the auction catalogues of the Hardy collections of G. B. McCutcheon (American Art Association, Inc., 1925), Jerome Kern (The Anderson Galleries, 1929), Paul Lemperly and A. Edward Newton (Parke-Bernet, 1940 and 1941), and Clement Shorter, Sir Edmund Gosse, and Sir Sydney Cockerell (Sotheby, 1928, 1928, and 1956 respectively). Portions of the Bliss collection have appeared at various auctions, mainly Sotheby's.

Guerard, only an indifferent or even soporific nod. Conversely, what these same elders overlooked or chided (Hardy's "foreshortening" of reality through the macabre and melodramatic, his stress on psychological perversities and irresistible passion) now deserves to be considered anew. Hardy, like so many Victorians, today is being regarded as a forerunner of modern literary techniques; he is numbered among the victims of our contemporary malaise. Nonetheless, little has been done to re-examine the elements of worth in earlier treatments of his novels and to relate, if not reconcile, the differing critical estimates by these two generations.

The three earliest full-length studies, informal and appreciative in the best sense of both words, look toward what has become a main area of interest in Hardy's work: his awareness of a living past, and his conception of human nature and the natural forces that quicken the province and inhabitants of Wessex. Annie Macdonnell's *Thomas Hardy* (1894) has some sensible and still relevant comments, particularly those on the novelist's "pessimistic" outlook in Chapter X. Lionel Johnson's *The Art of Thomas Hardy* (1894), which first cited certain features now widely recognized in the novels (Hardy's concern for the entrance of urban discord into rural order, his interruption of a tale with declamatory reasonings, the simple central design of his plots, and the kinship of his Wessex folk with Shakespearean rustics and the Greek chorus), discusses various characters according to common emotional traits; Johnson begins to group them within the now familiar clans and families. More important historically, Johnson uses Hardy's work to weigh the aesthetic trends of the "decadent" nineties and finds them wanting: "It is a sick and haggard literature, this literature of throbbing nerves . . . simplicity is exchanged for fantastic ingenuities. Emotions become entangled with the consciousness of them: and after-thoughts or impressions, laboured analysis or facile presentation, usurp the place of . . . older workmanship." That Hardy can depict "souls of a somewhat pagan severity, grand in the endurance of dooms" and yet suggest the modern "complexity of things, the clash of principles and of motives, the encounter of sub-tile emotions" serves to explain the power of his art: he has preserved the "massive" and "ardent austerities" of Words-worth. Johnson's study, appearing in the year before his own *Poems* (1895), also has a biographical value as the first major prose work of a minor poet. His censure of Hardy's indictment of divine providence, along with such references as the "grim genius of Puritanism," proceed from his con-version to Catholicism during the previous year. Even so, the poet of "The Dark Angel" and "The Dream of an Age" found in Hardy a "reasonable sadness."

Lascelles Abercrombie's *Thomas Hardy: a Critical Study* (1912) proffers much the same blend of biographical and historical interest and graceful remarks on particulars; pub-lished just before the poetry of his *Speculative Dialogues* (1913), it went so far as to defend prose fiction as an art capable of serious metaphysical statement. Abercrombie's account of Hardy's "tragic apprehension of the world," while sketchy, is sensitive. This tragedy he sees as a condi-tion of all activity, beginning not "in the persons who are most concerned in it" but rather as "an invasion into human consciousness of the general tragedy of existence, which thereby puts itself forth in living symbols." With varying success he follows Hardy's growth from *Far from the Mad-ding Crowd* through *Jude the Obscure* by noting a regular alternation from large to slight designs (minor novels as "annexes" to the central edifice) and by observing Hardy's change from "dramatic form," characterized by some system of relationships among a group of characters, to "epic form," the chronicled history of a single individual — Henchard, Tess, and Jude.

Abercrombie's "critical algebra" for the most frequent quartet of Hardy character types (masculine and feminine simplicity, masculine and feminine complexity) was extended to geometric graphs of the narrative action by H. C. Duffin in *Thomas Hardy* (1916; rev. ed., 1937) and then to charts of romantic rivalries in J. W. Beach's *The Techniques of Thomas Hardy* (1922), which though too elementary in its handling of abstract terms and the idea of technique is good on larger issues within certain novels. Antitheses and proto-types in Hardy's novels have been recorded in many German dissertations; the two most readable are Amélie von Behr's *Der Typen-Konflikt in Thomas Hardys Romanen* (Marburg, 1936) and Alice Reinhard-Stocker's *Charakterdarstellung und Schicksalsgestaltung in den Romanen Thomas Hardys* (Winterthur, 1958). Arthur Symons in *A Study of Thomas Hardy* (1927) goes behind all these shifting patterns of emo-tional affinity to find Hardy "concerned with one thing, seen under two aspects: not civilization, not manners, but the prin-ciple of life itself, invisibly realized as Sex, seen visibly in the world as what we call Nature." As might be expected from the laureate historian of the Symbolist poets, Symons writes well about Hardy's immense capacity for visualization. None of these early essays in criticism, however, consistently pro-vides any close reading of the novels.

The more valuable recent critiques have concentrated less on a philosophy allegedly imported into Wessex than on Hardy's fictional devices, the deeper psychology of his characters, and the varied kinds of relationships (social, eco-nomic, moral, and imaginative) between life in Wessex and actual conditions in the southwestern counties centering on nineteenth-century Dorset. Personal appreciations in Edmund Blunden's biography (1942) hark back to an earlier day. Lord David Cecil's *Thomas Hardy: An Essay in Criticism* (1943) has an ease which hides his real grasp of Hardy's habits of storytelling. Frank Chapman in "Hardy the Novelist" (*Scrutiny*, 1934) refurbishes many of the standard judgments. Other directions, however, had already been anticipated in the issue of *La Revue nouvelle* which commemorated the novelist's death ("Hommage à Thomas Hardy," 1928, with short contributions by Proust and Joyce). Charles du Bos in "Quelques traits du visage de Hardy" skillfully shows how the visible and invisible in his land were envisaged, and Ramon Fernandez' "Le Romancier" emphasizes Hardy's oblique realism (contrasted with French naturalism) in his presentation of space and time, especially the use of highly charged sense impressions to form an interior landscape and a "psychologie de position." The two main observances of Hardy's centenary are quite dissimilar. *John O'London's Weekly,* June 7, 1940, except for Sir Arthur Quiller-Couch on "The Dynasts" and H. M. Tomlinson on the novels, is occupied casually with biographical matters, whereas the critical analyses in the *Southern Review,* 1940, especially those by Auden, Barzun, Leavis, Tate, and Zabel, assume the value of bringing Hardy's poems to bear on his fiction; this can be done despite the difficulties cited by R. W. King in "Verse and Prose Parallels in the Work of Thomas Hardy" (*RES,* 1962). More than most poet-novelists, Hardy was all of a piece, and studies of his poetry which offer access to the novels, such as Samuel Hynes's *The Pattern of Hardy's Poetry* (1961), must therefore be included in any guide to research. J. I. M. Stewart's chapter on Hardy in *Eight Modern Writers* (1963), though separating the novels from the poetry, has some incisive comments on the direction of Hardy's development and on the unexpected turns which *Tess* and *Jude* give to the interplay of human responsibility and cosmic determinism.

Most prominent in scope and promise is Guerard's *Thomas Hardy* (1949), the first of a critical trilogy to deal with Hardy, Conrad, and Gide and to follow the move in modern fiction "away from orthodox realism, classical psychology, and conventional structure." Vigorously and with considerable acumen Guerard sets out to correct, by touching on the minor works and stories as well, the notion that Hardy "wrote depressing but profound and technically admirable realistic novels." His indifference to the major concerns of form, says Guerard (himself a practicing novelist), represents an inability to control certain impulses, often diverging: a penchant for the homely and the occult, a great yearning to realize the spiritual rather than the scientific view of life, and mixed feelings toward both the fickle and rebellious, the constant and self-denying. Unfortunately, in his fiction the "indifferently rational realist, who loved to classify and demonstrate, always threatened to suppress the dramatic, haunted, or nostalgic poet." From this treatment Hardy emerges as a wayward anti-realist in technique and outlook. But throughout it all Guerard remains curiously trapped by a method his task need not have imposed; while seeking to re-dress a balance between the features in Hardy's work over-praised by post-Victorians and the lapses discovered by exact-ing modern exegesis Guerard limits himself too much to con-trast and opposition and to what this mode of discussion can fix upon and evaluate. What remains to be done, clearly, is to examine more within its own fictional world, on its own terms and in its whole integrity, the mind that could express these traits instinctively and simultaneously.

Guerard's account of the central situation in the typical Hardy novel, some disruption of rural stabilities by urban and often strangely infernal outsiders, further refines the categories in J. O. Bailey's survey of Satanism as a structural device: "Hardy's 'Mephistophelian Visitants'" (*PMLA*, 1946). Bailey later in "Hardy's Visions of the Self" (*SP*, 1959) counts the apparitions that confront characters with their own irresponsibility and delusions. These issues and others Guerard carries resolutely into the hazardous psychoanalytic terrain seen from a distance by F. A. Hedgcock in *Thomas Hardy: penseur et artiste* (1911), P. d'Exideuil in *Le Couple humain dans l'oeuvre de Thomas Hardy* (1928; trans. with intro. by Havelock Ellis, 1930), and L. de Ridder-Barzin in *Le Pessimisme de Thomas Hardy* (1932). Hardy's interest was in psychic oddities not real neuroses and yet, Guerard maintains, all of his males except Henchard and Jude fail as characters through an "almost pathological unaggressive-ness" and "sexlessness," caught in roles of peeping and over-hearing that have "no little in common with the neurotic voyeur." There is more to be said on this matter. Guerard is not so extreme in reviewing Hardy's dramatization of the female temperament, which he sees developing from the oversimplified (women as "personalities": their evasive, vain gestures and respect only for immediate energy) to the in-creasingly complex (women as "characters": their motives and wider responses). His charted genealogy of Hardy's heroines indicates how each becomes heiress and ancestor within an ever more diverse clan; his portraits of Henchard and Jude open many new questions.

The question of Wessex has never been closed. What is Hardy's relationship to other Victorian connoisseurs of remnants and vestiges? To what extent does Hardy re-create the way of life, social and agricultural, that really existed in the southwestern counties during the time when the novels purport to occur or when they were written? Do all the indirect references to forced seasonal migrations and to foreclosed cottage lifeholds record the uprooting of a yeoman class between, say, 1830 and 1900? Or is Hardy's anxiety for the peasants only aesthetic, his interest only in the disappearance of picturesque traditions from villages which are becoming, in truth, ever more prosperous? Guerard asserts that the loss of old customs and the gnarled eccentricities useful for local color "was more significant to Hardy the novelist than the amelioration of the laborer's lot," and he refers to Hardy's "The Dorsetshire Labourer" in *Longman's Magazine* (1883). But an impressive amount of historical evidence — House of Commons papers, reports of agricultural commissioners, and travel journals — has been assembled by W. J. Hyde in "Hardy's View of Realism: A Key to the Rustic Characters" (*VS*, 1958) to show that deteriorating conditions in Wessex reflect accurately, if obliquely, the actual economic distresses of rural England. Hyde attributes the special authenticity of these rustics to certain notions of realism implicit in the notes of *Early Life* and *Later Years* and in three articles by Hardy: "The Profitable Reading of Fiction" (1888) in *The Forum*, and "Candour in English Fiction" (1890) and "The Science of Fiction" (1891) in *The New Review*. The scars left by city life have been magnified by G. W. Sherman in "The Influence of London on *The Dynasts*" (*PMLA*, 1948) and "The Wheel and the Beast: The Influence of London on Thomas Hardy" (*NCF*, 1949).

The historical context of this agricultural tragedy (debates on the Corn Laws and Free Trade, depression and crop failure in the seventies, prices lowered by competition from

American prairie harvests, and the need for cheap food in industrial centers) has been presented, and the novels sensitively read, in Douglas Brown's *Thomas Hardy* (1954). Brown asserts that "each of the great Wessex novels treats in imaginative form of the defeat of our peasantry and the collapse of our agriculture." This claim, along with the attempt to prove that Hardy's intimate knowledge of country ballads and folklore can account for his most characteristic methods, puts primary importance where only emphasis belongs; the same flaw appears in Donald Davidson's otherwise admirable article "The Traditional Basis of Thomas Hardy's Fiction" (*Southern Review*, 1940). The declining vitality of the rural order was used by John Holloway in "Hardy's Major Fiction" (*From Jane Austen to Joseph Conrad*, ed. R. C. Rathburn and M. Steinmann, 1958) to explain Hardy's abandonment of novel writing after 1895. Wessex and its natives, he felt, lacked the "inner resources" needed to survive in fact or to inspire new fiction.

"Nature" in Wessex, evoked wonderfully by John Livingston Lowes's "Two Readings of Earth" in *Essays in Appreciation* (1936), receives its classic treatment in Holloway's *The Victorian Sage* (1953), which numbers Hardy among the writers (such as Carlyle, Newman, George Eliot, and Arnold) who compel assent by their mastery of the nonlogical resources of language: the right word instead of the right argument. Wessex is more than a static and decorative backcloth; it is conceived as an "organic living whole," vast and exceedingly complex, which works through subtly unified natural processes to encompass and diminish humankind. Everywhere nature is seen in "what it *does*," and society is its microcosm. Those who refuse to live in accord with the land and its seasons, who become deracinated or fall prey to some "self-generated dream," will perish; such is natural law.

D. H. Lawrence in his "Study of Thomas Hardy" (published in the posthumous papers, *Phoenix*, 1936) meditates to the contrary: "Upon the vast, incomprehensible pattern of some primal morality greater than ever the human mind can grasp, is drawn the little pathetic pattern of man's moral life and struggle . . . The little fold of law and order, the little walled city within which man has to defend himself from the waste enormity of nature, becomes always too small, and the pioneers venturing out with the code of the walled city upon them, die in the bonds of that code, free and yet unfree, preaching the walled city and looking into the waste." The nature of Wessex, for Lawrence, becomes the rhythmic life surge which mocks rather than determines our social conventions. His essay is a long, fitfully brilliant rumination on Hardy's themes and the groupings of his characters.

Despite every sort and size of denial by Hardy much stress has been placed on the "thought" of his works, their metaphysical implications and weight, frequently as if they contained a detachable and paraphrasable philosophy of life. Helen Garwood in *Thomas Hardy: An Illustration of the Philosophy of Schopenhauer* (1911), though disclaiming direct indebtedness, finds a "noteworthy and observable sympathy" in the purposelessness and irrational disharmony which both men sense in the universe. Ernest Brennecke in *Thomas Hardy's Universe: A Study of a Poet's Mind* (1924) also refers to Schopenhauer when discovering in the novels certain foreshadowings of the "Immanent Will" of *The Dynasts*; he anticipates as well many of the speculations later weighed by J. O. Bailey in *Thomas Hardy and the Cosmic Mind* (1956). Harvey C. Webster's *On a Darkling Plain: the Art and Thought of Thomas Hardy* (1947) begins with a fine discussion of the intellectual conflicts in the fifties and sixties and the "pessimistic" literature of the seventies which may have affected the young Hardy, but he tries similarly to trace the growth of Hardy's "melancholy" philosophy and measure the impress of thought on art, of an abstracted content on form, without showing also the varied ways in which his technique itself contributes to the fictional meaning. The impact of Darwinism on Hardy can be assessed in such studies as Douglas Bush's *Science and English Poetry* (1950), Leo Henkin's *Darwinism in the English Novel* (1940), Lionel Stevenson's *Darwin among the Poets* (1932), and Georg

Roppen's *Evolution and Poetic Belief* (1956). Any attempt, however, to state with assurance and accuracy the influence of Kant, Schopenhauer, and von Hartmann (or Comte or Bergson) on Hardy meets one obstacle: the biographical evidence is not adequate for precise and final judgment — even of the kind made by C. J. Weber in "Hardy's Copy of Schopenhauer" (*Colby Library Quarterly*, 1957) about *On the Four-fold Root of the Principle of Sufficient Reason*. Efforts to label Hardy a fatalist, a determinist, or evolutionary meliorist could be redirected toward the novels themselves.

Hodgson's "Catalogue of the Library of Thomas Hardy" (1938) has all the volumes lumped together in auction lots; few are carefully identified. What can be learned of Hardy's personal library, his reading and how it may have shaped his fiction and poetry, is assembled in William R. Rutland's *Thomas Hardy: A Study of His Writings and Their Background* (1938), which describes the tenor of the books he owned and his marginalia in them. Rutland considers the use Hardy made of the Bible, the Greek and Roman classics, and the English poets (Crabbe, Wordsworth, Keats, Shelley, and Swinburne) as well as his acquaintance with the works of Darwin, Huxley, Spencer, Stephen, Mill, and many others; he connects the main issues of each novel to late Victorian life and culture. Phyllis Bartlett in "Hardy's Shelley" (*Keats-Shelley Journal*, 1955) discusses the underlinings in his earliest copy of Shelley's poetry, and her " 'Seraph of Heaven': A Shelleyan Dream in Hardy's Fiction" (*PMLA*, 1955) sets out the visionary strain more in detail. Hardy can testify still further to the affiliations between Romantic and Victorian literature.

It is clear, as Eugene Goodheart observes in "Thomas Hardy and the Lyrical Novel" (*NCF*, 1957), that "Hardy's story-telling is midway between lyric poetry, the affirmation of the individual personality" against threatening social or natural forces, and the novel in its traditional emphasis on the manners and bonds of life in society. But few distinctions have been made among the diverse and quite contradictory ways in which Hardy dramatizes the "seemings" often mistaken for his individual philosophy: the many different senses of the past in Wessex, the many different influences of Christian and pagan vestiges, and the widely varying impressions of outer and inner nature. His range of suggestion and hypothesis is greater than generally assumed; his dilemma in controlling their import must seem to our age all too familiar.

Most of the centennial critics *(Southern Review,* 1940) conceive of Hardy, like so many Victorians, as caught between a yearning for spiritual visions and the sad necessity of acknowledging the mindless, material universe of physical science, the "neutralized" nature later accepted by I. A. Richards in *Science and Poetry* (1926). As a result, according to Howard Baker in "Hardy's Poetic Certitude," Hardy was led to posit a "mechanistic determinism" or, according to Delmore Schwartz's "Poetry and Belief in Thomas Hardy," was left to construct some sort of "Dialectical tension" between the Christian idea of God and a "First or Fundamental Energy." In any case he is held by R. P. Blackmur in "The Shorter Poems of Thomas Hardy" to be the "great example of a sensibility violated by ideas," yet "locked enough in life" to survive the violation. Katherine Anne Porter, answering T. S. Eliot's *After Strange Gods* in "Notes on a Criticism of Thomas Hardy," would place his unorthodoxies in the tradition of plain-styled dissent. Jacques Barzun's "Truth and Poetry in Thomas Hardy" looks to the most likely state of "betweenness" in Hardy's fiction: he was pragmatic in his Romanticism, knowing that "Truth and Poetry do not fight a manichean fight which will leave Science or Ignorance master of the field: they merge into each other by degrees and constitute together the sum total of mind-measured reality."

Perhaps it would help if we were to suspend our diagnoses of Hardy's world view until we have considered a basic problem. To some extent, eventually, in the work of every novelist there will appear certain relationships, something in common or some sort of kinship, between the qualities of his prose writing and all the emphases in his ordering

of the narrative. What style and structure come to share,
even if they share it by chance and begrudgingly, can reveal
the source of a novelist's very being — what Hardy calls his
"idiosyncratic mode of regard." For Hardy himself these
relationships remain undefined because neither his prose
nor his plots have been examined carefully in their inter-
workings. Obviously we must avoid reducing the substance
of any novel to the sum of its stylistic and structural elements; but their qualities, when considered together, offer
us another chance to develop ways of comprehending the
"old novel" and all its rich disparities without invoking or
imitating the specialized disciplines employed in the criticism of modern fiction.

If, with T. S. Eliot, we agree that Hardy's style "touches
sublimity without ever having passed through the stage of
being good," we have yet to discover exactly how Hardy
manages to parlay ineptness into the sublime. His diction,
curiously stratified, has been inspected and discussed: stilted
elegances in the fashionable mode, fulsome elaborations of
Carlyle, Macaulay, or Burke, and bookish or technical pseudo-
terms, all mixed with archaic or Wessex dialect phrases and
the terse simplicities of the King James Bible. Besides the
observations by Frank Chapman (in *Scrutiny*, 1934), Lord
David Cecil (in *Thomas Hardy*, 1943) and Douglas Brown
("The Uniqueness of His Art" in *Thomas Hardy*, 1954)
there are valuable comments on Hardy's language in Vernon
Lee's *The Handling of Words* (1923), Virginia Woolf's "The
Novels of Thomas Hardy" in *The Common Reader* (second
series, 1932), and the articles in the *Southern Review*, 1940,
by Katharine Anne Porter and F. R. Leavis. P. Aliesch's
Studien zu Thomas Hardys Prosastil (Schiers, 1941) lists examples in the expected rhetorical categories. Hildegard Litt-
man's *Das Dichterische Bild in der Lyrik George Merediths
und Thomas Hardys in Zusammenhang mit ihrer Weltan-
schauung* (1938), shortened in another edition of the same
year to *Die Metaphor in Merediths und Thomas Hardys
Lyrik*, contains a tabulation of poetic imagery (from super-
human forces through nature to human "seemings," cold.

music, and color) which is relevant for the novels, especially the last chapter, "Der Dinge." The sudden richness of Hardy's prose in *The Return of the Native*, says S. F. Johnson in "Hardy and Burke's 'Sublime'" (*Style in Prose Fiction: English Institute Essays, 1958*, ed. H. C. Martin, 1959), can be attributed to the influence of Burke's *Enquiry into the Sublime and Beautiful.* Many of the components of Burkean sublimity (terror, obscurity, power, vastness, infirmity, pain) add to the weightinesses of Hardy's vocabulary, which are otherwise tabulated in John Paterson's *The Making of "The Return of the Native"* (1960). J. O. Bailey's "Hardy's 'Imbedded Fossil'" (*SP*, 1945) illustrates his penchant for the terminology of biology, geology, and astronomy.

Seldom, however, have critics tried to infer from this strange amalgam the traits of mind that preside over Hardy's choice of words and give form to his fictions. Two distinct idioms of prose, the poetic and the Latinized scientific, mark out what M. A. Goldberg calls "Hardy's Double-Visioned Universe" (*EC*, 1957), which arises from his simultaneous awareness of "two major Victorian concepts — the Darwinian world of mechanical science and natural law, and Arnold's world of culture and poetry." Both "concepts" guide the plotting on Egdon Heath.

Equally significant in its approach is M. D. Zabel's "Hardy in Defense of His Art: The Aesthetic of Incongruity" (*Southern Review*, 1940), which begins by specifying with superb concision the components of this "radical" art.

It derives from the conjunction, in his temperament, of conformist and eccentric tendencies; in his humanism, of stoic acquiescence and moral protest; in his understanding of human character, of a kinship with local, rudimentary, and naturally stable types ("humors" developing toward symbolism) and a sympathy with gifted, rebellious, or destructive aberrations from the human norm. In his thought it appears in his leaning toward cosmic simplifications so large and unwieldy that their grandeur becomes inflexible (and thus an impediment to critical thinking and an oppression to art) and in his humble loyalty to the claims of life in all its elusive and stubborn deviations — its vital struggles and appeals that protest and so make bearable the mindless negation of the universe. What this ambivalence of temper conferred on his style is apparent on almost every one of his pages. Their salt, tang, and sincerity is continuously accompanied by habits of rhetoric, pretentiousness, and straining grandeur — even by astonishing repetitions and labourings of effect — that exceed those in most of the greater literary masters.

Such incongruities, Zabel goes on to show, come not from bewilderment of a citified Dorset countryman or the unresolved "antipathies" of the age but rather from Hardy's endeavor to defend "casual vitality" and the instinctive against the intellect, even if it meant carelessness in his writing and rough contrivances. Other relationships of this sort could be found in all the novels, and certainly extended to include Hardy's offhand allusions to the contemporary Victorian scene: somehow they too are drawn into the erratic movement of his prose between the particular and general, the provincial and cosmic, present and past. Yet the pace and typical phases of his style are undetermined. These incongruous varieties of diction and allusiveness, often condemned, participate oddly in the central action of his narratives; they support the implications of certain attitudes in the characters and redefine their world by providing an unspoken, eccentric response to its nature.

Although no full-length study of Hardy's prose imagery has been published, the initial lines of inquiry are clear enough. In the working of Hardy's fiction "imagery" appears not only in figurative language, varying from abrupt, exaggerated similes, conceits almost, to the occasional pattern of subdued metaphor, but also in his peculiar manner of visualizing objects and persons. Richard C. Carpenter in "Hardy's 'Gurgoyles' " (*Modern Fiction Studies*, 1960) points out the grotesqueries of Hardy's Gothic fancy, "rank gardens and obscene ephemerons," and his "disproportioning" of reality by images which connote some violent or perverse yoking of man and his environs. In "Thomas Hardy and the Old Masters" (*BUSE*, 1961) Carpenter assesses the "painterly" (framing, form, scale, and light) and his typical compositions of place; fuller references to specific art works are included in Alastair Smart's "Pictorial Imagery in the Novels of Thomas Hardy" (*RES*, 1961).

The wayward suggestiveness of Hardy's language is handled adroitly by John Holloway in *The Victorian Sage* (minutiae of nature and bizarre intimations reveal the earth to be a living creature) and in his article in *From Jane Austen to Joseph Conrad* (Henchard and Tess are like animals tamed and hunted). This imagery is not in words alone; scenes in the novels can assume the shape of dramatized metaphor and present human actors according to an unfamiliar scale, the "hawk's vision" and panoramic view from a great height or the microscopic close-ups described in W. H. Auden's "A Literary Transference" and Bonamy Dobrée's "The Dynasts" (both in the *Southern Review*, 1940). Carol R. Andersen goes so far as to assert in "Time, Space, and Perspective in Thomas Hardy" (*NCF*, 1954) that "we must take all the ordinary elements of the novel (landscape, character, plot) and accept them as metaphoric equivalents of the theme"; she classifies and describes briefly some of these "equivalents" — metaphors "accumulative" and "premonitory," metaphors of "enlargement" and "diminution," and "direct symbols." But plot and character in Hardy are not simply "theme," and useful as such categories are, Hardy's imagery needs to be followed more on the move, watched as it reflects or brings an effect to bear on the course of action — watched, that is, in its essential function: showing how the individual subdues himself to some general tendency.

Elements of "counterpointing" in the structure of Hardy's fiction have been attributed to his architectural practice, to his feeling for the arc of classical Greek drama and Biblical parable, to an interest in the rhythms and refrains of ballad and folk music, and to the exigencies of serial publication and example of Wilkie Collins. His plots are conceived as symmetric designs which record the quirks of an inscrutable fatality; they consist, it is said, mainly of misunderstandings, thwarted reconciliations, and letters gone fatally astray. Beyond these devices, though, the actual workings of Hardy's narratives have been somewhat neglected, partly because he seems the provincial raconteur, partly because we still lack (except for analogies pilfered from other arts or the criticism of poetry) any set of consistent terms and techniques for discussing how the literal "plot" of a novel and its blocks of incident gradually cohere and create some larger figurative significance. Few of the Wessex novels have been scrutinized to discover the precise way in which action does proceed, its real sequence of psychological cause and effect, and the means by which social sanctions are brought to bear on choice and gesture. Nor have we discovered why Hardy's editorial comments so often simplify, misrepresent, or mythologize the more complicated human logic of motive and act in his characters. Improbable coincidences are commonly taken for diagrams of determinism or anti-realism, although they may occur strangely in response to some predisposition or to a motive revealed only by the recurrent failure of its contrary. Possibly more careful reading (proposed in at least two articles on specific novels) will show that these jagged narrative outlines follow the bias of flaws in the will and, similarly, that the qualities active overpoweringly in the minds of passive characters are involved as well in Hardy's prose. Utterances of the impersonal commentator could then be treated as Emma Clifford has treated the accents of the chorus in "The Impressionistic View of History in *The Dynasts*" (*MLQ*, 1961).

Hardy's place in the development of Victorian and modern fiction has not received an estimate directly based on a comparative study of specific scenes and relating his concerns and primary assumptions to those of other novelists. Something might be gained, for instance, by comparing certain of Hardy's methods and attitudes with Scott's mannerisms as a chronicler, George Eliot's agnosticism and compassionate defense of her characters, and the hallucinations and satire of the Dickens world. Though Hardy rejected the naturalists and their descriptive inventories ("life garniture," he said, "not life"), his own treatment of heredity, environment, and chance moves at moments in their direction —

how far is measured by W. Newton in "Chance as Employed by Hardy and the Naturalists" (*PQ*, 1951) and "Hardy and the Naturalists: Their Use of Physiology" (*MP*, 1951). Furthermore, the boundaries are unsurveyed between Wessex and the many provinces found in Romantic and Victorian literature. Hardy's tract of human nature, its contours and underpresence, stands in strange proximity to the lake country and Scots highlands, Meredith's idyllic valleys and the Brontës' moors; it is variously bordered by Barsetshire and Shropshire, Middlemarch and Loamshire, and by all the territories which extend in time and space even as far as D. H. Lawrence's midlands and the native grounds settled by American novelists. How and why, one begins to wonder, is regionalism bound up with the growth of the novel? What limits are there psychologically to the sense of place? Likewise it might be interesting to compare certain features of Hardy's writing with that of near contemporaries — Tennyson, Browning, and Arnold, even Pater and the younger Yeats.

The fortunes of Hardy abroad are recounted in the bibliographies. French critics reacted more quickly than the English to queer twists in his handling of traditional materials, but one would hope that Hardy has been read to advantage in Germany by writers other than doctoral candidates.

V. *Studies of Individual Novels and Stories*

Though most of the better commentaries on individual Hardy novels and stories are contained in longer studies or in shorter, more general essays, there are many articles of varying degrees of interest or value, or both, which are directed primarily at some one work. J. F. Danby in "Under the Greenwood Tree" (*Critical Quarterly*, 1959) finds Hardy's ultimate view of things implicit in the "narrative procedure" he adopts in this early idyl, his handling of personal experience as it passes into communal wisdom. Clarice Short's plea for the comedy in *The Hand of Ethelberta*, "In Defense of *Ethelberta*" (*NCF*, 1958), would leave most prosecutions unmoved. Leon Boucher's "Le Roman pastoral en Angleterre" (*Revue des deux mondes*, 1875), which centers on *Far from the Madding Crowd*, and Havelock Ellis' "Thomas Hardy's Novels" (*Westminster Review*, 1883), which covers everything through *Two on a Tower*, are typical of the response to Hardy's fiction before the mid-eighties.

The Return of the Native, predictably, has been much examined. Its internal time scheme, extolled for consistent accuracy by C. J. Weber's "Chronology in Hardy's Novels" (*PMLA*, 1938), has been shown defective by J. P. Emery in "Chronology in Hardy's *Return of the Native*" (*PMLA*, 1939), and by A. A. Murphee and C. F. Strauch in a similar reply (*MLN*, 1939). M. A. Goldberg, in "Hardy's Double-Visioned Universe" (*EC*, 1957), finds that its poetic and scientific diction heightens the conflict between two kinds of Beauty (the joyous ideal of Paris and Egdon's somber reality) and Time (historical-geological and the "fluid Now"), both of which define the "world external to the self and the world of aspiration within the self." R. W. Stallman maps out in "Hardy's Hour-Glass Novel" (*Sewanee Review*, 1947) a figured crisscross of concatenations in the plot without seeing anything but "deterministic machinery."

The original antagonism between Christian and Pagan elements, according to J. Paterson in *"The Return of the Native* as Antichristian Document" (*NCF*, 1959), Hardy weakened somewhat by altering the manuscript and also the serialized version before the first edition, but in it he still permitted the daemonic to appear powerfully (Eustacia the witch and "avatar of the heroic Greek sense of life") and overshadow an impotent piety (Clym the martyr and a preacher of Christian resignation). In "The 'Poetics' of *The Return of the Native*" (*Modern Fiction Studies*, 1960) Paterson cites many of the references to classical mythology that "transvaluate" the heath into a Tartarean underworld and Eustacia into the "idea" of a "generic heroine of Greek tragedy." Promethean fire imagery helps to locate a "domestic action peculiar to ballad and pastoral romance" within a "medium of analogy, a frame of reference, that creates an illusion of antique nobility and grandeur."

These pretentions to tragic stature collapse, or are deflated by Hardy himself, far more frequently than Paterson's thesis would allow him to admit: Leonard W. Deen in "Heroism and Pathos in Hardy's *Return of the Native*" (*NCF*, 1960) shows that the novel "begins heroically, but slips more and more into the diminishing ironic and pathetic mode" which prevails throughout Hardy's later prose and poetry. After the opening chapters Eustacia "does little to demonstrate or to justify the dazzling array" of exaggerated analogues for her Romantic *Weltschmertz*. Deen goes on to distinguish carefully between Eustacia's "outer" identity, mysterious when she remains off in darkness, isolated and distant, the persecuted Goddess, and her "inner" flaws revealed in ritualistic or symbolic scenes (her dream, the mummers' play, and the moonlight dancing) which enact her longing for euphoric oblivion. But if she is a victim of some less than heroic, self-destructive urge, what then of chance and fate? Implausible coincidences, Deen explains, make up the "parody of Providence" Hardy inserted to indict the universe and absolve Eustacia and Clym of the responsibility clearly asserted by the psychology of events. Much the same conclusion is reached by Charles C. Walcutt in "Character and Coincidence in *The Return of the Native*" (*Twelve Original Essays on Great English Novels*, ed. C. Shapiro, 1960), though he tends to relate mischance more to stubborn frailty and unconscious motives. John Hagan in "A Note on the Significance of Diggory Venn" (*NCF*, 1961) sees the reddleman's "unintentional devilishness" as an "emblematic expression" of the contingent. Clym, who replaces Eustacia on Rainbarrow (the future in "psychological time" rather than the past), is shown to be equally incomplete in R. C. Schweik's "Theme, Character, and Perspective in Hardy's *The Return of the Native*" (*PQ*, 1962). Despite the "appurtenances of tragedy," says S. F. Johnson in "Hardy and Burke's 'Sublime'" (*Style in Prose Fiction*, 1959), the novel becomes — as Northrop Frye's *Anatomy of Criticism* (1957) would suggest — another of Hardy's "ironic romances."

The Mayor of Casterbridge, perhaps because of a strange, ungainly appeal and its diverse elements along a single arc, continues also to attract a large number of critics, many of them with quite special cases to plead. H. O. Brogan in "'Visible Essences' in *The Mayor of Casterbridge*" (*ELH*, 1950) misuses this phrase of Hardy's (*Early Life*, p. 232) as critical longhand for symbol and argues that places, persons, and events are under the control of a didactic purpose involving fallen man, commercial rivalry, and an inexorable past. "The central *agon* of the novel, Henchard's struggle with Donald Farfrae," says D. A. Dike in "A Modern Oedipus: *The Mayor of Casterbridge*" (*EC*, 1952), "recalls the antagonism between Oedipus and Creon and also the sacred combat between the old god, priest, or father and the new, around which was constructed the primitive rite of the Seasonal King." The market place and cash nexus triumph over instinctive feeling until, finally, Newson enters as a kind of latter-day Greek messenger. Julian Moynahan introduces another analogue more moderately in "*The Mayor of Casterbridge* and the Old Testament's First Book of Samuel: A Study of Some Literary Relationships" (*PMLA*, 1956). "Through a strategy of association," he maintains, "Henchard's career is connected with the career of Saul" and Farfrae's with that of David; extensive parallels in character and incident suggest this Old Testament counterpart as a kind of "framing action" which re-enacts the recurrent strife between generations.

These two articles comparing Henchard with afflicted monarchs in Greek drama and the Bible provide a convenient cue for J. Paterson, who in "*The Mayor of Casterbridge* as Tragedy" (*VS*, 1959) contends that Hardy presents here, as he does not in *Tess* and *Jude*, a tragic narrative "in its olden, in its Sophoclean or Shakespearean, sense": traditional in assuming a universal moral order which informs man, nature, and society. Henchard's decline and fall, it is claimed, bears witness to the righteous indignation of a supernatural power outraged by the selling of his wife; the harvest storms show nature "instrumental" to this "just and morally-intelligent fate," and Casterbridge's "brutalized populace" and dark precincts register analogically the "corruption and demoralization of its chief magistrate." Such stylized pleading, of course, must ignore or rework certain facts — the lack of any moral connection between the sale of Henchard's wife and, twenty years later, the spoiled wheat, harvest storms, and Mixen Lane depravity; the defiant rancor of Henchard's last will and the superstitious fetishism, not orthodox acquiescence, of his few thoughts about the supernatural; and frequent demonstrations throughout the plot that "Character is Fate." [12]

This sort of emphasis on the "traditional," however eccentrically the novel may be reduced as a result, does remind us that its conflict, a primitive combat between two men differently flawed and ambiguously good, stands a world apart from the apparent martyrdoms in Hardy's other novels. In an otherwise favorable reply (*VS*, 1960) to Paterson's article H. C. Webster cites its rigid conception of tragedy and other small errors. No theoretical speculating, Norman Friedman observes apropos of Henchard in "Criticism and the Novel" (*Antioch Review*, 1958), can go further than the actualities of the plot will permit. Brief, but more balanced in its view of the protagonist (one of those who "anticipate the nemesis of their own failings"), is W. H. Gardner's "Some Thoughts on *The Mayor of Casterbridge*" (English Association Pamphlet, 1930). An objection to Hardy's "covering" for some of Henchard's misdeeds is entered by Derwent May in "The Novelist as Moralist and the Moralist as Critic" (*EC*, 1960). Other discrepancies between Hardy's editorial explanation and the scene itself are cited by Robert B. Heilman in his introduction (Riverside ed., 1962), which isolates also the contradictory stylistic and narrative elements in the portrayal of Henchard. Douglas Brown in *Thomas Hardy: The Mayor of Casterbridge* (1962), an excellent chapter-by-chapter analysis with much historical material, asserts that the narrative focus is on the calamities befalling the whole agricultural community rather than merely a single individual.

[12] W. E. Yuill's "Character is Fate: A Note on Thomas Hardy, George Eliot, and Novalis" (*MLR*, 1962) cites one line of indebtedness.

To show the movement in fiction from social document to psychological history, Frederick R. Karl in "*The Mayor of Casterbridge*: A New Fiction Defined" (*Modern Fiction Studies*, 1960) compares Henchard with figures from other nineteenth-century novels. There was little in Adam Bede's experience, for example, that he "could not understand, George Eliot leads us to believe, provided he was mature and intelligent enough to extend himself." This is also true of "Dickens' protagonists, Thackeray's middle-class gentlemen, Jane Austen's genteel provincials, and Meredith's romantic heroes: the world holds few secrets from those who would banish ego and vanity in favor of common sense." Michael Henchard's life of self-willed compulsion, "played out in a fabulous puppet show" of Fair Ground and Roman Amphitheater, unfolds the irrational egoism of one who insists on destroying himself in "muddle and non-comprehension."

Not guilt or compulsive egoism, argues Donald Davidson in "Futurism and Archaism in Toynbee and Hardy" (*Still Rebels, Still Yankees, and Other Essays*, 1957), brought Henchard's downfall — but his own proud anger and the rationalistic calculations of Donald Farfrae, whose paltry commercial "regime" prefigures the loss of larger traditional values. Whether the cause be Henchard's instinct for self-punishment or the fortunes of cultural combat, Richard Beckman in "A Character Typology for Hardy's Novels" (*ELH*, 1963) points out that the four main characters of the *Mayor* constitute, like the seasons of the year, a "full cycle" of temperaments — from a neutral-toned and wintry acceptance (Elizabeth-Jane), through vernal assurance (Farfrae) and summer wilfullness (Henchard), to an autumnal over-ripeness and melancholy (Lucetta). These seasonal archetypes he traces in the other novels, convincingly at times, along with the "quasi-evolutionary gradations of consciousness" from rustics to tragic protagonist. The ironic, though, is "systematically" the norm in Hardy's universe.

The Woodlanders, according to William H. Matchett in "The Woodlanders, or Realism in Sheep's Clothing" (*NCF,*

1955), shows Hardy weaving four sentimental threads into a completely unsentimental fabric, a "fierce reiteration of wounds and sorrow and disease." The fretful evasiveness of Dr. Fitzpiers and Mrs. Charmond, the two outsiders re-examined in George Fayen's "*The Woodlanders*: Inwardness and Memory" (*Studies in English Literature*, 1961), consists in their attempt to fashion for themselves an identity out of literary materials; even as "composites," though, they render far more inclusive all that nature in Little Hintock comes to signify. The woodlanders in their affinities are moved by "sights and sounds that constantly throw the mind back in upon itself." All are subjected to an "effect upon the faculties" which may account for Hardy's special version of pastoral and the reminiscing of his narrative manner. M. J. Collie in "Social Security in Literary Criticism" (*EC*, 1959) suggests that any just estimate of the gaucheries in this novel (staginess, silhouettes instead of depth in character portrayal, monologues to disclose vital information) must depend on establishing the relationship between an author's use of language and the public "state of the language." And that, he shows, will be no easy task.

The collections of short stories have been somewhat neglected. Although little per se has been written on *Wessex Tales*, Mary C. Richards in "Thomas Hardy's Ironic Vision" (*NCF*, 1949) touches on *Life's Little Ironies* as symptomatic of the contradictions Hardy explored in the novels and stories "between *seems* and *is*" and "between *is* and *ought to be*." *A Group of Noble Dames* has been shunned except for historical annotation; the links to *Tess* may merit some attention. *The Well-Beloved* provides an example of simple plot for E. K. Brown in *Rhythm in the Novel* (1950). Its "remarkable resemblance" to Proust's conception of love as a "purely subjective phenomenon and recurrent process" is set forth by L. A. Bisson's "Proust and Hardy: Incidence or Coincidence" in *Studies in French Language, Literature, and History Presented to R. L. Graeme Ritchie* (1949).

Tess of the d'Urbervilles gives rise to much thoughtful inquiry in Dorothy van Ghent's *The English Novel: Form and Function* (1953); her intricate essay and "Problems for Study and Discussion" offer the most suggestive reading of any Hardy novel. She quickly brushes aside his authorial polemics to concentrate on the internal and essential in "Hardy's vision," which is "abruptly articulated" through incidents which have an "almost ideographical simplicity": the blood of Tess's horse, Prince, splashing over her dress; the May Day "club-walking" and Tess in white left alone; and the profusely luxurious garden where Angel plays his harp. "It is Hardy's incorruptible feeling for the actual that allows his symbolism its amazingly blunt privileges and at the same time subdues it to and absorbs it into the concrete circumstance of experience, real as touch." Tess incarnates the "dilemma of morally individualizing consciousness in its earthly mixture." The earth is her antagonist, her first and "Final Cause," defying motive and intent at Talbothays and Flintcomb-Ash, its "long stretches" of distance rendering difficult her every move. Through its coarse surfaces and cruelly insistent force the terrain itself seems physically to control the nature of Hardy's prose: "not as a specifically verbal quality but as a quality of observation and intuition."

By locating the coincidences and accidents of an episodic narrative on such solid ground Hardy never lets us "forget that what is most concrete in experience is also what is most inscrutable." Mischance, furthermore, tends to be justified by Hardy's shrewd management of the Wessex peasantry, who apprehend everything magical under the sun and accept mishap as what "was to be"; even their violent gestures are instinctive, unreflecting adaptations to what in life seems "the given." This irrationale of folk magic and superstition (things coexistent in space or time interpreted as cause and effect) makes known the way of Hardy's world, full of mere correspondences rather than moral congruence, and the direction of his symbolic impulse — at best to predict or interpret, but always to imitate and mimic.

Dancing as such a mimicry and lore is followed by Langdon Elsbree in "Tess and the Local Cerelia" (*PQ*, 1961). The parallels with Milton's Eve meet in Allan Brick's "Paradise and Consciousness in Hardy's *Tess*" (*NCF*, 1962). Arnold Kettle's thesis in *An Introduction to the English Novel* (vol. II, 1953) that Hardy treats not the fate of a "pure woman" but the "destruction of the English peasantry" is convincingly revised by Ian Gregor and Brian Nicholas in their chapter ("The Novel as Moral Protest: *Tess of the d'Urbervilles*" in *The Moral and the Story*, 1962). Two dramatizations of the novel are edited and discussed by Marguerite Roberts in *"Tess" in the Theatre* (1950). George Wing's "Tess and the Romantic Milkmaid" (*Review of English Literature*, 1962) locates some of its obvious resemblances to Hardy's earlier *Romantic Adventures of a Milkmaid*.

The violent outcry caused by the publication of *Jude the Obscure* (1895) still prevails as the common judgment that it is, in too many ways, a frightful piece of work. J. H. Raleigh's "Victorian Morals and the Modern Novel" (*Partisan Review*, 1958) places Hardy's last novel in the context of censorship and relates it to certain schools of fiction. Havelock Ellis in "Concerning *Jude the Obscure*" (*Savoy*, 1896; reprinted, 1931) was among the first to defend its challenge (relatively bold at the time) to idealized Victorian marriage and to Victorian ideals of social perfectibility. But the novel's jagged symmetries, dense topicality, and bleakly sentimental protests have deterred any sustained effort at reappraisal — either in itself or in relation to the "religious" or "university" novel or to the intellectual controversies in newspapers and periodicals of the late eighties and nineties.

Hardy's handling, for fictional purposes, of literary and philosophic allusions should be examined in detail and depth. The obvious tenets of his unorthodoxy have been listed by Norman Holland, who in *"Jude the Obscure*: Hardy's Symbolic Indictment of Christianity" (*NCF*, 1954) translates the names and gestures of the characters into an allegory which depreciates the concept of Christian self-sacrifice and depicts, allegedly, the "sensual, aspiring, religious pre-Christian Jew." The specters haunting Jude's mind in the shape of empty hopes are identified by Kathleen R. Hoopes in "Illusion and Reality in *Jude the Obscure*"

(*NCF*, 1957). That the novel, far from being symbolic, reads primarily as a naturalistic chronicle of a "worthy man's education" is Arthur Mizener's case in "*Jude the Obscure* as a Tragedy" (*Southern Review*, 1940). Because Jude comes to realize that the circumstances which prevented his entrance to Oxford are changing, the narrative cannot be termed a "tragedy"; it is "not a carefully devised representation of life the purpose of which is to contrast, at every turn, the permanently squalid real life of man with the ideal life." Mizener spells out this position with further refinements in "The Novel of Doctrine in the Nineteenth Century: Hardy's *Jude the Obscure*" (in *The Sense of Life in the Modern Novel*, 1964). One writer's "tragedy" is another's "irony," and Hardy's own use of these words only complicates the issue: it will remain so until we have differentiated among the many variants of "tragedy" which are all found in his novels.

Reacting against Holland's stress on allegory and Mizener's on naturalistic realism, Frederick P. W. McDowell in "Hardy's 'Seemings or Personal Impressions': The Symbolical Use of Image and Contrast in *Jude the Obscure*" (*Modern Fiction Studies*, 1960) sets out to prove that Hardy was rendering a symbolic account of a "time of moral, intellectual, and spiritual dislocation." Though he is a little eager to find simple objects (the well–womb) and episodes (meetings at casement and window) endowed with "nuance" and "resonance," McDowell does a thorough job of organizing those aspects of the novel which deepen or amplify its purely naturalistic content: images of animals and music, the Bible and ecclesiastical paraphernalia, scenes repeated and sites revisited, jealousies in counterpoint, the disease of "modern restlessness," the theme of an uncertain cultural past, the opposed energies of life and death, and signs of Sue's moral ambiguity. It is, says McDowell, a kaleidoscope. So surveyed, and little more, these elements leave us wondering whether they ever converge at all to form not an example of this or that genre but some new thing. We need to know if the novel has any central coherence — whether, for instance, apart from "dislocation," there are any essential facts of human experience implied by all its fictional techniques. A. Alvarez, for instance, in a fine afterword to *Jude the Obscure* (New American Library, 1961; reprinted in *Hardy: A Collection of Critical Essays*, 1963, ed. A. J. Guerard) looks into its "loneliness" and obsession with "misfulfillment." But even if *Jude* is not merely naturalistic, how is it therefore a better novel — better, say, than a working-class novel like Gissing's *Thyrza?* Better or worse, it is seen by John Holloway in *The Victorian Sage* (1953) as an anomaly for being away from the natural background of Wessex. Guerard's comments (in *Thomas Hardy*) on the last testaments of Jude and Henchard, and D. H. Lawrence's comparison of Tess and her two men with Jude and his two women (in his "Study of Thomas Hardy") will explain this movement away from the provincial.

The best single discussion (along with Dorothy van Ghent's of *Tess*), not only in intrinsic worth but also because of the approach it suggests for reviewing Hardy's fiction, is Emma Clifford's "The Child: The Circus: and *Jude the Obscure*" (*Cambridge Journal*, 1954), which begins by observing the many weirdly aged children in his novels and goes on (after glancing with respectful subtlety at Hardy's own childhood) to consider the artistic "seeming" of the life which he creates. This semblance is never still: an imagery covers "his melodramatic stories, his stock characters and his absurd and ridiculous situations, with a complex ever-moving cloud of intensely personal impression." It is somehow childlike, a realm where "all things exist for themselves alone without relationship to one another, and where things and people are anonymous, highly coloured, over-simplified, and often over-sized." Sometimes it is a frenetic, almost hellish nightmare. In *Jude the Obscure*, especially, "Hardy has a great liking for shows, fairs, processions, models, brass bands and other activities easily associated with a childlike awareness of nomadic existence": hence, one might add, the novel's pattern of drifting and encounter.

By her dexterity and tact Miss Clifford shows the value in

exploring the essential conditions, the most commonly selected processes of knowing and feeling that pervade a novel and limit or enlarge the choices and capabilities of its inhabitants. Studies of manuscripts and texts, of structure, style, image, and theme, and the tracing of sources and influences and intellectual backgrounds all have their rewarding and intermediate worth. Many of these still are needed in Hardy — particularly studies of causation and the radical strains in the psychology of his characters, as well as a much closer awareness of the continuities he can reveal between Romantic and modern literature and between certain provinces of English and American fiction. But only when these elements are more fully related to one another will we see better the contours of Hardy's mind and begin to understand the novel of abundance, all the many-mindedness that prevails in the Victorian era.

12 ॐ

George Moore
George Gissing

Jacob Korg

GEORGE MOORE and George Gissing both took part in the transition between the period of Meredith and George Eliot and that of Conrad, Bennett, Galsworthy, and Wells, but they have little in common, and the resemblances between them turn out, upon examination, to be deceptive. Though each began his career in a spirit of reaction against the older novelists, they were reacting against different things and in different ways. Gissing sought new sources of material in slum life, while Moore attempted a series of stylistic innovations. Although each wrote novels of poverty, Gissing's have neither the fierce naturalism of *A Mummer's Wife* nor the quiet sympathy of *Esther Waters*. Both authors were influenced by foreign writers, but while Moore undertook vigorous campaigns on behalf of French literary theories, Gissing unobtrusively assimilated the influences of certain French, Russian, and Scandinavian novelists into a fictional style that remained essentially English. Both participated in the publishing revolution of the early nineties which resulted in the passing of the three-volume novel and of the moral dictatorship imposed by Mudie's, but Moore was a leader in this cause, while Gissing was a somewhat dubious follower.

On the whole, the contrasts between the two men are more striking than the similarities. Moore was active, gregarious, self-dramatizing; Gissing gained a reputation as a recluse. Moore's education was largely a collaboration between the military-school crammer and the café companion, and he was said to have had little patience for reading. Gissing was a thoroughly trained classical scholar and an encyclopedic reader. Moore wrote much in other forms, including drama, criticism, verse, and autobiography; Gissing's ventures into nonfiction, though distinguished, were comparatively rare. Finally, Moore lived far into the twentieth century, frequently changing his interests and his style, whereas Gissing died in 1903, only occasionally, in his twenty-three-year writing career, departing from the realistic novel of contemporary life which was his favorite medium.

MOORE

I. *Editions and Bibliographies*

Nearly all of Moore's work has gone through numerous editions. According to "George Moore's Revisions of *The Lake, The Wild Goose,* and *Esther Waters,*" by Royal A. Gettmann (*PMLA*, 1944), all of the novels, with the exception of *Mike Fletcher,* were revised before republication, and eight were revised twice. The Uniform Edition, whose volumes were published separately between 1924 and 1933, is incomplete because Moore, intending this edition to form his canon, excluded some of his most important novels from it. The two other collected editions, both more nearly approaching completeness, are the Carra Edition (1924) in twenty volumes (*Ulick and Soracha* was published in the format of this set in 1926), and the Ebury Edition (1937) in twenty volumes.

There is no satisfactory bibliography, either of Moore's works in general or of his novels. None of the existing ones lists the revised editions accurately, and all of them are incomplete on other grounds as well. A complete bibliography, which will describe all revised editions as well as the first English and American editions, is being compiled by

Edwin Gilcher. It will also list the publications of letters and ephemera by Moore and his contributions to books by other authors. The most complete bibliography appears as appendix II of *The Life of George Moore*, by Joseph Hone (1936). Also useful is Henry Danielson's descriptive bibliography of first editions published between 1878 and 1921, which is found in *A Portrait of George Moore in a Study of His Work*, by John Freeman (1922).

The most notable listing of works on Moore (in spite of its many typographical errors) is the exhaustive annotated bibliography, containing about a thousand entries, compiled by Helmut E. Gerber and others, and published in two parts as the Summer-Fall 1959 number of *English Fiction in Transition*. The best selected bibliography of Moore criticism is the one in *The Critic's Alchemy*, by Ruth Z. Temple (1953). The selected bibliography in *George Moore: A Reconsideration*, by Malcolm Brown (1955), is strong on biographical sources.

II. *Letters and Biographies*

Moore's letters to his long-time friend John Eglinton (William Kirkpatrick Magee), written between 1909 and 1932 and published as *Letters of George Moore* (n.d.) with an introduction by Eglinton, contain many allusions to the books written during that period. The correspondence in *Letters from George Moore to Edouard Dujardin, 1886–1922* (1929) was written in French, but translated for publication by Eglinton, who also supplied a preface containing personal impressions of Moore. The letters are concerned with the translation and publication of Moore's work in France, with his current projects, and with the Biblical interests he shared with Dujardin. *George Moore's Letters to Lady Cunard, 1895–1933* (1957) are mainly occupied with nonliterary activities; the frequent references to Moore's writing are casual and uninformative. However, the volume contains a useful introduction and notes by the editor, Rupert Hart-Davis.

Other letters by Moore appear in William Rothenstein's *Men and Memories* (3 vols., 1931–1939); Hone's *Life of George Moore*; "Letters from George Moore," by P. J. Dixon (*London Mercury*, 1934); and "George Moore: Letters of His Last Years," by V. M. Crawford (*London Mercury*, 1936).

Moore's extensive autobiographical writings offer a fund of information that is both indispensable and unreliable. Susan L. Mitchell in *George Moore* (1916) denies that *Hail and Farewell* has any factual value at all. She describes it as a new kind of *roman à clef* invented by Moore, "a work of fiction improvised upon his friends and himself." John Freeman in *A Portrait of George Moore in a Study of His Work* regards the autobiographies as the expression of a romantic sensibility "equally admirable and inexcusable," but he welcomes Moore's fabrications on the ground that they are more revealing, when properly interpreted, than the facts themselves could be. Joseph Hone's biography leans heavily on Moore's information, but Hone is fully aware that it is untrustworthy, and even raises the question of whether Moore's autobiographies are not satires, a question which Malcolm Brown in *George Moore: A Reconsideration* unhesitatingly answers in the affirmative.

The three biographies of Moore written before his death are gossipy and digressive; they may once have seemed informative, but they have been superseded by Hone's. The stated purpose of Susan L. Mitchell's *George Moore*, that of studying Moore as an Irishman, is a limitation that excludes much of interest and importance. Nevertheless, the book gives an eyewitness' survey of the Dublin scene in Moore's day, and opinions based on a personal knowledge of Moore and his friends. Miss Mitchell is the only biographer to devote an entire chapter to the delicate subject of Moore's attempts at painting; but it is exactly four and a half lines long. John Freeman's *A Portrait of George Moore in a Study of His Work* falls into the trap of relying heavily on Moore's writings, as the title suggests, but it contains some striking and original critical estimates. Humbert Wolfe, in *George Moore* (1932), offers much speculation, but little information. Probably the most enthusiastic of all Moore's critics, Wolfe has high praise for Moore's criticism, calls *The Brook Kerith* "the greatest prose book, except the Bible, in the English tongue," and attributes to Moore "the widest human sympathy of any English novelist."

The task of writing Moore's official biography was undertaken by Joseph Hone after being declined by John Eglinton and by Charles Morgan, both of whom wrote shorter reminiscences after his death. Hone's *Life of George Moore* draws its facts from Moore's autobiographies (which are used with caution), from correspondence and conversation with Moore's contemporaries, and from unpublished documents. Hone follows Moore's personal, financial, amorous, and literary relationships in detail, illustrating many of them with unpublished letters. This biography is particularly strong in dealing with Moore's childhood and education, and with the effects of such pre-Paris influences as Shelley, Jim Browne and the Moore family. It also gives a clear account of the changes of attitude which constituted Moore's intellectual development. It contains little original criticism; Hone usually tells when each novel was written, describes the relevant circumstances and summarizes the contemporary reaction, but adds few evaluations of his own.

As a striking and original personality, Moore usually found a place in the reminiscences of his friends and acquaintances. W. B. Yeats, in *Dramatis Personae, 1896–1902* (1936; republished as a part of Yeats's *Autobiography*, 1938) reports Moore's vindictive behavior toward himself and other friends in some detail, and describes some of his deficiencies of taste, manners, and education. Yeats seems to have had a better opinion of Moore at an earlier period, for most of the references to him in *The Letters of W. B. Yeats* (1955) are at least respectful. Yeats apparently regarded Moore as an equal, valued his contributions to the work of the Irish Literary Theatre, and praised his revision of *The Bending of the Bough*. A review of the relationship between the two men, "George Moore and His Friendship with W. B. Yeats" by Walther Gilomen (*English Studies*, 1937), contrasts their characters effectively.

Barrett H. Clark's *Intimate Portraits* (1951) contains a lively reminiscence about Moore by a man who collaborated with him in preparing a dramatic version of *Esther Waters*; it gives some clear insights into his creative methods, and describes his concern about such matters as plausibility and transitions. *GM: Memories of George Moore*, by Nancy Cunard (1956), though slight and digressive, conveys many valuable impressions and shrewd opinions of the older Moore. Miss Cunard's volume contains a number of unpublished letters, and records Moore's evaluations of such twentieth-century writers as Proust, Joyce, Pound, and Wyndham Lewis.

Other informative reminiscences are: *Conversations with George Moore*, by Geraint Goodwin (1930); "Souvenirs sur George Moore," by Mary Duclaux (*Revue de Paris*, 1933); "A Visit from George Moore" by Philip Gosse (*London Mercury*, 1933); "Contrasts: Memories of Galsworthy and George Moore," by Ford Madox Ford (*Atlantic Monthly*, 1933); "Recollections of George Moore" from *Irish Literary Portraits*, by John Eglinton (1935); *Epitaph on George Moore*, by Charles Morgan (1935); a chapter from *Portraits of a Lifetime*, by Jacques-Emile Blanche (1937); and "George Moore," by Max Beerbohm (*Atlantic Monthly*, 1950).

III. *Criticism*

Moore was no longer considered a particularly shocking author after 1900, but the question of his moral views still formed a significant topic of criticism well into the twentieth century. A representative example of this type of criticism appears in Stuart P. Sherman's *On Contemporary Literature* (1917). According to Sherman, the influences Moore brought across the Channel were all pernicious. The decadence of the *Confessions* was nothing but "aesthetic egoism," and the naturalism which Sherman finds in *Esther Waters* he takes to be merely a special case of the same impulse, the cynical contemplation of the grotesque as it is exhibited in a helpless creature.

However, some of Moore's early critics were able to take a more tolerant view of his work, though they did not always approve of it. The young James Joyce, briefly considering Moore in connection with the Irish Literary Theatre in "The Day of the Rabblement" (1901; republished in *Two Essays,* 1957), dismisses him as a possible source of the renewal of Irish literature. But Arnold Bennett, in his chapter on Moore in *Fame and Fiction* (1901), sees in the detailed and precise realism of *A Modern Lover* and *A Mummer's Wife* a successful rebellion against the conventions of English fiction. Forrest Reid, in "The Novels of George Moore" (*Westminster Review,* 1909), praises the novels for their strong characters and wide range of observation, and singles out *Esther Waters* as a masterpiece of honest and straightforward narration; but he disapproves of the flat impressionism of Moore's style, and declares that Moore's contentious realism hampers his popularity. An excellent French assessment, "George Moore," by Federico Olivero (*Revue Germanique,* 1910), praises his method of isolating the essential elements in characterization and description. Olivero compares the design of Moore's novels, a dominant figure against a subordinate background, to the work of the Goncourts, and relates his method of presenting unified impressions to the style of Flaubert. His treatment of spiritual crises, says Olivero, is like Pater's, for both implant seeds of thought which later lead to significant intellectual developments.

The American critic James Huneker shared Moore's interest in music, met him on one occasion, and devoted a number of essays to the man and his work. "The Later George Moore," which appears in *The Pathos of Distance* (1913), discusses *The Untilled Field* and *The Lake,* and recommends Moore's writings on music and musicians. "The Reformation of George Moore" from *Unicorns* (1917) explores the doctrinal implications of *The Brook Kerith.* A pair of essays on Moore in *Overtones* (1904) praises the music criticism in *Evelyn Innes* and detects both in that novel and in *Sister*

Teresa a style of handling inner conflicts resembling that of Huysmans. A study of the relations between Moore and Huneker and a number of Moore's letters to Huneker appear in "Irish Author and American Critic," by Arnold T. Schwab (*NCF*, 1954).

The nature and value of Moore's contribution to the novel is a matter of dispute among his critics. John Freeman, in *A Portrait of George Moore in a Study of His Work*, disapproves of nearly all the stylistic experiments Moore attempted before *The Brook Kerith*; he characterizes the prose of *A Mummer's Wife* as lifeless, and thinks the style of *Evelyn Innes* and *Sister Teresa* shows "aesthetic disintegration." He objects to *Evelyn Innes* on moral grounds, but vigorously defends *Esther Waters*, praising it for its unity, clarity of development, and fidelity to real life, and arguing that its detached, apparently unsympathetic tone is appropriate to naturalism. Thomas McGreevy, in "George Moore" (*Scrutinies*, ed. Edgell Rickword, 1928), challenges Freeman's claim that Moore gave form to the English novel. In general, says McGreevy, Moore's sense of form cannot be compared with that of Henry James and James Joyce, and it grew weaker in the later novels. H. V. Routh in *Towards the Twentieth Century* (1937) finds little to praise in any of Moore's novels except *Esther Waters*, but he does make a serious attempt to formulate the philosophy they imply. According to Routh, Moore was an agnostic humanist whose novels elaborate the mystery of the human personality, showing it dominating its culture and environment, an effect Routh finds particularly conspicuous in the historical novels. He describes Moore's realism as a search for the aesthetic aspect of everyday life.

The section on Moore in vol. IX of Ernest A. Baker's *History of the English Novel* (1938), after discussing influences, offers a good short analysis of the prose style of *The Untilled Field* and *The Lake*, and suggests that Moore's uncertainty, which made him aware of his deficiencies and ready to experiment, enabled him to develop his originality. Malcolm Elwin also gives Moore credit for self-improvement

in *Old Gods Falling* (1939), but he attributes Moore's progress to diligent reading, a view which is contradicted by the
many reports of his inability to read with attention, or to
assess other writers objectively. Elwin asserts that it was
Charles Reade, rather than Moore, who introduced naturalism into England. He implies that Moore turned to it as a
means of capitalizing upon the success of Reade's play of
1879, *Drink*, which was based on *L'Assommoir*.

Madeleine Cazamian's *Le Roman et les idées en Angleterre*, vol. II (1935), and Graham Hough's "George Moore
and the Nineties," *Edwardians and Late Victorians* (English
Institute Essays, 1959), examine Moore in relation to his
literary period. Mme. Cazamian details his importance as a
transmitting and reflecting agent by dividing his career into
five stages. The first was marked by his declaration of athe-
ism, the second by his conversion to Gautier, Baudelaire,
and Poe, the third by his adherence to realism, inspired first
by Balzac and later by Zola, the fourth by the influence of
Marius the Epicurean, and the last by a blend of aestheticism
and naturalism. Hough presents a persuasive case for considering Moore the most representative figure of the nineties,
on the ground that the three qualities his work drew from
the varied influences of Gautier, Baudelaire, Pater, Zola, and
Flaubert, namely, realism, rebellion against convention, and
attention to form, corresponded with the most pronounced
tendencies of the period as a whole.

The only full-length critical study of Moore written since
Freeman's book of 1922 is Malcolm Brown's *George Moore:
A Reconsideration* (1955). It traces his development in detail,
explaining the motivations that led him to the various stages
of his career, and making surprisingly good, if not strictly
logical, sense of the contradictory doctrinal affiliations that
marked it. According to Brown, naturalism interested Moore
because he was struck by Zola's program of scientific objectivity, and because it seemed to parallel French Romanticism
in attacking bourgeois morality, but he broke with it because
he discovered that it had revolutionary and libertarian implications which conflicted with his conservatism. *Esther*

Waters, according to Brown, is not the objective account of the futility of a servant's life, the English *Germinie Lacerteux* which Moore says, in the *Confessions*, he would like to write, but an attempt to recapture a public through the sympathetic treatment of ordinary life. Brown explains the new qualities of Moore's later novels as the results of an attempt to achieve "universality." One of the chief elements of this new manner was a tone of gentle pathos generated by a conviction of the futility of life, and suggested by the melancholy of classical elegies, contemporary Russian writers, and the "official mood of the Celtic twilight." Brown considers Moore's most decisive contribution to the development of the novel to be the rejection of the "evangelical" views of human nature and morality in favor of franker and more realistic ones.

There is considerable justification, in Moore's case, for the large proportion of scholarship devoted to study of influences. "No human being," says Ernest A. Baker of Moore, "was ever more plastic." During the eighties and nineties he was known as an emissary of French styles as well as of French lubricity and decadence. Information about his activities in gaining acceptance for Zola's work in England is to be found in *The Victorian Conscience,* by Clarence R. Decker (1952), in *Le Mouvement esthétique et "décadent" en Angleterre (1873–1900)*, by Albert J. Farmer (1931), and in Elwin's *Old Gods Falling*. Although the relation between Moore's work and that of a number of French authors is usually considered highly important, Freeman in his *Portrait of George Moore* dissents, asserting that Moore's French experiences delayed the development of his prose style. The naturalist influence upon each of Moore's relevant novels is briefly examined in *L'Influence du naturalisme français sur les romanciers anglais de 1885 à 1900*, by William C. Frierson (1925).[1] Frierson, whose opinion is followed by most subsequent critics, feels that *A Mummer's Wife* manifests the

---

[1] See also the same author's *The English Novel in Transition, 1885–1940* (1942), and his article "George Moore Compromised with the Victorians" (*Trollopian*, 1947).

influence of Zola more clearly than any other novel by Moore, principally because it acknowledges the determinist power of environment. After this novel, says Frierson, Moore retreated from naturalism, though *A Mere Accident* has the "spiritual naturalism" (described by Durtal) of Huysmans' *Là-bas*, a mode which is to reappear in *Evelyn Innes* and *Sister Teresa*.

Albert J. Farmer's chapter on Moore in *Le Mouvement esthétique et "décadent" en Angleterre (1873–1900)* describes him as the spokesman of a generation, who found expression for the revolutionary impulses of his time by serving as the transmitter of both naturalism and symbolism, and by making important contributions to the decadent movement. The controversy which followed the publication of *A Mummer's Wife* showed Moore to be a vigorous defender of the principle of the autonomy of art. During his symbolist period, that is, between 1886 and 1890, Moore, according to Farmer, was under the influence of Huysmans' *A Rebours. A Mere Accident,* an attempt to emulate the sensuous mysticism of Huysmans' novel, introduced the Des Esseintes character type which was to become important in England in the nineties. The *Confessions* was the most wholly symbolist of Moore's books, and the most effective in expressing tastes and attitudes which had originated in France. Farmer describes Moore's development after the *Confessions* as a movement away from symbolism and the French influence; *Esther Waters*, in spite of certain naturalistic features, fails to illustrate naturalist theory, and Farmer takes the view that it is primarily a novel of personality, and thus a return, on Moore's part, to the main tradition of the English novel.

In *On Contemporary Literature* Stuart P. Sherman had sought to demonstrate the influence of Huysmans on Moore by quoting from *A Drama in Muslin* a description of dress fabrics beginning with "white silks," which makes use of the symbolist device of synesthesia, comparing the various colors to sounds. The passage has become a crux among Moore's critics. Farmer attributes particular significance to it, pointing out that although the principle involved originated with Baudelaire, and was exploited in a famous sonnet by Rimbaud, Moore derived it from René Ghil's *Traité du verbe* (1886), where it is developed at length.[2] Farmer concludes that Moore was an initiator who left to others the development of the fictional modes he introduced. By bringing together the parallel tendencies of English Paterism and French symbolism, he effected a focusing and clarification of the vague impulses toward novelty that were to converge in the decadence of the nineties.

In *L'Idée de l'art pour l'art* (1931) Louise Rosenblatt describes Moore as an important partisan of the principle which is the theme of her study. Like his battle against publishing restrictions, his aestheticism was both a protest against prudery and a way of claiming freedom for art. Miss Rosenblatt maintains that *A Modern Lover* and *A Mummer's Wife* belong to the aesthetic tradition of Flaubert rather than to that of Zola, and that Moore's interest in moral issues arose from the fact that they offered conflicts for his characters, and not from a concern with their social consequences. She concludes that Moore's real commitment was to such aesthetic considerations as harmony, rhythm, and formal development.

The most thorough study of the influence of French writers on Moore is *George Moore et la France*, by Georges-Paul Collet (1957). After a useful review of Moore's friends, associations, and interests in his Paris years, Collet passes to an examination of the effects of individual authors on his work. He believes that *Mademoiselle de Maupin* was the first French book Moore knew, and that Gautier's introduction interested him in the doctrine of the supremacy of art. In his chapter on the influence of Zola, Collet agrees with the general opinion that *A Mummer's Wife* is the most natural-

---

[2] Hone, in *Life of George Moore*, also attributes the passage to the influence of Ghil, but he does not mention the background of the "correspondances" principle. Georges-Paul Collet in *George Moore et la France* (1957) quotes it in order to *deny* a suggested resemblance to a passage from Zola's *Au Bonheur des dames*, mentioning Baudelaire and Ghil. S. M. Steward in "J.-K. Huysmans and George Moore" (*Romanic Review*, 1934) cites this passage as evidence that *A Rebours* had suggested new fields of imagery to Moore.

istic of Moore's novels; its translation was received in France as an example of naturalism. About 1886–87, says Collet, Moore moved from the influence of Zola to the less important influence of Flaubert, from whom he derived a "sacerdotal conception of art," and an attitude of fastidiousness in matters of style and technique. It was Edouard Dujardin, says Collet, who influenced Moore more strongly than any other French writer. He bases this opinion on the contention that Moore's abandonment of naturalism, his interest in music and in the problems of Christianity, and his attitude toward St. Paul, are all traceable to his friendship with the editor of *La Revue indépendante.*[3]

Though Moore wrote an introduction for a translation of Dostoyevsky's *Poor Folk,* the only Russian writer who is frequently mentioned as an influence upon him is Turgenev. He wrote an article on Turgenev, and often praised him vigorously in conversation. Royal A. Gettmann, in *Turgenev in England and America* (1941), describes the influence of Turgenev as a counterweight to that of Zola, for it showed Moore that intellectual processes could be more important than physical or emotional experiences. Gilbert Phelps, in *The Russian Novel in English Fiction* (1956), places the first signs of Turgenev's influence in *Evelyn Innes,* where the trick of combining a character's thoughts with an account of his physical sensations, a Turgenev device much admired by Moore, is in evidence. However, the influence of the Russian writer is much clearer in the work Moore did after reading *A Sportsman's Sketches,* namely, *Celibates, The Untilled Field,* and *The Lake.*

A Disciple of Walter Pater, by Robert Porter Sechler (1931), examines the influence upon Moore of the only English author he wholeheartedly admired. Sechler believes that *Marius the Epicurean* had three distinct effects upon Moore: it portrayed a calm and thoughtful figure, it demon-

---

[3] The influence of Dujardin in arousing Moore's skepticism about the accuracy of the Gospels and drawing his attention to Biblical materials is described in "George Moore and Edouard Dujardin," by Francesco Cordasco (*MLN*, 1947).

strated "the sensuous effect of words," and it drew his attention from French to English literature. *Marius*, according to Sechler, attracted Moore to the spectacle of a mind actively engaged with spiritual problems, and led him to devote a number of his novels to people whose lives are quests for some religious, philosophic, or artistic formulation. Pater's example was an enduring one, ultimately leading, says Sechler, to the distinctive later prose style. In a notable dissenting opinion, "Pater and Moore" (*London Mercury*, 1936), Sean O'Faolain describes Moore's later style as devoid of feeling and monotonously graceful. Developing a much needed contrast between the master and his acolyte, O'Faolain maintains that while Pater's aestheticism was an attempt to formulate a disciplining principle for art, Moore's was no more than a Wildean hedonism lacking moral convictions and a sense of valucs.

GISSING

I. *Editions and Bibliographies*

There has never been a collected edition of Gissing's novels. The first editions were published in small printings and have grown very scarce, and some have been republished only recently or not at all. Two of the later editions are of particular interest. Gissing began, but never completed, a revision of *Workers in the Dawn*; his intended changes are indicated by footnotes in the two-volume 1935 reprint edited by Robert Shafer. The 1895 edition of *The Unclassed* is a thorough revision of the original version; the alterations are analyzed in "Gissing's Revision of *The Unclassed*," by Joseph J. Wolff (*NCF*, 1953). Most, though not all, of the numerous short stories Gissing wrote for periodicals in England and America have been collected in six separate volumes.

A. C. Ward's *Gissing* (Writers and Their Work, no. 111, 1959) contains the most complete bibliography of Gissing's work, though it misleadingly fails to mention many reprints. Robert Shafer's introductory material for *Workers in the*

Dawn contains a list of letters and criticism with valuable annotations. The bibliography in Mabel Collins Donnelly's *George Gissing: Grave Comedian* (1954) gives all the "principal editions" of Gissing's work, as well as uncollected contributions to periodicals, manuscripts used as source material, published letters, and a good representation of criticism and scholarship. Supplementary listings of publications on Gissing appear in *English Fiction in Transition*, Fall-Winter, 1957; Spring-Summer, 1958; and Fall Special, 1958.

II. *Letters and Autobiographical Material*

The Letters of George Gissing to Members of His Family, edited by Algernon and Ellen Gissing (1927), though it is an invaluable biographical source, fails to represent Gissing fully, both because he did not take the relatives who were his correspondents into his confidence, and because much material of interest has been excised. The account of Gissing's death appended to the volume is misleading; it should be corrected by Morley Roberts' narrative in *The Private Life of Henry Maitland* (1912), by "The Death of Gissing: A Fourth Report," by Arthur C. Young (*Essays in Literary History*, ed. Rudolf Kirk and C. F. Main, 1961), and by the information in the Gissing Exhibition Catalogue of the New York Public Library (see below). *The Letters of George Gissing to Eduard Bertz, 1887–1903*, ed. Arthur C. Young (1961), contains a long correspondence with a German friend to whom Gissing freely confided his opinions, literary plans, and personal problems from month to month throughout most of his mature years. The editor's introduction and annotations provide a generous background of information, much of it newly developed, about Gissing, Bertz, and matters relevant to the letters. *George Gissing and H. G. Wells, Their Friendship and Correspondence*, ed. Royal A. Gettmann (1961), gives both sides of the correspondence the writers carried on after their meeting in 1896, as well as some letters from other people, and Wells's reviews of Gissing's work.

Scattered publications of letters by Gissing include eleven letters to Edward Clodd in the latter's *Memories* (1916) and seventeen letters to Ellen Gissing in "George Gissing to His Sister," by Jacqueline Steiner (*Bulletin of the Boston Public Library*, 1947). "The Letters of George Gissing," by Morley Roberts (*VQR*, 1931) describes the contents of fifty-two letters written to Roberts between 1894 and 1903.

Gissing's *Private Papers of Henry Ryecroft* is not autobiographical, though the retired man of letters who is supposed to be its author bears some striking resemblances to Gissing. *George Gissing's Commonplace Book*, ed. Jacob Korg (1962; also in *BNYPL*, Sept.–Nov. 1961) is a notebook closely related to the Ryecroft papers which enables the reader to see how closely Gissing's views parallel those of his character.

III. *Biography*

Three full-length biographies of Gissing have appeared. The earliest is an eccentric reminiscence imperfectly disguised as fiction, *The Private Life of Henry Maitland*, by Morley Roberts, a lifelong friend of Gissing. Written in a casual and rambling style, *Maitland* makes no pretense of completeness or continuity, and often gives disproportionate attention to details, yet it is an excellent source of first-hand information, not all of it, however, entirely accurate. A third edition, ed. Morchard Bishop (1958), gives useful facts in its footnotes and introduction, and a key to the pseudonyms, as well as an interesting defense of Roberts' biographical methods. *George Gissing: Grave Comedian*, by Mabel C. Donnelly, makes use of extensive unpublished manuscript material to tell the full story of Gissing's life for the first time. From Gissing's diary, correspondence, and other papers, Mrs. Donnelly develops detailed information about such mysterious aspects of Gissing's biography as his visit to America, his difficulties with his first wife, his early years in London, and his relationship with Gabrielle Fleury. She gives a critical discussion of each of the novels, and seeks to place Gissing in the general history of the novel, showing how he broke new ground by varying or reversing established conventions. In particular, she draws a good contrast between the long, typically Victorian novels of Gissing's early period and the more compact and economical ones of his later career. *George Gissing: A Critical Biography* by Jacob Korg (1963) emphasizes the contemporary ideas which occupied Gissing and provided him with subjects for many of his novels.

The catalogue prepared by John D. Gordan for the exhibition of Gissing material at the New York Public Library in 1953, *George Gissing: 1857–1903* (also published in three parts in the *BNYPL*, 1954), is an important source of information. In giving full notes about the items displayed, the catalogue tells a well-integrated narrative that amounts to a short biography. It is still necessary to warn readers that the article on Gissing in the *Dictionary of National Biography* (second supplement, 1912), by Thomas Seccombe, contains some inaccuracies, for at least one of them, the notion that Gissing spent some time in Germany after leaving America, has been widely disseminated. On the other hand, Seccombe's long introduction to *The House of Cobwebs and Other Stories* (1906), though incomplete, is free of errors. Robert Shafer's biographical summary in the 1935 edition of *Workers in the Dawn* has been corrected in some respects by later investigation, but it remains excellent, giving details not found elsewhere. Shafer's account of Gissing's changing opinions, and his view that he was a bookish man who was willing to contend with contemporary problems, go far toward capturing his individuality.

In spite of Gissing's reputation as a solitary, there is no lack of firsthand impressions of him. Among the best of these are two articles by his sister, Ellen Gissing, "Some Personal Recollections of George Gissing" (*Blackwood's Magazine*, 1929) and "George Gissing, A Character Sketch" (*Nineteenth Century and After*, 1927). Aware that Gissing's unconventional relations with women and his avoidance of ordinary society carried suspicious implications for the late-Victorian mind, Ellen Gissing takes pains to make it clear that he was not a libertine, but a victim of his own mistakes. Two accounts by Austin Harrison, "George Gissing" (*Nineteenth Century and After*, 1906), and a passage from *Frederic Harri-*

son: Thoughts and Memories (1926), give details about Gissing's appearance, personality, opinions, and relationships with others. However, the date of these impressions is not 1882, as Harrison gives it, but 1880, as Robert Shafer has pointed out, and the visit to Germany described by Harrison is, of course, erroneous.

H. G. Wells, who was generous enough as a critic of Gissing's novels, writes disapprovingly of Gissing's aristocratic tendencies in *Experiment in Autobiography* (1934), describes him as self-defeating and ineffectual, and records valuable information about his opinions and his relationship with Gabrielle Fleury. W. Robertson Nicoll, in a chapter on Gissing in *A Bookman's Letters* (1913), gives an account of Gissing's youthful crime and defends *Maitland*, pointing out, however, that Roberts badly underestimated the quality of Gissing's work. In a short vignette in *People and Books* (1926) Nicoll describes Gissing's appearance in the nineties as that of "the very last man to have cultivated an intimacy with the slums. He was well dressed, bland, debonair and communicative."

George Matthew Adams' "How and Why I Collect George Gissing" (*Colophon*, 1934) contains an interesting biographical item, a photographic reproduction of the account Gissing drew up showing his income from writing between 1880 and 1898. Bernard Bergonzi, in "The Novelist as Hero" (*Twentieth Century*, 1958), compares Wells's and Harrison's reports about Gissing as a means of evaluating *Maitland*. "George Gissing and Clara Collet," by Ruth M. Adams (*NCF*, 1956), describes a friend and confidante who shared Gissing's interest in social problems and may well have influenced his approach to them. Royal A. Gettmann's *A Victorian Publisher* (1960), in reviewing Gissing's transactions with the firm of Bentley and Company, shows how the moral restrictions imposed upon writers compelled Gissing to make revisions in his work.

IV. *Criticism*

A book-length evaluation of the whole range of Gissing's work appeared as early as 1912 in Frank Swinnerton's *George*

Gissing: A Critical Study (republished, 1923). The biographical chapter is both inaccurate and incomplete; Swinnerton does not mention any of Gissing's wives, for example, though there are signs that he knows more than he is willing to tell. In spite of a serious lack of information, he arrives at a shrewd, if severe, assessment of Gissing's character. Although he uses only the most conventional critical standards in examining his author's work, Swinnerton produces some impressive results, accurately formulating many of its strengths and weaknesses. He sees, for example, that Gissing's novels of character (which he calls "studies of abnormal temperament") are superior to his novels of environment, that *New Grub Street* is a balanced, realistic performance which displays all of Gissing's abilities, and that *Born in Exile* is a sound character study. Old-fashioned predilections sometimes lead him astray. For example, he praises the idealistic note in *Thyrza,* and admires *Isabel Clarendon* for a special authenticity in some of its psychology. In general, he is too hard on Gissing, unsympathetically castigating him for his critical attitude toward the poor, and giving a disproportionate emphasis to such minor Victorian faults as the expository stance, the contrived plot, and the thumbnail character sketch.

Swinnerton's superior and disapproving tone prompted two defenders of Gissing to make replies. The first of these, *Frank Swinnerton und George Gissing, Eine Kritische Studie,* by A. Rotter (Prague, 1930), says very little about Swinnerton's views, but unconvincingly attempts, through a comparative study of the novels of the two men, to demonstrate that Swinnerton's work owes much to Gissing's. Ruth Capers McKay, in *George Gissing and His Critic Frank Swinnerton* (1933), argues that most of the qualities of Gissing's temperament Swinnerton objected to were really virtues. Her defense of Gissing involves an examination of his use of the conventions of the Victorian novel, which she finds to be present in his later novels as well as in his early work. She challenges Swinnerton on two of the familiar Gissing issues: whether he should have been an essayist or teacher instead of a novelist,

and whether the "Gissing man," the type represented by
Osmond Waymark and Godwin Peak, is merely a reflex of
Gissing's egotism or a valid representation of an existing
social group.

George Gissing: An Appreciation, by May Yates (1922),
takes the view that Gissing was an artist who was formed by
his hardships. Miss Yates's discussion of Gissing's personality
identifies a number of his leading characteristics, his "aristocratic" tendency, his neurotic scrupulousness, and his aver-
sion to contemporary industrial civilization. She describes
the typical Gissing hero as a poorly equipped warrior who
is ultimately compelled to accept defeat. It is a part of the
Gissing man's weakness that he idealizes women, a mistake,
as Miss Yates, points out, which Gissing himself made.

The reviewers usually treated Gissing's novels with respect,
though they occasionally disagreed violently with the opinions
expressed in them, and warned readers that they were
"gloomy" or "depressing." Contemporary analysts felt that
they had a sharply original quality, and most of the early
studies were attempts to place them in relation to more conventional fiction. "Two Philanthropic Novelists," by Edith
Sichel (*Murray's Magazine*, 1888), pairs Walter Besant and
Gissing as the Optimist and the Pessimist of the reform novel,
and accurately characterizes Gissing as a conservative who
fears industrial progress but, having no solutions to offer,
accepts current conditions with resignation. Frederick Dol-
man in "The Novels of George Gissing" (*National Review*,
1897) also recognizes that Gissing's portrayals of social conditions are authentic, but finds his attitude toward the common people inconsistent and his opinions about the social
role of women obscure. Henry James in "London Notes,
July, 1897" (*Notes on Novelists with Some Other Notes*,
1914) grants Gissing the merit of "saturation," that is, thorough knowledge of the lower-middle-class milieu, but expresses strong reservations about his technical and organiza-
tional powers, specifically deploring the tendency displayed
in *The Whirlpool* to resort to dialogue for much of the narration.

In "The Novels of Mr. George Gissing" (*Contemporary Review*, 1897) H. G. Wells perceptively points out that Gissing makes a social force the center of his story, in place of the heroic figure or plot device traditionally used as organizing principles in the English novel. Conceding that Gissing's novels have some weaknesses, particularly an ineffectual idealism, Wells nevertheless finds in them a valuable "contemporary" quality. In a second article, "George Gissing: An Impression" (*Monthly Review*, 1904), Wells gives the first informative sketch of Gissing's life and character ever published, refers to the structural elements of his novels, accurately describes them as "a synthesis of impressions," and mentions Gissing's plan for the unwritten last chapters of *Veranilda*.[4]

Thomas Seccombe's introduction to *The House of Cobwebs*, "The Work of George Gissing: An Introductory Survey" (1906), perceptively establishes relationships between Gissing's life and his books, nearly all of which are discussed in detail. Though he is somewhat glib in detecting influences, Seccombe is sensitive to Gissing's most distinctive qualities. Below the realism he feels a romantic, sentimental strain, yet he comments in another place, "there was always a flavour of scholarly, subacid and quasi-ironical modernity about his style." Paul Elmer More devotes one of his *Shelburne Essays* (fifth series, 1908) to a general analysis of Gissing's novels. Unlike Dickens, he says, Gissing was a principled realist, but his profound emotional involvement in the poverty he described prevented him from making successful artistic use of it. In the conflict of Gissing's people with poverty the reader feels a keen will to live and a strong moral sense. But More finds that in his later novels Gissing, misled by sinister Continental influences, turned from the struggle for survival to the less fundamental struggle against the evils of middle-class life. Ultimately, says More, he was saved by

[4] Articles written soon after Gissing's death also appeared in the *Fortnightly Review* (by Arthur Waugh) and the *Independent Review* (by N. Wedd) in 1904. Gissing's modernity was also stressed by Greenough White in "George Gissing" (*Sewanee Review*, 1898).

his classical training, which enabled him to command an aloof irony and lightness of touch.

In his discussion of Gissing in vol. XIII of the *CHEL* (1917), W. T. Young detects influences of Schopenhauer and Zola, but nevertheless places him in the tradition of Dickens and Meredith. The artificiality of Gissing's plots, says Young, shows that he was not at home with the old-fashioned novel of action, but he was, on the other hand, well equipped for the "study" of character and social scenes. Q. D. Leavis, in "Gissing and the English Novel" (*Scrutiny*, 1938) blames the traditional methods of Victorian fiction for imposing severe handicaps on Gissing, but she describes *New Grub Street* as a classic, one of a chain of great novels leading up to the modern period. Virginia Woolf discusses Gissing's ability to handle character in her essay on him in *The Common Reader, Second Series* (1932), observing that, in spite of his narrow range, he could achieve effective presentations of people confronted by vital issues.

Madeleine Cazamian in *Le Roman et les idées en Angleterre*, vol. I (1923), describes Gissing as the prisoner of a scientific age he detested. Though an aesthete by nature, he was strongly influenced by current thought, acknowledged the power of scientific analysis, and often alluded to contemporary intellectual history. Mme. Cazamian's views are supported by detailed accounts of the conflicts of ideas in Gissing's novels, which bring their substantial intellectual content to the fore. The passage on Gissing in vol. IX of *The History of the English Novel* (1938) by Ernest A. Baker characterizes the motive of Gissing's realism as resentment against the middle class. Baker feels that Gissing lacked sympathy for the poor, did not believe in the possibility of meaningful reform, and showed concern only for those characters in his novels who resembled himself. Conceding that they are weakened by such faults as authorial comment and lack of detachment, Baker nevertheless terms the novels "the fullest exposure extant in English of the hideous realities underlying modern civilization."

Most of Gissing's novels are addressed to such social themes as poverty, socialism, and the social role of women, but his opinions are difficult to formulate because they are often both complex and inconclusive. Stanley Alden, in "George Gissing, Humanist" (*North American Review*, 1922), begins his discussion of Gissing's general philosophy by pointing out that, though he is known as a realist, his own definition of realism as the communication of "impressions" has little to do with the methods of Zola or De Maupassant. In his idealization of women, his depiction of nature, and his progress from abstract social problems in his earlier novels to more specific problems of human nature in his later ones, Alden finds reasons for classifying him as a humanist rather than a coldly detached realist or naturalist. J. D. Thomas, in "The Public Purposes of George Gissing" (*NCF*, 1953), explains the inconclusiveness of Gissing's novels as the result of his conviction that the world is not ultimately intelligible. It was therefore natural that he should have no coherent social philosophy; his books, says Thomas, are "thesis novels without a thesis." Jacob Korg's "Division of Purpose in George Gissing" (*PMLA*, 1955) describes the conflict of didactic and aesthetic motivations as a disruptive element in Gissing's work. Though Gissing agreed with the theories of Shelley's "Defence of Poetry," his concern with social conditions prevented him from achieving the detachment it recommended.

A detailed analysis of Gissing's social ideas is given in *George Gissing und die Soziale Frage*, by Anton Weber (Leipzig, 1932). According to Weber, Gissing's social views originated in his scholarly and aesthetic interests, and his ultimate social standards were based on culture and art. The pessimistic and realistic tone of his social comment is described as a reaction against the sentimental socialism of earlier reformers. Gissing began with a scientific orientation, a belief in the overriding value of facts, and his earlier novels express a strong social determinism, but he later came to hold the view that science was the source of the evils of civilization. He was antidemocratic, regarding egalitarianism as an enemy of culture, and he considered popular education dangerous.

Gissing devoted considerable attention to what was called in his day "the woman-question," and his opinions on this subject, unlike most of his social views, were clear and consistent. Weber presents an analysis of them, and of his ideas about the related problems of marriage and the family. A monograph on the subject, *Die Darstellung der Frau bei George Gissing,* by Gerhard Haasler (Greifswald, 1938), classifies Gissing's female characters under such headings as "sympathetic working women" and "unsympathetic underworld types," and illustrates the categories at length. Haasler feels that Gissing generally idealized his women, but that he nevertheless succeeded in transcending the ordinary Victorian conception of such figures as the prostitute and the working girl. *The Odd Women,* he says, presents the condition of women as a reflection of obsolete social and religious principles. John Middleton Murry relates Gissing's treatment of women to his experiences in his essay "George Gissing" (*Katherine Mansfield and Other Literary Studies,* 1959), arriving at some ingenious, if debatable, conclusions. He points out that, in spite of his interest in oppressive women of the sort he had encountered himself, Gissing continued to idealize women in his novels.

The reader who knows Gissing as a social realist is usually surprised to learn that he was a strong student of the classics; this side of him has been treated in *George Gissing, Classicist,* by Samuel Vogt Gapp (1936). Observing that Gissing's interest in contemporary slum life and his attachment to the classics form a unique combination, Gapp establishes some relationships between the two. The classics offered an escape from the harsh realities of the nineteenth century, and guided Gissing in the pursuit of a humanist ideal. In addition, Gapp finds that they were responsible for his conservatism, and for his hatred of modern city life, which he contrasted with the pastoral atmosphere of certain ancient works.

Gissing, like Moore, was receptive to the influence of foreign writers. His debt to the French realists and naturalists has often been mentioned, but seldom analyzed in detail. William C. Frierson, in *L'Influence du naturalisme français*

sur les romanciers anglais de 1885 à 1900 (1925), takes up the
question with appropriate caution, admitting that it is
impossible to say exactly when Gissing read the French
authors or what their influence was. He finds reflections of
Zola in the descriptions of sordid scenes in *The Nether World*,
but points out that Gissing did not follow the principles of
the "experimental novel" because he was absorbed in problems of character, and really belonged to the English tradition. Gissing was as familiar with the Russian novelists as
any English writer of his time, and was for a period the
English correspondent of the Russian periodical *The Messenger of Europe*. In *Turgenev in England and America*
(1941) Royal A. Gettmann examines an aspect of this subject, attributing the economy and dramatic quality of Gissing's later style to his enthusiasm for Turgenev. Gettmann
suggests, however, that the resemblances between the self-
pitying and ineffectual heroes of the two authors are due,
not to direct influence, but to similar conditions in the life
of their time.

Although the essential quality of Gissing's mind is elusive,
critics who have attempted general evaluations of him tend
to agree that he is a significant illustration of the familiar
nineteenth-century phenomenon of alienation. André Maurois, in a respectful brief biography, "George Gissing"
(*Revue de Paris*, 1958), describes him as typical of the Eng-
lishmen of his time who suffered exclusion from the privileged classes; his trouble was, says Maurois, that he belonged
to too many irreconcilable worlds. Jacob Korg's essays
"George Gissing's Outcast Intellectuals" (*American Scholar*,
1950) and "The Spiritual Theme of George Gissing's *Born
in Exile*" (*From Jane Austen to Joseph Conrad*, 1958) discuss some of the novels in which characters experiencing
spiritual conflicts appear. Russell Kirk, in "Who Knows
George Gissing?" (*Western Humanities Review*, 1950), takes
the view that Gissing used these figures as a medium for
criticizing the modern spirit. Kirk's article, perhaps the
most successful brief formulation of Gissing's attitudes, presents him as a noble and lonely figure in an inhospitable

civilization, an Epicurean with a taste for contemplative pleasures, whose true bent is most clearly displayed in his restrained and discriminating prose style.

Among the questions about Gissing that await clarification are the textual status of his novels in their various editions, and the nature and extent of his contributions to periodicals. The biographical work is far from complete; some significant manuscripts and letters have not yet been published, and numerous details of his life require more investigation and intelligent correlation with his writings. Finally, many of the novels have not yet had the thoroughgoing critical analysis they deserve as representatives of a transitional period in English fiction.

Index

434 INDEX

156, 157, 158, 159–160, 162–164, 172, 179, 186

Raymond, E. T., on Disraeli, 25

Raymond, Ernest, on Brontës, 227–228

Read, Herbert, on Brontës, 228

Reade, Charles, 39, 196, 277, 279, 284–293, 396; *Cloister and the Hearth*, 288, 292; *Foul Play*, 292; *Griffith Gaunt*, 290, 293; *Hard Cash*, 288, 290, 292; *It Is Never Too Late*, 289–290, 292

Reade, C. L. and Compton, on Reade, 286, 291

Reeve, Wybert, on Collins, 280

Reichard, H. M., on *Tess*, 351

Reid, Forrest, on Moore, 394

Reid, J. C., on Dickens, 91, 109

Reid, T. W., on C. Brontë, 222

Reinhard-Stocker, Alice, on Hardy, 363

Reinhold, Heinz, on Dickens, 134

Reizov, B. G., on Dickens, 121

Renan, Ernest, 116

Rendall, Vernon, on Eliot, 313

Renton, Richard, on Forster, 71

Reuter, Fritz, 119

Reynolds, G. W. M., 107, 108

Richards, I. A.: *Practical Criticism*, 16; *Science and Poetry*, 370

Richards, M. C., on Hardy, 382

Richardson, Samuel, 289

Richter, J. P., 128, 332, 336, 342

Riddell, Mrs. J. H., 12

Ridder-Barzin, L. de, on Hardy, 365

Rimbaud, Arthur, 399

Ritchie, A. T.: on *Cranford*, 247; on Thackeray, 157, 159, 160–161, 178

Rives, Léone, on Reade, 285, 286, 291

Roberts, Marguerite, on *Tess*, 384

Roberts, Morley, on Gissing, 402, 403, 405

Robertson, J. L., on Disraeli, 22

Robertson, T. L., on Kingsley, 271

Robinson, A. M. F., on E. Brontë, 222, 228

Robinson, C. F., on Trollope, 211

Robinson, Carole, on *Romola*, 316, 321

Robinson, Kenneth, on Collins, 110, 279, 281

Rolfe, F. P., on Dickens, 48, 59

Romieu, E. and G., on Eliot, 301–302

Roppen, Georg, on Hardy, 368–369

Rosa, M. W., *The Silver-Fork School*, 31, 40

Rosenberg, Edgar, *From Shylock to Svengali*, 85, 321

Rosenberg, Marvin, on Dickens, 100, 104

Rosenblatt, Louise, on Moore, 399

Roth, Cecil, on Disraeli, 26, 30

Rothenstein, William, on Moore, 391

Rotter, F. A., on Gissing, 406

Roughead, William, on *Vanity Fair*, 179

Rouse, H. B., on Dickens, 112

Roussev, Russi, on Dickens, 139

Routh, H. V.: on Dickens, 132; on Moore, 395

Rubenius, Aina, on Gaskell, 251, 254–256

Rubinstein, E. L., on Eliot, 321–322

Rühl, Hans, on Disraeli, 29

Ruskin, John, 130

Russell, F. T., *Satire in the Victorian Novel*, 19

Russell, G. W. E., on *Lothair*, 34

Rust, J. D., on Eliot, 299, 305

Rutland, W. R., on Hardy, 356–357, 369

Sackville-West, Edward: on Dickens, 93; on Eliot, 318; on Meredith, 335

Sadleir, Michael: on Bulwer-Lytton, 37, 166; on Disraeli, 22–23; *Excursions in Victorian Bibliography*, 22, 245–246, 278, 282, 284, 285; *XIX Century Fiction*, 2–4, 22, 35, 50; on Thackeray, 166, 170; on Trollope, 188, 189, 190, 191, 192, 193, 194, 199–200, 203, 213

Saintsbury, George: on Dickens, 54, 72, 76, 88, 109; on the novel, 2; on Thackeray, 157, 166–167, 168, 170, 186; on Trollope, 198–199, 208

Samuel, H. B., on Disraeli and Bulwer-Lytton, 31, 40

Sand, George, 117, 262, 356

Sandberg, Leonard, on Dickens, 145

Winegarner, Lela, on Thackeray, 157
Wing, George, on *Tess*, 384
Winter, Albert, on Dickens, 109
Winter, Warrington, on Dickens, 92
Winter, William, on Collins, 280
Winterich, J. T.: on *Westward Ho!*,
264; on *Wuthering Heights*, 222
Wise, T. J., on Brontës, 215–216, 219,
220, 223
Wolf, Lucien, on Disraeli, 22, 26
Wolfe, Humbert, on Moore, 391–392
Wolff, J. J., on *The Unclassed*, 401
Wolff, Lucien, on Meredith, 332
Wolzogen, Ernst von, on Collins, 280
Wood, Butler, on Brontës, 216, 226
Wood, Mrs. Henry, 9
Woodall, Robert, on Dickens, 103
Woodring, C. R.: on Reade, 289; on
Wuthering Heights, 241
Woods, Alice, on Meredith, 338
Woollcott, Alexander: on Collins,
282; on Dickens, 75, 104
Woolf, Virginia: on Brontës, 229; on
Dickens, 78, 107, 114, 152; on
Eliot, 311; on Gissing, 409; on
Hardy, 371; on Meredith, 334–335,
340–341
Wordsworth, William, 338, 362, 369
Worth, G. J.: on Dickens, 96; on
Esmond, 181; on *Wuthering
Heights*, 241, 242
Wright, Thomas, on Dickens, 57,
62, 74, 131
Wright, W. F., on Eliot, 312–313; on
Meredith, 330
Wright, William, on Brontës, 226
Wroot, H. E., on C. Brontë, 230
Wyzewa, Téodor de, on Dickens, 119

Yamamoto, Tadao, on Dickens, 98,
146
Yamato, Yasuo, on Dickens, 146
Yang Yao-min, on Dickens, 139
Yates, Edmund, on Collins, 280
Yates, May, on Gissing, 407
Yates, W. W., on Brontës, 227
Yeats, W. B., 376; on Moore, 392–393
Yolland, A. B., on Dickens, 139
Yonge, C. M., 10
Young, A. C., on Gissing, 402
Young, G. M., on Dickens, 73
Young, W. J., on Gissing, 409
Yuill, W. E., on Hardy, 380

Zabel, M. D.: on Dickens, 45, 56, 88,
91, 114; on Hardy, 364, 372–373
Zech, Adolph, on Dilthey, 133
Zetland, Marquis of, on Disraeli, 23
Zimmerman, Erich, on *Last Days of
Pompeii*, 41–42
Zola, Emile, 18, 117–118, 289, 396,
397, 398, 399, 409, 410, 412
Zweig, Stefan, on Dickens, 133–134,
140